Test Bank for Crooks & Baur's
Our Sexuality

EIGHTH EDITION

KATHRYN NORCROSS BLACK

Purdue University
University of Arizona

with the assistance of
JOHN W. McCLURE

Australia • Canada • Mexico • Singapore • Spain • United Kingdom • United States

COPYRIGHT © 2002 Wadsworth Group. Wadsworth is an imprint of the Wadsworth Group, a division of Thomson Learning, Inc. Thomson Learning™ is a trademark used herein under license.

For more information about this or any other Wadsworth product, contact:
WADSWORTH
511 Forest Lodge Road
Pacific Grove, CA 93950 USA
www.wadsworth.com
1-800-423-0563 (Thomson Learning Academic Resource Center)

ALL RIGHTS RESERVED. Instructors of classes using *Our Sexuality, 8th Ed.,* by Crooks and Baur, as a textbook may reproduce material from this publication for classroom use. Otherwise, no part of this work covered by the copyright hereon may be reproduced or used in any form or by any means—graphic, electronic, or mechanical, including photocopying, recording, taping, Web distribution, or information storage and retrieval systems—without the written permission of the publisher.

For permission to use material from this work, contact us by
Web: www.thomsonrights.com
fax: 1-800-730-2215
phone: 1-800-730-2214

Printed in the United States of America

5 4 3 2 1

ISBN 0-534-57986-8

ACKNOWLEDGMENTS

John W. McClure, therapist (*board eligible* NCC) and attorney, has dedicated countless hours to the creation of this test bank. His expertise supplied invaluable contributions to the content of this work and his dedication and computer publishing skills helped produce the materials.

This eighth edition of the test bank makes extensive use of prior work by Lauren Kuhn. Jennifer Wilkinson was an informative and enthusiastic editor. Deirdre Black LeMire also provided valuable assistance.

Contents

To the Instructor

Part One: Introduction

Chapter 1:	Perspectives on Sexuality	1
Chapter 2:	Sex Research: Methods and Problems	21
Chapter 2:	Gender Issues	43

Part Two: Biological Basis

Chapter 4:	Female Sexual Anatomy and Physiology	67
Chapter 5:	Male Sexual Anatomy and Physiology	95
Chapter 6:	Sexual Arousal and Response	117

Part Three: Sexual Behavior

Chapter 7:	Love and the Development of Sexual Relationships	141
Chapter 8:	Communication in Sexual Behavior	163
Chapter 9:	Sexual Behavior	185
Chapter 10:	Sexual Orientation	207

Part Four: Sexuality and the Life Cycle

Chapter 11:	Contraception	231
Chapter 12:	Conceiving Children: Process and Choice	255
Chapter 13:	Sexuality During Childhood and Adolescence	283
Chapter 14:	Sexuality and the Adult Years	307

Part Five: Sexual Problems

Chapter 15:	The Nature and Origins of Sexual Difficulties	329
Chapter 16:	Sex Therapy and Enhancement	351
Chapter 17:	Sexually Transmitted Diseases	369

Part Six: Social Issues

Chapter 18:	Atypical Sexual Behavior	397
Chapter 19:	Sex Victimization	417
Chapter 20:	Sex For Sale	441

To The Instructor

This test bank, designed to accompany the eighth edition of Crooks and Baur's *Our Sexuality,* includes over 2400 multiple choice, true/false and short answer essay questions for the 20 chapters of the text. Each chapter begins with a listing of Learning Objectives as provided in the Instructors Manual. The test items that follow were constructed to provide comprehensive coverage of the text with varied levels of difficulty and include material presented in the boxed inserts as well as the main body of the text. You will notice that the true/false questions include two sets of instructions: one utilizes a more traditional format, and the other allows instructors to encourage more active student involvement. Some instructors like to include in their examinations an occasional multiple-choice question from the *Study Guide* in order to reinforce its use. To accommodate this preference, all of the multiple-choice questions from the *Study Guide* are included at the end of the multiple-choice section. For each chapter, 10 of the multiple choice test questions appear on a World Wide Web site: http://psychology.wadsworth.com/. The notation "WWW" in the margin to the left of the question indicates these.

Additionally, in the margin to the left of each multiple choice and true/false test item, the following information is provided: the test item number; a "K" or "A" to indicate a knowledge or application question; the letter that is the answer; the page reference in the textbook where the answer may be found; and the corresponding Learning Objectives number when this is applicable. A number of test items could not subsumed under any of the Learning Objectives and "n/a" indicates these. Only learning objective information follows the short answer essay questions.

The computerized test bank allows you to format exams to meet your personal specifications, which may entail editing, adding, and deleting questions. Computerized testing software is available for both the Windows and Macintosh platforms.

Kathryn Norcross Black
Purdue University, Professor Emeritus
The University of Arizona, Adjunct Faculty
23295 Grayshire Lane
Lake Barrington, IL 60010

1
Perspectives on Sexuality

Learning Objectives

After studying this chapter, the student should be able to:

1. Define the term "psychosocial" as it applies to the orientation of the text, and explain why the authors choose to emphasize this perspective.

2. Describe how the media both influences and reflects sexuality today.

3. Discuss how the sex-for-reproduction legacy has evolved historically, and explain how this theme affects sexual attitudes and behaviors today.

4. Discuss how the gender-role legacy has evolved historically, and explain how this theme affects sexual attitudes and behaviors today.

5. Describe the difficulty in determining what constitutes "normal" sexual behavior, citing specific cross-cultural examples to support your explanation.

6. Discuss the sexual attitudes and behaviors of the people in China, the Islamic Middle East and Sweden.

7. List several examples that illustrate how diversity exists in various subcultures within the United States.

8. Give examples of specific psychological, scientific and social advances within the last century that have affected sexual values and behavior in our society today.

Multiple Choice

1.
K
Answer: b
p. 2
Obj. #1

When discussing males and females
a. the text uses the traditional term "opposite sex".
b. the text uses "other sex" because the sexes are more alike than different.
c. we may assume there are some innate sexual differences.
d. the authors are being politically incorrect.

2.
K
Answer: a
pp. 2-3
Obj. #2

Which of the following is a suggestion offered for interviewing a parent or family member about their sexual experiences or beliefs?
a. Consider beginning by asking about their own sex education.
b. Only do this if you had a good sex education from them.
c. You probably should only talk with a same-sex relative.
d. They'll feel more comfortable if you reveal something of your own sex life.

3.
K
Answer: a
p. 2
Obj. #1

The authors use the term "other sex" instead of "opposite sex" because
a. they wish to emphasize that men and women are more similar than they are different.
b. the term "other sex" is politically more correct.
c. it is less confusing.
d. the term "other sex" includes a wider range of sexual orientations and lifestyles.

4.
K
Answer: b
p. 3
Obj. #1

According to the authors of the text, which of the following governs human sexuality to a greater degree?
a. hormones and instincts
b. social conditioning and psychological factors
c. sociobiological factors
d. anthropological factors

5.
K
Answer: c
pp. 2-3
Obj. #1
WWW

Which of the following statements **most** accurately reflects the authors' perspectives in writing this book?
a. Despite cross-cultural diversity, there are numerous universals in sexual experiences, attitudes and preferences.
b. The book reflects a primarily sociobiological orientation.
c. Our sexual attitudes and behaviors are strongly shaped by our society.
d. Human sexuality is influenced more by biological factors than by psychological factors.

6.
K
Answer: c
p. 4
Obj. #3

The cultural theme of sex-for-reproduction
a. is supported by the authors.
b. has its roots in Buddhist religious philosophy.
c. may devalue sexual behaviors other than intercourse.
d. may result in men feeling pressure to be "active" and women feeling pressure to be "passive".

7.
A
Answer: d
p. 4
Obj. #3

A man who feels his sex life has ended because he is no longer able to get an erection is a victim of
a. rigid gender-role conditioning.
b. imposed celibacy.
c. sociobiological conditioning.
d. the sex-for-reproduction legacy.

8.
A
Answer: a
p. 4
Obj. #4

Which of the following is the **best** example of a potential effect of rigid gender-role conditioning?
a. A woman may feel reluctant to express her sexual desires to her male partner.
b. A man may feel uncomfortable because his female partner prefers oral sex to intercourse.
c. As a result of her religious orientation, a woman feels guilty having sex for pleasure.
d. A man most enjoys sex with his partner when she initiates and takes control.

9.
K
Answer: a
p. 4
Obj. #3

Foreplay includes all of the following **except**
a. penile-vaginal intercourse.
b. kissing.
c. oral-genital contact.
d. manual genital stimulation.

10.
K
Answer: d
p. 4
Obj. #3

Which of the following was NOT suggested as a possible consequence of the view that reproduction is the only legitimate reason for sexual activity?
a. Kissing and manual manipulation of genitals are devalued.
b. It suggests that orgasm is supposed to occur during vaginal penetration.
c. Masturbation is not considered a viable sexual option.
d. It decreases the frequency of intercourse outside of marriage.

11.
A
Answer: b
p. 4
Obj. #5

Which of the following scenarios **best** illustrates the effects of rigid gender-role conditioning?
a. As a result of having prostate surgery, a man is no longer able to get erections, so he becomes celibate.
b. A man prefers to have his partner initiate and be sexually aggressive with him, but he hesitates to tell her this for fear of her rejection.
c. A woman prefers the manual stimulation of her partner to having intercourse, and he thinks this is abnormal.
d. A woman would like to spend some intimate time with her partner just touching and kissing, but he refuses to do this unless it culminates in intercourse.

12.
A
Answer: d
p. 4
Obj. #3, 4

With which of the following statements would the authors of your text **most** likely agree?
a. Emphasizing penile-vaginal intercourse as the focus of sexual expression can maximize orgasmic response in men and women.
b. Having sex for reproductive purposes is the most legitimate reason for sexual activity.
c. A clear distinction between male and female roles and expectations results in more creative and pleasurable sexual expression.
d. Masturbation, oral sex and engaging in sexual fantasy are viable options for people who choose them.

13.
A
Answer: d
p. 4
Obj. #3, 4
WWW

Which of the following scenarios **best** illustrates the effects of the sex-for-reproduction legacy as opposed to rigid gender-role conditioning?
a. A woman wants to ask a man out on a date, but she is afraid he will think she is too aggressive.
b. A man has sex with his partner even when he isn't really in the mood.
c. A man wants his partner to be on top when they have intercourse, but she is reluctant to do so.
d. A woman is orgasmic only during oral sex, and this is upsetting to her partner who wants her to be orgasmic during intercourse.

14.
K
Answer: d
pp. 4-5
Obj. #2

Which is **most** accurate with respect to sexualization of the media?
a. It is highly sexualized with the exception of magazines such as Men's Health and Prevention.
b. It is highly sexualized with the exception of coverage on TV and in newspapers of current events.
c. Movies have always been highly sexualized but recently other media have gone this route.
d. Printed and technological media are generally highly sexualized.

15.
K
Answer: a
pp. 5-6
Obj. #2

Which of the following is NOT true concerning sexuality on television?
a. Sexual bantering on TV occurs about half the time with married couples and half the time between singles.
b. About 2/3 of prime time shows contain sexual content.
c. Erectile dysfunction has been openly discussed in television ads.
d. The average 18 year old has watched TV for about 20,000 hours.

16.
K
Answer: b
p. 6
Obj. #2

Which one is **most** accurate with respect to television?
a. The sensationalistic discussions of daytime TV have no redeeming features.
b. The Media project advises shows on how to deal with date rape, condom usage, and unwanted pregnancy.
c. Daytime "soaps" are conservative and urge an abstinent approach.
d. The portrayal of gays and lesbians on TV has led to an increase in hate crimes.

17.
K
Answer: b
pp. 6-7
Obj. #2

Research on the effects of music videos have found that
a. they are not as widely watched as some had thought.
b. girls who watch videos of women in subordinate positions were more likely to accept teen dating violence than those who had not.
c. these videos only influence those who have a lower intellectual level or a low self-esteem.
d. these videos influence the views of males but not of females.

18.
K
Answer: b
pp. 6-7
Obj. #2
WWW

According to your text, which one of the following was NOT found in an analysis of music videos?
a. They are primarily designed to sell CDs and tapes.
b. Men dominate both in the numbers present and by their behavior.
c. Women are shown in a constant state of sexual arousal.
d. Many lyrics use guns and knives as metaphors for the penis.

19.
K
Answer: d
pp. 6-8
Obj. #2

With respect to Internet usage and images of sexuality, which is the **most** true?
a. Good research has not as yet been done on this area although it is needed.
b. Data has not found this to be a problem for people's lives.
c. Sites that show such things as sexual acts are banned from most college campuses.
d. About 9 million different people visit such sites daily.

20.
K
Answer: b
p. 7
Obj. #2

With respect to Internet usage all but which one is occurring now?
a. There are dating services and personal ads to determine if you wish to meet face to face
b. By paying a small amount extra you can go to many sites where people are guaranteed accurate information as to the gender and age of correspondents.
c. It is possible to have on-line extramarital affairs.
d. There are bulletin boards for transsexuals.

21.
K
Answer: b
p. 8
Obj. #4

Which one is NOT true concerning goddesses in early religions?
a. They were widely known as healers.
b. They were not portrayed as warriors or on the battlefield.
c. They were important from very early in history, i.e., thousands of years B.C.
d. They were persecuted by later religions which held male gods supreme.

22.
A
Answer: d
pp. 9-10, 12
Obj. #3
WWW

Which of the following groups of individuals would be **most** likely to share similar sexual values?
a. Augustine, Paul of Tarsus, and Theodore Van de Velde
b. Mary Wollstonecraft, John Calvin, and Aquinas
c. Martin Luther, Paul of Tarsus, and Aquinas
d. Theodore Van de Velde, Mary Wollstonecraft, and Havelock Ellis

23.
K
Answer: d
p. 9
Obj. #3

This person saw celibacy as superior to marriage.
a. Martin Luther
b. John Calvin
c. Mary Wollstonecraft
d. Paul of Tarsus

24.
A
Answer: b
p. 10
Obj. #3

Which one is true concerning "sex manuals"?
a. They originated in early Greece.
b. An early Hindu sex manual was called the Kama Sutra.
c. The originated after the invention of the printing press.
d. They are a very modern phenomenon.

25.
K
Answer: d
pp. 9-10
Obj. #4

Which one is NOT an accurate statement of the views of those within the Christian religion?
a. We know little about Jesus' views of sexuality.
b. Paul believed that celibacy was superior to marriage.
c. Martin Luther saw value in marital sex other than for procreation.
d. The Puritans disapproved of sexual activity even in marriage.

26.
K
Answer: b
pp. 9-10
Obj. #3

The writings of Augustine and Aquinas
a. were similar to those of Martin Luther.
b. emphasized sex for procreation.
c. advocated flexibility in gender roles.
d. encouraged a range of sexual expression.

27.
K
Answer: c
p. 10
Obj. #3, 4

All of the following attitudes regarding sexuality were embraced within the classical Islamic faith **except**
a. Celibacy was opposed.
b. Premarital intercourse was opposed.
c. Men and women were both expected to be monogamous.
d. Marital sexual pleasure was highly valued.

28.
K
Answer: b
p. 10
Obj. #6

If you were a person born in ancient China, you would be
a. encouraged to practice celibacy as a path to spiritual growth.
b. encouraged to participate in a range of sexual activities within marriage for spiritual growth as well as pleasure.
c. discouraged from engaging in masturbation.
d. severely punished for engaging in nonreproductive sex.

29.
K
Answer: d
pp. 9-10
Obj. #6
WWW

A comparison of the sexual views of religions and cultures from around the world would suggest which of the following?
a. They are surprisingly similar.
b. They often differ except in their views of premarital intercourse.
c. Some differences exist but they are alike in that they began with strict views and have loosened up in more recent times.
d. There are great differences with some religions and cultures suggesting sexual activity to promote spiritual growth.

30.
A
Answer: c
pp. 4, 9, 12
Obj. #3, 4

Which of the following statements is **most** accurate?
a. Gender roles became less rigidly defined in the Victorian era.
b. The notion that "real sex" equals penile-vaginal intercourse is a reflection of the gender-role legacy.
c. The idea of sex for reproduction is associated with Judaic and Christian tradition.
d. Oral contraceptives were first introduced at the turn of the century.

31.
K
Answer: d
p. 10
Obj. #3

Which of the following individuals was a writer during the Protestant Reformation who recognized that marital sex was acceptable for reasons besides procreation?
   a. Augustine
   b. Paul of Tarsus
   c. Aquinas
   d. John Calvin

32.
K
Answer: b
pp. 9, 10, 12
Obj. #3

Which of the following individuals would **most** disagree with the philosophies of Mary Wollstonecraft?
   a. Martin Luther
   b. Paul of Tarsus
   c. John Calvin
   d. Snoop Doggie

33.
K
Answer: a
p. 11
Obj. #8

Which one is NOT true concerning contraception?
   a. The oral contraceptive pill was introduced during the Second World War.
   b. It is contraception that increasingly allows the idea of the separation of sexuality and procreation.
   c. Contraceptive devices used by men in ancient times included goat bladders as condoms.
   d. Contraceptive devices used by women centuries ago included the use of pads to block the cervix.

34.
K
Answer: c
p. 10
Obj. #4

During the Protestant Reformation
   a. the ideas of Augustine and Aquinas dominated Western thought.
   b. the practice of courtly love flourished.
   c. the concept of sex for procreation was challenged.
   d. sexual decadence was at its peak.

35.
A
Answer: a
p. 10
Obj. #4

If you were among the very earliest Christians, how would your decision to marry have been perceived?
   a. It would be viewed as inferior to the choice of celibacy.
   b. It would be respected and celebrated.
   c. It would be honored as the path to spiritual salvation.
   d. It would be considered sinful.

36.
K
Answer: a
p. 11
Obj. #4

Which of the following statements regarding the practice of courtly love is false?
   a. It evolved during the Victorian era.
   b. It reflected an image of woman as pure and above reproach.
   c. It was the subject of many ballads throughout the courts of Europe.
   d. In its ideal form, the love remained unconsummated.

37.
K
Answer: c
p. 11
Obj. #4
WWW

Which of the following **best** describes the concept of "courtly love"?
a. promiscuous
b. religious
c. unconsummated
d. lewd

38.
K
Answer: b
pp. 11-12
Obj. #4

Which one is NOT true concerning gender role influences?
a. Both early Judaism and Christianity emphasized that women should be obedient and submissive to their husbands.
b. When England was rule by a beloved queen during the Victorian Era gender roles became more blurred.
c. Eve's perceived sinfulness in the Garden of Eden increased antagonism toward women.
d. In the United States women only received the right to vote after World War I.

39.
K
Answer: c
p. 12
Obj. #4

Witch hunts were the partial result of
a. exotic cults.
b. the practice of courtly love.
c. the portrayal of Eve as an evil temptress.
d. the clash in female roles that occurred during the Victorian era.

40.
K
Answer: a
pp. 11-14
Obj. #4

Which one is NOT true concerning stereotypical sexual contradictions?
a. They appear to exist more for men than women.
b. They include the Madonna image.
c. They gave slave owners a rationale for exploitation of Black women.
d. They were especially prevalent in nineteenth-century Western culture.

41.
K
Answer: d
p.12
Obj. #4

During the Victorian era
a. prostitution was even more infrequent than it is now.
b. women were finally given the right to vote in England.
c. although marriages were often arranged spouses frequently became good friends.
d. the majority of women experience both sexual desire and orgasm.

42.
K
Answer: d
p. 12
Obj. #4
WWW

Which of the following **best** describes Victorian attitudes toward morality?
a. progressive and experimental
b. expressive and uninhibited
c. rational and indifferent
d. hypocritical and repressive

43.
K
Answer: c
p. 12
Obj. #3

Which one of the following individuals asserted that premarital and extramarital sex were NOT sinful?
   a. John Calvin
   b. Queen Victoria
   c. Mary Wollstonecraft
   d. Aquinas

44.
K
Answer: b
p. 12
Obj. #4

During the Victorian era
   a. women enjoyed a new equality with men.
   b. prostitution flourished.
   c. the writing of Mary Wollstonecraft became popular.
   d. witch hunts were commonplace.

45.
K
Answer: d
p. 13
Obj. #4

Stereotypes concerning the sexuality of Black slaves in the United States
   a. were probably based on some average differences.
   b. included the need to have their bodies covered to avoid temptation.
   c. helped to keep White slave owners from abusing the women.
   d. existed for both male and female slaves.

46.
K
Answer: c
p. 13
Obj. #4

The constitutional amendment giving women the right to vote in the United States was passed in what year?
   a. 1880, not long after slavery was ended
   b. 1900, as a millennium celebration
   c. 1920, after the first World War
   d. 1940, just prior to the second World War

47.
K
Answer: d
p. 13
Obj. #4

Stereotypes of black slavery included
   a. the male buck who was very strong physically but not sexually powerful.
   b. the black Jezebel who lived to work in the fields.
   c. the singing Sammy who entertained the slaves in the evenings.
   d. Mammy who not only took care of white children but also cooked and cleaned.

48.
K
Answer: d
pp. 14-17
Obj. #7
WWW

Instances of sexual diversity include all but which one of the following?
   a. Countries differ greatly in the extent to which they have formal sex education.
   b. The idea of what is physically arousing varies greatly among different cultures.
   c. Women of all races are more stigmatized than are men for sexual expression.
   d. Most societies regulate sexual expression but a few do not.

49.
K
Answer: d
p. 14
Obj. #5

Which of the following statements concerning cross-cultural sexuality is false?
a. Exposed female breasts may trigger arousal in some societies but not others.
b. In some cultures sex is highly valued while in others it is considered shameful.
c. Within all societies, there are rules regulating sexual behavior.
d. A small minority of societies throughout the world allows sexuality to remain totally unregulated.

50.
K
Answer: d
p. 14
Obj. #5

Women would be most severely punished for engaging in extramarital sex in
a. Mangaia (in Polynesia).
b. China.
c. Sweden.
d. The Islamic Middle East.

51.
K
Answer: d
p. 15
Obj. #6

With respect to sexuality, China
a. became less restrictive when the Communists took over.
b. does not have an AIDS problem.
c. outlaws both adultery and divorce.
d. adolescents and young adults are less sexually active than the United States.

52.
K
Answer: c
p. 15
Obj. #6

All of the following are characteristic of sexuality in China **except**
a. Many men do not know that a woman has a clitoris.
b. Most married women view procreation as the reason for sex.
c. Adolescents and young adults are more sexually active than in the United States.
d. Little or no sex education exists in schools.

53.
K
Answer: c
p. 15
Obj. #6

Which one is NOT true concerning Islam?
a. Women are believed to be inherently sexual.
b. Arranged marriages are common.
c. Homosexuality is given a special privileged status in some countries.
d. By law, in some countries women must wear a veil.

54.
K
Answer: b
p. 15
Obj. #6

The world's fastest growing religion is
a. Buddhism.
b. Islam.
c. Catholicism.
d. Greek Orthodox.

55.
K
Answer: a
p. 15
Obj. #6

In China, rates of STDs are _____; premarital and extramarital sex are _____.
a. increasing; increasing
b. decreasing; increasing
c. increasing; decreasing
d. decreasing; decreasing

56.
K
Answer: b
p. 15
Obj. #6
WWW

In which culture is female sexual desire perceived to be many times greater then that of the male?
a. United States
b. Islamic Middle East
c. China
d. Sweden

57.
K
Answer: a
p. 16
Obj. #7

Which of the following groups would be generally **less** likely to engage in premarital intercourse?
a. Asian Americans
b. African Americans
c. Latinos
d. European Americans

58.
K
Answer: d
p. 16
Obj. #6

In Sweden
a. there is a high rate of teen pregnancy because of the open attitudes about sexuality.
b. half of all couples living together are unmarried.
c. law and custom promote the one-child family.
d. fathers are given equal responsibility for child care and this includes parental leave.

59.
K
Answer: c
p. 16
Obj. #4

All of the following describe the Native American "Two Spirit" **except**
a. They pursued traditional roles of the other gender.
b. They held a socially and economically prestigious role.
c. They had an exclusively homosexual orientation.
d. They were spiritual leaders.

60.
K
Answer: d
pp. 16-17
Obj. #7

Which of the following individuals would be generally **less** likely to engage in oral-genital sex?
a. a college-educated white female
b. a college-educated Latino male
c. a high-school educated white male
d. a high-school educated black male

61.
K
Answer: b
p. 17
Obj. #7

Which of the following **best** describes the concept of acculturation?
a. Replacing traditional beliefs with those of the dominant culture.
b. Integrating traditional beliefs with those of the dominant culture.
c. Refusing to relinquish traditional beliefs in favor of the dominant culture.
d. Attempting to recapture aspects of one's traditional culture.

62.
K
Answer: a
pp. 16-17
Obj. #7

With respect to diversity in the United States
a. educational level is often associated with differing sexual behaviors and attitudes.
b. probably because of the leveling effect of television, income does not appear to affect sexual expression.
c. Latinos seem to be more like one another than do those classified as African Americans.
d. It is not possible to make general statements about group differences.

63.
K
Answer: b
p. 17
Obj. #7

Which of the following would **most** significantly influence sexual attitudes and behaviors, even within the same ethnic group?
a. religious and political views
b. socioeconomic status and education
c. education and birth order
d. political views and socioeconomic status

64.
K
Answer: d
pp. 16-18
Obj. #7
WWW

Which one is NOT true for the United States?
a. Even within major religious groups such as Catholics or Judaism there is a wide range of views about sexuality.
b. Ethnic groups often become assimilated.
c. Latino culture in general places a higher value on chastity for both men and women.
d. Oral-genital sex is more common among those with less education.

65.
K
Answer: c
pp. 11, 17
Obj. #8

Which of the following events has had the **least** impact in bringing sexual decision-making into the personal domain?
a. invention of the Pill
b. 1973 Supreme Court decision on abortion
c. increased visibility of various "right-to-life" groups
d. homosexual men and women challenging the notion that sexual orientation should affect rights and responsibilities

66.
K
Answer: c
p. 17
Obj. #8

According to your text, which is the **most** true?
a. The sex for reproduction legacy is largely dead now.
b. Increased tolerance of diversity likely creates as many or more problems than it could solve.
c. Students in this class have more personal sexual choices than our ancestors and thus more responsibilities.
d. The impact of modern contraception is probably not as influential as our religious beliefs.

67.
K
Answer: b
p. 18
Obj. #8

Which one was NOT an influence on sexuality in the United States?
a. Penicillin, developed in the 40's, reduced the consequences of sexually transmitted diseases.
b. Prohibition in the 30's of both alcohol and access to contraceptive devices.
c. The mass produced automobile allowed privacy for sexual exploration.
d. Playboy, which emphasized sex as recreation.

68.
K
Answer: b
p. 18
Obj. #8

Which of the following people wrote "The Interpretation of Dreams"?
a. Havelock
b. Sigmund Freud
c. Van de Velde
d. Masters and Johnson

69.
K
Answer: a
p. 19
Obj. # 8

Which on of the following was NOT an important landmark for sexuality during the past century?
a. Christine Jorgensen is known for being the first woman athlete to come out as a lesbian.
b. Playboy began to be published in the 1950s and emphasized sex as recreation.
c. The American Psychiatric Association removed homosexuality from its diagnostic categories of mental disorders in the mid 70's.
d. Options in reproductive technologies, including test-tube babies, have boomed.

70.
K
Answer: d
p. 18
Obj. #8

The research of _____ contributed to greater understanding of the sexual response cycle.
a. Freud
b. Kinsey
c. Van de Velde
d. Masters and Johnson

Multiple Choice from Study Guide

1.
K
Answer: c
p. 3
Obj. #1

A psychosocial orientation reflects a concern with _____ factors in the study of human sexuality.
a. biological and anthropological
b. sociological and medical
c. psychological and social
d. psychiatric and sociobiological

2.
A
Answer: b
p. 4
Obj. #3

The sex for reproduction legacy is **most** clearly shown in which of the following statements?
a. Jorge believes that foreplay is an essential part of a sexual encounter.
b. Midori thinks she is still a virgin because she has done everything except penile-vaginal intercourse.
c. Sheila likes to initiate sexual activity with her partner.
d. Mike enjoys masturbating and does not feel guilty about it.

3.
A
Answer: a
p. 4
Obj. #4

Jamal believes that a "real" man always makes the first sexual advance in a relationship. Jamal's thinking **best** reflects
a. the gender role legacy
b. principles of courtly love
c. a lesser degree of acculturation
d. homophobia

4.
K
Answer: d
pp. 5-6
Obj. #2

Studies of television programming have demonstrated that prime-time shows
a. have substantially decreased the sexual content in recent years.
b. are complying with government issued restrictions on the use of sexual language.
c. have reduced the number of commercials with sexual imagery.
d. have more sexual content than previous years.

5.
K
Answer: a
p. 6
Obj. #2

The increase of gay and lesbian characters and story lines on incest and condom use illustrates that television
a. may help reduce taboos on the discussion of sensitive topics.
b. has failed to use realistic information about sexuality.
c. will soon include a rating system to alert viewers to homosexual content.
d. has completely failed to portray sexuality in a positive, healthy manner.

6.
K
Answer: d
pp. 6-7
Obj. #2

Research on the effects of music videos has shown that
a. watching videos promotes acceptance of dating violence.
b. filming techniques depersonalize women.
c. viewing encourages acceptance of exploitive beliefs about relationships.
d. all of the above

7.
K
Answer: a
p. 9
Obj. #3

Who is associated with the belief that celibacy is superior to marriage?
a. Paul of Tarsus
b. Solomon
c. Freud
d. Lao Tsu

8.
K
Answer: c
pp. 9-10
Obj. #3

Which of the following persons is NOT associated with the view that sex is sinful?
a. Thomas Aquinas
b. Augustine
c. Havelock Ellis
d. Paul of Tarsus

9.
K
Answer: d
p. 10
Obj. #3

What view did early Taoism and Hinduism have in common?
a. masturbation was encouraged
b. sex was primarily for procreation
c. celibacy was prohibited
d. sexual activity could help achieve spiritual growth and fulfillment

10.
K
Answer: b
p. 11
Obj. #4

The opposing images of women as the virgin Madonna and evil temptress Eve originated during
a. the Victorian era.
b. the Middle Ages.
c. the Roman Empire.
d. the Renaissance.

11.
K
Answer: b
p. 12
Obj. #4

Which statement **best** reflects gender roles during the Victorian era?
a. Men's and women's worlds were deeply intertwined.
b. Men's and women's worlds were clearly separated.
c. Men were expected to adhere to strict mores, even in business affairs.
d. Men were expected fulfill their families' need for moral and spiritual guidance.

Chapter 1 Perspectives on Sexuality   15

12.
Answer: d
p. 13
Obj. #4

Which of the following statements is inconsistent with the Jezebel stereotype of black women's sexuality under slavery?
    a. Black women were perceived as having an insatiable sexual appetite.
    b. Black women were thought to prefer short and scanty clothing.
    c. Black women were thought to lack self-respect.
    d. Black women were considered ladylike.

13.
K
Answer: c
p. 13
Obj. #4

Which of the following statements is consistent with prevailing stereotypes about black male sexuality during slavery?
    a. Black men were considered asexual.
    b. Black men were wanton seducers of white women.
    c. Black men were peaceful and meek.
    d. Black men were alleged to have smaller penises than White men.

14.
K
Answer: a
p. 14
Obj. #6

What basic generalization about world cultures and sexuality can be made, despite the fact that there is great diversity in human sexual expression?
    a. Every society regulates sexuality in some way.
    b. The world's cultures tend to universally view breasts as erotic.
    c. Sex is considered shameful in some way by all societies.
    d. Some form of kissing is considered arousing in each culture.

15.
K
Answer: b
p. 15
Obj. #6

Most married Chinese women believe that sex is
    a. the preferred path to spiritual enlightenment.
    b. for procreation only.
    c. permissible for adolescents.
    d. something that should be taught in college.

16.
K
Answer: c
p. 15
Obj. #6

Islamic customs such a wearing a veil and segregating the sexes until marriage are regarded as necessary because
    a. Islamic texts believe that men are rife with sexual desire.
    b. Urbanization has made it more difficult to follow Islamic teachings.
    c. Women have more sexual desire than men.
    d. Sex outside of marriage is increasing.

17.
K
Answer: d
p. 16
Obj. #6

Attitudes toward sexuality in Sweden are exemplified by
    a. the availability of free contraception.
    b. the acceptance of cohabitation.
    c. parental leave for fathers.
    d. all of the above

18.
K
Answer: d
pp. 16-17
Obj. #7

Diversity within a subculture or ethnic group is influenced by
    a. acculturation.
    b. education.
    c. socioeconomic status.
    d. all of the above

19.
K
Answer: a
p. 18
Obj. #8

Whose pioneering studies after World War II helped lead to a greater acceptance of a variety of sexual behaviors?
a. Kinsey
b. Klein
c. Van de Velde
d. Gagnon

20.
K
Answer: b
pp. 18-19
Obj. #8

Key events which helped change conceptions of gender roles during the latter part of the 20th century included all of the following **except**
a. the availability of "the Pill".
b. the reinstatement of Comstock laws.
c. the Roe vs. Wade decision.
d. the feminist movement.

21.
K
Answer: c
p. 19
Obj. #8

What key event of the 80's brought gay men and lesbians into the public limelight?
a. the Stonewall riots
b. publication of Evelyn Hooker's study
c. the first AIDS diagnosis
d. the murder of Matthew Shepherd

True/False

Students may be asked to answer these questions using the traditional format of marking their answers either "true" or "false". Or, to encourage more active involvement, you may choose to use the following instructions:

If the statement is true, place a "T" on the line preceding it. If the statement is false, place an "F" on the line preceding it and then change the statement to make it true by deleting incorrect information and/or adding accurate information.

1.
Answer: F
pp. 2-3
Obj. #1

___ The authors believe that human sexuality is governed more by biological factors than psychosocial ones.

2.
Answer: F
pp. 2-3

___ One good way to establish a better relationship with a relative to whom you are not close would be to ask them to be interviewed by you concerning their sexual views.

3.
Answer: T
p. 4
Obj. #3

___ The sex-for-reproduction view often leads to the view that anything other than a penis in a vagina is not "sex".

4.
Answer: T
p. 4
Obj. #4

___ The authors believe that the gender-role legacy produces a negative impact on our sexuality.

5.
Answer: F
p. 5
Obj. #2

___ The majority of sexual activity depicted in current television programming occurs between married or engaged people.

6.
Answer: T
p. 7
Obj. #2

___ Viewing only 10 minutes of a video displaying adversarial gender images has been shown to change beliefs about the nature of male-female relationships.

7.
Answer: T
p. 8
Obj. #4

___ In early history goddesses had important roles but these religions were suppressed by ones which held males gods to be supreme.

8.
Answer: T
p. 10
Obj. #3

___ Various Reformation groups believed that intercourse was for pleasure as well as for procreative purposes.

9.
Answer: T
p. 10
Obj. #3

___ Ancient Taoists and Hindus promoted sex for pleasure as well as for spiritual reasons.

10.
Answer: T
p.11
Obj. #4

___ The practice of courtly love, which evolved during the Middle Ages, reflected an idealized image of women.

11.
Answer: F
p. 12
Obj. #4

___ During the Victorian era, men and women enjoyed more gender-role flexibility than at previous times in history.

12.
Answer: T
p. 12
Obj. #4

___ Witches were condemned and burned in part because of their supposed sexual nature and behavior.

13.
Answer: F
p. 13
Obj. #4

___ The Mammy image of a nurturing woman was the predominant stereotype for Black female slaves and perhaps helped bring about their freedom.

14.
Answer: T
p. 14
Obj. #5

___ In most all societies, there are rules governing sexual behavior.

15.
Answer: F
p. 15
Obj. #6

___ In the Islamic Middle East, most men don't know that women have a clitoris, and women are largely viewed as asexual, providing sexual service for their husbands.

16.
Answer: T
p. 15
Obj. #6

___ In China, the rates of divorce, sexually transmitted diseases, and extramarital sex are all increasing.

17.
Answer: T
p. 16
Obj. #7

___ Oral-genital sex tends to be more common among college-educated whites than African-Americans with less education.

18.
Answer: F
p. 16
Obj. #8

___ Generally speaking, masturbation tends to be more common among people with less education.

19.
Answer: T
p. 14
Obj. #7

___ Generally speaking, Asian Americans are less likely to engage in premarital intercourse than Latinos or African Americans.

20.
Answer: F
p. 18
Obj. #8

___ Alfred Kinsey is best known for his work on sexual response cycles in men and women.

Short Answer Essay

1. The authors of your text believe that human sexuality is best viewed from a psychosocial orientation. Describe this perspective and contrast to other approaches. (Obj. #1)

2. The sex-for-reproduction legacy refers to the view that non-reproductive sex is sinful. How did this view arise? What factors impact it today? (Obj. #3)

3. Discuss some factors bringing about a rigid distinction between the roles for men and women (the gender-role legacy). What factors have reduced the prevalence of such a distinction? Describe whether or not the sex-for-reproduction legacy has impacted you or your distinction in this country. (Obj. #4)

4. Describe whether or not the sex-for-reproduction legacy has impacted you or your family. Do you agree with this legacy? Why or why not? (Obj. #3)

5. Describe how the gender-role legacy has impacted your life. To what extent do you agree with this legacy? (Obj. #4)

6. Describe how television has broken down some implicit taboos on sensitive sexual subjects including homosexuality, breast cancer, sexual health issues, etc. (Obj. #2)

7. Describe the messages that have been presented by television as viewed in the United States in the past decade. Consider both what is available for children and for adults. (Obj. #2)

8. How might heavy viewing of MTV affect adolescents' views of the other sex and their romantic or sexual interactions? (Obj. #2)

9. Give an overview of Internet usage with respect to sexuality sites. Specify possible problems and speculate about educational advantages. (Obj. #2)

10. Summarize the prevailing sexual attitudes for four of the five following periods: Biblical times; the Middle Ages; the Renaissance; the Victorian era; the twentieth century. (Obj. #3, 4)

11. Compare and contrast the views of Christianity and Islam with respect to sexuality. (Obj. #6)

12. Law and norms can influence but often do not control sexual behavior. Illustrate this general principle by describing Victorian England and present day China. (Obj. #6)

13. Cite specific examples of the sexual diversity that exists among various subcultures within the United States. What factors should be taken into account in explaining differences within various subcultures? (Obj. #7)

14. Your book suggests that the majority white culture used sexual stereotypes as a partial justification of the institution of slavery. What are the stereotypes that would support this view? (Obj. #4)

15. Choose a person you know well from one of the cultural subgroups described in the first chapter. (You may choose yourself.) Indicate in what ways this person fits the generalizations that are made in the chapter. Why might there be major differences? (Obj. #7)

2

Sex Research: Methods and Problems

Learning Objectives

After studying this chapter, the student should be able to:

1. Define sexology and describe three of its goals, providing examples of each goal.

2. Describe when and how the discipline of sexology originated.

3. Describe each of the following research methods, including advantages and disadvantages of each method, and provide an example of each type of research: case study, survey, direct observation, experimental

4. Define each of the following and distinguish among them: survey sample, target population, representative sample, and random sample.

5. Discuss two types of survey methods, and the strengths and limitations of each.

6. Explain how nonresponse, self-selection, demographic bias and inaccuracy present problems in sex survey research.

7. Summarize the available research on "volunteer bias."

8. Describe the research studies of Alfred Kinsey and his associates, including research methods used, subject populations studied, and strengths and limitations of this work.

9. Describe the National Health and Social Life Survey, including research methods used, subject populations studied, and strengths and limitations of this work.

10. Describe the results of surveys on violent pornography and alcohol use.

11. Describe Masters and Johnson's research, including the research method used, subject populations studied, and the strengths and limitations of this work.

12. Describe new technologies in sex research.

13. Distinguish between independent and dependent variables, providing examples of each.

14. Describe how the experimental method has been used to study the effects of alcoholism on sexual arousal.

15. Describe the experimental method that has been used to study the relationship between sexually violent media and rape attitudes and behavior.

16. Describe how feminist theory has influenced research in sexology.

17. Discuss the reliability of sex research published in popular magazines.

18. Identify some criteria that would be helpful in evaluating various kinds of research.

19. Summarize some of the research findings on ethnicity and sexual behavior.

20. Discuss some ethical considerations in conducting sex research.

21. Summarize some of the results of a national sex survey in China.

22. Summarize some of the results of the NHSLS research on American ethnicity and sexuality.

Multiple Choice

1.
K
Answer: d
p. 23
Obj. #1, 2

Which one is **most** true?
a. Sexology as a science began with Sigmund Freud.
b. There is probably little need for scientists in the United States to be able to understand and predict the sexual behavior of those in other countries.
c. Unlike other sciences those who study human sexuality have not in any major way been able to help control behavior.
d. The study of sexology heavily involves value judgments and ethics.

2.
K
Answer: b
p. 23
Obj. #1

All of the following are goals of sexologists **except**
a. understanding sexual behavior
b. promoting sexual behavior
c. predicting sexual behavior
d. controlling sexual behavior

3.
K
Answer: a
p. 23
Obj. #1

Which of the following goals of sexology is **most** difficult to comprehend?
a. controlling sexual behavior
b. predicting sexual behavior
c. defining sexual behavior
d. understanding sexual behavior

4.
K
Answer: c
p. 24
Obj. n/a

Cross-cultural research concerning AIDS
a. was the major focus of Ford and Beach's book Patterns of Sexual Behavior.
b. has been done primarily in Africa.
c. has found that French youth often do not use condoms because they are too expensive.
d. found that almost no one in the British Isle now has multiple sex partners because of their fears about AIDS.

5.
A
Answer: a
p. 25
Obj. #3

A science writer hears of a 35 year old male who lost his penis at circumcision. He interviews all family members, reads medical records, and writes a book about this. This is **most** likely an example of which of the following?
a. the case study
b. the survey method
c. direct observation
d. follow up to an experimental intervention

6.
K
Answer: d
p. 25
Obj. #3

The case study method has been used to study all but which one of the following?
a. the relationship between pornography and rape
b. whether or not alcohol increases sexual responsiveness
c. development of transsexualism
d. whether vaginal or clitoral orgasms are superior

7.
K
Answer: d
p. 25
Obj. #21

A national sex survey of 23,000 Chinese revealed all of the following **except**
a. The majority of respondents expressed approval of extramarital sex.
b. Women are more likely than men to initiate divorce proceedings.
c. Most Chinese couples engage in little or no foreplay prior to intercourse.
d. A small minority of young people engage in premarital intercourse.

8.
K
Answer: c
pp. 26-27, 36
Obj. #3

The survey method
a. allows for flexibility of procedures.
b. is objective and largely eliminates problems of falsification.
c. can be done with the use of technology such as computers.
d. can only be generalized to the people who were actually surveyed.

9.
K
Answer: d
pp. 25-27
Obj. #3
WWW

Which of the following statements regarding case studies is false?
a. They are often used to study atypical sexual behavior.
b. They allow for flexible data gathering.
c. The researcher is not easily able to generalize findings to broader populations.
d. Masters and Johnson's research is an example of the case study method.

10.
K
Answer: b
p. 26
Obj. #3

One advantage of the case study method is that
a. generalizations can be drawn to the rest of the population.
b. in-depth, highly subjective information about the subjects can be obtained.
c. the researcher is able to discover norms for specified groups.
d. representative sample populations are fairly easy to obtain.

11.
A
Answer: b
p. 26
Obj. #3

Since case study evidence demonstrates that rapists often report high exposure to sexually violent pornography, we can conclude that
a. viewing violent pornography causes men to rape women.
b. there is an association between the exposure to violent pornography and rape.
c. the rapists were sexually abused themselves as children.
d. more legislation banning pornography should be passed.

12.
K
Answer: b
p. 26
Obj. #3

Much of what is known about transsexuals, incest victims and sex offenders has been learned from
a. surveys.
b. case studies.
c. direct observation.
d. the experimental method.

13.
K
Answer: c
p. 26
Obj. #3

All of the following are limitations of the case study method **except**
a. Memory distortions in recalling past events.
b. Difficulty in generalizing what is learned to the larger population.
c. Inflexible data-gathering procedures.
d. Not as appropriate as other methods for addressing many kinds of research questions.

14.
A
Answer: d
pp. 25-27
Obj. #3

As a result of conducting therapy with several call girls, a psychologist becomes interested in the various backgrounds of these women and what factors contributed to their involvement in this activity. She conducts in-depth interviews with five additional call girls and eventually publishes her findings. The research method she has used is
a. the naturalistic observation method.
b. direct observation.
c. the experimental method.
d. the case study method.

15.
K
Answer: b
pp. 25-27
Obj. #3
WWW

The case study is a research method in which
a. individuals are carefully observed in their natural environments.
b. individuals are studied in great detail.
c. a representative sample of people is questioned regarding their attitudes or behaviors.
d. an investigator manipulates one or more variables that may affect behavior.

16.
A
Answer: d
pp. 25-27
Obj. #3

In order to understand the unusual sexual behavior of a client, a psychologist carefully investigates the client's current life situation and his social, physical and psychological history. What research method has the psychologist used?
a. the experimental method
b. direct observation
c. the survey method
d. the case study

17.
A
Answer: c
pp. 25-27
Obj. #3

In order to further understand how brain malfunctions influence sexual behavior, Dr. Morales thoroughly observed and questioned four stroke victims in depth. What method did Dr. Morales use?
  a. the experimental method
  b. the representative sample method
  c. the case study
  d. naturalistic observation

18.
A
Answer: a
pp. 25-27
Obj. #3

After helping two of her psychotherapy clients deal with the impact of viewing excessive amounts of pornography on their intimate relationships, Dr. Kamari began to grossly overestimate the negative effects of viewing sexually explicit materials. Dr. Kamari should be reminded of the limits of
  a. case studies.
  b. surveys.
  c. self-selection.
  d. direct observation.

19.
K
Answer: b
p. 27
Obj. #3

In which type of research is a representative sample of people asked to answer questions about their sexual attitudes or behaviors?
  a. case study
  b. survey
  c. direct observation
  d. experiment

20.
K
Answer: b
p. 24
Obj. #3

Most of our scientific information about human sexuality has been obtained by
  a. case studies.
  b. surveys.
  c. direct observation.
  d. experimental research.

21.
K
Answer: d
p. 25
Obj. #4

In a (an) _____ sample, subgroups are represented according to their incidence in the larger population.
  a. survey
  b. equivalent
  c. random
  d. representative

22.
K
Answer: d
p. 28
Obj. #1
WWW

A representative sample
  a. is also known as a target sample
  b. is also known as a random sample
  c. is also known as a volunteer sample
  d. is also known as a probability sample

23.
A
Answer: d
p. 27-28
Obj. #3

Which research method would be **most** appropriate for investigating the relationship between the religious beliefs of Americans and their attitudes toward sex education in the schools?
a. the case study
b. the experimental method
c. direct observation
d. the survey

24.
A
Answer: a
p. 28
Obj. #4

In order to learn about the sexual attitudes and behaviors of all of students attending Cleveland High School, Professor Brewer randomly selected and surveyed 50 of the school's students. In this case, all of the students attending the high school are called the
a. target population.
b. dependent variable.
c. representative sample.
d. independent variable.

25.
A
Answer: c
p. 28
Obj. #4

In order to generalize accurately, it is important to survey a _____ sample of cases.
a. self-selected
b. target
c. representative
d. diverse

26.
K
Answer: c
p. 29
Obj. #5

Which of the following is an advantage of using questionnaires instead of interviews?
a. The researcher can develop a rapport with the subject.
b. They provide opportunities for flexibility.
c. They are usually anonymous.
d. They usually take longer and are more thorough.

27.
K
Answer: c
p. 29
Obj. #5

Which one is NOT true concerning samples in sex survey research?
a. Women tend to be more willing to cooperate.
b. Volunteers for research tend to be more sexually experienced.
c. The white middle class has been disproportionately represented.
d. The refusal of selected subjects to participate is a common problem.

28.
K
Answer: a
p. 29
Obj. #5

Which of the following is an advantage of using interviews instead of questionnaires?
a. They provide opportunities for flexibility.
b. They are less expensive than administering questionnaires.
c. They preserve anonymity.
d. Subjects are less likely to distort information with an interviewer.

Chapter 2   Research: Methods and Problems   27

29.
A
Answer: d
pp. 28-29
Obj. #5
WWW

Assume that you wanted to research a sensitive subject and that you planned to have a fairly large sample population. Helping the respondents to feel at ease as well as giving them an opportunity to elaborate on their answers is crucial. Adequate funding for your study is not a problem. Which of the following research methods would **best** suit your needs?
- a. case study
- b. questionnaire
- c. experimental research
- d. interview

30.
K
Answer: a
p. 29
Obj. #6

One of the problems with sex survey research is _____ , or the refusal to participate in a study.
- a. nonresponse
- b. low self-efficacy
- c. the bystander effect
- d. diffusion of responsibility

31.
K
Answer: b
p. 29
Obj. #6

The degree to which research data may be biased as a result of the differences in the people who choose to participate in a study as opposed to those who do not is called
- a. the bystander effect.
- b. self-selection.
- c. demographic bias.
- d. ethnocentrism.

32.
K
Answer: b
p. 29
Obj. #7

Several studies indicate that volunteers for sex research tend to
- a. demonstrate less sexual interest and activity than non-volunteers.
- b. be more sexually experienced than non-volunteers.
- c. have lower levels of sexual self-esteem than non-volunteers.
- d. be in long-term, committed relationships more than non-volunteers.

33.
A
Answer: c
p. 28
Obj. #4

In written or oral surveys, a relatively small group, called the _____, is used to draw conclusions about a larger group, called the _____.
- a. experimental group; control group
- b. random sample; representative sample
- c. survey sample; target population
- d. dependent variable; independent variable

34.
A
Answer: d
p. 28
Obj. #4

A local radio talk show host asks his listeners to call in and report how frequently they engage in sexual intercourse. Which of the following **best** describes the validity of this information?
a. Because a random sample of the audience will call in, this will be valid information.
b. Because this is considered a demographically balanced sample, the information will be valid.
c. Because the host is utilizing the experimental method instead of the survey method, the information will not be valid.
d. Because this sample is not representative of the community, it will not be valid.

35.
K
Answer: b
p. 29
Obj. #7

All of the following statements regarding people who volunteer for sex research are true **except**
a. They tend to have more positive attitudes toward sex than nonvolunteers.
b. They tend to be less educated than nonvolunteers.
c. They tend to be more sexually experienced than nonvolunteers.
d. Women may be less likely than men to volunteer for sex research.

36.
K
Answer: c
p. 29
Obj. #6
WWW

The fact that the majority of participants in sex research have been white, middle-class volunteers illustrates the problem of
a. random sampling.
b. probability sampling.
c. demographic bias.
d. data discrimination.

37.
A
Answer: c
p. 29
Obj. #6

You are conducting a large scale sex survey and want to ensure that the results are representative of the larger population. In other words, you want to minimize the problem of
a. ethnographic bias.
b. replicability.
c. demographic bias.
d. equivalent sampling.

38.
K
Answer: d
p. 30
Obj. #8

Kinsey and his associates obtained their data by means of
a. direct observation.
b. case studies.
c. experimental research.
d. survey interviews.

39.
K
Answer: b
p. 30
Obj. #2

_____ conducted the first extensive survey of American sexual behaviors.
a. Masters and Johnson
b. Kinsey
c. Hefner
d. Havelock Ellis

Chapter 2   Research: Methods and Problems   29

40.
K
Answer: c
p. 30
Obj. #9

The National Health and Social Life Survey reported which of the following concerning ethnic differences?
a. There are no major differences with respect to giving or receiving oral sex.
b. There are sex differences but no group differences for masturbation.
c. Hispanics are more likely than white Americans or African Americans to have sexual partners out of their own ethnic group.
d. Those from another planet were least willing to discuss their sexual behavior.

41.
K
Answer: c
p. 30
Obj. #8

Which of the following statements regarding Kinsey's research is false?
a. His sample contained a disproportionately greater number of better-educated city-dwelling Protestants.
b. African Americans were omitted from his sample.
c. All of the respondents were married and age 30 or older.
d. All of Kinsey's subjects were volunteers.

42.
K
Answer: c
p. 30
Obj. #8

Which of the following statements regarding Kinsey's research is true?
a. Approximately two thousand men and women were included in the final subject population.
b. The study population was a representative sample of the American population at the time.
c. He published one report on male sexuality and another one on female sexuality.
d. He used a variety of research methods to obtain his data.

43.
K
Answer: c
p. 30
Obj. #8

Which of the following statements **most** accurately describes Kinsey's research?
a. discovered the causes of sexual dysfunction in men and women
b. described the physiology of sexual behavior in women and men
c. described patterns of sexual behavior in men and women
d. reported the incidence of deviant sexual behavior in men

44.
K
Answer: a
p. 31
Obj. #8
WWW

Which is true concerning the Kinsey research?
a. There were actually two volumes, one on male sexuality and one on female sexuality.
b. Subjects were paid.
c. Fifty years have passed and none of the findings have been replicated recently.
d. The findings that hold up are probably due to the use of a representative sample.

45.
K
Answer: a
pp. 31-32
Obj. #9

For which of the following is the National Health and Social Life Survey **best** known?
a. a low level of nonresponse and good demographic balance of the survey population
b. use of the direct observation method and broadest range of information about human sexual behavior to date
c. case studies of over 1500 individuals regarding their sexual histories and experiences
d. survey results that indicated American people are much more sexually active than was previously believed.

46.
K
Answer: a
pp. 31-32
Obj. #22

The NHSLS revealed which of the following regarding American ethnicity and sexuality?
a. Both oral sex and masturbation were least common among African Americans.
b. Oral sex was least common among Hispanic Americans and masturbation was least common among whites.
c. Oral sex was least common among African Americans and masturbation was least common among Hispanics.
d. Both oral sex and masturbation were least common among Hispanic Americans.

47.
K
Answer: a
pp. 31-32
Obj. #9

Which one is NOT true concerning the National Health and Social Life Survey?
a. This was a large, federally funded project.
b. The NHSLC was carried out by a team of researchers from the University of Chicago.
c. This involved both a national and a representative sample.
d. More than ¾ of the people contacted agreed to participate.

48.
K
Answer: c
p. 32
Obj. #9

The single best survey ever conducted of adult sexual behavior to date is
a. Kinsey's research.
b. Masters and Johnson's research.
c. The National Health and Social Life Survey.
d. The *Redbook* Survey.

49.
K
Answer: c
p. 32
Obj. #9

The single best sex survey conducted in the United States was probably
a. that done by Kinsey.
b. carried out by Playboy.
c. the NHSLS.
d. conducted by Havelock Ellis.

50.
K
Answer: d
p. 32
Obj. #10

Survey studies of various populations of men have indicated that exposure to sexually violent pornography may lead to all of the following **except**
   a. reduced sensitivity to rape victims.
   b. increased tolerance of sexually aggressive behavior.
   c. greater acceptance of the myth that women want to be raped.
   d. increased arousal (as measured physiologically) in nonviolent sexual encounters.

51.
K
Answer: d
p. 33
Obj. #10
WWW

Which of the following statements **most** accurately reflects the survey findings regarding the effects of alcohol on sexual responsiveness?
   a. Drinking alcohol did not significantly affect sexual pleasure in men or women.
   b. Drinking alcohol enhanced sexual pleasure in women, but not in men.
   c. Drinking alcohol enhanced sexual pleasure in men, but not in women.
   d. Drinking alcohol enhanced sexual pleasure in both men and women.

52.
K
Answer: a
p. 33
Obj. #3

An advantage of the direct observation method is that
   a. it essentially eliminates the possibility of data falsification by research subjects.
   b. it preserves anonymity.
   c. it involves the unbiased participation of the researchers.
   d. the subjects' behavior is rarely affected by the observation techniques employed.

53.
K
Answer: b
p. 33
Obj. #11

Which of the following statements regarding Masters and Johnson's research is true?
   a. Their subjects were paid to participate in their study.
   b. Their final sample population consisted primarily of individuals with above average intelligence from an academic community.
   c. They employed the case study method of research.
   d. They employed the survey method of research.

54.
K
Answer: b
p. 33
Obj. #8

The book *Human Sexual Response* was written by
   a. Alfred Kinsey.
   b. Masters and Johnson.
   c. John Bancroft.
   d. Dr. Ruth.

55.
K
Answer: b
p. 33
Obj. #11

Which of the following stimulus situations was NOT used in Masters and Johnson's research?
   a. coitus with a partner
   b. oral-genital stimulation
   c. masturbation
   d. breast stimulation

56.
K
Answer: c
p. 34
Obj. #3

A major advantage of the experimental method is
a. obtaining in-depth information on the subjects involved.
b. flexibility.
c. control over variables that influence the behavior being studied.
d. anonymity.

57.
A
Answer: d
p. 34
Obj. #11

Masters and Johnson's research findings would be **least** likely to be applied in
a. the treatment of premature ejaculation.
b. infertility counseling.
c. general sex education.
d. the treatment of sexually compulsive behavior.

58.
K
Answer: b
p. 34
Obj. #13

In the experimental method, the _____ variable is controlled by the researcher while the _____ variable is the outcome that the experimenter observes and records.
a. dependent, independent
b. independent, dependent
c. random, representative
d. representative, random

59.
K
Answer: d
p. 34
Obj. #10

Which one is **most** true concerning the effect of exposure to violent pornography upon sexually violent behavior?
a. This has only been investigated by means of case studies because of ethical concerns.
b. This is probably of primary interest only to feminist theorists.
c. This is best studied by direct observation so no one can lie.
d. This has been studied experimentally using exposure to films and later attitude questionnaires.

60.
A
Answer: a
p. 34
Obj. #11
WWW

If you wanted information on how men and women respond physiologically during sexual arousal and orgasm, your **best** source of information would be
a. Masters and Johnson.
b. Kinsey.
c. The National Health and Social Life Survey.
d. The *Redbook* Survey.

61.
A
Answer: c
p. 34
Obj. #13

A group of college men is exposed to films with nonviolent sexual themes. A second group is exposed to R-rated films in which men commit sexual violence against women. Several days later, all men complete an attitude questionnaire. The results demonstrate that the second group of men is more accepting of violence toward women than the first group. What is the dependent variable in this study?
a. the films with non violent sexual themes
b. the films with sexually violent themes
c. the subjects' responses to the questionnaire
d. the attitude questionnaire

Chapter 2   Research: Methods and Problems   33

62.
A
Answer: d
p. 34
Obj. #13

In one high school, condoms are freely available. In another similar high school, students must request condoms from the school nurse. The number of pregnancies among both groups of students are compared. The dependent variable is
   a. the freely available condoms.
   b. the condoms available by request.
   c. the high school students from the first school.
   d. the number of pregnancies.

63.
A
Answer: a
p. 34
Obj. #13

A matched group of rapists and nonrapists listen to different taped descriptions of sexual activity, one involving rape and the other involving consensual sexual interaction. The researcher measures the degree of penile engorgement in each group to each of the tapes. The independent variable is
   a. the taped descriptions.
   b. the penile tumescence among rapists.
   c. the penile tumescence among nonrapists.
   d. the group of nonrapists.

64.
A
Answer: b
p. 34
Obj. #15

Which of the following research strategies would provide the **most** effective way of demonstrating that sexually violent media may cause or contribute to some rapists' assaultive behaviors?
   a. the survey
   b. the experiment
   c. direct observation
   d. the case study

65.
A
Answer: c
p. 34
Obj. #13

A matched group of rapists and nonrapists listen to different taped descriptions of sexual activity, one involving rape and the other involving consensual sexual interaction. The researcher measures the degree of penile tumescence in each group to each of the tapes. The dependent variable is
   a. the taped description involving rape.
   b. the taped description involving consensual sexual activity.
   c. the penile tumescence among rapists.
   d. the group of rapists.

66.
K
Answer: b
p. 34
Obj. #3d

Which of the following research methods can **best** explore cause-and-effect relationships?
   a. survey via interviews
   b. experimental
   c. direct observation
   d. survey via questionnaires

67.
A
Answer: c
p. 34
Obj. #3d
WWW

Which of the following research methods would be **most** appropriate if you wished to examine the effects of different room temperatures on physiological sexual response?
   a. case study
   b. interview
   c. experimental research
   d. questionnaire

68.
K
Answer: c
p. 35
Obj. #14

According to research cited in the text, what are the effects of alcohol on physiological sexual arousal?
a. Arousal is reduced at low levels but increased at high levels of alcohol intake.
b. Arousal is increased at low levels and reduced at high levels of alcohol intake.
c. Arousal is reduced with increasing levels of alcohol intake.
d. Arousal is not affected by alcohol intake.

69.
K
Answer: a
p. 36
Obj. #12

A vaginal photoplethysmograph
a. measures increased vaginal blood volume.
b. measures increased vaginal lubrication.
c. measures increases in vaginal length.
d. records orgasmic contractions.

70.
K
Answer: c
pp. 35-36
Obj. #12

The penile strain gauge
a. is designed to measure the length of the penis.
b. has the disadvantage that a trained professional must attach it.
c. has been used to measure the dependent variable in experimental research.
d. has been developed only with the advent of 21st Century technology.

71.
K
Answer: d
pp. 36-37
Obj. #12

Which one is NOT true concerning computer-assisted self-interview technology?
a. This can be administered to those who are not literate.
b. This can be done in private.
c. This is preferred by teenagers over face-to-face interviews.
d. This has problems because of lack of standardization in self-administration.

72.
K
Answer: c
p. 38
Obj. #12

Which is NOT an advantage of Web based research?
a. Cyberspace questionnaires are cheaper to distribute and collect.
b. Data can be more quickly and efficiently sent to a database.
c. Researchers don't have to worry about ethical issues as they never see the respondents.
d. It may be easier to locate unusual populations not available locally.

73.
K
Answer: d
pp. 38-39
Obj. #16

Feminist theory has criticized sex research for all of the following **except**
a. excessive focus on penile-vaginal intercourse.
b. research has been dominated by white, middle-class men.
c. research on homosexuality has focused primarily on gay men as opposed to lesbians.
d. emphasis on qualitative, as opposed to quantitative, research.

Chapter 2 Research: Methods and Problems   35

74.
K
Answer: a
pp. 38-39
Obj. #16
WWW

Feminist sexology theorists
a. may be male or female.
b. are primarily interested in women's health.
c. are mainly interested in increasing our understanding of lesbians.
d. prefer the case study or interview methodology.

75.
K
Answer: b
p. 39
Obj. #12

A researcher using the Internet for sex research
a. should send e-mail to the home, not the person's work place.
b. should make provisions for referral services if participants become upset.
c. has the advantage of automatically providing anonymity to participants by having them give code names.
d. may reasonably expect a high response rate.

76.
K
Answer: d
pp. 40-41
Obj. #17

Which of the following **best** describes the results of the '74 *Redbook* survey?
a. due to its large number of respondents, highly representative of female sexual attitudes at that time
b. significant in that over 30% of the magazine's readers completed the survey
c. questionnaires with follow-up interviews of several thousand women revealed in-depth information on female sexual attitudes and behavior
d. noteworthy because of its huge sample size, despite the biased nature of its sample

77.
K
Answer: b
pp. 40-41
Obj. #17

Which of the following are two major criticisms of magazine sex surveys?
a. use of deception and biased samples
b. biased samples and failure to use scientific methodology
c. small sample sizes and researchers who lack credibility
d. failure to use scientific methodology and high level of nonresponse

78.
K
Answer: d
p. 41
Obj. #17

The magazine sex survey of college students published as Sex on Campus
a. had a very high completion rate of questionnaires distributed.
b. happily found that a good majority of the sexually active respondents practiced safer sex all of the time.
c. used a probability sampling of kinds of colleges.
d. reported that a majority of respondents listed love as the most important ingredient in quality sex.

79.
A
Answer: a
p. 42
Obj. #18

Which of the following criteria would be **most** useful evaluating a particular piece of research?
a. Find out if other research confirms or contradicts the study in question.
b. Check to see if the book or article is labeled "scientific".
c. Determine whether the researcher has a doctoral degree.
d. Check to see if the survey method was used to obtain information, since this method seems to be the most reliable.

80.
K
Answer: c
p. 42
Obj. n/a

Which one is probably NOT true of the future of sexology?
a. It will be interdisciplinary.
b. It will make use of distance education.
c. It will be more fact than theory oriented.
d. It will see increasing levels of government funding for research in social problems.

Multiple Choice from Study Guide

1.
K
Answer: b
p. 24
Obj. #1

Sexology first became a field of scientific study during the
a. late 1960's after Masters & Johnson's landmark study was published.
b. 20th century.
c. 19th century.
d. early 1700's.

2.
K
Answer: b
pp. 26-27
Obj. #3

If a researcher wanted to know how many teenagers consumed alcohol or drugs prior to engaging in sexual activity, which research method would be **best** to use?
a. case study
b. survey
c. direct observation
d. experiment

3.
K
Answer: c
pp. 25-26
Obj. #3

Much of what is known about persons with sexual difficulties comes from
a. experiments.
b. questionnaires.
c. case studies.
d. cross-sectional studies.

4.
K
Answer: d
p. 28
Obj. #4

A research team is conducting a survey on the marital adjustment of newlyweds. Which is the **most** representative sample?
a. couples who established a bridal registry at a local department store
b. volunteers who responded to a newspaper ad
c. friends, neighbors, and co-workers of the research team
d. couples who took out marriage certificates within the last year

Chapter 2 Research: Methods and Problems 37

5.
K
Answer: b
p. 29
Obj. #7

Studies suggest that all of the following are characteristics of persons who volunteer for sex research **except**
 a. Volunteers are more sexually experienced
 b. Females are more likely to volunteer than males
 c. College students are more willing to volunteer
 d. Volunteers hold more positive attitudes toward sexuality

6.
K
Answer: a
pp. 26-28
Obj. #5

Which of the following is NOT associated with the survey research method?
 a. independent variable
 b. nonresponse
 c. questionnaire
 d. target population

7.
K
Answer: a
p. 31
Obj. #8

Kinsey's studies on American sexuality were pioneering, but limited because his sample included
 a. a disproportionate number of better educated persons.
 b. non-volunteers.
 c. large numbers of rural dwellers.
 d. mostly older adults.

8.
K
Answer: c
pp. 40-41
Obj. #17

Readers of "Sports Illustrated" and "Maxim" magazines were asked to complete a survey regarding their attitudes toward extramarital sex, and mail the survey to an address listed in the magazine. Which of the following best describes a key problem of this survey?
 a. the artificial nature of the environment may adversely affect the responses
 b. problems with memory fallibility will contaminate the results
 c. demographic bias may adversely affect the study
 d. subjects' reactivity may positively sway the results

9.
k
Answer: c
pp. 31-32
Obj. #9

The National Health and Social Life Survey is considered noteworthy because
 a. large numbers of prostitutes and their customers agreed to participate.
 b. it examined the sexual practices of teenagers.
 c. a very high response rate was obtained.
 d. new physiological recording devices were utilized.

10.
K
Answer: c
pp. 33-34
Obj. #3

Direct observation is a highly desirable method for studying sexuality because the possibility of _____ is greatly reduced.
 a. demographic bias
 b. researcher interpretive bias
 c. data falsification
 d. self-selection

11.
K
Answer: d
p. 26
Obj. #3

Case studies are of limited usefulness to sex research because
 a. they require rigid data gathering methods.
 b. A controlled environment must be created.
 c. superficial information about behavior is often produced.
 d. findings cannot be generalized to a larger population.

12.
K
Answer: c
p. 26
Obj. #3

Which of the following methods allows causal relationships to be discovered?
a. case study
b. survey
c. experimental method
d. direct observation

13.
K
Answer: b
p. 34
Obj. #3

A research team is investigating the sexual response of women with spinal cord injury to two types of erotica. One group of women reads a short story, whereas another group of women sees a short film clip. Measures of heart rate, blood pressure and vaginal blood volume are taken. What is the independent variable in this study?
a. heart rate
b. the type of erotica
c. vaginal blood volume
d. type of spinal cord injury

14.
K
Answer: d
pp. 35-36
Obj. #12

The penile strain gauge and the vaginal photoplethysmograph both measure
a. strength of muscle contraction.
b. galvanic response.
c. body temperature in the pelvic area.
d. sexual arousal.

15.
K
Answer: c
pp. 36-37
Obj. #12

Which of the following is NOT an advantage of computer-assisted self-interviews (CASI)?
a. respondents do not have to be literate
b. CASI is a less threatening way to report sensitive behaviors
c. normative behaviors may be underreported
d. question presentation can be standardized for all respondents

16.
Answer: d
p. 27
Obj. #20

Ethical guidelines for doing sex research with humans require that
a. no pressure or coercion be applied.
b. subjects have the right of refusal.
c. informed consent be obtained.
d. all of the above are true.

17.
K
Answer: b
pp. 38-39
Obj. #16

Several feminist sex researchers believe that traditional sex research is limited because
a. lesbians have been studied more than gay men.
b. research is based upon a male model of sexuality.
c. qualitative data have been emphasized.
d. statistical methods have not been utilized.

18.
K
Answer: a
pp. 38-39
Obj. #12

Surveys administered over the Internet may be especially useful because
a. participants can be recruited from distant places.
b. it is easier to guarantee anonymity than with any other method.
c. demographic bias is greatly minimized.
d. response rates are much higher.

Chapter 2 Research: Methods and Problems   39

19.
K
Answer: d
pp. 40-41
Obj. #17

Surveys in popular magazines should be viewed with skepticism because
   a. surveys are done primarily to sell a product.
   b. sample sizes are large but biased.
   c. scientific methodology is not typically used.
   d. all of the above are true.

20.
A
Answer: b
pp. 41-42
Obj. #17

Roberto reads a newspaper article which claims that sexual harassment and date rape are declining among college students. What question should Roberto ask to evaluate the legitimacy of the research?
   a. Does the article seem scientific?
   b. What are the credentials of the researchers?
   c. Did the reporter ask good questions of the researchers?
   d. Was the article easy to understand?

True/False

Students may be asked to answer these questions using the traditional format of marking their answers either "true" or "false". Or, to encourage more active involvement, you may choose to use the following instructions:

If the statement is true, place a "T" on the line preceding it. If the statement is false, place an "F" on the line preceding it and then change the statement to make it true by deleting incorrect information and/or adding accurate information.

1.
Answer: T
p. 26
Obj. #3

___ An advantage of the case study method of research is the flexibility allowed in obtaining information.

2.
Answer: F
p. 26
Obj. #3

___ The nature of the case study method readily lends itself to exploring cause-and-effect relationships.

3.
Answer: T
p. 27
Obj. #3

___ If saving money and maintaining anonymity were important considerations in doing research, administering a questionnaire would be preferable to conducting interviews.

4.
Answer: T
p. 28
Obj. #4

___ Representative samples allow for more accurate generalizations to a target population than do random samples.

5.
Answer: T
p. 24
Obj. #7

___ "Volunteer bias" refers to the self-selection of research samples.

6.
Answer: F
p. 29
Obj. #7

___ Current research suggests that people who volunteer to participate in sex research often have personal sexual problems they are seeking to resolve.

7.
Answer: T
p. 31
Obj. #9

___ The National Health and Social Life Survey provided the most comprehensive information about adult sexual behavior to date in the United States.

8.
Answer: F
p. 30
Obj. #8

___ Kinsey's research exemplifies a representative sample of the American population.

9.
Answer: F
pp. 31-33
Obj. #11

___ Kinsey's research has been a valuable source of information regarding physiological patterns of sexual response in men and women.

10.
Answer: T
pp. 33-34
Obj. #11

___ Masters and Johnson utilized an observational approach in researching how men and women respond physiologically to sexual stimulation.

11.
Answer: F
pp. 33-34
Obj. #11

___ Masters and Johnson's final research population consisted of male and female prostitutes.

12.
Answer: F
p. 34
Obj. #3

___ Most of the information we have learned regarding human sexuality has been obtained through experimental laboratory research.

13.
Answer: T
p. 34
Obj. #3

___ A research method that is being used with increasing frequency and allows for more investigative control is experimental research.

14.
Answer: T
p. 37
Obj. #12

___ Both male and female arousal can be measured electronically.

15.
Answer: T
p. 37
Obj. n/a

___ Teenagers have been found to prefer research done with audio computer administered programs more than face to face interviews.

16. ___ An example of feminist research methodology would be to interview male subjects about their feelings concerning prostrate disease or cancer.
Answer: T
p. 38
Obj. #16

17. ___ One advantage of research on the Web is that participants can be guaranteed anonymity.
Answer: F
pp. 38-39
Obj. #12

18. ___ A recent survey reported in *Sex on Campus* found that the clear majority of sexually active respondents practiced safer sex all of the time.
Answer: F
p. 41
Obj. #17

19. ___ A major indication of a good research study is one that has a large sample.
Answer: F
pp. 41-42
Obj. #18

20. ___ One consideration to be aware of in evaluating a piece of research is whether the particular research method used may have biased the findings.
Answer: T
pp. 41-42
Obj. #18

Short Answer Essay

1. One of the goals of a scientific discipline is to control or influence events. Discuss some reasons why this might be desirable in human sexuality and why this might be a matter of concern. (Obj. #1)

2. Name, describe and contrast the three nonexperimental research methods described in your text. (Obj. # 3)

3. Describe what case study evidence has found concerning the relationship between exposure to sexually violent pornography and rape and compare this to experimental findings. (Obj. # 5)

4. Select a question that interests you in the area of sexuality and describe which methodology you would use to answer it. (Obj. #2)

5. Sexual research began with Kinsey in the 1940's. Compare his approach to that used by the recent National Health and Social Life Survey. (Obj.#8)

6. How has the research of Masters and Johnson contributed to our understanding of human sexuality? Include a consideration of methodology, and subject population as well as the information obtained. (Obj. # 11)

7. What are some of the ethical and legal safeguards that are in place to protect participants in sexual research? (Obj. #20)

8. If a friend asked you whether or not it would be a good idea to participate in an anonymous magazine survey concerning sexuality, what would be your answer? (Obj. #17)

9. Specify at least four criteria for evaluating a piece of research. (Obj. #18)

10. Would you yourself be willing to be a participating subject in a research project that investigated your sexual attitudes? Your sexual behaviors? Why, or why not? (Obj. n/a)

11. What is a penile strain gauge? A vaginal photoplethysmograph? How are these devices used in research settings? (Obj. #12)

12. Why might one choose to do an interview rather than administer a questionnaire? What are some reasons why information gathered in an interview might be erroneous? (Obj. #3)

13. Define a representative sample and a random sample and describe how one might obtain such samples. (Obj. #4)

14. Specify some potential advantages and potential problems with research conducted over the Internet? (Obj. #12)

15. What is a feminist approach to research? What could such an approach offer in the area of sexuality for women? For men? (Obj. #16)

3
Gender Issues

Learning Objectives

After studying this chapter, the student should be able to:

1. Define the key terms and concepts listed in the margin of the text and be able to integrate them with all relevant material outlined below.

2. Distinguish between gender identity and gender role and provide examples of each.

3. List and describe the six different levels of gender-identity formation from a biological perspective.

4. Discuss some of the abnormalities that may occur in prenatal sex differentiation, making specific reference to the following:
    a. Turner's syndrome
    b. Klinefelter's syndrome
    c. androgen insensitivity syndrome
    d. fetally androgenized females
    e. DHT-deficient males

5. Explain how social-learning factors influence gender-identity formation.

6. Define the interactional model of gender-identity formation.

7. Discuss transsexualism, making specific references to the following:
    a. the characteristics of transsexualism
    b. various theoretical explanations regarding what causes gender dysphoria
    c. treatment options for people with gender dysphoria
    d. the various phases involved in sex reassignment surgery
    e. what studies have revealed regarding post-operative follow-up of the lives of transsexuals

8. Define and give examples of gender-based stereotypes.

9. Explain how parents, peers, schools, textbooks, television and religion contribute to the socialization of gender roles, making reference to relevant research.

10. List and describe five gender-role assumptions and explain how these stereotypes affect sexual attitudes and behaviors in men and women.

11. Define the term "androgyny" and discuss research comparing androgynous individuals to people who are gender-typed masculine or feminine.

Multiple Choice

1.
K
Answer: b
p. 46
Obj. #1

Our biological maleness or femaleness is called _____, whereas the psychosocial concept of our maleness or femaleness is called _____.
a. gender; sex
b. sex; gender
c. chromosomal sex; androgyny
d. androgyny; chromosomal sex

2.
K
Answer: a
p. 46
Obj. #1

Sex chromosomes determine our
a. genetic sex.
b. anatomical sex.
c. gender identity.
d. gender assumptions.

3.
K
Answer: c
p. 46
Obj. #1

Two aspects of our biological sex are
a. gonadal sex and gender sex.
b. chromosomal sex and gender identity.
c. genetic sex and anatomical sex.
d. genetic sex and gender identity.

4.
A
Answer: b
p. 46
Obj. #2

Which of the following did Mead report as occurring in the Tchambuli society of New Guinea?
a. Men are aggressive and dominant; women are passive and nurturing.
b. Women are aggressive and dominant; men are passive and nurturing.
c. Both men and women are aggressive and controlling.
d. Both men and women are androgynous.

5.
K
Answer: a
p. 46
Obj. #1
WWW

Gender refers to _____ while sex refers to _____.
a. social and cultural aspects of maleness or femaleness; biological aspects of maleness or femaleness
b. biological aspects of maleness or femaleness; social and cultural aspects of maleness or femaleness
c. chromosomal make-up; sex-differentiated behavior
d. sexual preference; sexual orientation

6.
A
Answer: c
p. 47
Obj. #2

The assumption that a man would work to support his family while his wife would stay home to care for their children would be an example of
a. gender identity.
b. gender dysphoria.
c. gender role expectations.
d. androgyny.

7.
A
Answer: b
p. 47
Obj. #1

Roberto meets his female neighbor, and based on her sex, makes predictions about her behavior. He is
a. discriminating against her.
b. making gender assumptions.
c. asserting his gender identity.
d. exhibiting androgynous behavior.

Chapter 3 Gender Issues 45

8.
K
Answer: a
p. 47
Obj. #2

"Gender role" refers to
a. attitudes and behaviors considered appropriate in a specific society for people of a particular sex.
b. an individual's decision that they wish to be male or female.
c. the perception of others that you are masculine or feminine.
d. subtle demonstrations of sexuality.

9.
A
Answer: d
p. 47
Obj. # 1, 2

When asked whether she is a boy or a girl, 3-year-old Marga enthusiastically states "I'm a girl!" Marga's response indicates that she has a clearly formed
a. gender role.
b. sexual orientation.
c. gender type.
d. gender identity.

10.
A
Answer: c
pp. 46-47
Obj. # 1, 2

When his older sister teases him, 9-year-old Tyrone does not cry because he has learned that boys are not supposed to cry. This exemplifies the concept of
a. gender identities.
b. sexual orientation.
c. gender roles
d. gender types.

11.
K
Answer: d
pp. 46-47
Obj. #1, 2

Which of the following statements is true?
a. Gender identity is determined by some aspect of biological sex.
b. Gender role expectations are largely consistent across cultures.
c. Genetic sex and anatomical sex are two aspects of gender.
d. Genetic sex is determined by our sex chromosomes.

12.
K
Answer: b
pp. 47-48
Obj. #3
WWW

Which of the following **most** accurately reflects the chronological sequence of normal prenatal differentiation?
a. chromosomal sex; hormonal sex; sex of the internal reproductive structures; gonadal sex; sex of the external genitals; sex differentiation of the brain
b. chromosomal sex; gonadal sex; hormonal sex; sex of the internal reproductive structures; sex of the external genitals; sex differentiation of the brain
c. chromosomal sex; sex of the internal reproductive structures; sex of the external genitals; gonadal sex; hormonal sex; sex differentiation of the brain
d. chromosomal sex; sex of the internal reproductive structures; sex of the external genitals; hormonal sex; gonadal sex; sex differentiation of the brain

13.
K
Answer: d
p. 47-57
Obj. #3, 5, 6

The formation of our gender identity is a result of
a. biological factors.
b. developmental status.
c. psychosocial factors.
d. biological and social-learning factors.

14.
K
Answer: d
pp. 48-51
Obj. #3

Which of the following is NOT a level of sexual differentiation?
a. chromosomal sex
b. hormonal sex
c. sex differentiation of the brain
d. gender identity

15.
K
Answer: a
p. 48
Obj. #3

The sex chromosomes for males are _____ and those for females are _____.
a. XY; XX
b. XX; XY
c. XO; XYY
d. XYY; XO

16.
K
Answer: c
pp. 47-48
Obj. #3

At the first level of sexual differentiation, _____ determine our biological sex.
a. Hormones
b. gonads
c. chromosomes
d. autosomes

17.
K
Answer: c
pp. 48-49
Obj. #3

Which one of the following is false with respect to genetics and development?
a. Human body cells contain a total of 22 pairs of autosome that do not influence sex differentiation.
b. The Y chromosome is essential for male development.
c. No triggers are necessary for a fetus to develop into a female.
d. the female reproductive cell is called an ovum.

18.
K.
Answer: c
p. 49
Obj. #3

The _____ are part of the endocrine system.
a. Wolffian ducts
b. Müllerian ducts
c. gonads
d. external genital structures

19.
K
Answer: a
p. 49
Obj. #3

_____ influence the development of female physical sex characteristics and help regulate the menstrual cycle.
a. Estrogens
b. Progestational compounds
c. Androgens
d. Wolffian ducts

20.
K
Answer: d
p. 49
Obj. #3

Which of the following statements regarding prenatal sexual differentiation is **most** accurate?
a. Differentiation at this time is not very important.
b. Differentiation occurs for what will be external genitals but not for other parts of the body.
c. DHT (dihydrotestosterone) stimulates the development of the Müllerian ducts.
d. In the absence of male hormones, female external genitals will develop.

Chapter 3 Gender Issues 47

21.
A
Answer: b
p. 49
Obj. #3

Which of the following does NOT belong with the others?
a. endocrine system
b. autosomes
c. estrogen
d. progesterone

22.
A
Answer: c
p. 46
Obj. #3
WWW

_____ is to androgens as _____ is to estrogens.
a. Estradiol; progesterone
b. SRY; testosterone
c. Testosterone; estradiol
d. Estrogen; progesterone

23.
K
Answer: b
p. 49
Obj. #3

Which of the following statements regarding estrogens is false?
a. Estrogens influence the development of female physical sex characteristics.
b. A main function of estrogen is to stimulate the development of the uterine lining in preparation for pregnancy.
c. Small amounts of estrogens are secreted from the adrenal glands.
d. Estrogens are secreted by the ovaries.

24.
K
Answer: b
p. 49
Obj. #3

The original mass of sexual tissue differentiates into male or female gonads approximately _____ after conception.
a. one week
b. six weeks
c. twelve weeks
d. sixteen weeks

25.
K
Answer: d
pp. 49-50
Obj. #3

In the embryo, female sex structures develop from _____, and male sex structures develop from _____.
a. Skene's ducts; the prostate gland
b. the prostate gland; Skene's ducts
c. Wolffian ducts; Müllerian ducts
d. Müllerian ducts; Wolffian ducts

26.
K
Answer: d
p. 51
Obj. #3

The clitoris of the female corresponds to the _____ of the male.
a. testes
b. foreskin of the penis
c. shaft of the penis
d. glans of the penis

27.
K
Answer: c
pp. 51-52
Obj. #3

Differences between the male and female hypothalamus are associated with the presence or absence of _____ during prenatal differentiation.
a. Müllerian inhibiting substance
b. progesterone
c. testosterone
d. autosomes

28.
K
Answer: c
pp. 51-52
Obj. #3

Which of the following statements regarding sex differentiation of the brain is **least** accurate?
a. It has been suggested that females score higher on tests of verbal skills because of sex differentiation of the brain.
b. The left and right cerebral hemispheres of the brain appear to be affected by prenatal sex differentiation processes.
c. The presence or absence of circulating estrogens during prenatal differentiation leads to difference in the hypothalamic region of the brain.
d. Studies indicate that males and females differ in the hypothalamic region.

29.
K
Answer: c
p. 52
Obj. #3

The _____ plays a major role in controlling the production of sex hormones.
a. left cerebral hemisphere
b. cerebral cortex
c. hypothalamus
d. medulla

30.
A
Answer: c
p. 48
Obj. #3
WWW

If an individual is to be a genetic female, she must receive a/an
a. X chromosome from her father and a Y chromosome from her mother.
b. X chromosome from her mother and a Y chromosome from her father.
c. X chromosome from her mother and an X chromosome from her father.
d. Y chromosome from her mother and a Y chromosome from her father.

31.
K
Answer: d
p. 52
Obj. #3

The right hemisphere of the brain is **more** specialized for
a. verbal functions.
b. physical coordination.
c. sensory awareness.
d. spatial tasks.

32.
K
Answer: b
p. 56
Obj. #3

Which of the following is true concerning various examples of prenatal hormonal abnormal exposures?
a. AIS genetic males who are insensitive to androgens will still be most comfortable reared as males.
b. Chromosomal females who are masculinized by prenatal hormones will behave in a typically masculine manner even when reared as females.
c. The research in this area is consistently supportive of a strong biological influence upon gender identity.
d. The research in this area is consistently supportive of a strong socialization influence upon gender identity.

Chapter 3 Gender Issues   49

33.
K
Answer: d
p. 52
Obj. #3

Which of the following statements **most** accurately reflects recent research regarding sex differences in verbal and spatial skills?
a. The differences appear to be more pronounced than earlier evidence indicated.
b. The differences are largely due to psychosocial factors.
c. The differences are largely due to biological factors.
d. At this time we cannot conclude that there is either a solid biological or psychosocial basis for the differences.

34.
K
Answer: a
p. 53
Obj. #4

Which of the following statements is false?
a. People with ambiguous genital characteristics are referred to as hermaphrodites.
b. True hermaphrodites have both ovarian and testicular tissue in their bodies.
c. True hermaphrodites are more common than pseudohermaphrodites.
d. A pseudohermaphrodite may be the result of a chromosomal disorder or a hormonal abnormality.

35.
K
Answer: b
p. 53
Obj. #4

Pseudohermaphrodites
a. are extremely rare compared to true hermaphrodites.
b. are born with gonads that match their chromosomal sex.
c. possess both ovarian and testicular tissue in their bodies.
d. are more androgynous than true hermaphrodites.

36.
K
Answer: d
p. 53
Obj. #4a

In Turner's Syndrome, the chromosome combination is _____ , while in Klinefelter's Syndrome the combination is _____ .
a. XO; XYY
b. XXY; XO
c. XYY; XO
d. XO; XXY

37.
K
Answer: c
p. 53
Obj. #4a

All of the following are characteristic of individuals with Turner's Syndrome **except**
a. normal external female genitals.
b. lack of menstruation at puberty.
c. above average height.
d. female gender identity.

38.
K
Answer: a
p. 53
Obj. #4b
WWW

All of the following are characteristic of individuals with Klinefelter's Syndrome **except**
a. anatomically female.
b. usually sterile.
c. above average height.
d. little or no interest in sexual activity.

39.
K
Answer: b
p. 54
Obj. #4b

A man who has an extra "X" chromosome, manifests some gender-identity confusion, is sterile and has an undersized penis would **most** likely
a. have Turner's Syndrome.
b. have Klinefelter's Syndrome.
c. be a transsexual.
d. have androgen insensitivity syndrome.

40.
K
Answer: c
p. 55
Obj. #4c

As a result of androgen insensitivity syndrome,
a. external genitals of the male newborn are abnormally large.
b. external genitals of the female newborn are normal, but there are no ovaries present.
c. external genitals of the male fetus fail to differentiate, and so the newborn has normal-looking female external genitals.
d. external genitals of the female fetus fail to differentiate, and so the newborn has normal-looking male external genitals.

41.
K
Answer: d
p. 55
Obj. #4c
WWW

The condition of androgen insensitivity syndrome is typically diagnosed when
a. the testicles do not descend.
b. the external genitals appear to have both male and female characteristics.
c. the clitoris and labia are abnormally large.
d. menstruation does not occur.

42.
K
Answer: b
p. 55
Obj. #4c

A finding that individuals with androgen insensitivity syndrome acquire a female gender identity would support the importance of _____ in the formation of gender-identity.
a. biological factors
b. social learning
c. physical appearance
d. hormones

43.
K
Answer: c
p. 55
Obj. #4d

Which of the following statements regarding fetally androgenized females is false?
a. The prenatal female may be exposed to excessive androgen as a result of drugs the mother takes during pregnancy.
b. The prenatal female may be exposed to excessive androgen that is produced by her own adrenal glands.
c. This condition is the result of a chromosomal abnormality.
d. The external genitalia of the female are masculinized as a result of this condition.

44.
K
Answer: a
pp. 55-56
Obj. #4d

One study of fetally androgenized females raised as girls revealed that **most** of them were
a. interested in traditionally masculine activities.
b. interested in traditionally feminine activities.
c. androgynous in their attitudes and behavior.
d. interested in changing their sex.

Chapter 3 Gender Issues   51

45.
K
Answer: b
p. 56
Obj. #3, 4e

_____ is a hormone that is necessary for the normal development of male external genitals.
a. AGS
b. DHT
c. AIS
d. FSH

46.
K
Answer: c
pp. 55-56
Obj. #3, 4c

DHT is a hormone that is necessary for the development of the
a. Müllerian ducts.
b. gonads.
c. male external genitals.
d. female external genitals.

47.
K
Answer: a
p. 56
Obj. #4e

Which of the following statements regarding the Dominican Republic study of DHT-deficient males is true?
a. The individuals were raised as girls from birth.
b. The individuals had chromosomal abnormalities that made their internal reproductive structures fail to develop.
c. The study supported the idea that once gender identity is established, it is difficult to change.
d. Gender identity was influenced by their matriarchal culture.

48.
K
Answer: d
p. 56
Obj. #4d, 4e
WWW

That prenatal androgens may have masculinized their brains is a possible explanation for
a. androgen insensitivity syndrome and fetally androgenized females.
b. DHT-deficient males and androgen insensitivity syndrome.
c. fetally androgenized females and transsexualism.
d. fetally androgenized females and DHT-deficient males.

49.
K
Answer: c
p. 57
Obj. #5

Most children have developed a firm sense of being a boy or a girl by
a. 6 months.
b. 12 months.
c. 18 months.
d. 3 years.

50.
K
Answer: d
p. 58
Obj. #5

Margaret Mead's fieldwork in three societies in New Guinea revealed that
a. the men in these societies assume the active, dominant role.
b. the women in these societies assume the active, dominant role.
c. the men and women in these studies exhibit androgynous behaviors.
d. there is considerable variation in what is considered masculine or feminine, depending on the culture.

51.
K
Answer: b
p. 58
Obj. #5

According to the research John Money conducted in the mid-70s, most children whose assigned sex did not match their chromosomal sex developed
a. a strong desire to change their sex.
b. a gender identity consistent with the way in which they were reared.
c. adjustment difficulties.
d. into gays or lesbians.

52.
K
Answer: b
p. 58
Obj. #5

In Margaret Mead's classic book *Sex and Temperament in Three Primitive Societies*, differences between the sexes are explained in terms of
a. biological factors.
b. social learning factors.
c. sociobiological factors.
d. the interactional model.

53.
K
Answer: b
pp. 58-59
Obj. #5, 6

In the mid-70s, John Money published an unusual study of two identical twin boys, one of whom experienced a circumcision accident at eight months. Recent follow-up research on this case has revealed
a. that socialization plays an even greater role in gender-identity formation than was originally assumed.
b. that the effect of prenatal hormones on brain differentiation may be much more influential in gender-identity formation than was originally assumed.
c. clear evidence that gender identity is psychologically neutral at birth.
d. That twins were really not identical.

54.
K
Answer: d
pp. 59-60
Obj. #7

Which is false concerning recent findings or trends for intersexed children?
a. Some intersexed children left with ambiguous genitals have adjusted comfortable to this condition.
b. Genital altering surgery can impair the capacity for sexual pleasure.
c. The Intersex Society of North America argues that it is unethical to operate on intersexed babies who are unable to provide consent.
d. If sex reassignment surgery is chosen, adults (including professionals) should avoid discussion of this with the children until they are at least adolescents.

55.
K
Answer: a
p. 59
Obj. #4

Research on the development of 27 males born without penises and 25 sex reassigned after birth supports the conclusion that
a. those who were raised as males even without a penis were more well adjusted.
b. the original diagnosis of cloacal exstrophy was incorrect.
c. these sex reassigned children were tomboys, but clearly identified as girls.
d. things turned out better if sex reassignment had been done earlier.

Chapter 3 Gender Issues 53

56.
K
Answer: c
p. 61
Obj. #6

The term "interactional model" refers to
   a. a protocol for how to talk to cross sexed persons.
   b. a description of meiosis.
   c. an acknowledgement of the role of both biology and experience in the development of gender identity.
   d. guidelines for good gender role dating expectations.

57.
K
Answer: d
p. 62
Obj. #7

Another term for transsexualism is
   a. transvestism.
   b. homosexuality.
   c. hermaphroditism.
   d. gender dysphoria.

58.
K
Answer: b
p. 62
Obj. #7

A _____ crossdresses for sexual arousal, while a _____ crossdresses in order to feel comfortable and congruent.
   a. transsexual; transvestite
   b. transvestite; transsexual
   c. hermaphrodite; transsexual
   d. transvestite; hermaphrodite

59.
A
Answer: d
p. 63
Obj. #7a

Most male-to-female transsexuals would want to be romantically and sexually involved with a
   a. lesbian.
   b. heterosexual woman.
   c. gay man.
   d. heterosexual man.

60.
A
Answer: a
p. 63
Obj. #7a
WWW

The **majority** of transsexuals would describe their sexual orientation as
   a. heterosexual.
   b. homosexual.
   c. bisexual.
   d. asexual.

61.
A
Answer: c
pp. 62-64
Obj. #10

Which of the following is true concerning variant gender identity?
   a. Sexual orientation is an example of one variant gender identity.
   b. A transgenderist has no desire to alter his or her physical body.
   c. The transgendered community has about the same percentage of gays, lesbians and bisexuals as does the general population.
   d. Transexuals who do not have surgery are never really happy.

62.
K
Answer: a
p. 63
Obj. #7a

Most female-to-male transsexuals would probably describe their sexual orientation as
   a. heterosexual.
   b. homosexual.
   c. bisexual.
   d. asexual.

63.
K
Answer: c
p. 63
Obj. #7e

Which of the following **best** describes the sexual orientation of male-to-female transsexuals?
  a. predominantly homosexual
  b. predominantly bisexual
  c. usually heterosexual, but sometimes bisexual
  d. usually homosexual, but sometimes heterosexual

64.
K
Answer: a
p. 64
Obj. #7a

Most transsexuals first begin identifying with the other sex
  a. in early childhood.
  b. in early adolescence.
  c. in late adolescence.
  d. in early adulthood.

65.
K
Answer: d
p. 64
Obj. #7b

Which of the following is the **most** accurate statement regarding the cause of transsexualism?
  a. Prenatal exposure to hormones of the other sex probably leads to transsexualism.
  b. Unusual social learning experiences are the cause of transsexualism.
  c. A chromosomal abnormality has been shown to be associated with some transsexualism.
  d. There is insufficient evidence at this time to draw any definitive conclusions concerning the cause of transsexualism.

66.
K
Answer: c
p. 64
Obj. #7a, 7b

Which of the following statements is true?
  a. The majority of transsexuals have a chromosomal abnormality.
  b. The majority of transsexuals were emotionally abused as children.
  c. The majority of transsexuals are biologically normal.
  d. The majority of transsexuals were exposed to excessive amounts of androgen prenatally.

67.
K
Answer: d
pp. 65-67
Obj. #7d

Sex reassignment typically involves all of the following **except**
  a. screening interviews prior to surgery.
  b. hormone therapy.
  c. surgery.
  d. orgasm reconditioning therapy.

68.
K
Answer: d
pp. 65-67
Obj. #7c, 7d

Which of the following statements regarding transsexuals is false?
  a. When female-to-male transsexuals are given testosterone, menstruation is suppressed.
  b. Even though they are given drugs that inhibit testosterone production, most male-to-female transsexuals experience no lowering of vocal pitch.
  c. Most candidates for sex-reassignment surgery are required to live at least year or more as a person of the sex to which they wish to be reassigned.
  d. Once hormone therapy has begun, the changes that result cannot be successfully reversed.

69.
K
Answer: b
p. 67
Obj. #7e

Post operative studies of transsexuals have shown their adjustment to be
a. generally negative.
b. generally positive.
c. initially positive, but eventually problematic.
d. positive for those originally female but negative for those originally male.

70.
K
Answer: a
pp. 65-67
Obj. #7d

Surgical procedures for persons requesting sex reassignment are
a. most effective for men wishing to be women.
b. most effective for women wishing to be men.
c. equally effective for both sexes.
d. not effective for either sex.

71.
K
Answer: c
p. 67
Obj. #7e

Which of the following statements regarding orgasmic capacity in postoperative transsexuals is supported by research?
a. Orgasm is not likely to occur.
b. One study found an increase in the male-to-female group.
c. One study found an increase in the female-to-male group.
d. This topic has not been dealt with in research.

72.
K
Answer: a
p. 67
Obj. #8

Which of the following is NOT an example of a commonly held gender-based stereotype?
a. Women are logical.
b. Men are aggressive.
c. Women are emotional.
d. Men are competitive.

73.
K
Answer: d
p. 67
Obj. #8

Which of the following statements regarding gender-role stereotypes is true?
a. Gender-role stereotypes are becoming more rigid in our culture.
b. "Men are dependent" is an example of a commonly held gender-role stereotype.
c. Stereotypes take individuality into account.
d. Women appear to be somewhat more willing than men to believe that relations should be equal.

74.
A
Answer: c
p. 67
Obj. #8

Which of the following comments is **least** representative of stereotyped thinking?
a. "You can usually tell if someone is gay."
b. "She asks guys out so she must be very promiscuous."
c. "He wears his heart on his sleeve."
d. "Women are so illogical."

75.
K
Answer: c
p. 68
Obj. #9
WWW

Most theorists believe that gender roles are **primarily** a result of
a. brain differences.
b. hormonal variations.
c. socialization.
d. differences in reproduction roles.

76.
K
Answer: d
p. 68
Obj. #9

In which of the following ethnic groups would you most likely find a couple with a relationship characterized by egalitarianism?
   a. Caucasian
   b. Hispanic American
   c. Asian American
   d. African American

77.
K
Answer: b
p. 68
Obj. #9

Which one is false with respect to parent and offspring interaction, on the average?
   a. Girl babies get more attention than boy babies.
   b. Boys are encouraged to express emotions; both positive and negative.
   c. Parents are more protective of girls and allow boys more freedom.
   d. Fathers are more likely than mothers to convey gender role expectations.

78.
K
Answer: a
p. 70
Obj. #9

Recent research indicates that children currently
   a. respond to their peers in gender-stereotyped ways.
   b. tend to exhibit androgynous behavior during late childhood and adolescence.
   c. are not much affected by their peers' views of appropriate gender roles.
   d. exhibit sex-stereotyped behavior to a greater degree than previous generations.

79.
K
Answer: d
p. 70
Obj. #9

By first grade, children select same sex playmates about _____ percent of the time.
   a. 25
   b. 50
   c. 70
   d. 95

80.
K
Answer: c
p. 70
Obj. #9

Studies of the classroom treatment of boys and girls found that
   a. teachers treat boys and girls largely the same in the classroom.
   b. teachers call upon and encourage girls more than boys.
   c. teachers call upon and encourage boys more than girls.
   d. whether or not teachers treat boys and girls differently depends upon their own gender.

81.
K
Answer: b
p. 71
Obj. #9

Which of the following statements regarding the impact of education on gender roles is false?
   a. It is common for teachers to expect girls to excel in subjects like English and literature.
   b. Elementary school girls are more likely to receive praise, criticism, or help from their teachers than are elementary school boys.
   c. Teachers may expect boys to excel in subjects such as math and science.
   d. Girls who act dependent get their teachers' attention.

82.
A
Answer: a
pp. 71-72
Obj. #9

Which of the following would be **most** commonly found in an elementary school textbook in the late 1960s?
   a. girls portrayed as dependent and unambitious
   b. boys portrayed as sensitive and nurturant
   c. girls portrayed as strong and successful
   d. both boys and girls portraying flexibility in gender roles

83.
K
Answer: b
p. 72
Obj. #9

Research on gender role stereotypes in television has shown that
   a. one of the advantages of Sesame Street is that is not sexist.
   b. during the February 2000 sweeps prime time television was still largely a male dominated medium with women presented stereotypically.
   c. young girl TV watchers pay more attention to the competency of female television personalities that to their physical appearance, which is what males attend to.
   d. television is probably not as influential as the movies that children watch.

84.
K
Answer: d
p. 73
Obj. #9

It is suggested that the _____ presence of women on television may be a result of _____.
   a. decreased; a backlash effect against feminism
   b. decreased; product marketing that is directed toward men
   c. increased; efforts to reverse traditional gender-role typecasting
   d. increased; product marketing that is directed toward women

85.
K
Answer: c
p. 73
Obj. #9

Which of the following is NOT true concerning television watching?
   a. Men control the remote.
   b. Women are more likely to purchase products advertised on commercials.
   c. Men watch television more than do women in prime time.
   d. There are an increasing number of powerful women depicted on television.

86.
K
Answer: b
p. 73
Obj. #9

With respect to religion and gender, which one is true?
   a. Religious education probably has helped to bring about gender equality as much as anything in this country.
   b. Women were first ordained as clergy in the 1970's.
   c. The emphasis on Mary has made the Catholic church a leader in gender equality approaches.
   d. Catholicism and Judaism are alike in that they do not allow women to be priests or rabbis.

87.
K
Answer: a
p. 73
Obj. #9

Most religious organizations in the United States emphasize
   a. male dominance.
   b. female dominance.
   c. androgyny.
   d. undifferentiated gender roles.

88.
A
Answer: c
pp. 74-75
Obj. #10
WWW

A man quits dating a woman who openly expresses her interest in and enjoyment of sex, calling her a "sleaze". He behaves the same way and is perceived as a "stud". According to the text, the gender-role assumption underlying this behavior is
a. men as "sexperts."
b. women as controllers, men as movers.
c. women as undersexed, men as oversexed.
d. men as unemotional, women as nurturing.

89.
A
Answer: c
p. 75
Obj. #10

Tracey likes to ask men out, but she becomes frustrated when they assume she wants to have sex with them because of her assertiveness. Tracey is a victim of which of the following gender-role assumptions?
a. men as unemotional, women as nurturing
b. women as controllers, men as movers
c. men as initiators, women as recipients
d. men as "sexperts"

90.
A
Answer: c
p. 76
Obj. #10

Alex feels that making sure he and his wife have good sex is his "job," planning when and where, making sure they both enjoy it, etc. Despite his concerns, his wife has been reluctant to assume a more active role in their sexual relationship. This couple is a victim of which of the following gender assumptions?
a. women as undersexed, men as oversexed
b. men as strong, women as supportive
c. men as "sexperts"
d. women as controllers, men as movers

91.
A
Answer: b
pp. 77-78
Obj. #11

Which of the following is the **best** example of a child-rearing practice that is likely to lead to androgyny?
a. A girl is encouraged to do well in English and literature.
b. A boy is taught how to cook.
c. A boy is encouraged to compete in sports.
d. A girl is encouraged to express her feelings openly.

92.
K
Answer: c
pp. 77-78
Obj. #11

Which of the following statements regarding androgynous individuals is false?
a. They are more flexible in their behavior than people who are strongly gender-typed.
b. They are more nurturing than people who adhere to the masculine role.
c. They tend to be less achievement-oriented than people who are strongly gender-typed.
d. They are more independent than individuals who strongly identify with the feminine role.

Chapter 3 Gender Issues 59

93.
K
Answer: d
pp. 77-78
Obj. #11

Research on androgynous individuals indicates that
a. it is not really possible to develop a measure of this characteristic.
b. they experience less job-related stress than strongly gender-typed individuals.
c. they tend to be free of many of the potential problems that plague more gender-typed individuals.
d. they tend to demonstrate greater personal satisfaction than gender-typed individuals.

94.
K
Answer: d
p. 77
Obj. #11

Androgynous individuals tend to
a. have more negative attitudes toward sexuality than traditionally gender-typed individuals.
b. be more judgmental of the sexual behaviors of others.
c. be more sexually experienced than traditionally gender-typed individuals.
d. be more aware of their feelings of love and more able to express them.

95.
A
Answer: c
pp. 77-78
Obj. #11

A man who enjoys parenting his children, does laundry, competes in sports and changes the oil in his car would **most** likely be
a. bisexual.
b. gender dysphoric.
c. androgynous.
d. pseudohermaphroditic.

Multiple Choice from Study Guide

1.
A
Answer: b
p. 47
Obj. #2

Five-year-old Jorge and his friends are playing "dress-up" and wearing women's clothing. When his playmates ask him if he is a boy or girl, Jorge emphatically replies, "I'm a boy!". Jorge's answer **best** reflects his
a. gender assumptions.
b. gender identity.
c. gender role.
d. intersexed characteristics.

2.
K
Answer: c
p. 41
Obj. #1

When we say someone is female because she has a vulva and uterus, we are referring to
a. gender role.
b. gender identity.
c. sex.
d. autosomal sex.

3.
K
Answer: c
p. 48
Obj. #3

If a sperm carrying an _____ sex chromosome fertilizes an egg carrying an _____ sex chromosome, a male fetus is produced.
a. X; X
b. X; Y
c. Y; X
d. Y; Y

4.
K
Answer: a
p. 49
Obj. #3

The primary hormone products of the ovaries are _____ and _____ for the testes.
a. estrogens; androgens
b. estrogens; androgynous compounds
c. progesterone; DHEA
d. progesterone; androgynous compounds

5.
K
Answer: d
p. 49
Obj. #3

The male gonads are called _____ and the female gonads are called _____.
a. prostate glands; fallopian tubes
b. seminal vesicles; ovaries
c. Cowper's glands; Bartholin's glands
d. testes; ovaries

6.
K
Answer: b
pp. 49-50
Obj. #3

In a male fetus that develops normally, the _____ ducts become the internal reproductive structures.
a. Mullerian
b. Wolffian
c. Ejaculatory
d. Mullerian-inhibiting

7.
K
Answer: c
pp. 51-52
Obj. #3

The strongest support for sex differences in the brain comes from studies of the
a. hippocampus.
b. nucleus accumbens.
c. hypothalamus.
d. homunculus.

8.
K
Answer: d
p. 51
Obj. #4

Which of the following is considered a form of atypical prenatal differentiation due to a disorder of the sex chromosomes?
a. androgen insensitivity syndrome
b. DHT-deficient males
c. fetally androgenized females
d. Klinefelter's syndrome

9.
K
Answer: d
pp. 55-56
Obj. #3

What conclusion can be reached regarding the biological basis of gender identity formation, based on studies done with intersexed children exposed to abnormal prenatal hormones?
a. Gender identity is based upon chromosomal sex.
b. Gender identity is based upon the appearance of external genitalia.
c. Gender identity is based upon functional capacity of the gonads.
d. Studies provide contradictory evidence, so no firm conclusion can be reached.

10.
K
Answer: b
p. 57
Obj. #2

Most children have developed a firm gender identity by
a. one year of age.
b. 18 months of age.
c. three years of age.
d. five years of age.

Chapter 3 Gender Issues 61

11.
K
Answer: a
pp. 57-58
Obj. #5

Which of the following research findings does NOT support a social-learning view of gender identity formation?
a. Some intersexed children did not adopt a gender identity consistent with their assigned sex.
b. Parents treat newborn boys and girls differently.
c. Mead's studies showed that different societies had different views about what is deemed masculine or feminine.
d. Girls are encouraged to be cooperative, whereas boys are encouraged to be aggressive.

12.
K
Answer: c
pp. 60-61
Obj. n/a

Standard protocols for the treatment of intersexed children are being questioned because of
a. the difficulty of performing surgery on very young patients.
b. the number of new intersexed conditions being discovered.
c. The lack of long term outcome studies.
d. the growing acceptance of androgyny.

13.
K
Answer: b
p. 62
Obj. #7

Which of the following **best** describes a transsexual?
a. An intersexed person who agrees to genital altering surgery.
b. Someone whose gender identity does not agree with their biological sex.
c. A person who is sexually attracted to a member of the same sex.
d. A person who cross-dresses in order to achieve sexual gratification.

14.
K
Answer: c
p. 63
Obj. #7

Transsexuals have a predominantly _____ orientation.
a. homosexual
b. bisexual
c. heterosexual
d. psychosexually neutral

15.
K
Answer: a
p. 62
Obj. #7

Transgenderists can be distinguished from transsexuals because transgenderists
a. do not wish to change their bodies.
b. are more politically active.
c. have higher rates of mental illness.
d. are more likely to experience gender dysphoria.

16.
K
Answer: b
p. 65
Obj. #7

What statement **best** reflects current treatment options for transsexuals?
a. Psychotherapy can help change gender identity.
b. Psychotherapy alone cannot change gender identity.
c. Biological alteration is only necessary if there is the possibility of suicide.
d. Biological alteration is required in order for successful adjustment to occur.

17.
K
Answer: d
p. 67
Obj. #7

Studies of transsexuals who have undergone sex reassignment surgery have shown that
a. Adjustment is better for men becoming women.
b. Adjustment is better for women becoming men.
c. Adjustment is better when the period of living as the other sex is longer.
d. Adjustment is better for a substantial majority.

18.
A
Answer: a
p. 67
Obj. #8

Britta assumes that her new boyfriend will be able to fix her broken car, because she believes men are more mechanically inclined. Britta's behavior reflects
a. gender stererotypes.
b. gender identity.
c. androgyny.
d. marianismo.

19.
K
Answer: d
pp. 68-69
Obj. #9

Parents provide gender-role socialization by
a. giving girl babies more attention.
b. encouraging assertive behavior in sons.
c. using different communication styles with sons and daughters.
d. all of the above.

20.
K
Answer: b
pp. 70-71
Obj. #9

Peers influence the formation of traditional gender roles by
a. offering a haven relatively free from gender role stereotypes.
b. providing and withholding social acceptance.
c. encouraging rebellion against parents' efforts to engrain stereotypes.
d. encouraging play in mixed-sex groups.

21.
K
Answer: c
pp. 72-73
Obj. #9

Studies of television programming have demonstrated that
a. most Sesame Street characters are female.
b. advertising features more girls than boys.
c. women are valued primarily for physical appearance.
d. traditional stereotypes dominate primarily in sitcoms.

22.
K
Answer: a
pp. 68-69
Obj. n/a

Which of the following groups tends to have the **most** egalitarian relations between men and women?
a. African Americans
b. Hispanic Americans
c. White Americans
d. Asian Americans

23.
A
Answer: c
pp. 74-77
Obj. #10

Even though Leticia loves her partner very much, she frequently denies that she has feelings of sexual arousal, preferring to think that she is just tense from all the stress she is under. Leticia's behavior illustrates the negative impact of which gender-role expectation?
a. women as controllers, men as movers
b. men as "sexperts"
c. men as oversexed, women as undersexed
d. men as initiators, women as controllers

24.
A
Answer: b

pp. 74-77
Obj. #10

Kyle feels compelled to make the first sexual advance with a new date, even though he'd really prefer to get to know someone better first, yet Kyle is concerned his date will think he's weird. Kyle's dilemma reflects which gender-role expectation?
a. men as strong and unemotional, women as nurturing and supportive
b. men as oversexed, women as undersexed
c. men as movers, women as controllers
d. men as "sexperts"

25.
A
Answer: a
p. 77
Obj. #11

Baseball player Mark McGwire has cried at a press conference, hugged rival Sammy Sosa numerous times, expressing affection and admiration for this competitor. McGwire's behavior exemplifies
a. androgyny
b. misogyny
c. misanthropism
d. hegemony

True/False

Students may be asked to answer these questions using the traditional format of marking their answers either "true" or "false". Or, to encourage more active involvement, you may choose to use the following instructions:

If the statement is true, place a "T" on the line preceding it. If the statement is false, place an "F" on the line preceding it and then change the statement to make it true by deleting incorrect information and/or adding accurate information.

1.
Answer: F
p. 47
Obj. #2

___ Gender role refers to an individual's subjective sense of being female or male.

2.
Answer: F
p. 46
Obj. #3

___ Masculine and feminine refer to primarily innately determined characteristics.

3.
Answer: T
p. 48
Obj. #3

___ Two X chromosomes are needed for the complete development of both internal and external female structures.

4.
Answer: T
p. 49
Obj. #3

___ The gonads are part of the endocrine system, and include testes or ovaries.

5.
Answer: T
p. 49
Obj. #3

___ Androgen is secreted by the adrenal glands in both sexes.

6.
Answer: F
pp. 50-51
Obj. #3

___ Prenatal sexual differentiation appears to affect aspects of the endocrine system, but not the nervous system or brain.

7.
Answer: T
p. 49
Obj. #3

___ In the absence of androgens, the fetus develops female structures.

8.
Answer: T
p. 51
Obj. #3

___ The scrotum of the male is homologous to the labia majora of the female.

9.
Answer: T
pp. 53-54
Obj. #3

___ All persons with Turner's Syndrome are females and all persons with Klinefelter's Syndrome are males..

10.
Answer: F
p. 55
Obj. #4a

___ Individuals with androgen insensitivity syndrome are also chromosomally abnormal.

11.
Answer: F
p. 56
Obj. #4e

___ The Dominican Republic study of DHT-deficient males suggests that once gender identity is established during the formative years it is highly resistant to change.

12.
Answer: T
pp. 58
Obj. #5

___ The research of Margaret Mead supports a social-learning perspective regarding gender identity formation.

13.
Answer: F
p. 60
Obj. n/a

___ Intersexed children who are born with anomalous genitals should have surgery prior to the age of 18 months when they will have developed gender identify.

14.
Answer: F
p. 62
Obj. #7a

___ A person whose gender identity is opposite to his or her biological sex is called a transvestite, and usually has a heterosexual orientation.

15.
Answer: F
p. 63-64
Obj. #7a, 7c

___ Currently, more women than men request sex-reassignment surgery, probably because of the greater rewards of the male gender role.

Chapter 3 Gender Issues 65

16.
Answer: T
p. 64
Obj. #7a

___ Transsexuals are biologically normal and usually develop a sense of being at odds with their genital anatomy in early childhood.

17.
Answer: F
p. 64
Obj. #7b

___ Current research strongly supports a social learning explanation for what causes transsexualism.

18.
Answer: T
p. 67
Obj. #7e

___ Although it is costly and very time consuming, the great majority of transsexuals are satisfied and better socially adjusted after surgical alteration.

19.
Answer: F
p. 68
Obj. #9

___ As a result of the widespread influence of television there is little variation between ethnic groups in the United States with respect to gender roles.

20.
Answer: T
p. 73
Obj. #9

___ Although there were no female Protestant clergy until after 1970, almost 1/3 of seminarians are now women.

21.
Answer: T
p. 76
Obj. #10

___ A man complains about the feeling that it is his "job" to be knowledgeable, experienced and informed in his sexual relationship with his partner, and her attitude of sexual naiveté seems to reinforce this. They are both victims of the "men as 'sexperts'" gender-role stereotype.

22.
Answer: T
p. 77
Obj. #11

___ Androgynous individuals are more flexible in their behavior than those who are strongly gender-typed.

Short Answer Essay

1. Define and contrast the following: sex, gender, gender identity, and gender roles. (Obj. #1)

2. How are the terms masculine and feminine related to gender roles? Give examples of these as found in the US culture. (Obj. #1)

3. Two major brain areas are involved in prenatal sex differentiation. Specify these areas and state major findings concerning each. (Obj. #3)

4. Refer to appropriate research and build a case that the interactional model best explains the development of gender identity formation. (Obj. #4, 5, 6)

5. Turner's Syndrome and Klinefelter's Syndrome are two sex chromosome disorders. Choose one. Specify the chromosome cause, incidence, and characteristics of the individuals affected. (Obj. #4)

6. Findings with respect to the several disorders of prenatal hormonal processes are inconsistent with respect to whether they support biological or social factors in gender-identity formation. Describe these differing findings. (Obj. #6)

7. Suppose that you become the parent of an intersexed baby. What would you consider in assigning sex/gender? Would you have surgical intervention? Why, or why not? (Obj. n/a)

8. Define and contrast the following: transgendered, transsexual, and transvestite. (Obj. #7)

9. List the steps that are recommended prior to a final decision for sex reassignment surgery. What do post-operative follow-up studies find concerning the outcome for this surgery? (Obj. #7)

10. What does research say about how parents differentially treat their boy and girl offspring? How and to what extent would this be expected to influence gender roles? (Obj. #9)

11. Specify for each of the following ethnic groups one way in which gender roles often differ from the mainstream culture of white Americans of European origin: Hispanic Americans; African Americans; Asian Americans. (Obj. #8)

12. Give examples of gender typed images that you observed in school, on television, and in religious settings. State whether these appear to be typical according to your textbook. (Obj. #9)

13. List three stereotyped gender-role assumptions in the area of sexuality and give specific examples regarding how these assumptions may impact sexual attitudes and behaviors in women and men. (Obj. #10)

14. Using your own life, describe how the following contributed to gender-role socialization: parents, peers, schools, textbooks, television and religion. (Obj. #9)

15. Define androgyny. List some ways in which research has found androgynous persons to differ from others. (Obj. #11)

4

Female Sexual Anatomy and Physiology

Learning Objectives

After studying this chapter, the student should be able to:

1. List the reasons for doing a genital self-exam.

2. Briefly describe the process of doing a genital self-exam.

3. Define the terms "gynecology" and "vulva".

4. Identify and briefly describe the following structures of the vulva: mons veneris, labia majora, labia minora, clitoris, vestibule, urethral opening, introitus and hymen, perineum.

5. Identify the location, structure, and function of the following: vestibular bulbs, Bartholin's glands, vagina, cervix, uterus, fallopian tubes, ovaries.

6. Explain when and for what purpose Kegel exercises were developed.

7. Describe the steps involved in practicing Kegel exercises, and explain the benefits of doing these exercises.

8. Discuss the source and function of vaginal lubrication during sexual arousal.

9. List several factors that may inhibit vaginal lubrication, and explain how those situations might be remedied.

10. Identify the location and function of the Grafenberg spot.

11. Describe what function vaginal secretions serve.

12. Describe the chemical balance of the vagina, and discuss ways in which this balance may be altered.

13. Discuss the following in reference to urinary tract infections: incidence of, causes of, symptoms of, preventative measures.

14. Define vaginitis and discuss the following in relation to it: symptoms, factors increasing the susceptibility to vaginitis, ways to help prevent vaginitis.

15. Discuss the following in relation to a Pap smear: what purpose it serves, how it is done, how often it should be done, what steps may be taken if the results of a Pap smear are not normal, certain subgroups of women who are less likely to have routine Pap smears.

16. Describe which women may be at higher risk of cervical cancer, how common it is, and discuss available treatment options for women who receive this diagnosis.

17. Define the following terms: hysterectomy, oophorectomy.

68   Test Bank to Accompany *Our Sexuality*

18. Describe how a hysterectomy may affect a woman sexually, physically and emotionally.

19. Describe the controversy surrounding breast implants

20. Discuss the following in relationship to the breasts: structure and function of, self-exam — when, how and why, mammography, three types of breast lumps that may occur, breast cancer and treatment alternatives available for women who are diagnosed with it, high and low risk factors for breast cancer.

21. Discuss the following in regard to menstruation: attitudes toward it in American society; when it typically begins; the extent to which young women and men are informed about it; the length of the menstrual cycle; menstrual synchrony; the relationship among the hypothalamus, pituitary gland and adrenal glands; the proliferative, secretory and menstrual phases of the menstrual cycle; sexual activity and the menstrual cycle; premenstrual syndrome; primary and secondary dysmenorrhea; primary and secondary amenorrhea; self-help for menstrual problems; toxic shock syndrome

22. Describe symptoms of and treatment for Premenstrual Dysphoric Disorder.

23. Describe three types of genital mutilation, the reasons for doing it, the health consequences that may result, and the current controversy that surrounds it.

24. Explain how some other cultures have viewed menstruation, including American culture.

25. Define menopause as it relates to the climacteric.

26. Describe the physiosexual changes that women experience during menopause.

27. Define hormone-replacement therapy and explain its advantages and potential risks.

Multiple Choice

1.
K
Answer: d
pp. 82-83
Obj. #2

Each of the following is a suggestion related to doing a female genital self-exam **except**
a. Do it on a regular basis.
b. Use a hand mirror to look at your genitals.
c. As you proceed, be aware of your feelings regarding your genital anatomy.
d. After the visual exam, masturbate to orgasm.

2.
K
Answer: a
pp. 82-83
Obj. #1

Each of the following is discussed as a reason for doing a female genital self-exam **except**
a. to become sexually aroused.
b. to learn about your body.
c. to learn about your feelings related to your genital anatomy.
d. to enhance routine medical care.

Chapter 4 Female Sexual Anatomy and Physiology   69

3.
A
Answer: c
pp. 82-83
Obj. #1

As a result of practicing genital self-exam, which of the following would **least** likely occur?
    a. increased comfort with genital anatomy
    b. increased responsibility for health care
    c. increased strength of pelvic floor muscles
    d. increased awareness of genital sensitivity

4.
K
Answer: b
p. 83
Obj. #3

_____ is the medical specialty for female sexual and reproductive anatomy.
    a. Urology
    b. Gynecology
    c. Genitology
    d. Hysterology

5.
K
Answer: b
p. 83
Obj. #4

Vulva refers to
    a. the area covering the pubic bone.
    b. the female external genital structures.
    c. the vagina.
    d. the large outer lips.

6.
K
Answer: a
p. 83
Obj. #4

The vulva includes all of the following **except**
    a. vagina.
    b. clitoris.
    c. urethral opening.
    d. mons veneris.

7.
K
Answer: c
pp. 83-84
Obj. #4
WWW

Which of the following statements regarding the mons veneris is false?
    a. It consists of pads of fatty tissue between the bone and skin.
    b. Translated from Latin, it means "mound of Venus".
    c. Due to the absence of nerve endings, it is relatively insensitive to touch.
    d. At puberty it becomes covered with hair.

8.
K
Answer: d
p. 83
Obj. #4

The "Mound of Venus" refers to
    a. the vulva.
    b. clitoral engorgement resulting from sexual arousal.
    c. the female breast.
    d. the fatty tissue covering the pubic bone.

9.
A
Answer: a
p. 84
Obj. #4

A woman's partner caresses her labia majora. The woman would **most** likely experience
    a. sensual pleasure.
    b. little feeling due to the absence of nerve endings.
    c. a tickling sensation.
    d. a sense of pressure and being overstimulated.

10.
K
Answer: c
p. 84
Obj. #4

The labia majora
    a. contain the cavernous bodies.
    b. are a source of vaginal lubrication.
    c. surround the labia minora.
    d. join at the prepuce over the clitoris.

11.
K
Answer: b
p. 84
Obj. #4

The labia minora join at the
a. mons veneris.
b. prepuce.
c. vestibule.
d. introitus.

12.
K
Answer: d
p. 84
Obj. #4

The _____ is composed of the external shaft and glans and the internal crura.
a. vestibule
b. urethral opening
c. hymen
d. clitoris

13.
K
Answer: c
p. 84
Obj. #4

Which of the following is most descriptive of Judy Chicago's "The Dinner Party"?
a. Erotic photographs of food that represent various parts of a woman's genitals
b. A painting of pioneers in female health care and technology
c. Ceramic plates with vulval shapes that represent significant women in history
d. Erotic drawings of female genitals

14.
K
Answer: d
pp. 84-85
Obj. #4
WWW

Which of the following statements regarding the clitoris is false?
a. It has approximately the same number of nerve endings as the head of the penis.
b. The only purpose of the clitoris is sexual arousal.
c. Clitoral stimulation is the most common way women produce arousal and orgasm during self-stimulation.
d. It is located within the introitus.

15.
A
Answer: a
pp. 83-88
Obj. #4

All of the following are part of the vulva **except**
a. vagina.
b. clitoris.
c. introitus.
d. urethral opening.

16.
K
Answer: b
p. 84
Obj. #4

The labia majora encloses all of the following **except**
a. clitoris.
b. mons veneris.
c. introitus.
d. urethral opening.

17.
K
Answer: c
pp. 84-88
Obj. #4, 5

Which of the following terms does NOT belong with the others?
a. vagina
b. ovaries
c. clitoris
d. uterus

Chapter 4 Female Sexual Anatomy and Physiology   71

18. The cavernous bodies, or spongy structures are located in the
K
Answer: d   a. introitus.
p. 85   b. vestibule.
Obj. #4   c. labia minora.
   d. shaft of the clitoris.

19. _____ is the **most** common way women achieve arousal and
K orgasm when masturbating.
Answer: a   a. Clitoral stimulation
p. 85   b. Vaginal penetration
Obj. #4   c. Contracting the PC muscles
   d. Breast stimulation

20. Which of the following would have the **fewest** number of nerve
A endings?
Answer: b   a. the vaginal opening
p. 86   b. the inner two-thirds of the vagina
Obj. #4   c. the clitoris
   d. the labia minora

21. Which of the following statements regarding genital mutilation is false?
K   a. It can cause death.
Answer: c   b. It is practiced in parts of Africa, the Middle East and Asia.
pp. 85-86   c. Female circumcision is the most extreme.
Obj. # 22   d. In countries where genital mutilation is practiced, young girls
     are considered unmarriageable if they have not undergone the
     prescribed "surgery".

22. The vestibule
K   a. contains the clitoris and the prepuce.
Answer: c   b. refers to the clitoral shaft that houses the cavernous bodies.
p. 86   c. is where the urinary and vaginal openings are located.
Obj. #4   d. is the area between the introitus and the anus.

23. The opening of the vagina is referred to as the
K   a. vestibule.
Answer: c   b. os.
p. 87   c. introitus.
Obj. #4   d. vulva.

24. The introitus is located
K   a. between the urinary opening and the anus.
Answer: a   b. between the clitoris and the vaginal opening.
p. 87   c. where the labia majora converge
Obj. #4   d. in the shaft of the clitoris.

25.
K
Answer: a
p. 87
Obj. #4
WWW

An imperforate hymen
a. causes the menstrual flow to collect in the vagina.
b. refers to a hymen that has been punctured or partially torn.
c. indicates that a woman is no longer a virgin.
d. is very common in young women.

26.
K
Answer: d
p. 87
Obj. #4

The function of the hymen is
a. to protect urethral tissue in early stages of development.
b. to protect against early intercourse.
c. to enhance sexual arousal.
d. largely unknown.

27.
K
Answer: d
p. 87
Obj. #4

The hymen
a. begins to develop during adolescence.
b. typically covers the entire vaginal opening.
c. has several different physiological functions.
d. may serve to protect vaginal tissues early in life.

28.
K
Answer: b
p. 87
Obj. #4

Initial coitus is sometimes referred to as
a. circumcision.
b. deflowering.
c. episiotomy.
d. genital infibulation.

29.
A
Answer: c
p. 87
Obj. #4, 21

Twelve-year-old Daniella has been experiencing lower abdominal discomfort. A medical examination reveals that menstrual fluid has been collecting in her vagina and not being expelled as it should. This condition would **most** likely be explained as
a. vaginitis.
b. secondary dysmenorrhea.
c. an imperforate hymen.
d. secondary amenorrhea.

30.
A
Answer: b
pp. 87-88
Obj. #4

Which of the following is NOT an underlying structure of the vulva?
a. vestibular bulbs
b. introitus
c. pelvic floor muscles
d. Bartholin's glands

31.
K
Answer: d
p. 87
Obj. #4

Which of the following procedures is associated with the perineum?
a. laparoscopy
b. colposcopy
c. cryosurgery
d. episiotomy

32.
K
Answer: b
p. 88
Obj. #6

The vestibular bulbs
a. produce a drop or two of fluid just prior to orgasm.
b. engorge with blood during sexual arousal, causing the vagina to increase in length.
c. are located in the shaft of the clitoris.
d. contain the spongy structures called the cavernous bodies.

33.
K
Answer: a
p. 88
Obj. #5

The vestibular bulbs are active during
a. sexual arousal.
b. the birthing process.
c. menstruation.
d. menopause.

34.
K
Answer: c
p. 88
Obj. #6

Bartholin's glands are located on each side of the
a. cervix.
b. urethral opening.
c. vaginal opening.
d. clitoris.

35.
K
Answer: a
p. 88
Obj. #6

The _____ were once believed to be the source of vaginal lubrication.
a. Bartholin's glands
b. vestibular bulbs
c. perineal glands
d. Skene's ducts

36.
K
Answer: a
p. 89
Obj. #5

Each of the following is one of the layers of vaginal tissue **except**
a. endometrial tissue
b. mucous membrane
c. muscle tissue
d. fibrous tissue

37.
K
Answer: d
pp. 88-89
Obj. #4

The vagina includes all of the following **except** the
a. mucosa.
b. rugae.
c. Grafenberg spot.
d. clitoris.

38.
K
Answer: c
p. 89
Obj. #5

Rugae refer to
a. the fibrous connective tissues that hold the uterus in place.
b. the glands in the vaginal walls.
c. the folded walls of the vagina.
d. the color changes that occur during vasocongestion.

39.
K
Answer: a
p. 89
Obj. #5

The highest concentration of vaginal musculature is located
a. around the vaginal opening.
b. in the middle portion of the vagina.
c. in the back of the vagina, near the cervix.
d. along the inner two-thirds of the vagina.

40.
K
Answer: d
p. 90
Obj. #8

Which of the following statements regarding vaginal lubrication is false?
a. It is the first physiological sign of sexual arousal in women.
b. It seeps through the vaginal walls as vasocongestion occurs.
c. It occurs within 10 to 30 seconds after effective psychological or physical stimulation begins.
d. The primary source of the fluid is the vestibular bulbs.

41.
K
Answer: d
p. 90
Obj. #8

_____ refers to the blood engorgement that occurs during sexual arousal.
a. Myometrial swelling
b. Menarche
c. Proliferation
d. Vasocongestion

42.
K
Answer: a
p. 90
Obj. #8

Each of the following is a function of vaginal lubrication **except**
a. helps to make the vaginal environment more acidic.
b. enhances the possibility of conception due to its chemical composition.
c. increases sexual enjoyment.
d. prepares the vagina for entry of the penis.

43.
K
Answer: a
p. 91
Obj. #9

Which of the following would NOT be recommended to enhance vaginal lubrication?
a. Vaseline
b. saliva
c. K-Y jelly
d. lubricated condoms

44.
K
Answer: a
p. 91
Obj. #10

The _____ is located within the anterior wall of the vagina, one-third to one-half way in from the introitus.
a. Grafenberg spot
b. cervix
c. endometrium
d. os

45.
K
Answer: d
p. 83
Obj. #6
WWW

Kegel exercises
a. were named after the muscles that they are designed to strengthen.
b. can decrease sensation during intercourse if practiced too frequently.
c. were developed to help women improve their orgasmic capacity.
d. can increase genital sensitivity.

46.
K
Answer: c
p. 90
Obj. #6, 7

The _____ contract involuntarily at orgasm and can be strengthened by doing Kegel exercises.
a. clitoral muscles
b. Bartholin's glands
c. pelvic floor muscles
d. vestibular bulbs

47.
K
Answer: b
p. 90
Obj. #6

Kegel exercises were **originally** developed
- a. to help increase the frequency of orgasmic response.
- b. to help women regain control of urination after childbirth.
- c. to increase genital sensitivity.
- d. to help women take a more active role in childbearing.

48.
K
Answer: c
p. 90
Obj. #7

All of the following are benefits of doing Kegel exercises **except**
- a. regaining urinary control after childbirth.
- b. increasing overall genital sensitivity.
- c. increasing the ability to have multiple orgasms.
- d. increasing sensation during intercourse.

49.
A
Answer: d
p. 90
Obj. #6, 7

Maria has recently given birth and notices that she loses urine every time she coughs or sneezes. Her physician might suggest
- a. G spot stimulation.
- b. drinking a lot of cranberry juice.
- c. an episiotomy.
- d. Kegel exercises.

50.
K
Answer: b
p. 91
Obj. #10

The Grafenberg spot
- a. is located in the glans of the clitoris.
- b. is believed to be the female counterpart of the male prostate gland.
- c. consists of a system of nerve endings that surround the clitoris.
- d. develops from the same embryonic tissue as the penis.

51.
K
Answer: c
p. 91
Obj. #12

Douching
- a. is necessary for routine hygiene.
- b. can minimize vaginal infections if used in conjunction with feminine hygiene sprays.
- c. can increase susceptibility to infections if done too frequently.
- d. can make it impossible to become pregnant.

52.
K
Answer: d
p. 91
Obj. #12

According to recent research, genital deodorant sprays and body powders have been associated with increased risks of
- a. melanoma.
- b. cervical cancer.
- c. uterine cancer.
- d. ovarian cancer.

53.
K
Answer: b
p. 91
Obj. #11
WWW

Which of the following statements regarding normal vaginal secretions is false?
- a. The secretions are produced by the vaginal walls and the cervix.
- b. They are normally rather alkaline in nature.
- c. They vary throughout the menstrual cycle.
- d. They are a sign of vaginal health.

54.
K
Answer: b
p. 91
Obj. #12

Which of the following would be **most** beneficial in facilitating genital hygiene?
a. douching every day
b. washing the vulva regularly with a mild soap
c. using deodorant tampons
d. using a feminine hygiene spray

55.
K
Answer: a
p. 91
Obj. #5

A _____ is the instrument that is used to hold the walls of the vagina open during vaginal exams.
a. speculum
b. laparoscope
c. catheter
d. vaginal dilator

56.
K
Answer: c
p. 92
Obj. #5

The uterus
a. is where fertilization occurs.
b. is larger in women who have never had children.
c. is suspended in the pelvic cavity by ligaments.
d. is the site of an ectopic pregnancy.

57.
K
Answer: d
p. 92
Obj. #5

The inner lining of the uterus is the
a. perimetrium.
b. hymen.
c. myometrium.
d. endometrium.

58.
K
Answer: c
p. 92
Obj. #5

All of the following are layers of the uterus **except**
a. perimetrium.
b. endometrium.
c. perineum.
d. myometrium.

59.
K
Answer: a
p. 92
Obj. #5

Which of the following statements regarding a woman with a retroflexed uterus is **least** accurate?
a. She may have difficulty in becoming pregnant.
b. She may experience menstrual discomfort.
c. She may have difficulty inserting a diaphragm.
d. Her uterus is tipped back toward her spine.

60.
K
Answer: b
p. 92
Obj. #5

A woman with a retroflexed uterus
a. may have a difficult time conceiving.
b. may be more likely to experience menstrual discomfort.
c. may have an unusually difficult pregnancy.
d. may experience extreme hormone fluctuations.

61.
K
Answer: b
p. 92
Obj. #5

The fringe-like projections at the end of each fallopian tube are called
a. cilia.
b. fimbriae.
c. myometria.
d. ovarian receptors.

62.
K
Answer: c
p. 92
Obj. #5

Once the egg is released from the ovary into the fallopian tube, it remains viable for fertilization for approximately
a. twelve hours.
b. twelve to twenty-four hours.
c. twenty-four to forty-eight hours.
d. forty-eight to seventy-two hours.

63.
K
Answer: d
p. 93
Obj. #5

Which of the following statements regarding the ovaries is false?
a. The ovaries contain thousands of immature ova that are present at birth.
b. The ovaries are endocrine glands.
c. The ovaries produce sex hormones.
d. During each average menstrual cycle, each ovary releases an egg.

64.
K
Answer: c
p. 84
Obj. #21

The first time a woman begins to menstruate is called
a. mittelschmerz.
b. proliferation.
c. menarche.
d. the secretory phase.

65.
K
Answer: c
pp. 94-95
Obj. #21
WWW

The timing of menarche appears to be related to all of the following **except**
a. heredity.
b. altitude.
c. socialization.
d. general health.

66.
K
Answer: b
p. 95
Obj. #21

Despite differences in overall cycle length in women, which period of time is consistently the same?
a. The interval between the onset of menstruation and ovulation.
b. The interval between ovulation and the onset of menstruation.
c. The menstrual period itself.
d. There is no period of time throughout the cycle that is consistently the same.

67.
K
Answer: a
p. 95
Obj. #21

Menstrual synchrony is
a. when a group of women who live together develop similar menstrual cycles.
b. a consistent 28-day cycle.
c. when follicles erupt simultaneously.
d. an irregular menstrual cycle.

68.
K
Answer: a
p. 95
Obj. #21

The corpus luteum
a. secretes progesterone.
b. secretes estrogen.
c. develops during the proliferative phase.
d. develops during the menstrual phase.

69.
K
Answer: b
p. 95
Obj. #21

Menstrual synchrony may be related to
a. the sense of smell and the age of menarche.
b. close physical contact with women and the sense of smell.
c. close physical contact with men and the age of menarche.
d. the sense of smell and the regularity of the menstrual cycle.

70.
K
Answer: a
p. 97
Obj. #21

Mittelschmerz occurs during
a. ovulation.
b. menstruation.
c. fertilization.
d. implantation.

71.
K
Answer: b
p. 98
Obj. #21

During the secretory phase of the menstrual cycle, if _____ does not occur, the pituitary shuts down production of LH and FSH.
a. fertilization
b. implantation
c. ovulation
d. meiosis

72.
K
Answer: d
p. 98
Obj. #21

Which of the following **most** accurately describes sexual feelings and behavior throughout the menstrual cycle?
a. They increase around the time of ovulation.
b. They increase just prior to menstruation.
c. They increase during menstruation.
d. There is considerable variation from woman to woman.

73.
K
Answer: c
p. 99
Obj. #21

Premenstrual syndrome refers to _____ symptoms that women experience before menstruation.
a. physical
b. psychological
c. physical and psychological
d. psychosocial

74.
K
Answer: d
p. 100
Obj. #21

The causes of PMS are
a. attributed to the use of birth control pills.
b. related to excessive prostaglandin secretions.
c. attributed to an overproduction of FSH.
d. unknown.

75.
K
Answer: a
p. 100
Obj. #21

Dysmenorrhea refers to
a. painful menstruation.
b. absence of menstruation.
c. negative emotions experienced prior to menstruation.
d. pain at ovulation.

76.
K
Answer: a
p. 100
Obj. #21

_____ _____ is usually caused by the overproduction of prostaglandins.
a. Primary dysmenorrhea
b. Secondary dysmenorrhea
c. Primary amenorrhea
d. Secondary amenorrhea

77.
K
Answer: b
p. 100
Obj. #21

_____ is a normal condition during pregnancy, breast feeding, and women approaching menopause.
 a. Primary amenorrhea
 b. Secondary amenorrhea
 c. Primary dysmenorrhea
 d. Secondary dysmenorrhea

78.
K
Answer: c
p. 100
Obj. #21

Primary amenorrhea may be caused by all of the following **except**
 a. poor health.
 b. an imperforate hymen.
 c. not enough exercise.
 d. problems with the reproductive organs.

79.
A
Answer: a
p. 100
Obj. #21

A woman who is taking an antiprostaglandin medication is **most** likely being treated for
 a. primary dysmenorrhea.
 b. secondary dysmenorrhea.
 c. amenorrhea.
 d. pelvic inflammatory disease.

80.
K
Answer: b
p. 100
Obj. #21

Which of the following would be **least** likely to cause secondary dysmenorrhea?
 a. pelvic inflammatory disease
 b. rigorous athletic training
 c. presence of an IUD
 d. endometriosis

81.
K
Answer: b
p. 100
Obj. #21

_____ refers to the absence of menstruation.
 a. Dysmenorrhea
 b. Amenorrhea
 c. Dysmenarche
 d. Menstrual prolapse

82.
K
Answer: c
p. 100
Obj. #21

_____ is more common among athletes than among the general population.
 a. Pelvic inflammatory disease
 b. Endometriosis
 c. Amenorrhea
 d. Dysmenorrhea

83.
K
Answer: d
p. 100
Obj. #21

Adult women who engage in rigorous athletic training may experience
 a. primary dysmenorrhea.
 b. secondary dysmenorrhea.
 c. primary amenorrhea.
 d. secondary amenorrhea.

84.
K
Answer: b
p. 100
Obj. #21

A condition in which endometrial cells from the uterine lining implant in the abdominal cavity is referred to as
a. pelvic inflammatory disease.
b. endometriosis.
c. ectopic pregnancy.
d. toxic shock syndrome.

85.
A
Answer: c
p. 100
Obj. #21

Over the past year, Maggie has increased the intensity of her running and weight training program and has begun having her menstrual periods infrequently, if at all. This may put her at risk for
a. decreased bone density and atrophy of genital tissues.
b. irritable bowel syndrome.
c. secondary amenorrhea.
d. cervical cancer.

86.
A
Answer: d
p. 101
Obj. #21

All of the following appear to be effective in reducing PMS symptoms **except**
a. avoiding salt.
b. regular aerobic exercise.
c. some food supplements.
d. moderate increase in caffeine intake.

87.
A
Answer: c
p. 101
Obj. #21

To minimize the possibility of toxic shock syndrome a woman should
a. eat a high fiber diet.
b. practice stress management.
c. use sanitary napkins instead of tampons.
d. avoid using an IUD for birth control.

88.
K
Answer: a
p. 101
Obj. #24

The term _____ refers to the physiological changes that occur during the transition period from fertility to infertility.
a. climacteric
b. menopause
c. plateau phase
d. menarche

89.
K
Answer: b
p. 102
Obj. #24

_____ refers to the cessation of menstruation.
a. Climacteric
b. Menopause
c. Amenorrhea
d. Menarche

90.
K
Answer: c
p. 102
Obj. #25

The average life expectancy for a woman today is ____ years.
a. 70
b. 75
c. 82
d. 87

Chapter 4 Female Sexual Anatomy and Physiology   81

91.
K
Answer: d
p. 102
Obj. #26

Many of the menopause symptoms that women may experience are caused by
 a. an increase in progesterone.
 b. an increase in estrogen.
 c. a decrease in progesterone.
 d. a decrease in estrogen.

92.
K
Answer: c
p. 102
Obj. #26

"Hot flashes"
 a. are the side effects some women experience as a result of hormone replacement therapy.
 b. are one of the symptoms of PMS.
 c. are the result of rapid dilation of blood vessels.
 d. refer to migraine headaches that some women experience.

93.
K
Answer: c
p. 102-103
Obj. #26

Which of the following **best** describes possible symptoms of menopause?
 a. fatigue, irritability, water retention, orgasmic inhibition
 b. depression, hot flashes, nausea, dysmenorrhea
 c. sleep disturbances, hot flashes, severe headaches, short term memory loss
 d. nausea, hot flashes, short term memory loss, dysmenorrhea

94.
K
Answer: b
p. 103
Obj. #27

HRT involves
 a. participating in a daily regimen of physical therapy to reduce symptoms of menopause.
 b. taking estrogen and progesterone to compensate for the decrease in hormone production that occurs during the climacteric.
 c. taking daily doses of megavitamins and minerals to counteract the vitamin and mineral deficiencies that menopause creates.
 d. taking androgen to stabilize hormone fluctuations that occur during menopause.

95.
K
Answer: a
p. 103
Obj. #26

All of the following are potential benefits of hormone replacement therapy **except**
 a. protection against endometrial cancer.
 b. protection against osteoporosis.
 c. protection against cardiovascular disease.
 d. protection against loss of vaginal lubrication.

96.
K
Answer: c
p. 104
Obj. #13

All of the following are symptoms of urinary tract infections **except**
 a. a frequent need to urinate.
 b. a severe burning sensation when urinating.
 c. losing urine while coughing or sneezing.
 d. blood or pus in the urine.

97.
K
Answer: d
pp. 104-105
Obj. #13

Which of the following would be **least** likely to cause a urinary tract infection?
a. bacteria from the rectum
b. frequent intercourse during a relatively short period of time
c. bacteria from the vagina
d. an imperforate hymen

98.
K
Answer: b
p. 105
Obj. #13
WWW

Which of the following would be **least** likely to prevent urinary tract infections?
a. drinking cranberry juice
b. wiping from back to front after urination and defecation
c. using a sterile, water-soluble lubricant during intercourse
d. washing hands and genitals before sexual contact

99.
A
Answer: c
pp. 1-3, 104
Obj. #13

Which of the following statements regarding urinary tract infections is false?
a. They are usually treated with antibiotics.
b. Diabetes and pregnancy often predispose women to urinary tract infections.
c. Holding urine as long as possible as opposed to urinating frequently will strengthen the bladder muscles and minimize infection.
d. Urinating after intercourse can wash out potentially harmful bacteria.

100.
A
Answer: a
p. 105
Obj. #14

A woman experiences chronic vaginitis. Which of the following would be **least** likely to contribute to this problem?
a. a low carbohydrate diet
b. antibiotic medication
c. frequently wearing pantyhose
d. birth control pills

101.
A
Answer: d
p. 105
Obj. #14

To minimize the possibility of vaginal infections, a woman should
a. bathe regularly, using a strong deodorant soap.
b. douche twice daily.
c. use a lubricant such as Vaseline during intercourse.
d. wear cotton underpants rather than pantyhose.

102.
K
Answer: d
p. 105
Obj. #14

Vaginal health is enhanced by
a. regular douching.
b. use of feminine hygiene sprays.
c. wearing nylon underwear.
d. wiping from front to back, vulva to anus.

103.
K
Answer: c
p. 106
Obj. #15
WWW

Which of the following statements regarding the Pap smear is false?
a. It is not 100 percent accurate.
b. It is a relatively painless procedure.
c. It is used to detect ovarian cancer in women.
d. It examines cells taken from part of the cervix.

104.
K
Answer: d
p. 106
Obj. #15

A woman should have a Pap smear
a. every six months.
b. once a year.
c. once every two years.
d. as often as her health care provider recommends, depending on her history.

105.
A
Answer: b
pp. 106-107
Obj. #15

Which of the following women would generally be **more** likely than the others to have routine pap smears?
a. a single woman with three children, struggling to get by financially
b. a middle management executive in a large firm
c. a lesbian
d. a Native American woman

106.
K
Answer: d
p. 106
Obj. #15

_____ women are less likely than _____ to have routine pap smears?
a. Asian American women; Native American women
b. women with college degrees; women with high school diplomas
c. Caucasian women; Native American women
d. Lesbians; heterosexual women

107.
K
Answer: c
p. 107
Obj. #15

Which of the following procedures would **least** likely be used in treating cervical abnormalities?
a. cryosurgery
b. biopsy
c. oophorectomy
d. hysterectomy

108.
K
Answer: b
p. 107
Obj. #16

As stated in the text to describe treatment alternatives for various problems regarding female anatomy, cryosurgery involves
a. surgical removal of the cervix and uterus.
b. freezing and removing abnormal cells from the cervix.
c. removing endometrial tissue from the uterus.
d. surgical removal of vaginal adhesions.

109.
K
Answer: a
p. 107
Obj. #16

A woman with cervical abnormalities is treated by freezing some of the abnormal tissue and removing it. This procedure is called
a. cryosurgery.
b. colposcopy.
c. oophorectomy.
d. cervisectomy.

110.
K
Answer: b
p. 107
Obj. #16

Increased risk of cervical cancer has been associated with all of the following **except**
a. having had genital warts.
b. prolonged use of birth control pills.
c. having had several male sexual partners.
d. smoking or exposure to cigarette smoke.

111.
K
Answer: c
p. 107
Obj. #16
WWW

The risk of developing cervical cancer **increases** when a woman
a. has had an abortion.
b. is childless.
c. smokes cigarettes.
d. uses birth control pills.

112.
K
Answer: a
p. 107
Obj. #17

An oophorectomy is the surgical removal of
a. the ovaries.
b. the uterus.
c. cancerous cervical tissue.
d. the fallopian tubes.

113.
K
Answer: b
p. 107
Obj. #17

Approximately _____% of women have a hysterectomy by age 65.
a. 20
b. 33
c. 50
d. 66

114.
K
Answer: c
pp. 107-108
Obj. #19

Which of the following statements regarding the effects of hysterectomy on female sexuality is true?
a. Most women experience a decrease in sexual responsiveness.
b. Most women find that it enhances their sexual functioning.
c. The effects can vary, depending upon the woman.
d. There are no data available on this subject.

115.
K
Answer: c
p. 92
Obj. #20

The reason some breasts are larger than others is primarily a result of
a. larger amounts of glandular tissue.
b. larger pectoral muscles.
c. larger amounts of fatty tissue.
d. increased androgen output from the adrenals.

116.
K
Answer: b
p. 108
Obj. #20

Breasts are
a. primary sex characteristics.
b. secondary sex characteristics.
c. considered part of the external female genitalia.
d. considered part of the internal female genitalia.

117.
K
Answer: b
p. 108
Obj. #20
WWW

Variation in breast size is primarily a result of
a. the size of the mammary glands.
b. the amount of fatty tissue in the breasts.
c. the type of exercise program a woman uses.
d. the amount and type of food she consumes.

Chapter 4 Female Sexual Anatomy and Physiology 85

118.
A
Answer: c
pp. 108-109
Obj. #20

Which statement about breasts is true?
a. Variation in size is due primarily to the size of the mammary glands.
b. The best time for a woman to examine her breasts is right before she menstruates.
c. The glandular tissue in the breasts responds to sex hormones.
d. The areola is the opening in the nipple.

119.
K
Answer: d
p. 109
Obj. #20

_____ percent of breast lumps are found by women themselves.
a. Twenty-five
b. Forty
c. Sixty-five
d. Ninety

120.
K
Answer: c
pp. 109-110
Obj. #20

Which statement regarding mammography is false?
a. It is an X-ray screening test for cancerous breast lumps.
b. It can often detect a breast lump before it can be felt manually.
c. It is more effective for women under age 50 than in those over 50.
d. While mammography is highly effective, most breast cancer is detected by self-exam.

121.
K
Answer: b
p. 109
Obj. #20

The best time for a woman to do a breast self-exam is
a. once a month, right before her menstrual period.
b. once a month, right after her menstrual period.
c. once a month, as close to ovulation as possible.
d. twice a year.

122.
K
Answer: b
p. 111
Obj. #20

Fibroadenomas
a. are malignant breast tumors.
b. are benign breast tumors.
c. occur as the result of a high fiber diet.
d. are typically treated with radical mastectomy.

123.
K
Answer: c
p. 112
Obj. #20

Breast cancer affects approximately _____ North American women.
a. one in three
b. one in six
c. one in nine
d. one in twelve

123.
A
Answer: a
pp. 111-112
Obj. #20

A woman with fibrocystic breast disease would **most** likely be advised to
a. eliminate caffeine from her diet.
b. eat more red meat and whole milk.
c. undergo radical mastectomy.
d. undergo partial mastectomy.

124.
K
Answer: c
p. 112
Obj. #20

Which of the following is a **high** risk factor for breast cancer?
a. both ovaries removed early in life
b. early menopause
c. first child born after age 30
d. slenderness

125.
K
Answer: d
p. 112
Obj. #20

Which of the following is a **low** risk factor for breast cancer?
a. no pregnancies
b. never breast fed a child
c. onset of menstruation before age 12
d. more than 2 hours of exercise per week

Multiple Choice from Study Guide

1.
K
Answer: a
pp. 83-84
Obj. #4

Which of the following does NOT make up part of the vulva?
a. Grafenberg spot
b. Clitoris
c. mons veneris
d. urethral opening

2.
K
Answer: a
pp. 84-85
Obj. #4

Which structures are part of the clitoris?
a. glans, shaft, hood.
b. glans, shaft, introitus.
c. glans, fimbriae, shaft.
d. shaft, hood, vestibular bulbs.

3.
K
Answer: d
p. 85
Obj. #4

The primary function of the clitoris is
a. covering the urethral opening.
b. supplying the labia minora with blood.
c. secreting lubrication.
d. providing sexual pleasure.

4.
K
Answer: b
p. 84
Obj. #4

The _____ are hairless and contain sweat and oil glands.
a. labia majora
b. labia minora
c. crura
d. cavernous bodies

5.
K
Answer: c
p. 84
Obj. #4

Smegma may be found
a. along the areola.
b. along the rugae.
c. under the clitoral hood.
d. inside the vagina.

6.
K
Answer: c
pp. 88-90
Obj. #5

Which of the following statements about the vagina is false?
a. The vagina is about 3 to 5 inches in length when a woman is unaroused.
b. The vagina contains folded walls.
c. The greatest degree of musculature is found in the inner third.
d. Lubrication is produced by the vaginal walls.

7.
K
Answer: b
pp. 88-90
Obj. #5

The vaginal opening may be partially covered by the
  a. Skene's glands.
  b. Hymen.
  c. pubic symphysis.
  d. seminal sheath.

8.
K
Answer: a
p. 90
Obj. #6

Kegel exercises may increase sensation and promote urinary control by
  a. strengthening the pelvic floor muscles.
  b. contracting the clitoris.
  c. stimulating the production of prostaglandins.
  d. inhibiting the production of anti-diurectic hormone.

9.
K
Answer: d
p. 91
Obj. #8

Which of the following is false regarding vaginal secretions?
  a. They are normally rather acid.
  b. They are typically white or yellowish.
  c. The scent varies with a woman's cycle.
  d. The chemical balance is best maintained by regular douching.

10.
K
Answer: b
p. 91
Obj. #5

Which of the following is NOT associated with the cervix?
  a. os
  b. triangular and soft
  c. Pap smear
  d. mucus secreting glands

11.
K
Answer: d
p. 92
Obj. #5

This structure has a layer of muscle and is suspended in the pelvic cavity by ligaments.
  a. fallopian tubes
  b. ovaries
  c. fimbriae
  d. uterus

12.
K
Answer: a
p. 92
Obj. #5

Fertilization occurs
  a. in the fallopian tubes.
  b. in the uterus.
  c. in the cervical os.
  d. during mittelschmerz.

13.
K
Answer: c
pp. 93-94
Obj. #21

Which of the following statements regarding menstruation is true?
  a. Menstruation usually begins between 10 and 13 years of age.
  b. Menstrual cycle length typically spans 21 to 50 days.
  c. The amount of menstrual flow may vary from month to month.
  d. Menstrual synchrony has yet to be observed in humans.

14.
K
Answer: b
p. 95
Obj. #21

When the pituitary releases _____ the ovaries increase estrogen production and ova begin to mature.
  a. GnRH
  b. FSH
  c. LH
  d. Prolactin

15.
K
Answer: c
p. 95
Obj. #21

What is the correct ordering of the phases of the menstrual cycle?
a. proliferative phase, secretory phase, menstrual phase
b. secretory phase, menstrual phase, proliferative phase
c. menstrual phase, proliferative phase, secretory phase
d. secretory phase, proliferative phase, menstrual phase

16.
K
Answer: d
p. 97
Obj. #21

Ovulation
a. is triggered by a sudden spurt of LH.
b. occurs 14 days before the onset of the next menstrual period.
c. may be accompanied by discomfort in the lower abdomen.
d. all of the above are true.

17.
K
Answer: a
p. 98
Obj. #21

During the secretory phase of the menstrual cycle the corpus luteum
a. secretes progesterone.
b. produces LH.
c. signals the pituitary to make oxytocin.
d. promotes degeneration of the myometrium.

18.
K
Answer: c
pp. 98-99
Obj. #21

What can be concluded about studies which have examined sexual behavior and the menstrual cycle?
a. Sexual activity peaks near ovulation
b. Sexual activity rises during menstruation
c. Great individual variation is shown, so observing your own patterns is suggested
d. Little variation occurs in sexual behavior throughout the cycle

19.
K
Answer: a
p. 100
Obj. #21

Possible causes of dysmenorrhea include all of the following **except**
a. reduced FSH levels.
b. pelvic inflammatory disease.
c. endometriosis.
d. excess production of prostaglandins.

20.
K
Answer: b
pp. 101-102
Obj. #21

All of the following are associated with amenorrhea **except**
a. pregnancy.
b. being obese.
c. being an athlete.
d. anorexia nervosa.

21.
K
Answer: a
pp. 99-100
Obj. #22

Premenstrual syndrome may produce all of the following experiences **except**
a. increased weight loss.
b. breast pain.
c. irritability.
d. "tight-jeans" syndrome.

22.
K
Answer: a
p. 101
Obj. #24

In women the climacteric is associated with a range of symptoms produced by
a. declining estrogen levels.
b. increased testosterone production.
c. changes in free fatty acids in the blood.
d. decreased cortisol sensitivity.

23.
K
Answer: c
pp. 103-104
Obj. #26

Which statement best reflects current views regarding Hormone Replacement Therapy?
a. Women should begin HRT when perimenopause is first noticed.
b. Testosterone supplementation should be part of HRT for most women.
c. Women should consider the benefits and risks of HRT by discussing the matter with a health care provider.
d. Progesterone supplementation is not required for women with a uterus.

24.
K
Answer: b
p. 105
Obj. #13

A woman may reduce the chance of contracting a urinary tract infection by
a. douching after menstruation.
b. urinating as soon as she feels the urge.
c. wiping from back to front.
d. using petroleum jelly during intercourse.

25.
K
Answer: a
p. 105
Obj. #14

The risk of vaginitis increases if a woman
a. is using birth control pills.
b. wears cotton underpants.
c. uses mild soap when washing.
d. eats a low carbohydrate diet.

26.
K
Answer: c
p. 106
Obj. #15

A woman should begin having Pap smears
a. when she starts menstruating.
b. when she notices pelvic pain.
c. when she is 18 or begins having intercourse.
d. when she shows secondary sex characteristics.

27.
K
Answer: d
p. 107
Obj. #16

A woman who smokes and has multiple male sexual partners is at increased risk of developing
a. fibrocystic disease.
b. ectopic pregnancy.
c. Endometriosis.
d. cervical cancer.

28.
K
Answer: d
p. 107
Obj. #18

Which of the following is NOT true regarding hysterectomy?
a. It is the second most common surgical procedure for women.
b. It is used to treat cervical and uterine cancer.
c. It may affect sexual response.
d. The uterus and ovaries are removed.

29.
K
Answer: d
p. 108
Obj. #20

Breast size is primarily influenced by
a. the size of the mammary glands.
b. the amount of muscle tissue on the chest wall.
c. the number of milk ducts.
d. the amount of fatty tissue surrounding the glands.

30.
K
Answer: a
p. 111
Obj. #20

Most breasts lumps are NOT malignant tumors and may instead be a(n)
a. cyst or fibroadenoma.
b. axillary adhesion.
c. fibroidal mass.
d. mammary body.

31.
K
Answer: c
pp. 113-114
Obj. #20

Which of the following statements regarding breast cancer risk is false?
a. Approximately one in nine North American women is affected.
b. Environmental factors account for two times as much risk as genes.
c. Sedentary lifestyle does not seem to increase risk.
d. The risk of breast cancer rises with age.

True/False

Students may be asked to answer these questions using the traditional format of marking their answers either "true" or "false". Or, to encourage more active involvement, you may choose to use the following instructions:

If the statement is true, place a "T" on the line preceding it. If the statement is false, place an "F" on the line preceding it and then change the statement to make it true by deleting incorrect information and/or adding accurate information.

1.
Answer: T
p. 83
Obj. #4

___ The term "vulva" refers to all external female genital structures.

2.
Answer: T
p. 85
Obj. #4

___ The only purpose of the clitoris is sexual arousal.

3.
Answer: F
pp. 85 - 86
Obj. #4

___ The clitoris and the vaginal opening are located within the vestibule.

4.
Answer: F
pp. 85-86
Obj. #23

___ Female genital mutilation has been practiced in many parts of the world, but never in the United States.

5.
Answer: F
p. 90
Obj. #6

___ Kegel exercises were developed to help women increase their genital sensitivity.

6.
Answer: T
p. 90
Obj. #8

___ Vaginal lubrication serves two purposes: to help make the vagina more alkaline and to increase sexual pleasure.

7.
Answer: T
p. 91
Obj. #12

___ Using deodorant tampons serves no purpose as menstrual fluid has no odor until it is outside of the body.

8.
Answer: F
p. 95
Obj. #21

___ The length of the menstrual cycle varies from woman to woman, and the time differences occur in the interval between ovulation and the onset of menstruation.

9.
Answer: T
p. 95
Obj. #21

___ The "trigger" for uniform menstrual cycles among women appears to be related to the sense of smell.

10.
Answer: T
p. 97
Obj. #21

___ When ovulation occurs there are changes in the cervical mucus.

11.
Answer: F
p. 100
Obj. #21

___ Primary dysmenorrhea occurs prior to menstruation and is usually caused by pelvic inflammatory disease or endometriosis.

12.
Answer: T
p. 100
Obj. #21

___ Uterine contractions associated with dysmenorrhea are caused by an overproduction of prostaglandins.

13.
Answer: F
pp. 103
Obj. #26

___ Hormone replacement therapy may protect a woman from both cardiovascular disease and endometrial cancer.

14.
Answer: T
p. 104
Obj. #13

___ Urinary tract infections are typically caused by bacteria from the rectum or vagina.

15.
Answer: T
p. 107
Obj. #16

___ Women who have had genital warts may be at increased risk for cervical cancer.

16. ___ Some women may experience a decrease in their sexual responsiveness after having a hysterectomy.
Answer: T
p. 107
Obj. #18

17. ___ Variation in breast size among women is a result of the size of their mammary glands.
Answer: F
p. 108
Obj. #20

18. ___ The best time to do a breast self-exam is following menstruation.
Answer: T
p. 109
Obj. #20

19. ___ Fibroadenomas (solid, rounded breast tumors) are usually malignant.
Answer: F
p. 111
Obj. #20

20. ___ A high-fat diet and obesity are two factors that increase a woman's risk for breast cancer.
Answer: T
p. 111
Obj. #20

Short Answer Essay

1. Discuss the possible physical, personal and interpersonal benefits a woman can gain from knowledge and understanding of her body and how it functions. (Obj. #1, 14, 15, 16, 20, 21)

2. What are some of the reasons a woman might find it distressing or difficult to do a genital self-exam? What are some of the advantages to doing such an examination? (Obj. #1)

3. List and briefly describe the major structures of the vulva. (Obj. #2)

4. Discuss the following in reference to urinary tract infections: incidence of; causes of; symptoms of; and preventative measures. (Obj. #13)

5. For what purpose were Kegel exercises originally developed, and what added benefit was later realized? (Obj. #6, 7)

6. Describe some factors that may increase susceptibility to vaginal infections, and preventative measures that minimize the possibility of getting them. (Obj. #14)

7. What factors may put a woman at higher risk for cervical cancer, and what treatment options are available for women who receive this diagnosis? (Obj. #16)

8. List the three phases of the menstrual cycle and briefly describe what occurs in each phase. (Obj. #21)

9. Three menstrual problems that some women experience include premenstrual syndrome, amenorrhea, and dysmenorrhea. Select two and consider what causes them and what may be done to help alleviate these conditions? (Obj. #21)

10. Discuss the following in regard to female genital mutilation: where, how and why it is performed, health consequences that may result, and the current controversy surrounding it. (Obj. #22)

11. Citing specific examples, explain how menstruation has been viewed from a cross-cultural perspective. (Obj. #24)

12. With respect to women's breasts, what brings about variation in size? What is known about surgery to increase the size of the breasts (i.e., breast implants)? (Obj. #19, 20)

13. Suppose that a female friend learns that you are taking a course in human sexuality and ask you what you have learned about breast self-exam. What would you say to her about how and why these should be done? (Obj. #20)

14. Describe some of the changes that occur during risks and menopause and what, if anything may be done to counteract them. (Obj. #26)

15. Discuss the potential benefits and risks of hormone replacement therapy. (Obj. #27)

5

Male Sexual Anatomy and Physiology

Learning Objectives

After studying this chapter, the student should be able to:

1. Describe the structure and function of the following parts of the male sexual anatomy: the penis, the scrotum, the testes, the vas deferens, the seminal vesicles, the prostate gland, the Cowper's glands, semen.

2. Describe how Kegel exercises are done, and give three possible benefits of doing them.

3. Define cryptorchidism, including its incidence and how it is treated.

4. Discuss the possible relationship between heat and sperm production.

5. Define the cremasteric reflex, and discuss what types of situations may provoke this response.

6. Explain how to conduct a male genital self-exam.

7. Explain how and where sperm production and storage takes place.

8. Discuss in detail the physiological processes involved in erection and ejaculation.

9. Explain why penis size has historically been so important, and how that has affected men's masculinity and/or self-image. Describe the physiological facts of sexual interaction and penis size.

10. Define circumcision and discuss recent research regarding its necessity.

11. Discuss various cultural beliefs and practices regarding male genital modification and mutilation, referring specifically to the following: under what circumstances it is practiced; advantages and disadvantages of these procedures; how these procedures relate to sexual pleasure and function; cross-cultural beliefs and practices.

12. Discuss health care concerns regarding the penis.

13. Discuss benefits and costs of circumcision and recent AAP recommendations regarding circumcision.

14. Describe the incidence of, symptoms of and treatment alternatives for penile and testicular cancer, prostatitis and benign prostate hyperplasia.

15. Describe recent advances in treatment and management of prostate cancer.

Multiple Choice

1.
A
Answer: b
p. 118
Obj. #1

Which of the following **best** describes the composition of the penis?
a. blood vessels, skeletal tissue, nerves, spongy tissue
b. nerves, blood vessels, fibrous tissue, spongy tissue
c. muscular tissue, skeletal tissue, nerves, blood vessels
d. spongy tissue, skeletal tissue, fibrous tissue, nerves

2.
K
Answer: b
p. 118
Obj. #1

The penis consists primarily of
a. muscle tissue.
b. spongy tissue.
c. connective tissue.
d. skeletal tissue surrounded by muscle tissue.

3.
K
Answer: a
p. 118
Obj. #1

Which one is true concerning the penis?
a. The glans, or penis head, has a great many nerve endings.
b. The portion of the penis that is inside the pelvis is called the cavernous body.
c. One can do exercises to strengthen the muscles in the shaft of the penis.
d. Because of the small inside bone, erections are sometimes referred to as a "boner".

4.
K
Answer: d
pp. 118, 123
Obj. #1

Which of the following is NOT a part of the penis?
a. the root
b. the spongy body
c. the glans
d. the epididymis

5.
K
Answer: d
p. 119
Obj. #10, 11

Which of the following statements regarding circumcision is false?
a. Historically, records indicate that circumcision has taken place for thousands of years.
b. In some South Pacific cultures, a form of circumcision takes place when a boy reaches adolescence.
c. The majority of male infants in the U.S. are circumcised.
d. Circumcision is widely practiced in Europe and Africa.

6.
K
Answer: c
p. 119
Obj. #1
WWW

The _____ of the penis can be retracted, and circumcision involves the permanent removal of this sleeve of skin.
a. glans
b. frenulum
c. foreskin
d. crura

7.
K
Answer: c
p. 120
Obj. #11

Which one is NOT true concerning castration?
a. This refers to removal of the testes.
b. This was done in the Middle Ages to preserve the high voices of choirboys.
c. This is a Jewish religious rite.
d. This may be done as treatment for prostate cancer.

Chapter 5   Male Sexual Anatomy and Physiology   97

8.
A
Answer: d
pp. 120-125
Obj. #1

All of the following are a part of internal male sexual anatomy **except**
   a. prostate gland.
   b. seminal vesicles.
   c. epididymis.
   d. frenulum.

9.
K
Answer: c
p. 120
Obj. #11

Castration has been performed in recent decades for all of the following reasons **except**
   a. to treat prostate cancer.
   b. to allegedly deter sex offenders.
   c. as a supposed "cure" for masturbation.
   d. to prevent a mentally disabled person from having offspring.

10.
K
Answer: c
pp. 121-122
Obj. #1

Cold temperatures or sexual stimulation may cause it to move closer to the body.
   a. spermatic cord
   b. glans of the penis
   c. scrotum
   d. vas deferens

11.
K
Answer: c
p. 121
Obj. #1

The tunica dartos, which is composed of smooth muscle fibers and fibrous connective tissue, is an inner layer of the
   a. penis.
   b. vas deferens.
   c. scrotum.
   d. prostate gland.

12.
K
Answer: d
pp. 121-122
Obj. #1

All of the following are found in the scrotal sac **except**
   a. testicles.
   b. spermatic cord.
   c. cremasteric muscle fibers.
   d. Cowper's glands.

13.
K
Answer: d
p. 121
Obj. #2

All of the following statements regarding Kegel exercises are true **except**
   a. a man locates the muscle by stopping the flow of urine several times while urinating.
   b. better ejaculatory control may be experienced as a result of doing these.
   c. women can do these exercises too.
   d. results will be noticed within one week of regular practice.

14.
A
Answer: b
p. 121
Obj. #2

Kegel exercises
   a. are used for women but not for men.
   b. strengthen the muscles usually only contracted during ejaculation.
   c. are primarily done by males to deal with incontinence problems.
   d. if overdone may result in premature ejaculation.

15.
A
Answer: a
p. 121
Obj. #2

A man is having difficulty with premature ejaculation. One strategy he could use in order to deal with this problem would be to
a. practice Kegel exercises.
b. reduce his caffeine intake.
c. practice retrograde ejaculation.
d. exercise his cremasteric muscle.

16.
K
Answer: a
p. 119
Obj. #1

The spermatic cord contains the
a. vas deferens.
b. seminal vesicles.
c. prostate gland.
d. Cowper's glands.

17.
K
Answer: b
pp. 121-122
Obj. #5

All of the following stimuli cause the scrotum to draw closer to the body **except**
a. sexual arousal.
b. warm temperatures.
c. sudden fear.
d. stroking the inner thighs.

18.
A
Answer: c
p. 122
Obj. #1

All of the following involve the testes **except** the
a. cremasteric muscle.
b. seminiferous tubules.
c. frenulum.
d. epididymis.

19.
K
Answer: c
p. 122
Obj. #5

The cremasteric muscle fibers
a. can be strengthened by doing Kegel exercises.
b. are located at the base of the prostate gland.
c. may be voluntarily contracted.
d. cause the testicles to move away from the body when contracted.

20.
K
Answer: d
p. 122
Obj. #5

The response that occurs when the testicles move closer to the body as a result of sexual stimulation is called
a. testicular contraction.
b. cryptorchidic contraction.
c. phimosis.
d. the cremasteric reflex.

21.
K
Answer: d
p. 123
Obj. #1

The route that the testes take as they move from the abdomen to the scrotum is called the
a. cremasteric canal.
b. testicular tunnel.
c. scrotal canal.
d. inguinal canal.

22.
K
Answer: a
p. 123
Obj. #2

The condition whereby one or both testicles fail to descend is called
a. cryptorchidism.
b. phimosis.
c. testicular retraction.
d. prostatitis.

23.
K
Answer: a
p. 123
Obj. #3
WWW

Which of the following statements regarding cryptorchidism is false?
a. Fifteen to twenty percent of men are born with this condition.
b. This condition often corrects itself.
c. Infertility may be a consequence of this condition.
d. This condition is often associated with increased risk of developing testicular cancer.

24.
A
Answer: a
pp. 123-125
Obj. #1

Which of the following courses does a sperm cell follow on its way to the exterior body of the male?
a. testes, epididymis, vas deferens, urethra
b. vas deferens, epididymis, ejaculatory duct, urethra
c. testes, vas deferens, epididymis, urethra
d. testes, vas deferens, urethra, epididymis

25.
K
Answer: a
p. 123
Obj. #7

The major sources of androgen are the
a. interstitial cells.
b. bulbourethral glands.
c. seminal vesicles.
d. cavernous bodies.

26.
K
Answer: c
p. 123
Obj. #7

_____ takes place within the seminiferous tubules.
a. Blood engorgement
b. Androgen production
c. Sperm production
d. The production of seminal fluid

27.
K
Answer: c
p. 123
Obj. #7
WWW

Which of the following statements regarding sperm production is false?
a. It takes place within the seminiferous tubules.
b. It usually begins after the onset of puberty.
c. It constitutes approximately 70% of the seminal fluid.
d. It usually continues until death.

28.
A
Answer: a
p. 124
Obj. #6

Which of the following conditions would a man be **most** likely to prevent as a result of regular genital self-examination?
a. testicular cancer
b. cryptorchidism
c. priapism
d. phimosis

29.
K
Answer: c
p. 124
Obj. #1

The vas deferens
a. is a tube through which urine passes from the bladder to the outside of the body.
b. is located inside the penis.
c. is the tube that is severed in a vasectomy.
d. is where sperm production takes place.

30.
K
Answer: b
p. 124
Obj. #1

Which one is NOT true concerning male genital self-examination?
a. This may enable early detection of penile cancer.
b. One danger sign is to have testicles that vary in size.
c. A good time to conduct such an exam is after a hot shower.
d. A small hard mass may be an early sign of testicular cancer.

31.
K
Answer: c
p. 124
Obj. #7

All of the following are related to sperm production and storage **except**
a. seminiferous tubules.
b. testes.
c. Cowper's glands.
d. epididymis.

32.
K
Answer: d
p. 125
Obj. #1

The **major** portion of seminal fluid comes from the
a. prostate gland.
b. Cowper's glands.
c. vas deferens.
d. seminal vesicles.

33.
K
Answer: b
pp. 125-126
Obj. #1

Both ejaculatory ducts and the urethra pass through the
a. Cowper's glands.
b. prostate gland.
c. testes.
d. epidymis.

34.
K
Answer: d
p. 126
Obj. #1

The _____ is located at the base of the bladder and secretes about 30 percent of the seminal fluid released during ejaculation.
a. vas deferens
b. bulbourethral gland
c. seminal vesicle
d. prostate gland

35.
K
Answer: b
p. 126
Obj. #1

The Cowper's glands secrete a fluid when a man becomes sexually aroused
a. that is acidic in nature.
b. that may contain active sperm.
c. that functions as a vaginal lubricant during intercourse.
d. that is released during the emission phase of ejaculation.

36.
K
Answer: c
p. 126
Obj. #1

The Cowper's glands are located
a. at the base of the bladder.
b. adjacent to the seminal vesicles.
c. on each side of the urethra.
d. on each side of the vas deferens.

37.
K
Answer: d
p. 126
Obj. #1

Which of the following statements regarding Cowper's glands secretions is false?
a. They are not experienced by all men.
b. They occur just prior to orgasm.
c. They occur immediately after erection.
d. They occur immediately following the expulsion phase of ejaculation.

38.
K
Answer: a
p. 126
Obj. #1
WWW

Which of the following **best** describes the function of Cowper's glands secretions?
a. Buffers the acidity of the urethra and facilitates flow of semen through the urethra.
b. Facilitates flow of semen through the urethra and helps to lubricate the vagina.
c. Helps to lubricate the vagina and buffers the acidity of the urethra.
d. Buffers the acidity of the urethra and makes up the largest portion of the fluid in semen.

39.
K
Answer: b
p. 127
Obj. #1

Which of the following statements concerning seminal fluid is true?
a. It is composed primarily of fluids secreted by the prostate gland.
b. The amount of fluid is influenced by the length of time since the last orgasm.
c. It functions as a vaginal lubricant during intercourse.
d. The amount of fluid is approximately three tablespoons.

40.
K
Answer: d
p. 127
Obj. #1
WWW

Which of the following statements regarding the male ejaculate is true?
a. The fluid is highly alkaline in nature.
b. The major portion of the fluid is derived from the prostate gland.
c. The amount of fluid a man ejaculates is approximately three tablespoons.
d. It consists of fluids that come from the seminal vesicles, prostate and Bartholin's glands.

41.
K
Answer: d
p. 127
Obj. #8

Which of the following statements concerning penile erection is false?
a. It is a process coordinated by the autonomic nervous system.
b. The capacity for erection is present at birth.
c. Nighttime erections occur during the rapid-eye movement stage of sleep.
d. Morning erections occur as the result of a full bladder.

42.
K
Answer: b
p. 127
Obj. #8

Which one is NOT true concerning erections?
a. They sometimes occur in infant boys.
b. Morning erections are probably due to a full bladder.
c. They may be enhanced by fantasies.
d. This results from the penis engorging with blood.

43.
A
Answer: c
pp. 127-128
Obj. #8

In which of the following situations would a man be **least** likely to experience an erection?
a. while riding a bike
b. while lifting heavy weights
c. while swimming in a cold pool
d. while having a sexual fantasy

44.
A
Answer: a
p. 127
Obj. #8

A man wakes up in the morning with an erection. Which of the following would be **least** likely to be associated with this?
a. He has a full bladder.
b. He has just completed a REM stage of sleep.
c. He has been dreaming about his lover.
d. His lover has been kissing him while he was asleep.

45.
K
Answer: a
pp. 128-129
Obj. #8

During the _____ phase of ejaculation, a man will usually experience the "point of no return".
a. emission
b. retrograde
c. expulsion
d. rapid-eye movement

46.
K
Answer: c
p. 129
Obj. #8

In the _____ stage of ejaculation, the collected semen is expelled from the penis by strong rhythmic contractions.
a. emission
b. retrograde
c. expulsion
d. rapid-eye movement

47.
K
Answer: b
pp. 127-128
Obj. #8
WWW

The "point of no return" or "ejaculatory inevitability" occurs during
a. the expulsion phase.
b. the emission phase.
c. the rapid-eye movement stage.
d. nocturnal emission.

48.
K
Answer: b
p. 129
Obj. #8

In _____, semen is expelled into the bladder.
a. spermatogenesis
b. retrograde ejaculation
c. penile inhibition
d. seminal retraction

49.
K
Answer: d
p. 129
Obj. #8

Occasionally a male will experience orgasm without direct genital stimulation. The most familiar of these occurrences is called
a. REM expulsion.
b. insominal emission.
c. ejaculatory expulsion.
d. nocturnal emission.

50.
K
Answer: d
p. 129
Obj. #8

Ejaculation
a. occurs in three stages.
b. is synonymous with orgasm.
c. is basically a psychological response.
d. usually takes three to ten seconds in the expulsion phase.

51.
K
Answer: d
p. 129
Obj. #8

Retrograde ejaculation may occur as a result of all of the following **except**
a. prostate surgery.
b. using certain drugs.
c. a congenital abnormality.
d. doing Kegel exercises.

52.
K
Answer: c
pp. 130-131
Obj. #9

Which of the following statements concerning penis size is true?
a. Most women say that larger penis size is an important factor in their sexual gratification.
b. Due to research findings on penile anatomy, few men worry about penis size anymore.
c. Smaller flaccid penises tend to expand proportionately more in size during erection than ones that are larger when flaccid.
d. Penis size is related to race, but not to virility or body build.

53.
A
Answer: b
p. 130
Obj. #9
WWW

A woman's partner penetrates her very deeply during intercourse, causing her to experience sharp pain. This pain would **most** likely be attributed to
a. cervical sensitivity.
b. jarring of the ovaries.
c. vaginal sensitivity near the cervix.
d. an infection of the Bartholin's glands.

54.
K
Answer: b
pp. 130-131
Obj. #9

With respect to penises which one is NOT true?
a. Penises that are smaller when flaccid increase more in size during erections than those that are originally larger.
b. Women tend to be more sexually aroused by pictures of larger penises than by ones that are smaller.
c. Your book chooses not to give information about the average dimensions of penises.
d. Many men and women erroneously believe that penis size is related to being a desirable lover.

55.
K
Answer: d
p. 131
Obj. #9

According to the text, the average penis is approximately _____ in length when erect.
a. four inches
b. five inches
c. six inches
d. The authors do not report this information because they do not think it is important.

56.
K
Answer: d
pp. 119, 131-132
Obj. #10, 11

Which of the following statements concerning circumcision is false?
a. It is the surgical removal of the foreskin.
b. It is widely practiced throughout the world for religious or hygienic reasons.
c. In the United States, circumcision is usually performed the second day after birth.
d. Superincision, a variation of circumcision, is common in Europe.

57.
K
Answer: a
pp. 119, 131-132
Obj. #11

From a cross-cultural perspective, which of the following statements regarding male circumcision is true?
a. It is practiced for religious as well as hygienic reasons.
b. Circumcision was first known to be practiced in the mid eighteenth century.
c. Circumcision is relatively uncommon in Middle Eastern and African societies.
d. Circumcision is widespread in Europe.

58.
K
Answer: c
pp. 131-132
Obj. #11

Circumcision
a. is primarily performed as part of the clean up process after delivery.
b. is done in about 80% of newborn male babies in the United States.
c. is presently moderately opposed by the American Academy of Pediatrics.
d. is sometimes medically referred to as phimosis.

59
K
Answer: a
p. 132
Obj. #10, 11, 15
WWW

Uncircumcised men are at higher risk for developing _____ than circumcised men.
a. penile cancer
b. testicular cancer
c. prostate cancer
d. benign prostatic hyperplasia

60.
K
Answer: c
p. 132
Obj. #10, 11

A recent study revealed that uncircumcised men were more likely to have _____ than were circumcised men.
a. problems with premature ejaculation
b. problems with ejaculatory inhibition
c. gonorrhea and syphilis
d. herpes and chlamydia

61.
K
Answer: c
p. 132
Obj. #10

Which of the following statements is **least** accurate?
a. The incidence of cervical cancer may be higher in women who have sex with uncircumcised men.
b. Bacteria from the foreskin can cause vaginal infections in women who have sex with uncircumcised men.
c. The pain of circumcision helps to inure little boys against other kinds of pain.
d. Uncircumcised men may be more likely to become infected with HIV through heterosexual intercourse than circumcised men.

Chapter 5 Male Sexual Anatomy and Physiology 105

62.
K
Answer: b
pp. 132-133
Obj. #10, 11

Which of the following statements regarding circumcision is true?
a. Recent research concludes that sexual performance and satisfaction is greater among men who have not been circumcised than among men who have.
b. Infants who undergo circumcision without anesthesia feel and respond to pain.
c. Recent research has demonstrated that the foreskin of the penis serves an important sexual as well as hygienic function.
d. Men who have been circumcised are more at risk for penile cancer than those who have not.

63.
K
Answer: c
p. 133
Obj. #10, 11

Several studies have reported that uncircumcised boys have a higher rate of _____ than circumcised boys.
a. preputial discharge
b. penile adhesions
c. urinary tract infections
d. testicular cancer

64.
K
Answer: d
pp. 132-133
Obj. #10, 11

Arguments against routine circumcision include which of the following?
a. It increases the likelihood of acquiring viruses.
b. Data by Masters and Johnson suggest that the uncircumcised experience more sexual pleasure.
c. This should be reserved for groups that wish to use it for religious reasons.
d. Infants experience pain and some health risks when circumcised.

65.
K
Answer: b
p. 133
Obj. #11

A condition known as _____ exists when a man has an extremely tight foreskin.
a. cremasteric constriction
b. phimosis
c. cryptorchidism
d. glans constriction

66.
A
Answer: b
p. 133
Obj. #5

A man experiences aching sensations in his testicles and a burning sensation while urinating. The medical specialist best able to diagnose his condition would be a
a. gynecologist.
b. urologist.
c. entomologist.
d. endocrinologist.

67.
K
Answer: a
p. 134
Obj. #10, 12

A cheesy substance known as _____ can accumulate under the prepuce of the penis, causing discomfort and possible infection.
a. smegma
b. preputial discharge
c. phimonal abscess
d. frenulum fungus

68.
A
Answer: c
p. 134
Obj. #11
WWW

For an uncircumcised male, retracting the foreskin and practicing daily hygiene can help avoid the problem of
a. coronal eczema.
b. prostatitis.
c. smegma build-up.
d. phimosis.

69.
K
Answer: c
p. 134
Obj. #1

Which of the following statements regarding smegma is false?
a. It consists of glandular secretions and dead skin cells.
b. It may be physically irritating.
c. It accumulates in the urethral opening of the penis.
d. It may have an unpleasant odor.

70.
K
Answer: b
p. 134
Obj. #5

Which of the following statements concerning a penile fracture is true?
a. It is a fairly common occurrence.
b. It involves a rupture of the cavernous bodies when the penis is erect.
c. It happens most frequently during masturbation.
d. Erectile functioning in most men is seriously impaired as a result of it.

71.
K
Answer: b
p. 134
Obj. #5

Which one is NOT one of the possible penile reactions?
a. They may be fractured (ruptured) during coitus.
b. "Cock rings" may destroy penile tissue.
c. Smegma is part of the ejaculate.
d. It is possible for the penis to become allergic to vaginal secretions.

72.
K
Answer: a
pp. 134-135
Obj. #10, 14

Which of the following statements regarding penile cancer is false?
a. It is rare, but nearly always fatal.
b. It is not as common as prostate cancer.
c. Uncircumcised men are more at risk for it than circumcised men.
d. A long history of tobacco use can increase a man's risk of developing it.

73.
K
Answer: c
p. 135
Obj. #13

All of the following are risk factors for developing penile cancer **except**
a. being over age 50.
b. history of multiple sex partners and genital herpes.
c. history of prostate infections.
d. long-term tobacco use.

74.
A
Answer: c
p. 135
Obj. #14

Which of the following statements regarding testicular cancer is false?
a. It is one of the most common malignancies among young men in the 15–34 age group.
b. The survival rate among men treated for testicular cancer is very high if detected early.
c. The first symptom of testicular cancer is a painful chancre that appears on the scrotum.
d. Regular genital self-exam is recommended in order to identify early symptoms.

75.
K
Answer: a
p. 135
Obj. #14

Which of the following would be **least** symptomatic of testicular cancer?
a. a lesion on the scrotum
b. a mass within the testicle
c. tender breasts and nipples
d. swelling in the scrotum

76.
K
Answer: d
p. 136
Obj. #14

Which of the following statements concerning prostatitis is false?
a. It may occur in men of any age.
b. The prostate gland will enlarge as a result of the infection.
c. It is commonly treated by antibiotics.
d. It may be detected by a blood test for PSA (prostate-specific antigen).

77.
K
Answer: b
p. 136
Obj. #15

The second leading cause of cancer death among men in the United States is
a. testicular cancer.
b. prostate cancer.
c. rectal cancer.
d. penile cancer.

78.
K
Answer: a
pp. 136-137
Obj. #15

Prostate cancer
a. may lack obvious symptoms in the early stages.
b. is more common among black men than white men.
c. is relatively rare.
d. is usually fatal, even with early diagnosis.

79.
K
Answer: c
p. 136
Obj. #15

All of the following are risk factors associated with prostate cancer **except**
a. old age.
b. diet high in saturated fats.
c. being Asian American.
d. a prior history of sexually transmitted diseases.

80.
K
Answer: b
p. 137
Obj. #15

All but which of the following might be used to detect prostate cancer?
a. a blood test
b. genital self-exam
c. needle biopsy
d. digital rectal examination by a physician

81.
K
Answer: b
pp. 137-138
Obj. #15
WWW

Treatment for prostate cancer may include all of the following **except**
a. orchidectomy.
b. PSA (prostate-specific antigen) injections.
c. radiation therapy.
d. expectant management.

82.
K
Answer: d
p. 138
Obj. #15

Which of the following statements regarding treatment of early detected prostate cancer is **most** accurate?
a. Expectant management is the preferred treatment in the U.S., especially for young men.
b. Radical prostatectomy is the most common treatment of choice.
c. Outside of the U.S., radiation therapy and surgery are the most common treatment strategies.
d. At this time, there is considerable controversy regarding the optimum treatment approach to use.

83.
K
Answer: b
p. 138
Obj. #15

Brachytherapy
a. is another term for expectant management.
b. is a term for internal radiotherapy seed.
c. is another term for antiandrogen treatment.
d. is a kind of chemotherapy.

84.
K
Answer: d
p. 137-138
Obj. #15

A recommended health strategy discussed in your text includes
a. an annual rectal exam for men beginning at age 40 and women at age 60.
b. using a PSA, which is more accurate than a rectal exam.
c. Radical prostatectomy only for men 70 or older.
d. Antiandrogen therapy for several months after either surgery or radiotherapy.

85.
K
Answer: d
p. 123
Obj. #14

Which one is NOT true?
a. High school health classes rarely give instruction for testicular self-examination.
b. The testicles can be affected by a variety of diseases, most of which have observable symptoms.
c. Apparently fewer than 10% of male college students examine their testicles regularly.
d. Men should be encouraged to begin self-examination of the testicles on a regular basis beginning at about age 40.

Multiple Choice from Study Guide

1.
K
Answer: a
p. 118
Obj. #1

The interior of the penis contains
a. the cavernous bodies and spongy body.
b. an extensive network of muscle tissue.
c. a cylinder-shaped piece of cartilage.
d. all of the above.

2.
K
Answer: c
p. 118
Obj. #1

The exterior of the penis includes the
a. glans, shaft, and vas deferens.
b. crura, shaft, and glans.
c. foreskin, glans, and shaft.
d. corona, root, and ureter.

Chapter 5 Male Sexual Anatomy and Physiology 109

3.
K
Answer: d
p. 118
Obj. #1

The glans contains two areas that are quite responsive to stimulation. These are the
a. corona and crura.
b. foreskin and frenulum.
c. meatus and ampulla.
d. corona and frenulum.

4.
K
Answer: b
pp. 119-120
Obj. #4

Male genitals have been altered using all of the following procedures except
a. castration.
b. Infibulation.
c. superincision.
d. circumcision.

5.
K
Answer: c
p. 121
Obj. #2

Which of the following is NOT one of the benefits of doing Kegel exercises?
a. increased pelvic sensation
b. increased ejaculatory control
c. more rapid erection
d. stronger orgasm

6.
K
Answer: c
pp. 121-122
Obj. #1

Which of the following structures is not associated with the scrotum?
a. testis
b. spermatic cord
c. seminal vesicles
d. interstitial cells

7.
K
Answer: d
p. 123
Obj. #1

The testicles may be drawn closer to the body when
a. the scrotum is cooled.
b. straining during a bowel movement.
c. experiencing sudden fear.
d. all of the above.

8.
K
Answer: b
p. 123
Obj. #1

The two major functions of the testes are
a. controlling ejaculation and producing seminal fluid.
b. producing male sex hormones and making sperm.
c. making sperm and initiating the erectile response.
d. manufacturing seminal fluid and urine.

9.
K
Answer: a
p. 123
Obj. #1

Sperm are produced in tightly coiled structures called the
a. seminiferous tubules.
b. seminal vesicles.
c. vas deferencs.
d. epididymis.

10.
K
Answer: b
p. 123
Obj. #1

Most of a man's androgen is made in the
a. adrenal glands.
b. interstitial cells.
c. Cowper's gland.
d. prostate gland.

11.
K
Answer: a
pp. 124-125
Obj. #1

During a vasectomy a section of the _____ is removed, resulting in sterilization.
a. vas deferens
b. spongy body
c. urethra
d. spermatic cord

12.
K
Answer: a
p. 125
Obj. #1

The majority of the seminal fluid is produced by the
a. seminal vesicles.
b. seminiferous tubules.
c. prostate gland.
d. Leydig's cells.

13.
K
Answer: d
pp. 125-126
Obj. #14

Which walnut-shaped structure at the base of the bladder may cause problems with urination when enlarged?
a. ejaculatory ducts
b. urethral bulb
c. seminal vesicles
d. prostate gland

14.
K
Answer: b
p. 126
Obj. #1

The fluid from this gland is often confused with semen and may contain live sperm.
a. ejaculatory gland
b. Cowper's gland
c. prostate gland
d. ampulla gland

15.
K
Answer: a
p. 127
Obj. #7

Sperm comprise _____ percent of total semen volume.
a. 1%
b. 10%
c. 46%
d. about 63%

16.
K
Answer: c
p. 127
Obj. #1

Which of the following influences the amount of seminal fluid?
a. type of sexual activity that lead to ejaculation
b. exposure of the testicles to warmer temperatures
c. length of time since the last ejaculation
d. presence of bioflavinoids in the diet

17.
K
Answer: c
pp. 127-128
Obj. #8

In order for the penis to become erect, which of the following must occur?
a. swelling of the penis bone
b. stiffening of the spermatic cord
c. blood must accumulate in the cylinders of the penis
d. activation of the penis muscle fibers must exceed threshold

Chapter 5 Male Sexual Anatomy and Physiology 111

18.
K
Answer: d
pp. 128-129
Obj. #8

The first phase of ejaculation is _____ whereas the second is called
a. intromission; expulsion
b. expulsion; intromission
c. expulsion; emission
d. emission; expulsion

19.
K
Answer: d
p. 130
Obj. #9

Research has shown that penis size appears to be related to
a. age at puberty.
b. height.
c. set point weight.
d. none of the above.

20.
K
Answer: b
pp. 132-133
Obj. #10

Which of the following is NOT an argument against routine circumcision?
a. the procedure is traumatic for infants.
b. penile cancer rates are the same for circumcised and uncircumcised men.
c. sexual function may be altered by the removing the foreskin.
d. the foreskin may serve a function not known at this time.

21.
K
Answer: c
pp. 132-133
Obj. #10

Proponents of circumcision cite all of the following as reasons to continue circumcision **except**
a. female partners of uncircumcised men have increased risk of cervical cancer.
b. organisms living under the foreskin may cause vaginal infections women who are partners of uncircumcised men.
c. few health risks are associated with circumcision.
d. uncircumcised men are at greater risk of contracting HIV.

22.
K
Answer: d
p. 133
Obj. #12

Luis has been experiencing pain in his penis when urinating and has an aching lower back. What type of health care provider would be best for him to see?
a. internist
b. proctologist
c. endomologist
d. urologist

23.
K
Answer: b
p. 134
Obj. #12

Cleaning under the foreskin may remove _____, which may cause irritation, unpleasant odor, or infection.
a. condyloma accuminata
b. smegma
c. sebaceous cysts
d. urethral granuloma

24.
K
Answer: d
p. 136
Obj. #14

Symptoms of prostatitis and prostate cancer include all of the following **except**
a. lower back pain.
b. difficulty urinating.
c. pelvic pain.
d. a mass in the testicle.

112   Test Bank to Accompany *Our Sexuality*

25.
K
Answer: d
p. 137
Obj. #12

Men are hesitant to have rectal examinations because
a. of discomfort about homosexual overtones if the doctor is male.
b. they fear of the examination's results.
c. they anticipate that treatment will impair sexual functioning.
d. all of the above

True/False

Students may be asked to answer these questions using the traditional format of marking their answers either "true" or "false". Or, to encourage more active involvement, you may choose to use the following instructions:

If the statement is true, place a "T" on the line preceding it. If the statement is false, place an "F" on the line preceding it and then change the statement to make it true by deleting incorrect information and/or adding accurate information.

1.
Answer: T
p. 118
Obj. #1

___ The head of the penis is known as the glans.

2.
Answer: F
p. 120
Obj. #11

___ The practice of castration involves removal of the penis and the testicles.

3.
Answer: T
p. 120
Obj. #11

___ Castration is sometimes performed as a medical treatment for prostate cancer and genital tuberculosis.

4.
Answer: T
p. 121
Obj. #2

___ Both men and women can increase sexual pleasure by practicing Kegel exercises.

5.
Answer: T
p. 123
Obj. #3

___ The condition of cryptorchidism often corrects itself within the first two years of life.

6.
Answer: T
p. 123
Obj. #1

___ The testicles not only produce sperm but also secrete male sex hormones.

7.
Answer: F
p. 124
Obj. #6

___ Men are encouraged to practice regular self-exam in order to diagnose early prostate cancer.

Chapter 5 Male Sexual Anatomy and Physiology

8. Answer: T
p. 125
Obj. #1, 7

___ The C-shaped structure that serves as a storage chamber for sperm is called the epididymis.

9. Answer: F
p. 125
Obj. #1

___ The major portion of seminal fluid is derived from the prostate gland.

10. Answer: T
pp. 126
Obj. #1

___ The fluid secreted by the Cowper's glands may contain active sperm.

11. Answer: T
p. 127
Obj. #1

___ Seminal fluid is derived from the prostate, Cowper's glands and seminal vesicles.

12. Answer: T
p. 127
Obj. #8

___ Nighttime erections occur during the rapid-eye movement stage of sleep.

13. Answer: T
p. 127
Obj. #1

___ Although usually semen is not harmful if swallowed, it can transmit the HIV virus from an infected male.

14. Answer: F
p. 129
Obj. #8

___ During the emission phase of ejaculation, semen is expelled from the penis.

15. Answer: F
p. 129
Obj. #8

___ Retrograde ejaculation may potentially be harmful because of the buildup of seminal fluid in the bladder.

16. Answer: T
p. 131
Obj. #9

___ Small, flaccid penises tend to increase more in size when erect than do larger, flaccid penises.

17. Answer: F
p. 132
Obj. #10, 11

___ Some research has shown that circumcised men are slightly more at risk for penile cancer than uncircumcised males.

18. ___ Accumulation of smegma can result in phimosis.
Answer: F
p. 133
Obj. #11

19. ___ The incidence of testicular cancer is on the increase.
Answer: T
p. 135
Obj. #14

20. ___ Prostate cancer is relatively uncommon, but can be fatal if left untreated.
Answer: F
p. 136
Obj. #15

Short Answer Essay

1. Discuss the **structure** and **function** of **five** of the following: scrotum, testes, vas deferens, seminal vesicles, prostate gland, Cowper's glands, semen, and the penis. (Obj. #1)

2. Trace the route taken by sperm, beginning from production and through storage and expulsion. (Obj. #1)

3. Discuss the condition of cryptorchidism, including how common it is, what the effects are if left untreated, treatment alternatives, and its relationship to other types of medical conditions. (Obj. #3)

4. Discuss some of the bodily symptoms or changes that a man should be looking for in doing a genital self-exam. (Obj. #6)

5. Explain the physiological processes that occur during penile erection. (Obj. #8)

6. Discuss the general procedures and potential benefits of male Kegel exercises. (Obj. #2)

7. Discuss some of the reasons why preoccupation with penis size occupies many people's minds. What are some of the possible effects of such thinking? In actuality, how important is penis size to women? (Obj. #9)

8. Describe the emission and expulsion phases of ejaculation. (Obj. #8)

9. Outline some of the key issues surrounding the question of male circumcision, making references to relevant research studies. (Obj. #11)

10. If you were to become the parent of a baby boy would you want to have him circumcised? Why, or why not? Would it matter if your partner had a different view? (Obj. #11)

11. Describe three types of male genital alteration and mutilation, making reference to the various reasons why these procedures are performed. (Obj. #11)

12. Discuss prostate cancer, making specific reference to the following: how common it is; risk factors with which it is associated; symptoms; and treatment alternatives. (Obj. #13)

13. If you or your partner were to be diagnosed with prostate cancer what information would you want before deciding on treatment? (Obj. #13)

14. When did you first hear of nocturnal emissions? How did what you heard match with what you now have learned from the text? (Obj. n/a)

15. Your book discusses cultural messages about the importance of penis size. Give some examples from your life of what you have observed with peers, in the media, in humor, etc. Does this confirm your text's position? Do you believe that you were previously affected by this? What is your belief now? (Obj. #9)

6

Sexual Arousal and Response

Learning Objectives

After studying this chapter, the student should be able to:

1. Explain the role of hormones in male sexual behavior, including the following: definition of androgens and their source; how testosterone affects male sexuality; definition of orchidectomy and what research has revealed regarding the effects of this procedure on sexual functioning; definition of antiandrogens and what research has demonstrated regarding the use of antiandrogens in the treatment of sex offenders; definition of hypogonadism and how research on this condition has contributed to our understanding of the relationship between androgens and sexual motivation

2. Explain the role of hormones in female sexual behavior, making specific reference to estrogens and testosterone, and citing relevant research studies.

3. Discuss the amount and type of testosterone that is necessary for hormonal sexual functions in men and women.

4. Discuss the signs of testosterone deficiency and issues involved in seeking testosterone replacement therapy.

5. Discuss the role of the brain in sexual arousal.

6. Describe the role of the following senses in sexual arousal: touch, vision, smell, taste and hearing.

7. Assess each of the following in regard to their aphrodisiac effects: various foods (oysters, eggplant, etc.), alcohol, amphetamines, barbiturates, cantharides, cocaine, psychedelic drugs, marijuana, amyl nitrate, L-dopa, yohimbine hydrochloride, Libido.

8. List at least seven substances that inhibit sexual behavior (anaphrodisiacs).

9. Describe the influence of pheremones on sexual response in humans and animals.

10. Describe Kaplan's three-stage model of sexual response.

11. List the four phases of Masters and Johnson's sexual response cycle and briefly describe the physiological changes that occur in each stage for women and men.

12. Discuss how female orgasmic response has been analyzed and explained over time, beginning with Freud's interpretation.

13. Define the Grafenberg spot and explain the controversy surrounding it.

14. Describe changes in the sexual response cycle of women as they age.

15. Describe changes in the sexual response cycle of men as they age.

16. Identify at least three significant differences in sexual response between men and women.

17. Discuss sexual arousal from a cross-cultural perspective, citing specific examples.

Multiple Choice

1.
K
Answer: a
p. 142
Obj. n/a

Human sexual arousal and response
a. is probably more determined by psychosocial factors than biological ones.
b. is probably more determined by hormonal influences than other factors.
c. is probably more determined by sensory and central nervous system factors than others.
d. is apparently more determined by psychosocial factors in women and hormonal factors in men.

2.
K
Answer: c
p. 142
Obj. #1

Approximately 5 percent of the androgens produced by males are secreted by the
a. testes.
b. hypothalamus.
c. adrenal glands.
d. Cowper's glands.

3.
K
Answer: b
pp. 142-143
Obj. #1

In men, the primary source of androgens is the _____, while the _____ is/are where the remaining androgens are produced.
a. Cowper's glands; hypothalamus
b. testes; adrenal glands
c. adrenal glands; hypothalamus
d. testes; hypothalamus

4.
K
Answer: c
pp. 142-143
Obj. #1, 2
WWW

Which of the following statements regarding hormones in men and women is false?
a. Male testes produce estrogens as well as androgens.
b. A woman's ovaries and adrenals produce androgens as well as estrogens.
c. The dominant estrogen in males and females is also called Depo-Provera.
d. The dominant androgen in males and females is testosterone.

5.
K
Answer: c
p. 142
Obj. #2

Both the _____ and _____ produce androgens in the female body.
a. ovaries; hypothalamus
b. adrenal glands; hypothalamus
c. ovaries; adrenal glands
d. adrenal glands; Bartholin's glands

Chapter 6 Sexual Arousal and Response 119

6.
A
Answer: a
p. 143
Obj. #3

A low testosterone level in men would be **most** likely to have which of the following effects?
a. little interest in sexual activity
b. difficulty in achieving and maintaining erections
c. problems with premature ejaculation
d. problems with ejaculatory inhibition

7.
K
Answer: d
pp. 143-144
Obj. #1, 2, 3
WWW

Which of the following statements regarding testosterone is false?
a. Erectile difficulties may sometimes be associated with testosterone deficiency.
b. Testosterone deficiency may result in decreased genital sexual pleasure for men.
c. Women experience a loss of testosterone after menopause or surgical removal of the ovaries.
d. Men but not women may experience increased sexual desire with remedial administration of testosterone.

8.
K
Answer: d
p. 143
Obj. #1

The medical term for castration is
a. vasectomy.
b. cryptorchidism.
c. prostatectomy.
d. orchidectomy.

9.
K
Answer: d
p. 143
Obj. #1

Castration might be performed for any of the following reasons **except**
a. as a treatment for genital tuberculosis.
b. for sex offenders who agree to it.
c. as a treatment for prostate cancer.
d. as a treatment for hypogonadism.

10.
K
Answer: c
p. 143
Obj. #1
WWW

The effect of castration on sexual desire and erotic functioning in men is
a. always negative, usually resulting in the total or near total elimination of all sexual activity.
b. rarely significant as human male sexual behavior is largely independent of gonadal function.
c. highly variable, ranging from complete cessation of sexual activity to only moderately reduced levels of erotic arousal and expression.
d. impossible to estimate as no legitimate experimental investigations of this question have been conducted.

11.
K
Answer: c
p. 143
Obj. #1

One of the problems in using drugs such as Depo-Provera to treat sex offenders is that
a. its effect on reducing testosterone circulation is highly variable.
b. its use may be associated with increased risk of prostate cancer.
c. some sexual assaults occur as the result of nonsexual motives.
d. while it has been used successfully in Europe, it has not met with FDA approval in the United States.

12.
K
Answer: c
pp. 143-144
Obj. #2

Estrogen replacement therapy
- a. can increase sexual desire in both men and women.
- b. does not have any apparent effect on sexuality although it prevents some medical problems.
- c. has sometimes been found to increase sexual desire and sometimes to have no effect.
- d. is one way to bring about the occurrence of multiple orgasms.

13.
K
Answer: a
pp. 143-144
Obj. #1

If hypogonadism occurs before puberty
- a. maturation of the primary and secondary sex characteristics will be retarded.
- b. the testicles will become infected and swell.
- c. orchidectomy is usually indicated.
- d. the results are more variable than if this condition occurs in adulthood.

14.
K
Answer: d
p. 143
Obj. #1

Information on the impact of testosterone on male sexuality has been obtained from all of the following **except**.
- a. research involving the use of Depo-Provera and other antiandrogens.
- b. research on hypogonadism.
- c. studies of men who have undergone castration.
- d. research on limbic system stimulation.

15.
A
Answer: d
p. 143
Obj. #1, 2

A woman has been dating a man for some time who, although he appears to enjoy her company, seems sexually apathetic toward her. Which of the following would **most** likely enhance his sexual desire?
- a. L-dopa
- b. cantharides
- c. any drug used to treat high blood pressure
- d. androgen

16.
K
Answer: b
p. 143
Obj. #1

Which of the following biological factors play the **most** important role in male sexual motivation?
- a. pheromones
- b. androgens
- c. estrogens
- d. aphrodisiacs

17.
K
Answer: b
p. 143
Obj. #1
WWW

When hormone replacement therapy is administered to hypogonadal men,
- a. sexual interest and activity decline.
- b. sexual interest and activity is restored.
- c. sexual interest and activity remain the same.
- d. the results are highly variable but most are unaffected.

Chapter 6 Sexual Arousal and Response 121

18.
K
Answer: d
pp. 143-144
Obj. #8

Which of the following statements concerning estrogen and its replacement therapy is **most** accurate?
  a. Most women who receive ERT experience increased sexual desire and orgasmic capacity.
  b. Most women who receive ERT experience "mood mellowing" benefits that make them more receptive to sexual interaction.
  c. Most women who receive ERT experience no discernible effects in sexual desire or activity.
  d. The role of estrogens in female sexual motivation and behavior remains unclear.

19.
K
Answer: d
pp. 143-144
Obj. #2

Which of the following statements **best** describes the relationship between estrogens and female sexual motivation and behavior?
  a. Estrogens play an insignificant role in female sexual activity.
  b. Estrogen replacement therapy increases female sexual desire.
  c. Estrogen replacement therapy increases orgasmic capacity.
  d. At this time, research findings are contradictory.

20.
K
Answer: a
p. 145
Obj. #3

Which of the following statements is true?
  a. Women have less testosterone than men but are more sensitive to it than men are.
  b. Men and women have similar levels of testosterone but men are more sensitive to it, so they tend to have stronger sex drives than women.
  c. Raising the level of testosterone above a normal range in men and women increases the sexual motivation in both sexes.
  d. As men and women age, testosterone deficiency is usually more acute and occurs more quickly in men.

21.
K
Answer: b
p. 145
Obj. #3

Which of the following is **most** influential in sexual motivation in both men and women?
  a. attached (bound) testosterone
  b. unattached (free) testosterone
  c. total testosterone
  d. our beliefs about our testosterone level

22.
A
Answer: a
p. 145
Obj. #4

Erika has just turned fifty and has noticed a decrease in sexual desire and orgasmic capacity as well as a decrease in her overall energy level. She may ask her physician to assess her
  a. free testosterone level.
  b. bound testosterone level.
  c. total testosterone level.
  d. blood libido level

23.
A
Answer: d
pp. 146-147
Obj. #4

Under which of the following circumstances would testosterone replacement therapy probably be **least** appropriate?
a. when a woman goes through menopause
b. when a woman has her ovaries removed
c. when a woman has noticed decreased sexual desire, less intense orgasms and diminished energy levels
d. when a woman is satisfied with her level of sexual desire and responsiveness

24.
A
Answer: c
p. 147
Obj. #6

The fact that some women have claimed to have experienced orgasm while listening to their favorite musician at a concert can be attributed to
a. the vibration of their chairs as a result of the amplified sound.
b. an excess of estrogen intake, probably as the result of being on birth control pills.
c. the capacity of their brains to engage in fantasy.
d. being on antidepressant medication.

25.
K
Answer: a
pp. 147-148
Obj. #16

Which of the following statements regarding cross-cultural sexual arousal is false?
a. Kissing on the mouth is a universal source of sexual arousal.
b. Healthy skin, hair and teeth are universally viewed as attractive.
c. In most parts of Africa, oral sex is viewed as unnatural or disgusting.
d. In many societies bare female breasts are not generally viewed as sexually stimulating.

26.
K
Answer: a
p. 147
Obj. #5

Mental events like fantasies are the product of the _____, the gray matter in the brain that controls reasoning and language abilities.
a. cerebral cortex
b. septal area
c. limbic system
d. hippocampus

27.
K
Answer: c
pp. 148-149
Obj. #5
WWW

Which of the following **best** describes the effects of "pleasure center" stimulation on rats and humans?
a. The rats experienced intense sexual pleasure but the human subjects found it irritating.
b. The rats appeared unaffected but the human subjects experienced intense pleasure.
c. The rats worked to exhaustion for such stimulation and the human subjects reported intense sexual pleasure.
d. Both the rats and the human subjects were unaffected by the stimulation.

28.
K
Answer: c
p. 149
Obj. #5

The "pleasure centers" that James Olds referred to in his research with rats was in reference to
a. primary erogenous zones.
b. secondary erogenous zones.
c. parts of the limbic system.
d. gonads and adrenal glands.

Chapter 6 Sexual Arousal and Response 123

29.
K
Answer: c
p. 150
Obj. #5

The effects of stimulation of the human hypothalamus
 a. has not been studied because of ethical reasons.
 b. strengthens the conclusion that we should not make use of animal research when talking about humans.
 c. has been reported in case studies to produce intense sexual pleasure.
 d. has led to the conclusion that this is the sex center of the brain.

30.
K
Answer: b
p. 150
Obj. #6

Of the main senses, _____ tends to predominate during sexual sharing.
 a. taste
 b. touch
 c. smell
 d. vision

31.
K
Answer: a
p. 150
Obj. #6

The mouth and the genitals are examples of _____ erogenous zones, while the upper and lower back are examples of _____ erogenous zones.
 a. primary; secondary
 b. secondary; primary
 c. sensate; affectional
 d. affectional; sensate

32.
K
Answer: a
p. 150
Obj. #6

The breasts, inner thighs, neck and mouth are all examples of
 a. primary erogenous zones.
 b. secondary erogenous zones.
 c. "pleasure centers".
 d. "G" spots.

33.
K
Answer: b
p. 150
Obj. #6

The upper back and the back of the knees are both examples of
 a. primary erogenous zones.
 b. secondary erogenous zones.
 c. "pleasure centers".
 d. "G" spots.

34.
A
Answer: b
p. 150
Obj. #6

If a person's shoulder were consistently stroked during each pleasurable sexual experience, it would soon become a source of sexual arousal. This part of the body would then be **most** appropriately labeled
 a. a primary erogenous zone.
 b. a secondary erogenous zone.
 c. a G spot.
 d. a pleasure center.

35.
K
Answer: b
p. 150
Obj. #6
WWW

Which of the following is the **most** accurate summary of research on the effects of visual erotica on men and women when measured physiologically?
   a. Men show strong responses while women generally have no reaction.
   b. There are strong similarities in how men and women respond to visual erotica.
   c. Women consistently manifest higher arousal levels than men.
   d. Women consistently manifest lower arousal levels than men.

36.
K
Answer: a
p. 150
Obj. #6

Which of the following **best** describes how men and women respond sexually to visual erotica?
   a. When measured by self-reports, men respond more than women; when measured physiologically, both men and women have similar responses.
   b. When measured by self-reports, men respond more than women; when measured physiologically, women respond more than men.
   c. When measured by self-reports, men and women have similar responses; when measured physiologically, men respond more than women.
   d. When measured by self-reports, women respond more than men; when measured physiologically, men respond more than women.

37.
K
Answer: c
p. 151
Obj. #6

With respect to odors and sexual arousal, which one is NOT true?
   a. Pheromones are an example of odors related to reproductive functioning.
   b. Sexual response in animals is often more elicited by odors than by visual stimuli.
   c. The odor of genital secretions serves as a sexual stimulant for most people.
   d. Both men and women possess a sensory input channel that may be activated by pheromones.

38.
A
Answer: b
pp. 151-153
Obj. #6

Which of the following statements **most** accurately represents current research findings in regard to pheromones?
   a. There is conclusive evidence that pheromones exist in humans as well as in animals.
   b. There is tentative evidence that pheromones exist in humans and conclusive evidence that pheromones exist in animals.
   c. There is only tentative evidence that pheromones exist in humans or in animals.
   d. There is no convincing evidence that pheromones are natural attractants for humans or animals.

Chapter 6 Sexual Arousal and Response 125

39.
K
Answer: d
p. 153
Obj. #6

Experimental research on synthetic human pheromones
a. has yet to be done.
b. has been done with women, who need them, but not men, who rarely need an increase in sexual desire.
c. found that their administration led to increased masturbation by those using the pheromones.
d. demonstrated an increase in sexual/affectionate behaviors and intercourse.

40.
K
Answer: b
p. 154
Obj. #6

In one research study, many women reported that their male partner's silence during sex play _____ their own sexual arousal.
a. heightened
b. inhibited
c. did not affect
d. Women responded in all of the ways described above; no one particular pattern predominated.

41.
K
Answer: a
pp. 154-156
Obj. #7

Which one is NOT true of aphrodisiacs?
a. Alcohol is one of the readily available and inexpensive aphrodisiacs.
b. Foods that resemble male genitalia have often been tried as aphrodisiacs.
c. Marijuana has erroneously been reported to stimulate sexual desire.
d. The term derives from the name of the Greek goddess of love.

42.
K
Answer: d
p. 155
Obj. #7

Which of the following has demonstrated aphrodisiac properties in rats and to some extent in humans?
a. amphetamines
b. L-dopa
c. cantharides
d. yohimbine hydrochloride

43.
K
Answer: d
pp. 155-156
Obj. #7

Which of the following statements concerning yohimbine hydrochloride is false?
a. It is derived from the sap of a tree.
b. It may be an aphrodisiac for rats.
c. It increases sexual desire in males with erective dysfunction.
d. It is now illegal in some states

44.
K
Answer: b
pp. 155-156
Obj. #7

Which one is NOT true concerning the commercial product, Libido?
a. It is derived in part from fertilized chicken eggs.
b. The effects have been primarily studied in women.
c. No unpleasant side effects have so far been reported.
d. It has been shown to increase sexual desire in both those with no problems and many with low desire.

45.
K
Answer: d
p. 156
Obj. #7

Which of the following has been known to induce priapism (constant, unwanted erection)?
a. amyl nitrate
b. marijuana
c. cantharides
d. L-dopa

46.
K
Answer: b
p. 156
Obj. #7I

According to preliminary research findings, which of the following appears to have the most genuine aphrodisiac effects on sexually functioning men?
a. L-dopa
b. Libido
c. cantharides
d. alpha androstenal

47.
K
Answer: a
p. 157
Obj. #8

Substances known to inhibit sexual behavior are called
a. anaphrodisiacs.
b. antierectiles.
c. potassium nitrates.
d. pheromones.

48.
K
Answer: c
pp. 157-158
Obj. #8

Which of the following would be **least** likely to inhibit sexual behavior?
a. antihypertensives
b. tranquilizers
c. saltpeter
d. nicotine

49.
K
Answer: c
pp. 157-158
Obj. #8
WWW

Nicotine slows sexual motivation and function by
a. dilating the blood vessels.
b. impairing hypothalamic and pituitary functioning.
c. constricting the blood vessels and decreasing testosterone in the blood.
d. Recent evidence demonstrates that use of nicotine does not retard sexual motivation, as was earlier believed.

50.
A
Answer: b
pp. 157-158
Obj. #8

Miguel has been experiencing both a delay and a decrease in his level of sexual arousal. Which of the following would **most** likely contribute to this?
a. using amyl nitrate
b. smoking high-nicotine cigarettes
c. using cocaine
d. taking L-dopa

51.
A
Answer: b
pp. 155-157
Obj. #4

Which of the following statements is false?
a. Significant amounts of alcohol can negatively affect sexual functioning.
b. Cocaine is a known aphrodisiac.
c. Antihypertensives may reduce sexual interest in both men and women.
d. Love is the best aphrodisiac of all.

52.
A
Answer: d
p. 157
Obj. #7

Gwyneth has experienced decreased sexual desire over the past year. This could be explained by any one of the following **except**
   a. she uses birth control pills as her method of contraception.
   b. she has been taking antidepressant medication.
   c. she smokes high nicotine cigarettes.
   d. she ingests Libido on a regular basis.

53
K
Answer: b
pp. 156-158
Obj. #10

Which one is true concerning "desire?
   a. It is the first stage in Masters and Johnson's model.
   b. Not all sexual expression is preceded by desire.
   c. It can be enhanced by progesterone.
   d. Lack of desire may be treated by amphetamines.

54.
A
Answer: c
p. 158
Obj. #9

A man never initiates sex with his partner, although when she initiates with him he is sexually responsive (has an erection and eventually ejaculates). This man is having difficulty with the _____ phase of sexual response.
   a. refractory
   b. plateau
   c. desire
   d. excitement

55.
K
Answer: c
p. 158
Obj. #10

Which of the following statements regarding the desire phase of sexual response is true?
   a. It is included in Masters and Johnson's model.
   b. All sexual expression is preceded by desire.
   c. When people have desire problems, they do not necessarily have excitement and/or orgasm problems.
   d. Excitement is part of the desire phase.

56.
K
Answer: a
p. 159
Obj. #11

All of the following are phases in Masters and Johnson's sexual response cycle **except**
   a. desire.
   b. excitement.
   c. plateau.
   d. resolution

57.
A
Answer: a
p. 159
Obj. #11

In which of the following areas would Masters and Johnson's research on sexual response be **least** helpful?
   a. compulsive sexual behavior
   b. infertility counseling
   c. general sex education
   d. sex therapy for couples and individuals

58.
K
Answer: d
p. 160
Obj. #11

_____ is the engorgement with blood of body tissues that respond to sexual excitation.
   a. Labioscrotal swelling
   b. Mytonia
   c. Tumescence
   d. Vasocongestion

59.
K
Answer: b
p. 160
Obj. #11

Which of the following is the **best** example of vasocongestion?
a. uterine contractions
b. erection of the penis
c. clitoral retraction
d. muscular spasms during orgasm

60.
K
Answer: b
p. 160
Obj. #11

Sexual facial grimaces are an example of
a. vasocongestion.
b. myotonia.
c. sex differences.
d. a lack of desire.

61.
K
Answer: a
pp. 159-160, 164
Obj. #11

Which one is NOT true concerning the four-phase sexual response model?
a. Secondary sexual areas such as the nipples are not affected.
b. There is tremendous variability in subjective responses.
c. Paradoxically, the plateau level is a changing state.
d. The basic responses of men and women are very similar.

62.
K
Answer: a
pp. 160-161
Obj. #11

All of the following occur during the excitement phase **except**
a. clitoris retracts underneath the hood.
b. labia minora increase in size.
c. scrotum elevates.
d. penis becomes erect.

63
K
Answer: b
p. 163
Obj. #11

Which of the following occurs **most** frequently in the plateau phase?
a. uterine contractions
b. orgasmic platform
c. vaginal lubrication
d. testes return to their normal size

64.
K
Answer: b
p. 163
Obj. #11

Which of the following **most** accurately describes the plateau phase?
a. Physiological reactions stabilize and level off.
b. Physiological reactions become more pronounced.
c. Sexual systems return to their nonaroused state.
d. Rhythmic muscular contractions occur at 0.8-second intervals.

65.
K
Answer: d
p. 163
Obj. #11

The orgasmic platform
a. refers to the increased muscle tension that develops during the excitement phase.
b. refers to the pink or red rash that men and women experience just prior to orgasm.
c. is manifested in the engorgement of the testicles.
d. refers to the increased engorgement of the outer third of the vagina during plateau phase.

66.
K
Answer: c
p. 164
Obj. #11

_____ is the shortest phase of the sexual response cycle.
a. Plateau
b. Excitement
c. Orgasm
d. Refractory

67.
A
Answer: d
p. 164
Obj. #11

Women who become highly aroused but never achieve orgasm do not move beyond the _____ stage of sexual response.
a. desire
b. refractory
c. excitement
d. plateau

68.
A
Answer: b
pp. 164-165
Obj. #10

Sex differences in orgasm include which of the following?
a. Men enjoy them more.
b. Female orgasms last slightly longer than male orgasms.
c. Women enjoy them more.
d. The sexes have a tendency to describe them in different fashion although physiologically they are indistinguishable.

69.
K
Answer: c
p. 165
Obj. #10

Freud's theory of orgasm held that _____ orgasm was more mature, and thus more preferable, than _____ orgasm.
a. vulval; uterine
b. uterine; vaginal
c. vaginal; clitoral
d. clitoral; vaginal

70.
K
Answer: d
p. 165
Obj. #11

Sometimes the areola becomes so swollen that it appears that nipple erection is diminishing. This occurs during the
a. resolution phase.
b. desire phase.
c. excitement phase.
d. plateau phase.

71.
K
Answer: d
p. 165
Obj. #11
WWW

Research indicates that when men and women are asked to write their subjective descriptions of orgasm,
a. women's responses are distinguished by the intense imagery they use to describe their experiences.
b. men's responses are distinguished by the graphic way in which they describe their physical sensations.
c. women's responses are distinguished by the graphic way in which they describe their physical sensations.
d. male and female descriptions are, on the whole, indistinguishable.

72.
K
Answer: b
p. 166
Obj. #12

The Singers have proposed with respect to orgasm
a. a model for men to complement that of Freud for women.
b. that one should take women's emotional satisfaction into consideration.
c. that there are four kinds.
d. that the uterine orgasm is more mature.

73.
K
Answer: b
p. 166
Obj. #12

All of the following are types of orgasms described by Singer and Singer **except**
a. vulval.
b. clitoral.
c. uterine.
d. blended.

74.
K
Answer: c
p. 166
Obj. #12

An orgasm induced by vaginal penetration followed by a woman involuntarily holding her breath and exhaling as she climaxes has been labeled by Singer and Singer a _____ orgasm.
a. vaginal
b. blended
c. uterine
d. clitoral

75.
K
Answer: b
p. 166
Obj. #11, 12, 13

Research on vaginal sensitivity indicates that
a. most women prefer vaginal to clitoral stimulation.
b. the anterior wall of the vagina may be much more sensitive to stimulation than was originally believed.
c. due to the lack of nerve endings throughout the vagina, it is relatively insensitive to stimulation.
d. the density of nerve endings is concentrated around the cervix, which is where women typically experience the most sensitivity.

76.
K
Answer: c
p. 168
Obj. #13

A woman who ejaculates after G-spot stimulation expels the fluid from her
a. vagina.
b. Bartholin's glands.
c. urethra.
d. cervix.

77.
K
Answer: a
pp. 167-168
Obj. #13

Which of the following statements concerning the Grafenberg spot is true?
a. When this area is stimulated, some women ejaculate a fluid that is chemically similar to male prostate secretions.
b. The erotic significance of this area was first discussed in the medical literature at the end of the 19th century.
c. It is an area approximately the size of a dime, located on the cervix.
d. Very gentle stimulation of the area should be used in order for a woman to respond.

78.
K
Answer: c
p. 168
Obj. #11

Which of the following statements regarding the refractory period is true?
a. It usually lasts several hours for men and several days for women.
b. It occurs after the plateau phase of the response cycle.
c. The frequency of prior sexual activity will affect the length of this period.
d. Vasocongestion occurs during this period.

Chapter 6 Sexual Arousal and Response 131

79.
K
Answer: c
p. 168
Obj. #11

Which of the following influences the duration of the resolution phase in a male?
a. the method of sexual stimulation
b. the time of day
c. the length of arousal prior to orgasm
d. the frequency of previous sexual activity

80.
K
Answer: a
p. 168
Obj. #11

Which of the following would be **least** likely to affect the length of the refractory period?
a. the method of sexual stimulation
b. the age of the man
c. the degree of sexual desire for the partner
d. the frequency of previous sexual activity

81.
K
Answer: a
p. 168
Obj. #10

The final phase of Masters and Johnson's sexual response cycle is
a. resolution.
b. refractory.
c. orgasm.
d. plateau.

82.
K
Answer: b
p. 169
Obj. #14

All of the following are physiosexual changes in the aging female **except**
a. decreased vaginal lubrication.
b. cessation of uterine contractions at orgasm.
c. decrease in length and width of the vagina.
d. decrease in the number of orgasmic contractions.

83.
K
Answer: d
p. 170
Obj. #14

Which of the following statements concerning survey findings on orgasm in older women is false?
a. Some women continue to experience multiple orgasms.
b. Some women report inability to experience orgasm.
c. The majority of women still consider orgasms to be important.
d. Most women no longer experience contractions of the orgasmic platform.

84.
K
Answer: a
p. 169
Obj. #14

All of the following are physiosexual changes that occur in the excitement phase of the aging female **except**
a. the uterus ceases to elevate.
b. the vaginal blood-volume increase is smaller.
c. the vagina mucosa becomes thinner.
d. the ability of the inner vagina to expand is diminished.

85.
K
Answer: d
p. 170
Obj. #14
WWW

Which of the following statements **most** accurately summarizes the effects of aging on female sexuality?
a. Because there is no longer the risk of pregnancy or the problems involving menstruation, women experience a new sexual freedom that enhances their sexual desire and response.
b. Due to the reduction in vaginal lubrication and loss of vaginal elasticity, intercourse is extremely uncomfortable, and so women lose interest in sexual expression.
c. Intercourse is replaced by masturbation as a primary mode of sexual expression.
d. There is considerable variation in the effect of aging on female sexuality.

86.
K
Answer: c
p. 170
Obj. #15

All of the following are characteristic of plateau phase changes in the aging male **except**
a. reduced myotonia.
b. testicle elevation not as high.
c. unable to sustain plateau phase to the degree that was possible when younger.
d. full erection not obtained until just prior to orgasm.

87.
A
Answer: c
p. 170
Obj. #14

A woman in her mid-seventies is extremely sexually active. Based on what is known about sexuality and older women, which of the following inferences could **most** likely be made?
a. The woman must be engaging in sexual behavior other than intercourse, because vaginal atrophy as a result of the aging process would have occurred by now.
b. The woman was probably not very sexually active when she was younger, and so she is compensating for that now.
c. The woman has probably been sexually active on a regular basis for many years.
d. This behavior is probably the result of a hormonal abnormality.

88.
K
Answer: a
pp. 171-172
Obj. #15

Which of the following statements concerning the orgasm phase in the aging male is false?
a. Sensations of ejaculatory inevitability become more intense.
b. The number of muscular contractions during orgasm is reduced.
c. Orgasm may be less intense.
d. The force of ejaculation is reduced.

89.
K
Answer: d
pp. 170-171
Obj. #11

In one study, the majority of older men reported that orgasm was _____ in their sexual experiences.
a. virtually nonexistent
b. no longer considered a factor in sexual pleasure
c. not as important as it used to be
d. very important

90.
A
Answer: c
p. 170
Obj. #15

A 65-year-old man comments that his sexual relationship with his wife is better than it has ever been. To which of the following aspects of his sexual experience would he **most** likely be referring?
a. more intense orgasms
b. renewed interest in sex due to increases in testosterone production after age 60
c. better ejaculatory control as the result of a more prolonged plateau phase
d. more rapid erectile response to sexual stimuli

91.
K
Answer: a
p. 171
Obj. #16

Which of the following statements is true?
a. Generally speaking, women experience more variability in their sexual response than men do.
b. Generally speaking, men experience more variability in their sexual response than women do.
c. The variability in male and female sexual response is roughly comparable.
d. There are currently no research data available on the variability in male and female sexual response.

92.
K
Answer: a
p. 171
Obj. #15

As men grow older, the resolution phase _____ and the refractory period _____.
a. occurs more rapidly; lengthens
b. occurs more slowly; shortens
c. occurs more rapidly; shortens
d. occurs more slowly; lengthens

93.
K
Answer: b
p. 172
Obj. #16

Which of the following explanations for the existence of the refractory period is **best** supported by research at this point in time?
a. There is an evolutionary advantage as females can continue to copulate with other males, enhancing the possibility of impregnation.
b. Ejaculation triggers a short-term neurological inhibitory mechanism.
c. The loss of seminal fluid during orgasm results in significant hormone reduction that prevents further sexual activity.
d. The expelled seminal fluid results in an energy drain.

94.
K
Answer: d
pp. 172-173
Obj. #16
WWW

Which of the following statements concerning multiple orgasms is true?
a. Women who masturbate are less likely to have multiple orgasms than those who do not.
b. Multiple orgasms are more common among males than females.
c. Men who have multiple orgasms ejaculate a small amount of seminal fluid each time.
d. The majority of women have the capacity for multiple orgasms.

95.
A
Answer: a
p. 173
Obj. #16

According to several researchers, which of the following would be **most** likely to experience multiple orgasms?
a. Women who are sexually relating to other women.
b. Women who experience both vulval and uterine orgasms.
c. Women who prefer G spot stimulation.
d. Women with relatively high androgen levels.

96.
A
Answer: d
pp. 173-174
Obj. #16

Men who report multiple orgasms
a. have never been studied in a laboratory.
b. can only do this when masturbating.
c. have only discovered this skill late in life.
d. have a variety of ejaculatory patterns for orgasm.

97.
A
Answer: c
pp. 173-174
Obj. #16

Which one is NOT true concerning "multiple orgasms"?
a. This refers to having more than one orgasmic experience within a short time interval.
b. This experience occurs in about 15% of women sampled.
c. They are the preferred expression for females and why they masturbate so much.
d. They occur much less frequently in men than women.

Multiple Choice from Study Guide

1.
K
Answer: a
p. 142
Obj. #1, 2

Estrogen is produced
a. in both men and women.
b. only during a woman's reproductive years.
c. primarily by the adrenal glands in women.
d. primarily by the Cowper's gland in men.

2.
K
Answer: c
p. 142
Obj. #1

Which statement about testosterone and male sexual function is true?
a. Sexual behavior completely stops after castration.
b. Antiandrogens stop sexual behaviors motivated by anger or the desire to control.
c. Sexual interest declines when testosterone levels decrease.
d. If sexual interest and activity decline due to hypogonadism, the decline is permanent.

3.
K
Answer: d
pp. 143-144
Obj. #2

Current research demonstrates clearer and stronger evidence regarding the role of _____ in female sexuality.
a. progesterone
b. estrogen
c. adrenaline
d. testosterone

4.
K
Answer: c
p. 144
Obj. #2

Women who receive testosterone replacement therapy show
a. increased genital sensitivity.
b. increased sexual desire.
c. more frequent sexual activity.
d. all of the above

Chapter 6 Sexual Arousal and Response 135

5.
K
Answer: b
pp. 144-145
Obj. #3

Which form of testosterone plays the greatest role in libido?
a. bound
b. free
c. total
d. alpha-androstenal

6.
K
Answer: b
p. 146
Obj. #4

Testosterone deficiency is characterized by all of the following **except**
a. reduced genital and breast sensitivity.
b. increased body hair.
c. lowered sexual desire.
d. diminished energy levels.

7.
K
Answer: b
p. 148-149
Obj. #5

Stimulation of the _____ has resulted in increased sexual activity in rats and feelings of sexual arousal in humans.
a. hippocampus
b. hypothalamus
c. cerebral cortex
d. histamine blocking system

8.
K
Answer: b
p. 150
Obj. #6

When women view visual erotica, ratings of sexual arousal are likely to be higher when
a. old style "porn" films are used.
b. arousal is measured using physiological recording devices.
c. arousal is measured by self reports.
d. films are made by female directors.

9.
K
Answer: a
pp. 151-153
Obj. #6

Current research evidence seems to indicate that humans do secrete _____, yet it is still uncertain if they influence sexual behavior.
a. pheromones
b. olfactory hormones
c. libidinial compounds
d. vomeronasal enhancers

10.
K
Answer: d
p. 154
Obj. #8

Which of the following seems to have true aphrodisiac qualities?
a. alcohol
b. Spanish fly
c. rhinoceros horn
d. vohimbine

11.
K
Answer: c
p. 157
Obj. #8

Blood pressure medicines and psychiatric medications may
a. increase vasocongestion.
b. promote a stronger orgasmic response.
c. impair erectile function.
d. elevate sexual desire.

12.
K
Answer: b
p. 157
Obj. #8

Nicotine affects sexual behavior by
a. promoting feelings of relaxation through reduction of central nervous system activity.
b. slowing vasocongestion.
c. elevating testosterone levels.
d. increasing sexual desire.

13.
K
Answer: b
p. 158
Obj. #10

Which phase of sexual response is found only in Kaplan's model?
a. excitement
b. desire
c. plateau
d. refractory period

14.
K
Answer: d
p. 160
Obj. #11

Which of the following is the **best** example of vasocongestion?
a. orgasmic platform contractions
b. spasms of the hands or feet
c. facial grimaces
d. vaginal lubrication

15.
K
Answer: c
p. 159
Obj. #11

The correct order of Masters and Johnson's model is
a. plateau, excitement, orgasm, resolution.
b. excitement, orgasm, plateau, resolution.
c. excitement, plateau, orgasm, resolution.
d. excitement, orgasm, resolution, plateau.

16.
K
Answer: c
p. 168
Obj. #11

A sex flush may appear during all of the following phases of the sexual response cycle **except**
a. excitement.
b. orgasm.
c. resolution.
d. plateau.

17.
K
Answer: c
pp. 164-168
Obj. #11

Which statement regarding the orgasmic platform is true?
a. It forms in the upper two-thirds of the vagina.
b. It is present primarily in multi-orgasmic women.
c. It develops during the plateau phase.
d. It is a diving event that will debut in the 2004 Olympics.

18.
K
Answer: b
pp. 162-163
Obj. #11

The rectal sphincter contracts
a. primarily in homosexual men.
b. in both men and women during orgasm.
c. in men only during orgasm.
d. during orgasm only if anal intercourse has occurred.

19.
K
Answer: a
pp. 164-168
Obj. #11

The testes become completely engorged and elevated during
a. plateau.
b. orgasm.
c. excitement.
d. the expulsion phase of orgasm.

20.
K
Answer: d
pp. 164-168
Obj. #11

Which statement about female orgasm is true?
a. Vaginal orgasms are more mature than clitoral orgasms.
b. Clitoral orgasms are more mature than vaginal orgasms.
c. Uterine orgasm may result from clitoral stimulation.
d. There is only one kind of orgasm, physiologically speaking.

21.
K
Answer: a
pp. 166-168
Obj. #11

Orgasms that result from stimulation of the Grafenberg spot
   c. may result in the ejaculation of fluid from the urethra.
   d. are similar to vulval orgasms.
   e. are similar to uterine orgasms.
   f. are psychologically similar to blended orgasms.

22.
K
Answer: a
p. 168
Obj. #11

The period of time following orgasm when no additional stimulation will produce orgasm is called the
   a. refractory period.
   b. resolutory period.
   c. erectile inhibition interval.
   d. remission period.

23.
K
Answer: b
pp. 169-170
Obj. #14

Which statement regarding older women and sexual response is false?
   a. vaginal lubrication occurs more slowly
   b. sexual enjoyment declines
   c. vaginal mucosa becomes thinner
   d. resolution occurs more rapidly

24.
K
Answer: c
pp. 170-171
Obj. #15

Which of the following is true regarding older men and sexual response?
   a. resolution occurs more slowly
   b. orgasm becomes more intense
   c. ejaculatory control may improve
   d. erection occurs as rapidly as when younger

25.
K
Answer: b
pp. 172-174
Obj. #16

Which statement regarding multiple orgasms is true?
   a. The majority of women regularly experience multiple orgasms.
   b. The majority of women are capable of having multiple orgasms.
   c. Men cannot experience multiple orgasms.
   d. Kinsey's subjects reported the highest rates of multiple orgasms.

True/False

Students may be asked to answer these questions using the traditional format of marking their answers either "true" or "false". Or, to encourage more active involvement, you may choose to use the following instructions:

If the statement is true, place a "T" on the line preceding it. If the statement is false, place an "F" on the line preceding it and then change the statement to make it true by deleting incorrect information and/or adding accurate information.

1.
Answer: T
p. 142
Obj. #1, 2

___ The dominant androgen in both males and females is testosterone.

2.
Answer: T
p. 143
Obj. #1

___ It appears that orchidectomy usually results in reduced sexual interest and activity, although the amount of reduction can vary.

3.
Answer: F
p. 143
Obj. #1

___ Antiandrogen drugs have been used to treat hypogonadism.

4.
Answer: F
p. 147
Obj. #16

___ Oral sex is practiced universally as a source of sexual pleasure.

5.
Answer: T
p. 149
Obj. #6

___ Of the major senses, touch tends to be the most important during sexual sharing.

6.
Answer: F
p. 150
Obj. #6

___ When measured physiologically, men tend to respond to visual erotica more than women.

7.
Answer: F
p. 155
Obj. #7

___ Research has demonstrated that, when measured physiologically, minimal amounts of alcohol intake will increase sexual arousal, but increasing levels of alcohol intake will decrease arousal.

8.
Answer: T
p. 155
Obj. #7

___ Yohimbine hydrochloride appears to be an aphrodisiac for rats, although its effect on humans is more variable.

9.
Answer: F
p. 156
Obj. #7

___ Cantharides ("Spanish fly") functions as an aphrodisiac by stimulating genital tissue.

10.
Answer: T
p. 158
Obj. #8

___ Smoking high nicotine cigarettes can significantly decrease sexual desire and response.

11.
Answer: F
p. 160
Obj. #11

___ The most obvious signs of myotonia during sexual response are erection in men and vaginal lubrication in women.

12.
Answer: T
pp. 164-165
Obj. #10

___ In the orgasm phase of the sexual response cycle for women, the uterus, orgasmic platform and rectal sphincter all contract rhythmically.

13. Answer: F p. 165 Obj. #11	___	When subjective reports of men and women's orgasmic experiences are analyzed, they are clearly distinguishable from each other because men relate their experiences in a much more graphic, visually disruptive manner.
14. Answer: T p. 165 Obj. #12	___	Freud viewed "vaginal" orgasms as superior to "clitoral" orgasms.
15. Answer: T p. 167 Obj. #13	___	A woman who responds to Grafenberg spot stimulation may ejaculate a fluid from her urethra.
16. Answer: F p. 169 Obj. #16	___	Men and women have similar refractory periods.
17. Answer: T p. 171 Obj. #11	___	Generally speaking, women have more variety in their sexual response patterns than men do.
18. Answer: F p. 171 Obj. #16	___	To date, the best explanation for the male refractory period involves the energy depletion that results from the loss of seminal fluid during orgasm.
19. Answer: T p. 172 Obj. #12	___	Several surveys have revealed that less than twenty percent of women regularly have multiple orgasms.
20. Answer: T p. 173 Obj. #16	___	Those women who masturbate are more likely to experience multiple orgasms.
21. Answer: T pp. 173-174 Obj. #15	___	Men experience multiple orgasms, although much less commonly than women do.

Short Answer Essay

1. Discuss the role of testosterone and estrogen in male sexuality. (Obj.#1, 2, 3)

2. Discuss the role of testosterone and estrogen in female sexuality. (Obj. #1, 2, 3)

3. List 5 signs of testosterone deficiency. What are some issues in testosterone replacement therapy? (Obj. #4)

4. Select two of the five senses and indicate how important these seem to be with respect to sexual arousal. Would you expect these senses to be equally important for all people? Why, or why not? (Obj. #6)

5. Imagine that you are going to a foreign students mixer. What differences might you expect with respect to what the people present would find arousing in terms of interaction with the others also present? What about with their sexual partners? (Obj. #17)

6. Imagine that you are celebrating your Golden (50th) Wedding Anniversary. You decide that you will rent a honeymoon suite for the night and make love. What differences, if any, might you expect between the actual honeymoon and this anniversary celebration. (Obj. #15, 16)

7. Discuss various conceptions of female orgasm, beginning with Freud and concluding with current research in this area. (Obj. #12, 13)

8. What is the data concerning the frequency of multiple orgasms in women? What explanations can one give as to why this frequency rate occurs? (Obj. #16)

9. What is the data concerning the frequency of multiple orgasms in men? What explanations can one give as to why this frequency rate occurs? (Obj. #16)

10. What are the stages of sexual response as proposed by Kaplan? As proposed by Masters and Johnson? What is the significance of any difference between these? (Obj. #10, 11)

11. What would you say to a friend who asked you to suggest for them an aphrodisiac? Give your general advice; also be sure to list some things that you would state are NOT aphrodisiacs, and some that MIGHT be aphrodisiacs. (Obj. #7)

12. Imagine that you are a doctor about to prescribe some new medication for a patient. List at least four frequently prescribed medications that have the potential for decreasing sexual desire or disrupting sexual response. Choose one and give some specific examples of negative side effects that have been reported. (Obj #8)

13. There is considerable speculation as to why only men have a refractory period. Outline some of the hypotheses that have been put forth, indicating those which you consider to be most plausible and why. (Obj. #16)

14. You are trying to decide whether to buy for your significant other a perfume that advertises that it contains pheromones. What will you take into consideration when making this decision? Cite data from your textbook as well as value decisions. (Obj. #9)

15. Your book discusses three major differences between the sexes in sexual response. List and describe these differences. How might either lack of knowledge or an awareness of these differences influence a couple's sex life? (Obj. #16)

7

Love and the Development of Sexual Relationships

Learning Objectives

After studying this chapter, the student should be able to:

1. Explain how Zick Rubin attempted to measure love, including a list and description of the three components of his love scale and what his findings revealed.

2. Describe the characteristics of passionate love.

3. Describe the characteristics of companionate love.

4. Explain Sternberg's triangular theory of love.

5. List and describe six styles of loving as proposed by John Lee.

6. Discuss the factors that affect with whom we fall in love, making specific reference to the following: the chemistry of love; proximity; similarity; reciprocity; physical attractions.

7. Discuss sociobiological accounts of gender differences in mate selection.

8. Describe the role self-love plays in the development of intimacy.

9. List and describe each of the following phases of a relationship as it develops and becomes more intimate: inclusion; response; care; trust; affection; playfulness; genitality.

10. Discuss what research findings reveal regarding how women and men, both heterosexual and homosexual, perceive the relationship between love and sex.

11. Discuss strategies for determining personal values and guidelines regarding sexual expression.

12. Define jealousy, and discuss the role it plays in love relationships and how to manage jealous feelings.

13. Summarize research findings regarding sex differences in jealousy.

14. Discuss some of the factors that contribute to maintaining relationship.

15. Discuss differences in love and marriage in collectivistic vs. individualistic cultures.

16. From a cross-cultural perspective, discuss men's and women's preferences in mate selection.

17. Describe research findings that clarify whether romantic love is a universal experience.

Multiple Choice

1.
K
Answer: d
p. 179
Obj. #1

According to Rubin's love scale, _____ refers to an individual's concern for the other's well-being, while _____ is the desire for close, confidential communication.
a. attachment; inclusion
b. inclusion; attachment
c. sympathy; bonding
d. caring; intimacy

2.
K
Answer: a
p. 179
Obj. #1

Rubin's love scale revealed that "strong lovers"
a. made more eye contact with each other than "weak lovers".
b. held hands more than "weak lovers".
c. made more suggestive remarks to each other than "weak lovers".
d. laughed together more than "weak lovers".

3.
K
Answer: b
p. 179
Obj. #1

According to Rubin's love scale, _____ refers to a person's desire for the physical presence and emotional support of the other person.
a. inclusion
b. attachment
c. intimacy
d. bonding

4.
A
Answer: c
p. 181
Obj. #1

One plausible explanation offered for the increase in love research in recent years is that
a. major universities have allocated more funds for research in this area.
b. an increasing number of therapists have demanded it in order to better serve their clients.
c. there are an increasing number of female scientists in the field of sexology.
d. we are concerned about the increase in cohabitation.

5.
K
Answer: b
p. 179
Obj. #3

Philia refers to
a. a passionate sexual relationship.
b. love between friends.
c. unrequited love.
d. love between parent and child.

6.
K
Answer: c
pp. 179-180
Obj. #2

All of the following are characteristics of passionate love **except**
a. generalized physiological arousal.
b. usually occurs early in a relationship.
c. friendly affection and a deep attachment based on familiarity.
d. usually does not last long.

Chapter 7 Love and the Development of Sexual Relationships 143

7.
K
Answer: c
p. 179
Obj. #2

Which of the following would be **least** likely to appear on a scale measuring passionate love?
a. "I think about _____ all the time; I just can't seem to get enough of him (her)."
b. "I get extremely depressed when things don't go well in my relationship."
c. "We have so many interests and activities in common."
d. "No one could love _____ like I do."

8.
K
Answer: a
p. 179
Obj. #2

_____ usually occurs early in a relationship.
a. Passionate love
b. Altruistic love
c. Pragmatic love
d. Consummate love

9.
K
Answer: d
p. 180
Obj. #2

When Erich Fromm said, "[it] is a delicious art form but not a durable one", he was referring to
a. consummate love.
b. altruistic love.
c. companionate love.
d. passionate love.

10.
K
Answer: b
p. 180
Obj. #2

Anthropological research has used all but which one of the following to investigate the presence of romantic love?
a. elopement because of feelings
b. premarital pregnancy
c. love songs about romantic involvement
d. an anthropologist's statement about the culture

11.
K
Answer: a
pp. 180-181
Obj. #3, 4, 5

All of the following characterize companionate love **except**
a. according to Sternberg, this type of love lacks passion and commitment.
b. according to Lee, this type of love usually begins as a friendship.
c. less intense emotionally than passionate love.
d. more enduring than passionate love.

12.
K
Answer: d
p. 183
Obj. #17
WWW

The recent research of two anthropologists, Jankowiak and Fischer, revealed that romantic love
a. is primarily limited to Western culture.
b. existed in about half of the cultures they studied.
c. was more evident in cultures in which male and female roles were clearly defined.
d. occurred in a clear majority of cultures.

13.
K
Answer: b
p. 181
Obj. #4

The three components of Sternberg's theory of love are
a. friendship, trust and intimacy.
b. passion, intimacy and commitment.
c. caring, inclusion and commitment.
d. passion, friendship and trust.

14.
K
Answer: c
p. 181
Obj. #4

For Sternberg, intimacy
a. refers to a relationship with sexual component.
b. is essential in any kind of relationship that we call love.
c. involves emotional closeness and sharing private thoughts and feelings.
d. is the behavioral component of his triangular theory.

15.
K
Answer: b
p. 182
Obj. #4

The way we feel toward casual acquaintances is what Sternberg refers to as
a. empty love.
b. nonlove.
c. fatuous love.
d. consummate love.

16.
A
Answer: a
pp. 182-183
Obj. #4

Elonda and Zach met on a Caribbean cruise, fell madly in love with each other and are making plans to get married within three months. According to Sternberg, the type of love they are experiencing is
a. fatuous love.
b. romantic love.
c. infatuation.
d. companionate love.

17.
A
Answer: d
pp. 181-183
Obj. #4
WWW

The physical chemistry that existed when Linh and Bryan met at a psychology conference was overwhelming for both of them. They are enjoying the sexual energy in their relationship and are becoming more intimate as they take time to get to know one another, but neither one is discussing long-term plans or commitments, as they both wish to pursue their education and careers. Sternberg would characterize their love experience as
a. infatuation.
b. fatuous love.
c. empty love.
d. romantic love.

18.
A
Answer: a
pp. 182-183
Obj. #2, 3

Marriage for love is **most** likely in which of the following countries?
a. Australia
b. India
c. the Phillippines
d. Thailand

19.
A
Answer: c
pp. 182-183
Obj. #4

Toni and Jodie have lived together for many years and enjoy an intimate, committed relationship with one another, although their relationship is no longer the priority it once was. Sternberg would characterize this type of love as
a. non-love.
b. consummate love.
c. companionate love.
d. friendship love.

Chapter 7 Love and the Development of Sexual Relationships 145

20.
K
Answer: b
pp. 182-183
Obj. #4

The love style in which all three components of passion, intimacy and commitment are present is called
a. romantic love.
b. consummate love.
c. ideal love.
d. complete love.

21.
A
Answer: c
pp. 182-183
Obj. #4

Chantarra and Eli met while vacationing in Mexico. Their physical attraction was immediate, and in spite of spending just several days together, they made a commitment to carry on a long-distance relationship. Since he lives in Boston and she lives in San Francisco, the reality is that they will see one another very infrequently. Sternberg would characterize their love as
a. romantic.
b. infatuation.
c. fatuous.
d. consummate.

22.
A
Answer: b
pp. 182-183
Obj. #4

Beryl and Roger have made a lifetime commitment to one another, despite the fact that the passion and intimacy they once shared has eroded over time. They lead separate lives in may ways but would never consider divorce and have vowed to stay together "until death do us part." Sternberg would characterize this type of love as
a. nonlove.
b. empty love.
c. fatuous love.
d. companionate love.

23.
A
Answer: c
pp. 182-183
Obj. #15

Which one is NOT true?
a. In collectivist cultures marriages unite families and not just two people.
b. In collectivist cultures family needs may take precedence over individual feelings.
c. Most people refuse to marry without love, either in collectivist of individualistic cultures.
d. The United States is an individualistic culture that tends to stress individual goals over group interests.

24.
A
Answer: c
pp. 182-183
Obj. #6

Sternberg's triangular theory of love has revealed all of the following **except**
a. intimacy did not decline in long-term relationships.
b. passion declined for women over time.
c. the passion and commitment components were predictive of relationship stability and longevity.
d. passion did not decline for men over time.

25.
K
Answer: b
p. 183
Obj. #4

According to one study of dating couples, which of the following love components were predictive of relationship stability and longevity?
a. intimacy only.
b. intimacy and commitment.
c. passion and commitment.
d. passion and intimacy.

26.
K
Answer: c
p. 184
Obj. #5

According to John Lee, an altruistic love style is characterized by
a. having a good time, but with no commitment.
b. taking a rational, practical approach to compatibility.
c. selfless, giving love with no expectation of reciprocity.
d. placing emphasis on physical attractiveness to the exclusion of other qualities.

27.
K
Answer: d
p. 184
Obj. #5
WWW

John Lee believes that, in order to maximize satisfaction and success in a relationship, you should find a partner who
a. would score similarly on Rubin's love scale.
b. is high on ludus.
c. has interests and values that would complement yours.
d. would share your same approach to loving.

28.
K
Answer: a
p. 184
Obj. #5

According to a study that investigated the relationship between styles of loving and relationship satisfaction in different life stages, which of the following statements is true?
a. Possessive and pragmatic love were not related to relationship satisfaction for any life stage group.
b. Companionate and pragmatic love were positively associated with relationship satisfaction for all life stages.
c. Romantic and altruistic love were associated with relationship satisfaction only for young childless married adults.
d. Altruistic love was significantly related to relationship satisfaction only for married couples with children at home.

29.
K
Answer: d
p. 185
Obj. #6

The euphoric intensity associated with passionate love may be due, at least in part to
a. release of pheromones.
b. testosterone surge from the adrenal glands.
c. neurotransmitters called endorphins.
d. neurotransmitters such as PEA and norepinephrine.

30.
K
Answer: b
p. 185
Obj. #6
WWW

The neurotransmitters that are partially responsible for the "high" that is associated with passionate love are chemically similar to
a. morphine.
b. amphetamines.
c. anti-depressants.
d. psychedelic drugs.

31.
K
Answer: d
p. 186
Obj. #6

The brain chemicals called endorphins are **most** likely
a. associated with passionate love.
b. associated with sexual intimacy.
c. a partial explanation for homosexuality.
d. associated with long term loving relationships.

Chapter 7 Love and the Development of Sexual Relationships 147

32.
K
Answer: d
p. 187
Obj. n/a

According to the NHSLS nationwide survey by Laumann and associates, which group was least likely to choose a same-race intimate heterosexual relationship?
   a. white respondents
   b. African American respondents
   c. Southern respondents
   d. Hispanic American respondents

33.
K
Answer: d
p. 187
Obj. #6

What can we NOT conclude concerning partner choice and race?
   a. This has not yet been studied scientifically.
   b. Different studies found different results.
   c. All studies have found that minority races are more likely to choose out of group partners than are white.
   d. Aliens are gradually infiltrating the human race because of their exotic sexual parts and practices.

34.
K
Answer: c
p. 186
Obj. #6
WWW

When we are repeatedly exposed to a person who lives or works near us, we tend to find them more appealing. This is called
   a. the equidistant effect.
   b. reciprocity.
   c. the mere exposure effect.
   d. the proximal relationship effect.

35.
K
Answer: b
pp. 187-188
Obj. #6

Which of the following would be **least** likely to explain why we are attracted to particular individuals?
   a. proximity
   b. opposites attract
   c. physical attractiveness
   d. brain chemistry

36.
A
Answer: b
pp. 186-189
Obj. #6

Given the reasons discussed in the text for why people fall in love with whom they do, a romance would be most likely to develop in all of the following situations **except**
   a. they were both very attracted to one another physically.
   b. she likes to dance and attend parties; he enjoys spectator sports and refurbishing classic cars.
   c. he was flattered by her interest in and attraction to him, and as a result he found himself wanting to spend more time with her.
   d. she likes to kayak, snow ski and hike; he enjoys river rafting and snow skiing.

37.
K
Answer: d
pp. 188-189
Obj. #6

According to one study of college men and women, when selecting a partner for a sexual or long-term relationship, women placed more emphasis on
   a. physical appearance.
   b. socioeconomic status.
   c. playfulness and sense of humor.
   d. interpersonal warmth and personality characteristics.

38.
K
Answer: b
p. 189
Obj. #16

According to Buss' cross-cultural study on sex differences in partner preferences, men placed more value on _____, and women placed more value on _____.
a. attractiveness and financial prospects; attractiveness and intelligence
b. youth and attractiveness; financial responsibility and dependability
c. chastity and intelligence; attractiveness and sociability
d. youth and good character; financial responsibility and chastity

39.
K
Answer: b
p. 189
Obj. #16

Which one is NOT true concerning the role of physical attractiveness in mate selection?
a. This may be important to men because it is an indicator of good health and reproductive value.
b. This is of highest importance for men in both early and long-term stages of a relationship.
c. Sociobiology has been used to explain the importance for men of physical attractiveness.
d. Men in all cultures surveyed have placed greater emphasis on attractiveness than do women.

40.
K
Answer: c
p. 190
Obj. #8

According to several authors, intimacy within a relationship begins with
a. totally committing yourself to the happiness of your partner.
b. bonding sexually with your partner.
c. self-love.
d. reciprocal self-disclosure.

41.
K
Answer: c
p. 191
Obj. #9

The **best** example of inclusion is
a. glancing away when someone makes eye contact with you.
b. having a pillow fight with your partner.
c. hugging after an absence.
d. co-hosting a party.

42.
A
Answer: b
p. 191
Obj. #9

Remembering to do the little things that make your partner feel loved and appreciated is an example of
a. reciprocity.
b. inclusion and response.
c. attachment-appreciation.
d. self-love.

43.
K
Answer: a
pp. 191-192
Obj. #9

Which of the following is NOT a phase of a relationship as outlined in the text?
a. bonding
b. inclusion
c. genitality
d. trust

Chapter 7 Love and the Development of Sexual Relationships 149

44.
K
Answer: c
p. 191
Obj. #9
WWW

The _____ phase of a relationship is characterized by feelings of warmth and attachment, and may be expressed by sitting close, holding hands, etc.
   a. prelude
   b. inclusion
   c. affection
   d. foreplay

45.
K
Answer: d
p. 191
Obj. #9

Positive _____ and _____ are the foundation for the development of subsequent phases in a relationship.
   a. attachment; intimacy
   b. responses; bonding
   c. reinforcement; affection
   d. inclusions; responses

46.
K
Answer: a
p. 191
Obj. #9

Being enthusiastic about seeing the other person is an example of the _____ phase of a relationship.
   a. response
   b. inclusion
   c. playfulness
   d. genitality

47.
K
Answer: b
p. 192
Obj. #9

The _____ phase extends the relationship to include genital contact.
   a. consummate
   b. genitality
   c. intercourse
   d. bonding

48.
A
Answer: b
p. 192
Obj. #9

Which of the following is **least** likely to be an indicator of closeness in a couple's relationship?
   a. They share opinions on all major decisions.
   b. They have sex frequently.
   c. They are concerned about each other's problems.
   d. They engage in most of their leisure activities together.

50.
K
Answer: d
p. 191
Obj. #9

The phase of a relationship in which you can count on your partner to act consistently and to contribute to the stability of the relationship is called the _____ phase.
   a. cognitive consistence
   b. inclusion
   c. reciprocity
   d. trust

51.
A
Answer: a
p. 192
Obj. #9

Casey and Nicole like to laugh and tease and act goofy with each other. They are in the _____ phase of a relationship.
   a. playfulness
   b. regressive
   c. romantic
   d. affection

52.
A
Answer: b
p. 192
Obj. #9

Which one is NOT true of sexual relationships as compared to nonsexual friendships?
a. They have more conflict.
b. They have more acceptance.
c. They have more criticism.
d. They have more discussions about the relationship.

53.
K
Answer: c
p. 193
Obj. #9

According to surveys of college students in the authors' human sexuality classes, approximately _____% of women and _____% of men indicated that love is a necessary component of sexual relationships.
a. 86; 85
b. 86; 25
c. 36; 12
d. 13; 13

54.
K
Answer: c
pp. 193-194
Obj. #10
WWW

Which of the following **best** summarizes recent research findings regarding how heterosexual men and women view love and sex in relationships?
a. Men are placing much more value on love and sex in sexual relationships while women are placing much less on it.
b. Women are placing much more value on love and sex in sexual relationships while men are placing much less on it.
c. There is a trend toward convergence of men's and women's attitudes about the value of love and sex in a sexual relationship.
d. Both men and women are placing much less emphasis on the value of love and sex in sexual relationships.

55.
K
Answer: b
p. 194
Obj. #10

For which of the following relationships would an individual involved be **most** likely to separate sex and love?
a. a lesbian pair
b. a gay male pair
c. a cohabiting heterosexual couple
d. a married heterosexual couple

56.
K
Answer: a
p. 194
Obj. #10

Sexologist John Money maintains that _____ is the essential ingredient that distinguishes being homosexual from being heterosexual.
a. loving someone of the same sex
b. having sex with someone of the same sex
c. coming out to family and friends
d. having same sex sexual fantasies that are congruent with same sex sexual behavior

57.
K
Answer: c
pp. 194-195
Obj. #11

If you would like to better understand the role that sex and relationships play in your life, you should ask yourself all of the following **except**
a. "How comfortable am I with some of the contemporary approaches to sex and relationships?"
b. "Which of the more traditional norms do I value?"
c. "How can I alter my values to be more in harmony with my partner's?"
d. "Where do my sexual values come from — family, church, etc.?"

58.
K
Answer: c
p. 195
Obj. #11

The authors suggest that, when making a decision about whether or not to have sex with a particular individual, you should ask yourself
a. "Does this person like me as much as I like him/her?"
b. "Will he/she respect me in the morning?"
c. "Will it create positive feelings about myself and my partner?"
d. "Will this lead to a long-term commitment or marriage?"

59.
K
Answer: c
p. 195
Obj. #11

One of the risks of understanding and acting on your own feelings and values is that
a. you must be willing to tell those who differ that they are wrong.
b. people may lose respect for you.
c. the other person may not agree, requiring you to compromise or end the relationship.
d. you may become more selfish by not considering others.

60.
K
Answer: b
p. 196
Obj. #10

Which one is NOT true with respect to the commencement of sexual relations after first contact?
a. People who are quick to have sex are more likely to have brief relationships (i.e., a month or less).
b. People who are so passionately aroused that they have sex quickly are more likely to have an intense affair for a year or so.
c. Many of the married NHSLS respondents knew future spouses for more than a year before they shared sex.
d. Men and women have different ideas about how long a couple should wait before engaging in sex.

61.
K
Answer: d
p. 197
Obj. #11

All of the following are suggestions for letting a person know you would like the relationship to progress slowly in terms of sexual involvement **except**
a. indicate that you find the person attractive.
b. say that you might eventually want to be sexually intimate, but that you're not ready yet.
c. let the person know what kind of physical contact you want at a given point in the relationship.
d. wait until the person initiates sexual contact and then say no and set limits.

62.
K
Answer: a
p. 197
Obj. #11
WWW

The majority of students in the authors' sexuality classes indicate that when someone does not want to continue a relationship with them, they would prefer to receive that information
a. by clearly being told.
b. by having the person just not call or answer the phone anymore.
c. through a friend.
d. by voice or e-mail.

63.
K
Answer: b
pp. 197-198
Obj. #11

An effective strategy for managing feelings of rejection when another person says "no" to a relationship with you is to
a. tell the other person what your strong points are that they seem to be overlooking.
b. recall that your self-worth does not depend on everyone approving of you.
c. ask the person if he/she is afraid of commitment.
d. accept the "no" for now, but explore the possibilities for a "change of heart" in the future.

64.
K
Answer: b
p. 198
Obj. #12

One survey indicated that, in general, men were more envious of
a. athletic and physical abilities.
b. wealth and fame.
c. wealth and attractiveness.
d. socioeconomic status and emotional security.

65.
K
Answer: b
p. 198
Obj. #12

In rivals for their partner's affection, women tend to be most envious of _____ while men tend to be most envious of _____.
a. socioeconomic status and intelligence; attractiveness and athletic ability
b. attractiveness and popularity; wealth and fame
c. emotional security and wealth; popularity and attractiveness
d. attractiveness and popularity; intelligence and educational level

66.
K
Answer: d
p. 198
Obj. #12
WWW

Which of the following was NOT one of the traits possessed by people prone to jealousy?
a. having low self-esteem
b. seeing a large discrepancy between who they are and who they would like to be
c. placing a high value on wealth, fame, popularity and attractiveness
d. growing up in a single-parent family

67.
K
Answer: d
pp. 198-199
Obj. #12

Which of the following statements concerning jealousy is false?
a. Jealousy is usually defined as an aversive emotional reaction.
b. Many people think that jealousy is a measure of devotion.
c. Some writers believe that jealousy is related more to people's fear of losing what they want to possess than it is to love.
d. Jealous people are rarely able to change their attitudes or behavior.

Chapter 7 Love and the Development of Sexual Relationships 153

68.
K
Answer: b
p. 199
Obj. #12, 13

Research reveals that violence precipitated by jealousy is **most** commonly directed towards
a. one's self.
b. one's partner or lover.
c. the third party rival.
d. anyone or anything within range.

69.
K
Answer: b
p. 199
Obj. #12

In general, men are **more** likely to _____ jealous feelings.
a. project
b. deny
c. rationalize
d. acknowledge

70.
K
Answer: c
pp. 199-200
Obj. #13

In response to feeling jealous, women would be **more** likely to blame _____, whereas men would be more likely to blame _____.
a. the third party or their partner; themselves
b. their partner; the third party
c. themselves; the third party or their partner
d. the third party; their partner

71.
K
Answer: d
p. 199
Obj. #13

_____ appear to be **more** inclined than _____ to provoke jealousy in their partners in order to _____.
a. Men; women; maintain control of the relationship
b. Men; women; bolster their self-worth
c. Women; men; maintain control of the relationship
d. Women; men; bolster their self-worth

72.
A
Answer: c
p. 200
Obj. #12

According to one therapist, people will be **most** likely to work on their jealous behavior when
a. their partner reassures them that they have no reason to feel jealous.
b. they understand that the jealousy stems from their low self-esteem and are willing to accept responsibility for that.
c. their partner makes references at different times to being together in the future.
d. their partner gets angry and attempts to make them feel guilty for their jealous behavior.

73.
A
Answer: c
p. 200
Obj. #13

A woman is feeling jealous because her male partner is spending a great deal of time at the office working on a project with a female colleague. According to the text, the woman would **most** likely respond to this situation by
a. telling her partner that he was deliberately spending much more time with this colleague than he needed to, and to start being home by six o'clock in the evenings or he could expect to find her elsewhere.
b. confronting the other female with her suspicions.
c. increasing her efforts to be more attractive.
d. hiring a private investigator to observe her husband's whereabouts after work.

74.
K
Answer: d
pp. 201-202
Obj. #14

In the survey of 300 happily married couples, all of the following were frequent reasons given for the success of the marriage **except**
a. My partner is my best friend.
b. Marriage is a long-term commitment.
c. My partner has grown more interesting over time.
d. Our sexual intimacy is the best it has ever been.

75.
A
Answer: b
p. 201
Obj. #14

Which one of the following was NOT found to be characteristic of long-term successful marriages?
a. The parents of both had had happy marriages.
b. The couple had at least one child.
c. There was an adequate and steady income.
d. They had similar attitudes and personality styles.

76.
A
Answer: b
pp. 201-202
Obj. #14

A lasting love relationship
a. is facilitated by avoiding conflict.
b. requires frequent positive interaction.
c. is probably easier today than in the past.
d. won't happen if you are aware of your partner's flaws.

77.
A
Answer: c
p. 203
Obj. #14

Which one is **least** likely true concerning working on a relationship?
a. This can facilitate individual growth.
b. This is easier if you view problems as challenges to overcome.
c. This will work best if you work out a solution and then stick to it from that time on.
d. You should expect both individual and partner change over time.

78.
K
Answer: a
pp. 203-204
Obj. #14

All of the following were discussed regarding sexual variety **except**
a. sexual variety is essential for a quality long-term relationship.
b. communication is an important aspect of sexual variety.
c. planning for sexual time can help maintain closeness.
d. reading books together on sexual techniques may enhance sexual relationships.

79.
K
Answer: d
p. 204
Obj. #14
WWW

According to the authors, couples should be having sex _____ in order to maintain intimacy.
a. at least twice a week
b. at least one every two weeks
c. at least once a month
d. as often as they like

80.
K
Answer: c
pp. 203-204
Obj. #14

Which of the following is NOT a suggestion for maintaining sexual variety?
a. sharing fantasies
b. avoiding the routine of time and place
c. making your partner just a little jealous
d. planning for intimate time

Multiple Choice from Study Guide

1.
K
Answer: c
p. 179
Obj. #1

Which of the following is NOT an aspect of love measured by Zick Rubin's love scale?
a. caring
b. attachment
c. concern
d. intimacy

2.
K
Answer: b
p. 179
Obj. #1

What quality did Rubin observe among "weak" lovers or those less deeply in love?
a. more episodes of conflict
b. less eye contact
c. increased personal space
d. poorer communication skills

3.
K
Answer: d
pp. 179-180
Obj. #2

Generalized physiological arousal and strong sexual desire are components of
a. compassionate love.
b. companionate love.
c. paraphiliac love.
d. passionate love.

4.
K
Answer: a
p. 181
Obj. #4

According to Sternberg's triangular theory of love, _____ declines in a relationship whereas _____ builds gradually over time.
a. passion; intimacy
b. infatuation; philia
c. passion; philia
d. fatuous love; companionate love

5.
K
Answer: d
p. 182
Obj. #4

Faye and Suzanne share a strong commitment to each other that they expressed in a holy union ceremony over 12 years ago. The passion in their relationship has slowly decreased over the years, nonetheless they still feel a deep emotional connection to each other. In Sternberg's framework this couple shows
a. empty love.
b. consummate love.
c. romantic love.
d. companionate love.

6.
K
Answer: c
p. 184
Obj. #5

Ever since Thach met his new girlfriend at school, he feels that his life is like a roller coaster. He can't stop thinking about Anh and feels intensely jealous whenever he sees her talking to any other men. According to Lee, Thach's style of loving is
a. romantic love.
b. altruistic love.
c. possessive love.
d. game playing love.

7.
K
Answer: c
p. 184
Obj. #5

Now that Erika is dating again, she is determined to find the very best looking man around, and she fantasizes about how she will enjoy sensual exploration of this handsome man's body after she finally meets him. Erika's behavior reflects Lee's _____ style of loving.
    a. possessive
    b. game-playing
    c. romantic
    d. pragmatic

8.
K
Answer: a
p. 185
Obj. #6

The popular saying "love is a drug" has received some support through research, as studies have shown that when we are in love, the body makes _____ that are chemically similar to amphetamine drugs.
    a. neurotransmitters
    b. estrogens
    c. enzymes
    d. androgens

9.
K
Answer: d
p. 186
Obj. #6

When our attraction to someone grows because we see them regularly and they become familiar is called the
    a. social distance effect.
    b. similarity effect.
    c. familiarity gradient.
    d. mere exposure effect.

10.
K
Answer: d
p. 187
Obj. #6

Which statement below **best** reflects the findings from two recent studies that examined partner choice and race?
    a. White Americans preferred white partners more than African Americans preferred African American partners.
    b. Hispanic Americans preferred White partners more than any other group.
    c. Asian Americans were the most likely to find partners outside their ethnic group.
    d. People generally prefer to form partnerships with people of similar race and ethnicity.

11.
K
Answer: a
pp. 188-189
Obj. #7

Several studies have demonstrated that _____ placed greater emphasis on a partner's physical attractiveness and _____ placed greater importance on a mate's financial status.
    a. men; women
    b. women; men
    c. men; men
    d. women; women

12.
K
Answer: b
p. 191
Obj. #9

Returning someone's gaze with a smile and greeting is an example of the _____ phase of a relationship.
    a. inclusion
    b. response
    c. affection
    d. care

13.
K
Answer: c
p. 190
Obj. #8

Which of the following is NOT consistent with the authors' conceptualization of self-love?
   a. respect
   b. interest
   c. conceit
   d. concern

14.
K
Answer: d
p. 192
Obj. #9

Which of the following describes the final phase of relationship growth?
   a. feelings of exhilaration and abandon
   b. feelings of warmth and attachment
   c. holding the belief that a partner will act consistently
   d. expressing feelings through genital sex

15.
K
Answer: c
pp. 192-194
Obj. #10

Research has revealed that _____ find it easier than _____ to have sex without an emotional commitment.
   a. lesbians; gay men
   b. bisexuals; lesbians
   c. men; women
   d. women; men

16.
K
Answer: a
p. 194
Obj. #9

A study of lesbians showed a preference to postpone sexual involvement with a partner until
   a. emotional intimacy is present.
   b. they have known each other at least one month.
   c. both have received STD screenings.
   d. they have agreed to cohabitate.

17.
K
Answer: d
p. 196
Obj. #9

Findings from over 1800 married persons in the National Health and Social Life Survey demonstrated that _____ knew their spouse less than one month before having sex.
   a. 76%
   b. 51%
   c. 23%
   d. 10%

18.
K
Answer: c
p. 197
Obj. N/A

Citing their experience with their classes, the authors suggest which strategy to end a relationship?
   a. Relay the information through a third party, in order to avoid hurting the other more.
   b. Write a letter and honestly share your feelings.
   c. Tell the other clearly and unmistakably that you don't wish to be involved.
   d. Avoid the other by failing to return phone calls.

19.
K
Answer: a
p. 198
Obj. #12

Several writers believe that jealousy is closely related to all of the following **except**
   a. feelings of love.
   b. injured pride.
   c. fear of abandonment.
   d. fear of losing control.

20.
K
Answer: d
p. 199
Obj. #13

Men whose jealousy is aroused are **more** likely to
a. deny their feelings.
b. confront a third party rival.
c. retaliate by seeking extrarelationship involvement.
d. all of the above are true

21.
K
Answer: b
p. 199
Obj. #13

Jealous women are **more** inclined to
a. be more concerned about a partner's sexual fidelity than emotional involvement.
b. blame themselves.
c. suppress attempts to provoke jealousy in their partner.
d. ignore their feelings.

22.
K
Answer: c
p. 198
Obj. #12

People who are **more** prone to feel jealous have
a. parents who had distressed marriages.
b. higher distrust of others.
c. low self-esteem.
d. feelings of guilt.

23.
K
Answer: d
p. 201
Obj. #14

When researchers reviewed studies on marital satisfaction they found that successful marriages had which of the following qualities?
a. The parents of the partners had happy marriages.
b. The woman was not pregnant when they married.
c. Partners had similar interests and personalities.
d. all of the above are true.

24.
K
Answer: a
p. 201
Obj. #14

A study of over 300 happily married couples revealed that
a. fewer than 10% thought that good sexual relations kept their relationships together.
b. most dated extensively prior to marriage.
c. seeing one's partner as a best friend was not considered important by a majority.
d. marriage encounter weekends gave their relationships added zest when needed.

25.
K
Answer: c
p. 203
Obj. #14

Which of the following **best** exemplifies a strategy suggested by the authors for adding sexual variety to a relationship?
a. purchase sex toys at a boutique
b. provoke a little jealousy in your partner
c. make love in places other than the bed
d. concern yourself with what is considered normal to keep a quest for variety healthful

True/False

Students may be asked to answer these questions using the traditional format of marking their answers either "true" or "false". Or, to encourage more active involvement, you may choose to use the following instructions:

If the statement is true, place a "T" on the line preceding it. If the statement is false, place an "F" on the line preceding it and then change the statement to make it true by deleting incorrect information and/or adding accurate information.

Chapter 7 Love and the Development of Sexual Relationships 159

1.
Answer: T
p. 179
Obj. #1

___ Zick Rubin's research revealed that strong lovers made more eye contact than weak lovers did.

2.
Answer: F
p. 180
Obj. #17

___ Recent cross-cultural research by Jankowiak and Fischer supports the view that romantic love is a phenomenon of Western culture.

3.
Answer: T
p. 180
Obj. #15

___ In their cross-cultural research, Jankowiak and Fischer found that the vast majority of the societies they studied experienced romantic love.

4.
Answer: F
p. 181
Obj. #4

___ According to Sternberg, the three dimensions of love are passion, trust and commitment.

5.
Answer: T
p. 182
Obj. #4

___ According to Sternberg, if a person is very strongly attracted to someone, but doesn't experience intimacy or commitment in the relationship, it is the experience of infatuation.

6.
Answer: F
p. 183
Obj. #4

___ According to Sternberg, the couple who has been together for years because of their religious and family convictions, despite the lack of passion or intimacy in their relationship, is experiencing companionate love.

7.
Answer: T
p. 184
Obj. #5

___ Lee suggested that a successful loving relationship is more likely with a mate who share the same approach to and definition of love.

8.
Answer: F
p. 186
Obj. #6

___ Brain endorphins have been associated with the exciting high of passionate love.

9.
Answer: T
p. 187
Obj. #6

___ Contrary to the old saying that "opposites attract", people who fall in love often share strong similarities in their values and interests.

10.
Answer: T
p. 188
Obj. #6

___ Being interested in someone who has shown an interest in or attraction toward you is an example of reciprocity.

11.
Answer: F
p. 188
Obj. #6

____ Both men and women appear to be equally influenced by physical attractiveness in their selection of a partner.

12.
Answer: T
pp. 188-189
Obj. #16

____ Recent research indicates that men place greater value on women who are physically attractive while women place greater value on men who are somewhat older and are financially stable.

13.
Answer: F
p. 191
Obj. #9

____ According to the text, the first step in developing intimacy in a relationship is establishing trust.

14.
Answer: T
p. 191
Obj. #9

____ Complimenting or appreciating your partner, or sincerely asking "tell me about your day," are all examples of the inclusion phase of a relationship.

15.
Answer: T
p. 193
Obj. #10

____ A number of studies consistently reveal that women link love and sex to a greater extent than men do.

16.
Answer: T
p. 194
Obj. #10

____ Loving someone of the same sex rather than having same-sex physical encounters is what distinguishes a homosexual from a heterosexual.

17.
Answer: T
p. 196
Obj. #14

____ People who are quick to have sex are less likely to have lasting relationships.

18.
Answer: T
p. 198
Obj. #11

____ People who place a high value on wealth, fame, popularity and physical attractiveness tend to experience more jealousy in a relationship.

19.
Answer: F
p. 199
Obj. #13

____ In general, men are more likely to acknowledge their jealous feelings than women are.

20.
Answer: T
pp. 199-200
Obj. #12

____ According to the text, men and women generally tend to react to jealousy differently.

Short Answer Essay

1. Describe the differences between passionate and companionate love. (Obj. #2, 3)

2. Describe several research studies on love, and briefly summarize their findings. (Obj. #1, 4, 5, 12, 17)

3. Describe the three components of Sternberg's triangular theory of love and choose four patterns that exist with varying combinations of these components and describe them. (Obj. #4)

4. Discuss at least four factors that appear to play an important role in determining with whom we fall in love. (Obj. #6)

5. Choose a couple that you know well, e.g., your parents, friends, you and your partner, and after listing the four factors that your book proposes as important in determining why we fall in love, evaluate the role of these factors for this couple. (Obj. #6)

6. Explain why self-love is important in the development of intimacy. What might you look for, in yourself and others, in determining to what degree this has been achieved? (Obj. #8)

7. List and describe the seven phases of a relationship as it develops and becomes more intimate. (Obj. #9)

8. Citing relevant research, explain how men and women, both homosexual and heterosexual, view the relationship between love and sex. (Obj. #10)

9. Discuss the guidelines for determining personal values and making decisions regarding sexual expression. (Obj. #11)

10. Define jealousy and explain how it may be viewed within a relationship. Discuss sex differences related to people or situations that provoke jealousy, and how men and women react to jealous feelings. Finally, discuss some coping strategies for dealing with jealousy. (Obj. #12, 13)

11. Consider a relationship (family, friendship, or romance) in which you experienced jealousy and consider how the coping strategies discussed in your book might have helped in this situation. (Obj. #12, 13)

12. Describe some of the factors that contribute to relationship satisfaction over time. (Obj. #14)

13. Describe how recent physiological research has explained the "high" we experience in intimate relationships. (Obj. #6)

14. Is romantic love a universal experience? Cite research. You may also wish to give personal case study examples. (Obj. #17)

15. Citing recent research, describe men and women's differential preferences in mate selection and the theory used to explain these choices. (Obj. #15)

8

Communication in Sexual Behavior

Learning Objectives

After studying this chapter, the student should be able to:

1. Define mutual empathy and explain how it relates to effective sexual communication.

2. Discuss how each of the following may hinder effective sexual communication:
   a. socialization
   b. language
   c. gender-based communication styles
   d. sexual anxiety

3. Discuss three strategies that may be helpful to begin talking about sex.

4. Identify and describe at least six characteristics of effective listening and feedback.

5. List and expand upon four different strategies that could be used to discover what is pleasurable to your partner.

6. Describe three aspects of communication to consider in learning to make sexual requests.

7. Discuss seven aspects of communication to consider in order to give criticism effectively.

8. Describe five strategies to consider in order to receive criticism effectively.

9. Outline a three-step approach that can be used to effectively turn down offers for sexual involvement.

10. Discuss the effects of sending mixed messages and explain how to respond if receiving them.

11. Articulate four aspects of nonverbal communication that play an important part in the process of communication.

12. Enumerate and discuss several strategies for dealing with an impasse that may occur in sexual communication.

13. Discuss ethnic differences in intimate communication among white Americans, African Americans, Hispanic Americans and Asian Americans.

14. Discuss normal male alexithymia and treatment strategies to address this issue.

Multiple Choice

1.
K
Answer: b
p. 207
Obj. #1

The knowledge that each partner in a relationship cares for the other and knows the care is reciprocated is called
   a. reciprocal rapport.
   b. mutual empathy.
   c. inclusion.
   d. unconditional positive regard.

2.
A
Answer: c
p. 212
Obj. #1

Which of the following is the **best** example of mutual empathy?
   a. A woman assures her partner that, in spite of the sexual difficulties he is having, she loves him no matter what.
   b. A woman initiates sex with a man she has been dating and he responds with enthusiasm.
   c. Despite a crisis in their marriage, a couple enters into therapy with the knowledge that they both care for each other and are committed to the relationship.
   d. A man lets his partner know that it excites him when she is sexually aggressive.

3.
K
Answer: a
p. 207
Obj. #2

Which of the following childhood experience was NOT considered a contribution to later difficulties in talking about sex?
   a. Watching dogs or other pets copulate.
   b. Learning to keep our genitals covered.
   c. Learning that elimination of feces or urine is "dirty".
   d. Not talking about sex at home.

4.
K
Answer: a
p. 208
Obj. #2
WWW

"Penis" is an example of
   a. clinical terminology.
   b. street language.
   c. slang.
   d. a euphemism.

5.
K
Answer: d
pp. 207-208, 228
Obj. #2

Which of the following statements concerning sexual communication is false?
   a. Facial expression and interpersonal distance are both examples of nonverbal sexual communication.
   b. Clinical terms for sexual acts may fail to convey emotional feelings.
   c. Inadequate socialization may negatively affect sexual communication.
   d. According to the authors, the basis for effective sexual communication is reciprocal self-disclosure.

6.
K
Answer: a
p. 208
Obj. #2

In descriptions of genital anatomy, two extremes tend to predominate: _____ and _____.
   a. clinical terminology; street terms
   b. slang; euphemisms
   c. medical terminology; clinical terms
   d. slang; street terms

Chapter 8 Communication in Sexual Behavior 165

7.
K
Answer: b
pp. 207-211
Obj. #2

Which of the following is NOT discussed as one of the reasons why sexual communication is difficult?
a. lack of positive role models
b. the prevalence of childhood sexual abuse
c. lack of comfortable language for talking about sex
d. the differences in men's and women's communication styles

8.
A
Answer: b
p. 208
Obj. #13
WWW

"I'm sharing this sexual experience with you but getting my sexual needs met is important too." This statement is an example of
a. collectivism.
b. individualism.
c. mutual empathy.
d. reciprocity.

9.
A
Answer: d
p. 208
Obj. #13

"We are sharing this sexual experience together, and it is important that we both enjoy it and are satisfied." This statement is an example of
a. unconditional positive regard.
b. mutual empathy.
c. individualism.
d. collectivism.

10.
K
Answer: c
pp. 208-209
Obj. #13

Which of the following would be **most** likely to emphasize collectivism in their intimate relationships?
a. White Americans and African Americans
b. African Americans and Asian Americans
c. Asian Americans and Hispanic Americans
d. Hispanic Americans and white Americans

11.
K
Answer: c
pp. 208-209
Obj. #13

Which of the following individuals would be **most** likely to value communication competence in a relationship?
a. an African American woman
b. an Asian American woman
c. a white American woman
d. an Hispanic American woman

12.
K
Answer: d
p. 209
Obj. #13

In general, which of the following would be **most** likely to be comfortable acknowledging and resolving conflict in an intimate relationship?
a. African American couples
b. Asian American couples
c. Hispanic American couples
d. white American couples

13.
K
Answer: a
p. 209
Obj. #13

Which of the following tend to be **most** comfortable with the use of touch to convey sexual feeling or desire?
a. African Americans and Hispanic Americans
b. white Americans and African Americans
c. Asian Americans and white Americans
d. Hispanic Americans and Asian Americans

14.
K
Answer: a
p. 210
Obj. #2c

According to Tannen, women use language to _____, while men use language to _____.
a. achieve intimacy; convey information
b. achieve status in a group; to prevent others from pushing them away
c. gain control; achieve sexual intimacy
d. to prevent being pushed around; achieve status in a group

15.
K
Answer: c
p. 210
Obj. #2c

Men most commonly use language in all of the following ways **except**
a. to achieve status in a group.
b. to convey information.
c. to promote intimacy.
d. to avoid being put down.

16.
K
Answer: d
p. 210
Obj. #2c

Women most commonly use language in all of the following ways **except**
a. to create a sense of sharing and support.
b. to promote intimacy.
c. to prevent others from pushing them away.
d. to avoid being dominated or controlled.

17.
K
Answer: c
p. 210
Obj. #2c

According to linguistics professor Deborah Tannen, all of the following statements are true **except**
a. men use language to maintain power and status in a group.
b. it may be difficult for many men to ask for advice; they would rather give it.
c. women use language to avoid being dominated or controlled.
d. because women like to talk about their troubles doesn't necessarily mean they want men to offer suggestions.

18.
A
Answer: b
p. 210
Obj. #2c
WWW

Based on Tannen's position on gender-based communication styles, if a woman came home and wished to talk to her partner about her problems at work, in which of the following ways would she **most** like him to respond?
a. brainstorm possible solutions to the problem
b. empathize with her concerns
c. disclose the problems he was having at work
d. share advice on how he would approach the problem

19.
A
Answer: c
p. 215
Obj. #2c

Based on Tannen's position on gender-based communication styles, if a woman wanted her male partner to share in the completion of various household chores, she would be **most** likely to gain his cooperation if she
a. approached him indirectly by indicating how much her friend's husband shared household responsibilities.
b. complained how tired she was of doing most all of the work by herself.
c. asked for his help, gave him a list of chores, and asked him how he thought they could solve the problem.
d. prayed about this.

20.
K
Answer: a
p. 210
Obj. #2c

According to Deborah Tannen, which of the following statements is false?
   a. Women's communication style is better than men's for a good romantic relationship.
   b. Men tend to offer solutions to problems when women really just want to be listened to.
   c. Women use language to create rapport.
   d. Men often enter into conversations concerned about who has more status or control.

21.
K
Answer: c
p. 210
Obj. #5

A male and female decide to use nicknames for their genitals. This **most** likely
   a. means they are sexually dysfunctional.
   b. means they are inhibited.
   c. means they want playfulness in their communication about sexual matters.
   d. means they are fixated at an earlier Freudian level.

22.
A
Answer: d
p. 211
Obj. #3

Andre begins a conversation with his partner by saying, "I have been wanting to talk to you about our sexual relationship, but I feel awkward doing it. I've also been worried that you might pull away or become more distant if I tried to talk with you." He is using the "getting started talking" strategy of
   a. comparing notes.
   b. giving permission.
   c. mutual empathy.
   d. talking about talking.

23.
A
Answer: a
p. 211
Obj. #3

The authors discuss several strategies for getting started talking about sex: talking about why it is difficult to talk; sharing sexual histories; and
   a. reading articles and books about the subject.
   b. appraising the nonverbal behavior of your partner before talking.
   c. discreetly getting as much information from you partner about the subject prior to the discussion itself.
   d. using a good balance of "I" and "you" statements as you initiate discussion.

24.
K
Answer: d
p. 211
Obj. #3
WWW

Which of the following is NOT a suggestion for "breaking the ice" in regard to a sexual conversation?
   a. talking about talking
   b. reading and discussing
   c. sharing sexual histories
   d. demonstrating unconditional regard

25.
A
Answer: c
p. 211
Obj. #3

In an effort to get her partner to begin talking more openly about sex, Sharon asks questions about how he learned about sex at home and at school, how nudity and physical affection were dealt with at home, etc. She also shares information concerning herself. She is using the "getting started talking" strategy of
   a. reciprocal self-disclosure.
   b. unconditional positive regard.
   c. sharing sexual histories.
   d. mutual empathy.

26.
K
Answer: a
p. 212
Obj. #4

Which of the following is NOT a listening and feedback skill?
   a. self-disclosure
   b. expressing unconditional positive regard
   c. maintaining eye contact
   d. paraphrasing

27.
K
Answer: c
p. 212
Obj. #4

Which of the following is **most** closely associated with listening and feedback?
   a. using "I" language
   b. making specific requests
   c. maintaining eye contact
   d. self-disclosure

28.
K
Answer: d
p. 212
Obj. #4

People who respond to conversation by staring into space, perhaps murmuring an "uh-huh" now and then, are called _____; people who respond by making brief comments, asking questions and changing their facial expressions are called _____.
   a. paraphrasers; validators
   b. validators; paraphrasers
   c. active listeners; passive listeners
   d. passive listeners; active listeners

29.
A
Answer: d
p. 212
Obj. #4

Meredith is relating an incident that happened at work to her friend Josh. He responds by asking questions and making brief comments. He is using the communication skill of
   a. self-disclosure.
   b. paraphrasing.
   c. unconditional positive regard.
   d. active listening.

30.
K
Answer: c
p. 213
Obj. #4
WWW

When we value our partners regardless of what they say or do, we are
   a. expressing mutual empathy.
   b. using paraphrasing.
   c. expressing unconditional positive regard.
   d. practicing self-disclosure.

31.
A
Answer: c
p. 213
Obj. #4

"It seems like we rarely touch each other except when we have sex." A paraphrase of this statement would be
   a. "That's not true — we always cuddle when we watch TV."
   b. "When did you begin noticing that?"
   c. "You mean you don't think we have much physical contact except when we make love?"
   d. "Well, let's give each other a massage then."

32.
A
Answer: c
p. 213
Obj. #4

"It seems like sex has become kind of routine for us." A paraphrase of this would be
   a. "Yes, I think we should discuss this. But I want you to know that regardless of what issues may surface, I still love and care for you."
   b. "What do you mean by 'routine'?"
   c. "So you think we've allowed ourselves to fall into a sexual rut?"
   d. "I agree. Having kids and working full-time has seemed to put a damper on our sexual relationship."

33.
A
Answer: a
p. 213
Obj. #4

"Sometimes you're just too aggressive sexually." The **best** paraphrase of this statement would be
   a. "So what you're saying is that I push you to respond before you're ready?"
   b. "Tell me exactly what you mean by 'aggressive'."
   c. "Well, I would love it if you would take the initiative more often then."
   d. "I can't help it; you just excite me so much."

34.
A
Answer: b
p. 213
Obj. #4
WWW

"I am tired of being the only one that seems to be interested in sex around here." The **best** paraphrase of this statement would be
   a. "I know it seems like that, but it's just because I've been working extra hours lately."
   b. "You mean you feel you have to initiate sex all of the time?"
   c. "Even though I may not have the same level of sexual interest you do, I'm still very attracted to you."
   d. "I would be more interested if it weren't just the same old routine every time."

35.
A
Answer: b
p. 213
Obj. #4

"I have had some past sexual experiences that have been rather traumatic, so sex is a sensitive subject for me." Which of the following responses expresses unconditional positive regard?
   a. "You mean you find it difficult to talk about sex?"
   b. "Well, I'm glad you brought this up. But I want you to know that no matter what has happened, I still love you and care for you very much."
   c. "I can see that. Have you considered getting some counseling?"
   d. "I appreciate it that you can discuss this with me."

36.
K
Answer: a
p. 213
Obj. #4

The notion of unconditional positive regard was first referred to in a book written by
   a. Carl Rogers.
   b. Erik Erikson.
   c. Deborah Tannen.
   d. Bernie Zilbergeld.

37.
A
Answer: c
p. 213
Obj. #4

"Being on this medication has affected my interest in sex. I still love you and am attracted to you, but I just haven't been that interested in sex lately." Which of the following expresses unconditional positive regard in response to this comment?
   a. "I appreciate you letting me know what is going on. Have you considered trying a different medication?"
   b. "Yes, I know you haven't been that interested lately. Perhaps we should get some counseling."
   c. "I'm disappointed that we aren't having sex that often, but you know that I still love you very much and am very committed to our relationship."
   d. "I think you've been working too much too. Why don't we get away together for the weekend?"

38.
A
Answer: d
p. 214
Obj. #5

Which of the following is the **best** example of an open-ended question?
   a. "Was I gentle enough?"
   b. "Would you like to make love here or in front of the fireplace?"
   c. "Do you like it when I'm on top?"
   d. "What are your feelings about sharing our sexual fantasies?"

39.
K
Answer: b
p. 214
Obj. #5

If you were trying to elicit a specific response from your partner, which of the following types of questions would be **most** appropriate?
   a. open-ended
   b. yes or no
   c. probing inquiry
   d. positive inquiry

40.
K
Answer: d
pp. 213-218
Obj. #5

Which of the following is NOT discussed as a way to discover your partner's needs?
   a. asking questions
   b. self-disclosure
   c. comparing notes
   d. using "I" language

41.
A
Answer: c
p. 214
Obj. #5

Which of the following types of questions does NOT belong with the others:
   a. "Do you like to listen to music while we are making love?"
   b. "Is this your favorite position?"
   c. "What are your thoughts about having sex in the Jacuzzi?"
   d. "Do you like it when I talk to you while we're having sex?"

Chapter 8 Communication in Sexual Behavior 171

42.
A
Answer: a
pp. 215-216
Obj. #5

Which of the following is the **best** example of self-disclosure?
a. "I've been having this fantasy that we would both go out to the same bar but pretend that we didn't know each other. Then I would pick you up, bring you home, and seduce you. What do you think about that?"
b. "I realize that you are not real comfortable taking the initiative sexually, but I just want you to know that I find that very exciting, so anytime you want to experiment would be just fine with me."
c. "Would you prefer to make love in the back seat of the car or in that phone booth?"
d. "How would you feel about going nude sunbathing together?"

43.
A
Answer: a
pp. 216-217
Obj. #14

Normative male alexithymia is a result of
a. male gender role socialization.
b. prenatal hormonal influences.
c. being raised by at least one emotionally abusive caretaker.
d. a linguistic deficiency.

44.
K
Answer: c
pp. 216-217
Obj. #14

Treatment for normative male alexithymia involves all of the following **except**
a. exercises to increase the ability to empathize with others.
a. keeping an "emotional log" describing context and emotions.
b. biofeedback to help control physiological arousal during conflict.
d. exercises oriented toward expanding a client's emotional vocabulary.

45.
K
Answer: d
pp. 216-217
Obj. #14

Which of the following statements regarding normative male alexithymia is true?
a. It was first observed in men who had suffered a stroke in the left hemisphere of their brains.
b. Male alexithymia is associated with a recessive gene.
c. Mothers express more emotion to their sons than their daughters, which contributes to this problem.
d. In terms of treatment, the emphasis is on "emotional intelligence."

46.
K
Answer: b
p. 217
Obj. #5

Which one is true with respect to the sharing of sexual fantasies?
a. This is unhealthy.
b. Some people find this exciting and informative.
c. It's OK as long as it involves only movie stars and not animals.
d. Committed couples will even be able to comfortably share fantasies about other lovers.

47.
K
Answer: b
p. 218
Obj. #5

When you reassure your partner and encourage him or her to talk about specific needs or feelings, you are using the communication skill called
a. unconditional positive regard.
b. giving permission.
c. mutual empathy.
d. active listening.

48.
A
Answer: d
p. 218
Obj. #5
WWW

"I know that you feel self-conscious walking around the house in that lingerie, but I love watching you; it is so erotic for me. So feel free to experiment feeling less inhibited anytime you like!" This person is using the communication skill called
a. positive role modeling.
b. unconditional positive regard.
c. validating.
d. giving permission.

49.
K
Answer: a
p. 219
Obj. #6

When asking for what you want from a partner, it is **best** if you
a. are very specific about what you would like.
b. ask in the form of a yes/no question in order to get a definitive response.
c. practice "you" language while making your request.
d. be somewhat general in your request to avoid putting your partner on the defensive.

50.
A
Answer: d
pp. 218-219
Obj. #6

Which of the following attitudes is associated with taking responsibility for your own pleasure?
a. "We have been together for two years, and he usually knows what I want by now."
b. "I will make sure that you are always sexually satisfied."
c. "If you really loved me you would be able to satisfy me sexually."
d. "I know that I'm unable to orgasm consistently, but it's not your fault."

51.
K
Answer: c
p. 219
Obj. #6

In reference to the discussion on how to ask for what you want, which of the following requests would **most** likely be understood?
a. "I would like you to be more affectionate."
b. "I would like our intimate time to be sensual as well as sexual."
c. "I would like you to hold my hand or put your arm around me when we are out together."
d. "I would like you to touch me more when we make love."

52.
A
Answer: c
p. 220
Obj. #6
WWW

Which of the following is the **best** example of "I" language?
a. "I feel you're being insensitive."
b. "What do you think about oral sex?"
c. "I feel more aroused when you undress me before we make love."
d. "Sometimes I feel you are too aggressive sexually."

53.
A
Answer: c
p. 220
Obj. #7

If you wanted to improve your communication within a relationship, which of the following would be **most** helpful?
a. Keep the focus of the conversation general; avoid discussion of specifics.
b. When giving feedback, focus on aspects of the person's character rather than on his or her behavior.
c. Use "I" language in order to avoid blaming the other person.
d. Demonstrate conditional positive regard.

Chapter 8 Communication in Sexual Behavior 173

54.
A
Answer: c
p. 221
Obj. #7

A verbal statement of a complaint to your partner
    a. is perhaps best raised after they have just criticized you.
    b. should always be made if something really annoys you.
    c. should be done because a change can make the relationship better.
    d. is not a good idea until after you are married.

55.
A
Answer: c
pp. 221-225
Obj. #7

Sue needs to offer some constructive criticism regarding her partner's lovemaking. Which of the following would be **least** helpful as a guideline to follow in this endeavor?
    a. Focus on a positive aspect of her relationship with her partner and combine that with the criticism.
    b. Wait until her partner has completed a stressful project he is working on before she confronts him.
    c. Make a list of her concerns so she will remember to discuss all of them.
    d. Avoid asking "why" questions in the course of the discussion.

56.
K
Answer: c
p. 222
Obj. #7

When raising a concern or criticism with your partner
    a. it is really important to make sure that you follow through on a discussion right when it is raised.
    b. if your partner doesn't want to talk about it, then you should probably drop it.
    c. agree to a later specific time if your partner prefers some delay.
    d. both of you should have several drinks first so you'll feel more relaxed.

57.
K
Answer: a
p. 224
Obj. #7
WWW

According to the text, "why" questions
    a. are barely concealed efforts to criticize or attack our partners.
    b. are used to get to the heart of a problem in the relationship.
    c. typically induce positive changes in the relationship.
    d. are more effective than structured questions.

58.
K
Answer: b
p. 224
Obj. #7

_____ statements express how we feel without blaming the other person, whereas _____ statements are interpreted as attacks on the other person's character.
    a. "You"; "I"
    b. "I"; "you"
    c. "Why"; "you"
    d. "Why"; "I"

59.
K
Answer: a
pp. 222-224
Obj. #7

All of the following are discussed as a strategy for delivering criticism **except**
    a. use "why" questions to understand the person's motivation.
    b. combine praise with criticism.
    c. express anger appropriately.
    d. nurture small steps toward change.

60.
K
Answer: c
p. 224
Obj. #7

Asking a "why" question
a. lets the other person respond in a more open-ended way.
b. gleans more information regarding the subject at hand.
c. puts the other person on the defensive.
d. makes the other person feel like he or she is being actively listened to.

61.
A
Answer: b
p. 224
Obj. #7
WWW

"Why don't you ever initiate sex?" The problem with the way this is expressed is that
a. it is an open-ended question.
b. it is a disguised effort to attack the other person.
c. it exposes the selfishness of the partner.
d. it forces a communication impasse.

62.
K
Answer: a
pp. 224-225
Obj. #7

When raising issues or complaints
a. there should be just one complaint per discussion.
b. if things are going well then you should continue on to a number of major issues.
c. consider usually doing this in the afterglow of a good lovemaking session.
d. it is more effective to be able to present a list documenting examples of the behavior that concerns you.

63.
A
Answer: c
pp. 225-226
Obj. #8

Your partner is upset because you rarely initiate sexual interaction. According to the text, which of the following responses would be **least** effective?
a. "You're right — I haven't taken the initiative. I'm uncomfortable being that aggressive."
b. "So you're tired of being the one that is always pursuing me — is that right?"
c. "I would love to initiate if you wouldn't be after me all the time so I could have a chance to work up an appetite!"
d. "I know it must be frustrating for you that my sexual desire isn't as strong as yours."

64.
K
Answer: c
pp. 225-226
Obj. #8

Which of the following is NOT one of the strategies discussed for receiving criticism?
a. acknowledge the criticism
b. paraphrase the criticism
c. express unconditional positive regard
d. express your feelings

65.
K
Answer: d
p. 226
Obj. #8

Which of the following suggestions outlined in the text is a good closure to receiving criticism?
a. Compare notes on the conversation.
b. Discuss any negative feelings you might have.
c. Establish mutual empathy.
d. Focus on future changes the two of you can make.

Chapter 8 Communication in Sexual Behavior 175

66.
K
Answer: c
p. 226
Obj. #8

If you are upset by your partner's criticism and you know they love you
a. you should probably just not say anything and try to control yourself.
b. leave the room.
c. you should tell them how angry or hurt you are.
d. you probably really don't trust them enough for the relationship to work.

67.
K
Answer: d
pp. 226-227
Obj. #9

With respect to saying "no" in relationships
a. if we are really committed and it is not a moral or legal issue then we should comply although we really don't want to.
b. we should avoid this because the other person may feel hurt.
c. this is usually easier with people we care about as compared to mere acquaintances.
d. it helps to have a strategy in mind for doing this.

68.
K
Answer: d
p. 227
Obj. #9

Which of the following is NOT an example of a response according to the three-step approach to saying no outlined in your text?
a. "I'm flattered that you find me interesting."
b. "No, I never see students, even former ones, socially. "
c. "I'm not interested in making love tonight but what about tomorrow morning?"
d. "I'm sorry I can't have coffee with you but I've promised my boyfriend that I won't see anyone else."

69.
K
Answer: b
p. 227
Obj. #10

Jonas tells Shenan that he is not interested in a romantic relationship with her but he then invites her to watch a movie with him while lying on his waterbed with an arm around her. This is an example of
a. one of the stages of saying no.
b. a mixed message.
c. nonverbal validation.
d. implicit criticism.

70.
K
Answer: c
p. 228
Obj. #10

If you are the recipient of mixed messages, it is probably **best** to
a. respond to the first message.
b. respond to the second message.
c. discuss your confusion with your partner in hopes that he or she will clarify his or her intentions.
d. assertively state that you feel you are being manipulated.

71.
A
Answer: b
p. 228
Obj. #11

Although Jack says nothing is wrong, his frown, and lack of eye contact and physical affection give his partner another message. Despite what he is saying, she is being affected by his
a. lack of communication.
b. nonverbal communication.
c. subassertive behavior.
d. lack of unconditional positive regard.

72.
K
Answer: d
p. 228
Obj. #11

The distance we maintain between ourselves and people with whom we have contact is called
a. sensory space.
b. proximal space.
c. energy equilibrium.
d. interpersonal distance.

73.
K
Answer: d
pp. 228-229
Obj. #11

Which of the following is NOT an aspect of nonverbal communication discussed in the text?
a. facial expression
b. touching
c. interpersonal distance
d. proximal space

74.
K
Answer: b
pp. 229-230
Obj. #11

During sexual activity
a. loud sounds should be repressed in case you wake the children.
b. moans and cries are arousing for some individuals.
c. if a person doesn't cry out loudly you know they are not really aroused.
d. words are not as important or necessary as nonverbal communication.

75.
K
Answer: b
p. 230
Obj. #12

Indicating that you see how reasonable another person's viewpoint may seem is called
a. empathic paraphrasing.
b. validating.
c. compromising.
d. mutual empathy.

76.
K
Answer: a
p. 230
Obj. #12

Faced with a communication impasse, a couple may find it helpful to
a. grant each other the right not to change.
b. compare notes.
c. continue discussing the issue with the understanding that eventually it will be resolved.
d. practice self-disclosure.

Multiple Choice from Study Guide

1.
K
Answer: c
p. 207
Obj. #1

Which statement below **best** reflects the concept of mutual empathy?
a. Getting in touch with your partner's feelings.
b. Expressing your feelings no matter what they are.
c. Caring for another and knowing that such care is reciprocated.
d. Telling your partner you care about them no matter what they do or say.

2.
K
Answer: d
pp. 207-209
Obj. #2

Obstacles to effective communication about sex include
a. Anxiety.
b. lack of a suitable language for sex.
c. ethnic group differences in intimate communication.
d. all of the above are true.

Chapter 8 Communication in Sexual Behavior 177

3.
K
Answer: d
p. 210
Obj. #2c

Of the following strategies listed below, which is **most** effective in dealing with gender-based differences in communication?
 a. Males should suggest solutions to their female partner's problems.
 b. Women should let men push them around, since it is natural for men to do so.
 c. Males should refrain from seeking advice or looking vulnerable.
 d. Women should tell their male partners that they need someone to just listen.

4.
K
Answer: b
p. 209
Obj. #13

_____ American couples and _____ American couples are **least** likely to discuss sex and relationship issues with a partner.
 a. African; Asian
 b. Hispanic; Asian
 c. African; Hispanic
 d. Asian; white

5.
K
Answer: a
p. 211
Obj. #4

Nhat tells his partner that he is afraid to discuss their sexual relationship out of fear of embarrassing or hurting his partner. Nhat is using the communication strategy of
 a. talking about talking.
 b. mutual empathy.
 c. sharing sexual histories.
 d. Paraphrasing.

6.
K
Answer: b
p. 212
Obj. #4

Providing attentive body language, sympathetic facial expressions, nodding, and asking questions are ways to demonstrate
 a. unconditional positive regard.
 b. active listening.
 c. comparing notes.
 d. validating.

7.
K
Answer: b
pp. 212-213
Obj. #4

Which of the following was NOT suggested as a method of providing feedback to a partner?
 a. paraphrasing
 b. self-disclosure
 c. unconditional positive regard
 d. supporting a partner's communication efforts

8.
K
Answer: b
p. 214
Obj. #5

"What are some of the places where you'd like to make love?" is an example of a(n) _____ question.
 a. yes-or-no
 b. open-ended
 c. either/or
 d. mixed

9.
K
Answer: d
p. 214
Obj. #5

Which question type provides the **least** opportunity to discuss an issue?
a. either/or
b. clarifying
c. open-ended
d. yes-or-no

10.
K
Answer: a
p. 215
Obj. #5

Research has shown that when one partner begins self-disclosure the other partner
a. is likely to reciprocate.
b. will respond in kind only if the topic of fantasies is being discussed.
c. should avert eye contract in order to establish positive regard.
d. may experience a reduction in relationship satisfaction.

11.
K
Answer: d
pp. 216-217
Obj. #14

Normative male alexithymia may result in
a. difficulty communicating intimate feelings.
b. channeling of vulnerable feelings into aggression.
c. sexual sharing being the only place where love is expressed.
d. all of the above may occur.

12.
K
Answer: c
pp. 218-219
Obj. #6

Which statement **best** reflects taking responsibility for your own pleasure?
a. "If you loved me, you'd know what I want."
b. "If our relationship is healthy, we won't need to talk about sex."
c. "It's not your fault if I don't climax. Sometimes it's difficult for me to relax.'
d. "It is my job to satisfy you."

13.
K
Answer: a
pp. 218-219
Obj. #6

Saying "I would like it if you stayed inside me longer" is **more** likely to be understood and heeded than "I wish we could do something different" because
a. "I" language is being used.
b. a specific request has been made.
c. permission has been given.
d. a vague request communicates our desires more effectively.

14.
K
Answer: d
p. 220
Obj. #7

Expressing criticism is likely to be constructive when the motivation behind the criticism is
a. to assert one's needs as primary in the relationship.
b. giving a partner a taste of their own medicine, so that empathy can be established.
c. getting even with your partner so that equilibrium may be restored.
d. a genuine desire to make a relationship better.

15.
K
Answer: a
pp. 221-225
Obj. #7

Which of the following is out of place here among suggestions for giving criticism?
   a. withholding praise until criticism is received
   b. nurturing small steps toward change
   c. expressing negative emotions appropriately
   d. choosing the right time and place

16.
K
Answer: c
p. 224
Obj. #7

"Why" questions should be avoided because
   a. they are vague.
   b. it is important that a partner assume their fair share of the blame.
   c. they promote defensiveness and rarely bring about positive change.
   d. they represent simple, straightforward requests for information.

17.
K
Answer: c
p. 224
Obj. #7

Which of the following statements represents the **best** way to express negative emotions?
   a. "You never seem to want to touch me anymore."
   b. "You don't seem interested in sex any more."
   c. "I feel afraid for us when we go so long without sex."
   d. "You don't care about us and our problems."

18.
K
Answer: b
p. 225
Obj. #8

Receiving a criticism in a way that can strengthen the relationship begins with
   a. Defending your position.
   b. Empathizing with your partner's concern.
   c. Immediately venting your feelings of frustration.
   d. Withdrawing so that your and your partner can calm down and resume discussion later.

19.
K
Answer: d
p. 226
Obj. #8

The process of receiving criticism continues by
   a. finding something to agree with.
   b. asking clarifying questions.
   c. focusing on future changes that can be made.
   d. all of the above are true.

20.
K
Answer: c
p. 227
Obj. #9

The three-step approach for "saying no" consists of all of the following **except**
   a. expressing appreciation for the invitation.
   b. saying no in a clear, unmistakable manner.
   c. encouraging the person to engage in self-disclosure.
   d. offering an alternative.

21.
K
Answer: c
p. 227
Obj. #10

Which of the following **best** illustrates a mixed message?
a. "I don't want to date you, I want a nonsexual friendship instead."
b. "I'd like to make love, but I'd prefer to do so in the morning when I'm rested."
c. Your partner says "Let's crawl in bed and make love after I check my e-mail" and then they spend so much time on line that you have fallen asleep on the sofa.
d. "I don't want to hop into the shower. How about a dip in the jacuzzi?"

22.
K
Answer: b
p. 228
Obj. #11

Facial expression, personal space, touch and sounds refer to the _____ aspects of sexual communication.
a. gendered
b. nonverbal
c. semiotic
d. psychological

23.
K
Answer: a
p. 230
Obj. #12

Impasses in communication may be bridged by
a. validating.
b. continuing to talk until all concerns have been aired.
c. maintaining the reasonableness of your position until your partner yields.
d. letting negative emotions rise to the surface.

True/False

Students may be asked to answer these questions using the traditional format of marking their answers either "true" or "false." Or, to encourage more active involvement, you may choose to use the following instructions:

If the statement is true, place a "T" on the line preceding it. If the statement is false, place an "F" on the line preceding it and then change the statement to make it true by deleting incorrect information and/or adding accurate information.

1.
Answer: F
p. 208
Obj. #2

___ One of the few sources of models for meaningful verbal communication between lovers occurs from viewing movies.

2.
Answer: T
p. 208
Obj. #13

___ Asian American couples are more likely to value nonverbal and indirect over explicit verbal communication.

3.
Answer: F
p. 210
Obj. #1, 4

___ According to Tannen, men use language to promote closeness and to prevent others from pushing them away.

4.
Answer: T
p. 212
Obj. #4

___ Being an active listener, maintaining eye contact and providing feedback are all aspects of good listening.

5.
Answer: F
pp. 212-213
Obj. #4

___ "Paraphrasing" refers to the technique of telling your partner your reaction to his or her message.

6.
Answer: F
p. 213
Obj. #12

___ Unconditional positive regards entails paraphrasing what the other person is saying in order to prevent miscommunication from occurring.

7.
Answer: T
p. 214
Obj. #5

___ If you wanted to find out how your partner felt about your sexual relationship, that information could best be obtained by asking an open-ended as opposed to a yes or no question.

8.
Answer: T
p. 215
Obj. #5

___ Sexual and nonsexual self disclosure has been found to contribute to overall relationship satisfaction.

9.
Answer: T
p. 216
Obj. #14

___ Clinical observation has suggested that mild to moderate inability to put feelings into words is widespread among men.

10.
Answer: T
p. 218
Obj. #5

___ The communication skill of "giving permission" is one way to discover your partner's needs.

11.
Answer: F
p. 219
Obj. #6

___ When asking for what you want from your partner, it is preferable to ask in a general way in order to avoid putting your partner on the defensive.

12.
Answer: F
p. 220
Obj. #6

___ "I feel that you are being insensitive to my needs" is an example of "I" language.

13.
Answer: F
p. 221
Obj. #7

___ One good time to confront a lover with a problem in your relationship is when you are really feeling bothered by the issue.

14. ___ Your book recommends giving criticism by combining it with
Answer: T   praise followed by a request for feedback.
p. 223
Obj. #7

15. ___ If you are interested in discovering how your partner feels about
Answer: F   intimacy and commitment, asking a "why" question is a good way
p. 224   to initiate that type of discussion.
Obj. #5

16. ___ If there are several issues you would like to discuss with your
Answer: T   partner, it is best to limit yourself to one issue per discussion as
p. 225   opposed to talking about all of them at once.
Obj. #7

17. ___ One suggestion for receiving criticism is to find something about
Answer: T   the criticism with which you can agree.
p. 226
Obj. #8

18. ___ If you wish to turn down an invitation for intimate interaction, be
Answer: T   sure to say no in an unequivocal and clear fashion.
p. 227
Obj. #9

19. ___ The amount of "interpersonal distance" we maintain between
Answer: T   ourselves and others is one aspect of nonverbal communication.
p. 228
Obj. #11

20. ___ One problem with validating the others viewpoint is that you give
Answer: F   up your own position, even if only temporarily.
p. 230
Obj. #12

Short Answer Essay

1. Your text lists the following as reasons why many people find it difficult to talk about sex with their partner: socialization, the language available for talking about sex, fears about self-expression. For each of these give examples to illustrate what this means and how this came about. (Obj. #2)

2. Outline Deborah Tannen's suggestions about gender-based communication styles. What has empirical research found in this area? (Obj. #2)

3. Consider friendships or romantic relationships and describe how Deborah Tannen's suggestions concerning gender differences in communication styles match, or don't match, your own experience. (Obj. #2)

4. Briefly discuss three methods that people may use to get started talking about sex with their partners, giving specific examples to illustrate each method. Which of these do you feel has the most potential and why? (Obj. #3)

5. Describe five of the six characteristics of effective listening that your book discussed. (Obj. #4)

6. Discuss some of the communication skills you can use to discover your partner's needs, providing samples for each. (Obj. #5)

7. Describe and give examples of three strategies you can use in learning to ask for what you want sexually. (Obj. #6)

8. Imagine a situation in which something has been bothering you regarding your sexual relationship. Using the "giving criticism" skills discussed in the text, write a *verbatim* account of how you might confront your partner on this, noting in parenthesis the specific communication skill you are using as you proceed.(Obj. #7)

9. Imagine a situation in which your partner has criticized you on your sexual relationship, resulting in you feeling angry or hurt. Using the "receiving criticism" skills discussed in the text, write a *verbatim* account of how you might respond to the criticism, noting in parenthesis the particular communication strategy you are using as you proceed. (Obj. #8)

10. Summarize some of the differences in gender-based communication styles according to Tannen. Compare to the category of normal male alexithymia. Compare the treat methods suggested for dealing with these. (Obj. #2, 14)

11. Discuss some of the differences in intimate communication among white Americans, African Americans, Hispanic Americans and Asian Americans reported by empirical research. (Obj. #13)

12. Research has reported on-the-average differences between white American, African American, Hispanic Americans and Asian Americans. Does this match what you yourself have observed empirically? (Obj. #13)

13. Define and discuss normative male alexithymia, making specific reference to the following:
    a. its origins and how it is reinforced
    b. the treatment strategy used that was developed by Levant (Obj. #14)

14. Explain some of the options available to a couple when they reach an impasse in discussing an issue. (Obj. #12)

15. Select three items of information from the chapter on Communication in Sexual Behavior that you found either most interesting or most helpful. Specify these and indicate why these were of especial interest to you. (Obj. n/a)

9
Sexual Behaviors

Learning Objectives

After studying this chapter, the student should be able to:

1. Define the two types of celibacy and discuss some of the reasons a person might become celibate.

2. Discuss erotic dreams and fantasy, making specific reference to the following:
   a. how common they are in men and women
   b. what nocturnal orgasm is, and when and in whom it occurs
   c. what research has demonstrated on the content of erotic fantasy
   d. functions that fantasies serve
   e. similarities and differences in the fantasy lives of men and women
   f. research that supports both the positive and negative aspects of sexual fantasy

3. Define masturbation, and discuss the following in regard to it:
   a. traditional and contemporary views of masturbation
   b. reasons why people masturbate
   c. research regarding ethnic differences in frequency of masturbation
   d. characteristics of people who tend to masturbate more than others
   e. various self-pleasuring techniques

4. Explain the significance of the Maltz hierarchy of sexual interactions and briefly describe the six levels of sexual interaction according to this model.

5. Explain some of the benefits of kissing and touching, and discuss areas of the body that are especially sensitive to stimulation.

6. Define cunnilingus and fellatio, discuss the origin of negative attitudes toward these sexual behaviors, and cite research concerning frequency of oral sex in recent years.

7. Describe some of the considerations in practicing anal stimulation and cite research concerning frequency of this sexual practice.

8. Describe variations in gay and lesbian sexual expression.

9. Define intromission and discuss considerations in using various coital positions.

10. Summarize how different racial, educational and religious backgrounds may affect a person's experience with oral sex.

11. Describe the history and process of Tantric sex.

12. Identify and discuss Mosher's sexual styles.

Multiple Choice

1.
K
Answer: a
p. 234
Obj. #1

The two types of celibacy are _____ and _____.
a. partial; complete
b. religious; secular
c. short-term; long-term
d. permanent ; temporary

2.
K
Answer: a
p. 234
Obj. #1

In complete celibacy, a person
a. neither masturbates nor has sexual contact with another person.
b. engages in masturbation but does not have sexual contact with another person.
c. does not masturbate, and has no physical contact, sexual or affectionate, with another person.
d. engages in masturbation and oral sex but not sexual intercourse.

3.
A
Answer: d
p. 234
Obj. #3b

For which of the following reasons would a person be **least** likely to masturbate?
a. for the pleasure of arousal and orgasm
b. to relieve sexual tension
c. to deal with differences in sexual interest within a relationship
d. if the person was completely, as opposed to partially, celibate

4.
K
Answer: d
pp. 234-235
Obj. #1

All of the following are cited as reasons for why a person may choose celibacy **except**
a. concern about contracting a sexually transmitted disease
b. as part of a treatment plan for recovering from alcohol or drug dependency
c. to focus on personal development without the distraction of sexual involvement
d. to avoid physical as well as emotional intimacy with a spouse

5.
K
Answer: c
p. 235
Obj. #1

One disadvantage of celibacy is that
a. over time, men's sperm count may be diminished, when and if sexual activity is resumed.
b. women may discover that their capacity for orgasmic response is diminished, when and if sexual activity is resumed.
c. reestablishing sexual relationships may be difficult, when and if sexual activity is resumed.
d. for men, retrograde ejaculation may occur occasionally when and if sexual activity is resumed.

Chapter 9 Sexual Behaviors   187

6.
A
Answer: b
p. 235
Obj. #1

Sarah has recently begun dating Joe, who tells her on their third date that before meeting her he decided to be celibate for a while. Based on the information in the text, what would you be **most** likely to infer from this?
 a. Joe has sexual problems and wants to avoid facing them with Sarah.
 b. Joe wants to make sure his personal criteria for a good relationship are met before he engages in sex.
 c. Joe is not sexually attracted to Sarah and this is a way for him to get out of the relationship.
 d. Joe is hoping that Sarah will be more sexually aggressive in response to his decision.

7.
K
Answer: b
p. 235
Obj. #2
*WWW

Nocturnal orgasm is another term for
 a. having intercourse after midnight.
 b. "wet dreams".
 c. delayed ejaculation.
 d. retrograde ejaculation.

8.
K
Answer: d
p. 235
Obj. #2b

According to one study, women who had a **higher** frequency of _____ and _____ were **more** likely to experience and be aware of orgasms during sleep.
 a. masturbation; sexual fantasy
 b. oral-genital sex; orgasm with masturbation
 c. oral-genital sex; intercourse
 d. intercourse; orgasm with masturbation

9.
K
Answer: c
p. 235
Obj. #2b

Nocturnal orgasm is experienced by
 a. men.
 b. women.
 c. men and women.
 d. adolescent males only.

10.
K
Answer: d
p. 236
Obj. #2e

A study of common sexual roles that women like to play in their own private fantasies used all of the all of the following categories **except**
 a. "Pretty Maiden"
 b. "Victim"
 c. "Dominatrix"
 d. "Exhibitionist"

11.
K
Answer: d
p. 236
Obj. #2c

The **most** common fantasy that women have during masturbation is
 a. being forced to have sex.
 b. having intercourse with strangers.
 c. being observed engaging in sexual intercourse.
 d. having intercourse with a loved one.

12.
K
Answer: b
p. 236
Obj. #2d

The **most** commonly reported purpose of sexual fantasy during intercourse for both men and women was
a. to imagine activities that the couple typically did not engage in.
b. to facilitate sexual arousal.
c. to increase partner attractiveness.
d. to relieve boredom.

13.
K
Answer: c
p. 237
Obj. #2

With respect to masturbation fantasies, it has been found that
a. lesbians often fantasize about threesomes with another male and female.
b. over half of women have had same-sex fantasies.
c. about one in three men have had same-sex fantasies.
d. if homosexuals use heterosexual fantasy often enough it is likely that they will be able to switch sexual preferences.

14.
K
Answer: d
p. 237
Obj. #2
WWW

The hypothesized functions of sexual fantasies include all but which one of the following?
a. They allow mental rehearsal and anticipation of new sexual experiences.
b. They allow some forbidden wishes to be expressed without actually engaging in them.
c. They provide relief from gender-role expectations.
d. They make it possible for athletes to refrain from sex prior to important competitions.

15.
A
Answer: c
pp. 237-238
Obj. #2c, 2d

Based on information presented in the text, if a woman friend of yours confided that one of her favorite fantasies during masturbation was being forced to have sex, which of the following assumptions would be the **most** reasonable for you to make?
a. Your friend can be included with the majority of women who have similar fantasies.
b. Your friend needs counseling because many women who have similar fantasies are susceptible to becoming rape victims.
c. This kind of fantasy is common and harmless; it frees a woman from the responsibility and guilt of personal choice.
d. It is highly likely that your friend's fantasies will become progressively more violent and masochistic.

16.
K
Answer: a
p. 238
Obj. #2c

According to a recent research summary, which of the following was **most** characteristic of men's sexual fantasies?
a. explicit sexual acts and nude bodies
b. emphasis on emotional feelings
c. prolonged nongenital touching
d. being sexually submissive to their partners

Chapter 9 Sexual Behaviors 189

17.
K
Answer: a
p. 238
Obj. #2d, 2f

Which of the following statements regarding sexual fantasy is false?
a. Research reveals that people who experience more guilt about sex feel more arousal in response to sexual fantasies than people who do not experience as much guilt about sex.
b. Most research indicates that sexual fantasy is healthy.
c. Private fantasies during sex with a partner may erode trust and intimacy.
d. People who experience low levels of sexual desire do not usually engage in sexual fantasy.

18.
K
Answer: c
p. 238
Obj. #2e

According to a research summary of male/female fantasies, which of the following statements is true?
a. Women are more likely to fantasize about group sex than men are.
b. Men are likely to focus on women's interests in the male body but women do not focus on men's interest in the female body.
c. Men are more likely to have dominance fantasies while women are more likely to have submission fantasies.
d. Women are more likely to focus on explicit sexual acts than men.

19.
K
Answer: a
p. 238
Obj. #2a, 2d, 2f

Which of the following statements regarding sexual fantasy is false?
a. Use of sexual fantasy will usually increase anxiety in people who are concerned about their sexual functioning.
b. One study found that college students with liberal sexual attitudes had longer, more explicit fantasies.
c. More women than men fantasize about being forced to have sex.
d. Many sex therapists encourage their clients to use fantasy as a source of stimulation.

20.
A
Answer: b
p. 238
Obj. #2c

The fact that a significant number of women fantasize about being forced to have sex probably means that
a. subconsciously, women really want to be raped.
b. while they may enjoy the idea of being overpowered in fantasy, it does not mean that they would really want to be raped.
c. these women may tend to be predisposed toward masochism.
d. these women are probably gender dysphoric.

21.
A
Answer: c
p. 239
Obj. #2f

Carmen feels guilty regarding her frequent sexual fantasies, and although the content of her fantasies is unusual, it is not harmful to herself or others. What would the authors of the text be **most** likely to tell her?
a. Incorporate the fantasies into your real life to some degree in order to feel less inhibited.
b. Share the fantasies with your partner or a close friend in order to diffuse the guilt around it.
c. Remember that a fantasy is not the same as actions or behavior.
d. Seek professional help since sexual fantasy that makes a person feel guilty is usually a sign of potential deviant behavior.

22.
A
Answer: c
p. 239
Obj. #2f

Don feels guilty about some of the sexual fantasies he experiences. At what point should he feel concerned?
a. When the fantasies involve being forced to have sex.
b. When he wants to act out a sexual fantasy, even though the fantasy may be harmless to himself or others.
c. When the fantasy involves hurting another person, and he feels compelled to act on it.
d. When the fantasies involve sexually and emotionally dominating his lover.

23.
K
Answer: b
p. 239
Obj. #3

Autoeroticism is another word for
a. self-flagellation.
b. self-stimulation of one's genitals for sexual pleasure.
c. the use of sexual fantasy without additional stimulation to achieve arousal and orgasm.
d. masochistic sexual behavior.

24.
K
Answer: d
p. 240
Obj. #3a
WWW

In 1976, the Vatican issued a "Declaration on Certain Questions Concerning Sexual Ethics", which described masturbation as
a. "forgivable only in small children who were unaware of their behavior."
b. "forgivable as early adolescent exploration but condemnable for adults."
c. "an act which, if not done to excess, could clear the mind for the pursuit of God's work."
d. "intrinsically and seriously disordered."

25.
K
Answer: b
p. 240
Obj. #3a

Which of the following **most** closely corresponds to Freud's view of masturbation?
a. Because ejaculation reduces precious "vital fluids", it is discouraged in any form except intercourse.
b. Masturbation is normal during childhood, but if continued into adulthood, could result in the inability to form good sexual relationships.
c. Masturbation during childhood could result in an abnormal preoccupation with sex, but it is a healthy outlet for adults alone or with partners.
d. Masturbation is how we discover eroticism, so it should be learned and practiced throughout the life cycle.

26.
K
Answer: b
p. 240
Obj. #3b

The **most** common reason that people give for why they masturbate is
a. to deal with differences in sexual interest in a relationship.
b. to relieve sexual tension.
c. to increase orgasmic response.
d. to induce sleep.

27.
K
Answer: a
p. 241
Obj. #3b

Masturbation has been recommended in your text for all but which one of the following?
    a. as a possible aid to reduce depression and anxiety.
    b. helping to fall asleep at night.
    c. a help for men experimenting with ejaculatory control.
    d. a help for women learning to experience orgasm.

28.
K
Answer: b
p. 241
Obj. #3

Masturbation when married
    a. is often a sign of dissatisfaction with the partner.
    b. is common.
    c. is likely to cut down on the frequency of intercourse.
    d. is associated with dissatisfaction for women but not men.

29.
K
Answer: d
p. 241
Obj. #3

With respect to the frequency of masturbation,
    a. women and men both do this more in their teens than twenties.
    b. it is unhealthy to never do this.
    c. it is probably unhealthy (psychologically) to do it more than once a day.
    d. college men do this more frequently than do college women.

30.
K
Answer: a
p. 242
Obj. #3d

Which of the following individuals would be **most** likely to masturbate?
    a. a married, college educated white man
    b. a married, high school educated African-American man
    c. a single, college educated African-American woman
    d. a single, high school educated Hispanic woman

31.
K
Answer: c
p. 242
Obj. #3e

During self-pleasuring exercises
    a. you should always keep your eyes close so as not to be distracted.
    b. avoid lotions or oils so you can see how excited you are naturally.
    c. you should probably learn to be less genitally focused.
    d. you should avoid fantasies as they will distract you from body awareness.

32.
K
Answer: b
p. 242
Obj. #3e

With respect to self-pleasuring techniques, which one is NOT true?
    a. This is also known by some as masturbation.
    b. This is something that your authors believe everyone should try.
    c. This is likely to require at least an hour in time as well as privacy.
    d. This is often anxiety producing when first attempted.

33.
K
Answer: a
p. 243
Obj. #3e

Which of the following masturbatory techniques is **least** common among women?
    a. inserting a finger or penis-shaped object into the vagina
    b. stroking the mons or clitoris
    c. pressing the thighs together and tensing the pelvic floor muscles
    d. thrusting the clitoral area against a pillow

34.
K
Answer: c
p. 243
Obj. #3e

Vibrators, or sex toys
a. are often dangerous and should be avoided.
b. are primarily used by homosexuals.
c. are devices that women are even more enthusiastic about than are men.
d. are meant to be used only in the genital area.

35.
K
Answer: a
p. 243
Obj. #3e

With respect to techniques for masturbation,
a. both men and women may rub their genitals against a pillow.
b. men need lotion.
c. women should primarily stimulate the glans of the clitoris.
d. books detailing these are often on the NY Times bestseller list.

36.
K
Answer: d
p. 244
Obj. #3a

It is the authors' view that masturbation
a. should be practiced regularly by adults to increase sexual awareness and expression.
b. is healthy for adults but should be discouraged in children.
c. can detract from healthy adult sexual expression.
d. is an option for sexual expression.

37.
K
Answer: b
p. 244
Obj. n/a

A dildo
a. is a set of balls.
b. is an artificial penis.
c. is a latex simulation of female genitals.
d. is a medical device requiring a prescription.

38.
K
Answer: c
p. 244
Obj. n/a

The vibrator
a. was the first sexual toy.
b. has been around for thousands of years.
c. was originally a replacement for medical manual stimulation for the female genitals.
d. has been banned by the Catholic Church.

39.
K
Answer: c
p. 245
Obj. #4

The Maltz hierarchy of sexual interactions is a model that clarifies
a. the degree to which kissing, oral sex, intercourse, etc. are considered intimate sexual behaviors.
b. the frequency with which various sexual behaviors occur in heterosexual relationships.
c. the degree to which sexual energy is positively or negatively expressed.
d. the gender differences that exist regarding genitally focused and nongenitally focused sexual activity.

40.
K
Answer: d
p. 245
Obj. n/a

With respect to sexual practices, which is NOT true?
a. Females are more likely than males to prefer foreplay over coitus.
b. Foreplay may be thought of as how partners have treated one another since the last sexual experience together.
c. Gay men and lesbians sexual repertoire is often more expansive than heterosexuals.
d. Sex ending in orgasm is never an act of selfishness.

41.
K
Answer: c
p. 245
Obj. #4

Which of the following statements regarding the Maltz hierarchy of sexual interactions is true?
a. Sexual energy is viewed as a primarily positive force.
b. There are eight levels of sexual energy.
c. Authentic sexual intimacy may characterize an entire lovemaking experience or a momentary peak experience.
d. A person whose gender role largely defines their sexual experience is at level +3.

42.
A
Answer: c
pp. 245-247
Obj. #4

Raoul has forced Elissa to have intercourse with him on several occasions. According to the Maltz hierarchy, Raoul
a. cannot be rated as we don't know whether or not Raoul and Elissa are married.
b. Raoul is at a zero.
c. Raoul is at -2.
d. has probably selected a partner with a minus rating.

43.
A
Answer: c
pp. 245-247
Obj. #4

Janie is cohabiting with Louie. When they make love she feels that this is an erotic recreational experience that is helping to create intimacy. According to the Maltz hierarchy, Janie is
a. at a zero as she is not committed.
b. Trying Tantric sex.
c. At level +2.
d. Unable to be rated because we do not know what Louie thinks about this.

44.
A
Answer: b
pp. 245-247
Obj. #4

When Joel want to have sex with a woman, he encourages her to think that he cares about her more than he in fact does. According to the Maltz hierarchy, Joel
a. is at a zero level.
b. is at -1 level, impersonal interaction.
c. is at -2 level, abusive interaction.
d. is at -3 level.

45.
A
Answer: c
pp. 245-247
Obj. #4

Vernon sends cards saying he loves Joanne and shortly moves in to her condo. They have frequent sex that is satisfying for both of them. But in a few months when Joanne asks Vernon to pay for his share of the living expenses he moves out. According to the Maltz hierarchy, Vernon probably
a. cannot be rated as they weren't together long enough.
b. is. is a cad.
c. is at -1. impersonal interaction.
d. is at -2, abusive interaction.

46.
A
Answer: b
pp. 245-247
Obj. #4

When Lucille has sex with her husband, he prefers that he initiate and is pleased that both get their sexual needs met. According to the Maltz hierarchy, Lucille is at level
a. +1
b. +2
c. +3
d. +4

47.
A
Answer: b
pp. 245-247
Obj. #1
WWW

Rebecca has herpes, and although she is sexually active, she does not share this information with her partners for fear of their rejection. According to the Maltz hierarchy of sexual interaction, Rebecca would probably be at level
a. 0
b. -1
c. -2
d. -3

48.
A
Answer: b
pp. 245-247
Obj. #4

According to the Maltz hierarchy, a rapist is at the _____ level of sexual expression.
a. -4
b. -3
c. -2
d. -1

49.
K
Answer: c
p. 248
Obj. #5
WWW

A classic study (Harlow and Harlow) demonstrated that when baby monkeys were denied physical contact with their mothers,
a. they were able to readily transfer their affection and attachment to wire mesh substitute mothers.
b. it negatively affected their subsequent motor development and coordination.
c. they grew up to be extremely maladjusted.
d. they became vulnerable to a wide range of physical illnesses.

50.
K
Answer: c
p. 248
Obj. #5

Which of the following **best** reflects Masters and Johnson's views on touching?
a. Second only to what stimulates us visually, touch is an important aspect of sexual communication.
b. Touching is overemphasized; the emphasis should be on verbal communication during sex.
c. Touch is a primary form of communication — an end in itself.
d. The process of shared touching is what culminates in the ultimate goal of sexual union.

51.
K
Answer: d
p. 248
Obj. #5

Which of the following statements concerning breast stimulation is false?
a. Many men and women find breast stimulation arousing.
b. Some men and women find breast stimulation unpleasant.
c. Some women reach orgasm from breast stimulation alone.
d. The size of a woman's breasts is related to how erotically sensitive they are.

52.
K
Answer: b
p. 249
Obj. #5

All of the following are recommended as lubricants for manual stimulation **except**
a. K-Y jelly
b. Vaseline
c. a lotion without alcohol
d. saliva

53.
K
Answer: d
p. 249
Obj. #6

Which on is NOT true with respect to stimulation of the genital area?
a. This should not be done with a finger also used for anal stimulation.
b. Women differ from time to time in their preference for kind of genital touch.
c. Men may desire different kinds of strokes and touch at different times during arousal.
d. Oral-genital contact may result in orgasm for men, but it does not do so for women.

54.
K
Answer: c
p. 249
Obj. #6

"69"
a. is a sex practice largely restricted to lesbians.
b. is a sex practice largely restricted to gay males.
c. refers to simultaneous oral-genital stimulation.
d. refers to the grade required for passing this course.

55.
K
Answer: a
p. 250
Obj. #6

_____ is oral stimulation of the vulva.
a. Cunnilingus
b. Fellatio
c. Vulvalingus
d. Oralingus

56.
K
Answer: d
p. 250
Obj. #6

The reservations that some people have concerning oral sex usually stem from all of the following beliefs **except**
a. It is a homosexual act.
b. It is unsanitary.
c. It cannot result in pregnancy.
d. It is an activity in which lower class people are more likely to participate.

57.
K
Answer: d
pp. 250-252
Obj. #6

Which of the following statements regarding oral-genital stimulation is false?
a. HIV may be transmitted this way.
b. This behavior is illegal in some states.
c. This behavior is a type of sodomy.
d. According to Kinsey's research, fellatio was more common than cunnilingus among heterosexual couples.

58
K
Answer: b
p. 251
Obj. #6

Kinsey's research indicated that, in heterosexual couples,
a. men were less likely to stimulate their partners orally than the reverse.
b. women were less likely to stimulate their partners orally than the reverse.
c. men and women were equally likely to stimulate their partners orally.
d. oral sex was rarely practiced by men or women.

59.
K
Answer: d
p. 251
Obj. #10

Which of the following individuals would be **least** likely to experience oral sex?
a. an African-American, college educated man
b. a white, high school educated Catholic man
c. a white, college educated, conservative Protestant woman
d. an African-American, high school educated, conservative Protestant woman

60.
K
Answer: c
p. 251
Obj. #10
WWW

A recent study comparing rates of oral sex experience between African-American and white men indicated that _____ may be more important than race in sexual behavior.
a. religious affiliation
b. marital status
c. socioeconomic status
d. age

61.
K
Answer: a
p. 251
Obj. #10

Which of the following would be **least** likely to affect oral sex experience among various racial groups?
a. marital status
b. educational level
c. religious affiliation
d. socioeconomic status

62.
K
Answer: d
p. 251
Obj. #6
WWW

Kinsey's research revealed that the _____ was **most** likely to have experienced oral-genital sex.
a. person who has no formal education
b. grade school-educated person
c. high school-educated person
d. college-educated person

63.
K
Answer: a
p. 252
Obj. #7

_____ is one of the riskiest of all sexual behaviors associated with the transmission of HIV.
a. Anal intercourse
b. Fellatio
c. Cunnilingus
d. Penile-vaginal intercourse

64.
K
Answer: a
p. 252
Obj. #7

According to a 1991 study, anal intercourse is practiced regularly by about _____ percent of heterosexual couples.
a. 10
b. 20
c. 30
d. 40

65.
K
Answer: c
p. 252
Obj. #7

According to a 1994 survey, approximately _____% of adults have experienced anal intercourse at least once.
a. 5
b. 10
c. 25
d. 40

Chapter 9 Sexual Behaviors   197

66.
K
Answer: d
p. 252
Obj. #7

Which of the following statements concerning anal stimulation is false?
a. It is possible for a woman to experience orgasm during anal intercourse.
b. Oral stimulation of the anus is a high-risk behavior.
c. A lubricant should always be used with anal intercourse.
d. For women, the risk of contracting the AIDS virus through unprotected anal intercourse is the same as the risk through unprotected vaginal intercourse.

67.
A
Answer: a
p. 252
Obj. #7

For heterosexual couples who practice anal intercourse, which of the following recommendations would be **most** helpful?
a. If planning to have vaginal intercourse as well, do it prior to having anal intercourse.
b. Practice analingus prior to penetration.
c. Use a good lubricant such as Vaseline.
d. Contract the sphincter prior to penetration for ease of insertion.

68.
K
Answer: b
p. 252
Obj. #8

Homosexual sexual behaviors
a. are unique to homosexual relationships.
b. are very similar to heterosexual behavior.
c. do not typically result in orgasm.
d. require a certain degree of agility that discourages heterosexuals from trying them.

69.
K
Answer: b
p. 252
Obj. #8
WWW

Which of the following statements regarding lesbian sexual expression is true?
a. Lesbians tend to have more frequent sexual encounters with their partners than heterosexual women do.
b. Lesbians tend to have orgasms in a greater percentage of sexual encounters than heterosexual married women do.
c. Dildos are used extensively among lesbians.
d. Tribadism is practiced among a small minority of lesbians.

70.
K
Answer: a
pp. 252-253
Obj. #18

Research has demonstrated that lesbians have an orgasm rate that is _____ heterosexual women.
a. greater than
b. equal to
c. less than
d. significantly less than

71.
K
Answer: d
p. 253
Obj. #8

In a survey comparing lesbian vs. heterosexual women's most recent sexual experience, which of the following statements is false?
a. More lesbians than heterosexual women received oral sex.
b. Over twice as many lesbians as heterosexual women had experiences that lasted more than one hour.
c. Almost twice as many lesbians as heterosexual women had more than one orgasm.
d. For heterosexual women, the time interval between the most recent experience and the previous one was greater than that of lesbians.

72.
K
Answer: a
p. 253
Obj. #8

Which of the following is probably the **least** common form of sexual behavior among lesbians?
a. using dildos for vaginal penetration
b. manual stimulation
c. rubbing genitals against partner's
d. oral stimulation

73.
K
Answer: c
p. 253
Obj. #8
WWW

Many lesbians enjoy tribadism because
a. it enhances the possibility of G-spot stimulation.
b. the nerve endings that surround the vaginal opening are stimulated in this way.
c. it involves all-over body contact and generalized sensuality.
d. as a form of oral-genital stimulation, it maximizes the capacity for orgasmic response.

74.
K
Answer: b
p. 253
Obj. #8

The term for rubbing genitals against another person's body is called
a. sensate focus.
b. tribadism.
c. rimming.
d. body pressing.

75.
K
Answer: b
p. 253
Obj. #8

Which one is most likely true with respect to the frequency of lesbian couple and compared to heterosexual couple sex?
a. Lesbian couples have sex more frequently than heterosexual couples.
b. Lesbian couples have sex less frequently than heterosexual couples.
c. Lesbian couples have sex with the same frequency as heterosexual couples.
d. Research data have revealed contradictory findings.

76.
K
Answer: d
p. 254
Obj. #8

The **most** prevalent forms of sexual behavior between homosexual men are, in order of frequency,
a. mutual masturbation, fellatio, anal intercourse.
b. tribadism, anal intercourse, fellatio.
c. anal intercourse, fellatio, mutual masturbation.
d. fellatio, mutual masturbation, anal intercourse.

77.
K
Answer: d
p. 254
Obj. #8

A survey of gay men found that _____ % liked hugging, kissing, and snuggling.
a. 25
b. 45
c. 65
d. 85

78.
K
Answer: a
p. 254
Obj. #8

Which of the following is the **most** prevalent form of sexual behavior between homosexual men?
a. fellatio
b. manual stimulation
c. tribadism
d. anal intercourse

Chapter 9 Sexual Behaviors 199

79.
K
Answer: a
p. 255
Obj. #9

This is a good position to use during pregnancy.
a. rear-entry
b. face-to-face, side-lying
c. woman above
d. man above

80.
K
Answer: d
p. 255
Obj. #9
WWW

In a recent survey, when college men and women were asked to respond to the question, "What is your favorite intercourse position?", the majority of women said _____, and the majority of men said _____.
a. "woman on top"; "doggie style"
b. "woman on top"; "woman on top"
c. "man on top"; "doggie style"
d. "man on top"; "woman on top"

81.
K
Answer: b
p. 257
Obj. #9

_____ refers to entry of the penis into the vagina.
a. Introital penetration
b. Intromission
c. Coitus
d. Penile intrusion

82.
K
Answer: a
p. 257
Obj. #11

Tantric sex
a. emphasizes spiritual aspects.
b. was developed in Africa.
c. is done in temples.
d. should be done while fasting.

83.
K
Answer: c
pp. 257-258
Obj. #9

A 1998 survey of the United States found all but which one of the following?
a. The national average frequency of sex is once a week.
b. Sexual activity lasts on the average one half hour.
c. Unmarried adults have sex more often than married couples.
d. Persons who work more hours have sex more often.

84.
K
Answer: b
p. 258
Obj. #12

According to Mosher
a. Tantric sex should be practiced in the United States.
b. a couple's sexual compatibility can be influenced by their differences in sexual styles.
c. sexual styles are primarily defined by ones preferences for certain sexual behaviors.
d. individuals can be fairly easily and consistently categorized into one of three sexual styles.

85.
K
Answer: b
p. 258
Obj. #12

Which one is NOT true in Mosher's sexual styles system?
a. The sexual trance style usually finds talking more a distraction than an enhancement.
b. The role-play style seeks novelty and a variety of settings.
c. The partner-engagement style uses lots of face-to-face and full body contact.
d. The erotic-artistic style prefers fantasy and such things as dance or body paints.

Multiple Choice from Study Guide

1.
K
Answer: c
p. 234
Obj. #1

Since he joined Alcoholics Anonymous last month, Frank has decided to refrain from having sexual contact, although he continues to masturbate. Frank appears to have chosen
   a. asceticism.
   b. autoerotic exclusivity.
   c. partial celibacy.
   d. complete celibacy.

2.
K
Answer: b
p. 235
Obj. #1

Reasons for choosing celibacy include all of the following **except**
   a. Wanting to establish new relationships without the complications of sexual interaction.
   b. Having the desire to avoid forming new relationships, so celibacy is used as an excuse.
   c. The person is new to recovery from drug or alcohol dependency.
   d. Waiting until one's standards for a sexual relationship have been met.

3.
K
Answer: d
p. 236
Obj. #2c

The **most** common fantasy reported by men and women during masturbation is
   a. being forced to have sex.
   b. sexual activities that could not be done in real life.
   c. sex with more than one person.
   d. intercourse with a loved one.

4.
K
Answer: a
p. 236
Obj. #2d

Fantasies that occur during intercourse are **least** likely to serve the purpose of
   a. relieving boredom.
   b. facilitating sexual arousal.
   c. increasing a partner's attractiveness.
   d. imaging forbidden activities.

5.
K
Answer: b
p. 238
Obj. #2

Which of the following statements about sexual fantasies among women and men is true?
   a. Men have fantasies during sexual activity with a partner more frequently than women.
   b. Women are more likely to use romance in their sexual fantasies.
   c. Women are more likely to have fantasies involving dominance.
   d. Men are less likely to have fantasies involving multiple partners.

6.
K
Answer: c
p. 239
Obj. #2

Among college students, the **most** threatening fantasy a partner could have was about
   a. sex with a member of the same sex.
   b. sex with a famous person or movie star.
   c. sex with a mutual friend or classmate.
   d. oral sex.

Chapter 9 Sexual Behaviors 201

7.
K
Answer: a
pp. 239-240
Obj. #3

Which of the following persons did NOT espouse negative views about masturbation?
 a. Dodson
 b. Tissot
 c. Graham
 d. Kellogg

8.
K
Answer: c
p. 242
Obj. #3

Rates of masturbation are lowest among
 a. white women.
 b. college educated, Asian men.
 c. Hispanic women.
 d. African American women.

9.
K
Answer: c
pp. 241-242
Obj. #3

Which statement is true regarding masturbation among married and partnered persons?
 a. Masturbation is a sign that there is something wrong in the relationship.
 b. Masturbation rates decrease sharply during the first year of togetherness.
 c. Masturbation occurs more often among those who have partnered sex more frequently.
 d. Masturbation occurs more often among couples who have partnered sex less frequently.

10.
K
Answer: c
pp. 245-246
Obj. #4

Dave and Sam feel they can best express the profound love they feel for each other when they are sexually intimate, and they enjoy a sense of deep connection and spiritual ecstasy when they are together sexually. According to the Maltz Hierarchy, this couple is at
 a. Level +1, Positive Role Fulfillment.
 b. Level +2, Making Love.
 c. Level +3, Authentic Sexual Intimacy.
 d. Level -1, Impersonal Interaction.

11.
K
Answer: d
p. 250
Obj. #6

_____ is to penis as _____ is to vulva.
 a. penilingus; cunnilingus
 b. fellatio; vulvalingus
 c. penilingus; vulvalingus;
 d. fellatio; cunnilingus

12.
K
Answer: b
p. 250
Obj. #6

People feel ill-at-ease with oral-genital stimulation for all of the following reasons **except**
 a. Oral sex is considered a homosexual activity.
 b. The "69" position has a higher risk of HIV transmission.
 c. Genitals are thought to be dirty.
 d. Sodomy is illegal in many states.

13.
K
Answer: a
p. 251
Obj. #6

Who is **most** likely to participate in oral-genital sex?
 a. a college educated African American woman
 b. a high school educated African American woman
 c. an Hispanic woman without a high school diploma
 d. an Asian-American homemaker without a high school diploma

202 Test Bank to Accompany *Our Sexuality*

14.
K
Answer: a
p. 252
Obj. #7

Which statement is true regarding anal stimulation?
a. 25% of adults have experienced anal intercourse at least once.
b. nearly ¾ of gay men consider this their most preferred sexual activity.
c. women cannot reach orgasm from anal intercourse.
d. 5% of heterosexual couples practice anal intercourse regularly.

15.
K
Answer: c
pp. 252-254
Obj. #8

All of the following are characteristic of lesbian sexual expression **except**
a. lesbian sexual relations last longer than those of heterosexual women.
b. lesbians are more likely to experience orgasm.
c. the use of dildos is common in lesbian sexual encounters.
d. nongenital sexual interaction is more common among lesbians than heterosexual women.

16.
K
Answer: d
p. 254
Obj. #8

Research shows that the **most** common form of sexual expression among gay men is
a. interfemoral intercourse.
b. anal intercourse.
c. mutual masturbation.
d. fellatio.

17.
K
Answer: b
p. 255
Obj. #9

Which of the following coital positions would be **most** comfortable for a pregnant woman who wants to avoid pressure on her abdomen?
a. woman on top, woman lying down
b. rear-entry
c. man above, face to face
d. face to face, side lying

18.
K
Answer: a
p. 258
Obj. #12

Mosher's styles of sexual expression include
a. sexual trance, partner engagement, and role play.
b. sexual hypnosis, partner engagement, authentic enhancement.
c. sexual trance, romantic engagement, mutual role play.
d. sexual hypnosis, partner engagement, and role play.

True/False

Students may be asked to answer these questions using the traditional format of marking their answers either "true" or "false". Or, to encourage more active involvement, you may choose to use the following instructions:

If the statement is true, place a "T" on the line preceding it. If the statement is false, place an "F" on the line preceding it and then change the statement to make it true by deleting incorrect information and/or adding accurate information.

1.
Answer: F
p. 234
Obj. #1

___ There are two types of celibacy: celibacy as a result of religious devotion, and celibacy as a commitment to personal and physical health.

2.
Answer: T
p. 235
Obj. #2b

___ Women as well as men may experience nocturnal orgasms.

3.
Answer: T
p. 236
Obj. #2a

___ A recent research summary revealed that 95% of men and women reported having had sexual fantasies.

4.
Answer: F
p. 238
Obj. #2f

___ Although some sexual fantasy is generally considered healthy, most sexual fantasy is considered to be indicative of poor relationships or other sexual problems.

5.
Answer: F
p. 239
Obj. #3a

___ Tissot, a European physician during the eighteenth century, felt that masturbation was healthy during childhood but could result in unhealthy sexual relationships if practiced as an adult.

6.
Answer: F
pp. 240-241
Obj. #3c

___ Masturbation is generally considered a healthy practice throughout the life cycle, although it is discouraged while in a relationship because it excludes the other partner and deprives him or her of pleasure.

7.
Answer: T
p. 241
Obj. #3d

___ One recent study revealed that married women who masturbated to orgasm had greater marital and sexual satisfaction than women who did not masturbate.

8.
Answer: T
p. 242
Obj. #3d

___ White men and women masturbate more than African-American or Hispanic men and women.

9.
Answer: F
p. 243
Obj. #3e

___ A majority of women use vaginal penetration in addition to clitoral stimulation to reach orgasm during masturbation.

10.
Answer: F
p. 244
Obj. #3a

___ The authors recommend regular masturbation as a way to promote and maintain good sexual health and awareness.

11.
Answer: F
p. 246
Obj. #4

___ Level -1 in the Maltz hierarchy of sexual energy describes sex that is used to express anger.

12.
Answer: T
p. 247
Obj. #5

____ Open mouth kissing is also known as "French" kissing and is usually more sexually intense than kissing with closed mouths.

13.
Answer: T
p. 250
Obj. #6

____ Kinsey's research revealed that among heterosexuals, cunnilingus was more common than fellatio.

14.
Answer: T
p. 251
Obj. #6

____ Current research indicates that although oral-genital contact is more common than ever before, it is still practiced most frequently among college-educated couples.

15.
Answer: T
p. 251
Obj. #10

____ Socioeconomic status may be more important than race in comparing oral sex experience between African-American and white men.

16.
Answer: T
p. 252
Obj. #7

____ Some women experience orgasm as a result of being anally penetrated by their partners.

17.
Answer: T
p. 252
Obj. #7

____ Recent research indicates that approximately ten percent of heterosexual couples engage in anal intercourse on a regular basis.

18.
Answer: F
p. 253
Obj. #8

____ A slight majority of lesbian women commonly use a dildo for one or both of the partners

19.
Answer: T
p. 264
Obj. #8

____ Anal intercourse is the least common sexual behavior used by homosexual men.

20.
Answer: T
p. 264
Obj. #9

____ The favorite intercourse position for college men is woman on top while the favorite position for college women is man on top.

Short Answer Essay

1. Define celibacy, identifying two types of celibacy. Discuss what factors may contribute to a person becoming celibate. (Obj. #1)

2. Discuss the frequency and nature of sexual fantasies during either masturbation or intercourse. (Obj. #2)

3. Discuss differences between the sexes in the frequency, nature, or purpose of sexual fantasies. Speculate about why these reported differences might occur (Obj. #2)

4. Discuss both positive and negative aspects of sexual fantasies and some things that are important for individuals and couples to keep in mind concerning fantasies. (Obj. #2)

5. Compare historical and contemporary attitudes and beliefs about masturbation. Include both societal and religious views. (Obj. #3)

6. Discuss some of the reasons why people might masturbate. Consider both sexes, and unattached and coupled individuals. (Obj. #3)

7. Maltz has a six level model of sexual interaction that includes both positive and negative interactions. Describe the variables included in this model and indicate how it might be useful or significant. (Obj. #4)

8. Define cunnilingus and fellatio. Explain why some people may feel uncomfortable with or have negative views regarding these behaviors. Obj. #6)

9. What does research say concerning how experience with oral sex is associated with the factors of race, education, religion and socioeconomic status? (Obj. #6)

10. What does your book report concerning preference for the use of various coital positions? What are the reasons for why couples might choose as particular one? (Obj. #9)

11. How common is anal stimulation? What are some of the risks associated with this behavior and how can they be minimized? (Obj. #7)

12. How do gay males sexual experiences compare to those of heterosexual men's? (Obj. #8)

13. How do lesbians' sexual experiences compare to those of heterosexual women's? (Obj. #8)

14. Describe the history and process of Tantric sex. How might this practice benefit couples who have been familiar with primarily Western models of heterosexual intercourse? (Obj. n/a)

15. Mosher describes three "sexual styles". List and briefly describe these. (Obj. #12)

10

Sexual Orientations

Learning Objectives

After studying this chapter, the student should be able to:

1. Define the following terms: homosexual, gay, lesbian, sexual orientation, and bisexual.

2. Describe Kinsey's continuum of sexual orientation and discuss how his estimates of the incidence of homosexuality in the general population compare to the findings in the National Health and Social Life Survey.

3. Discuss bisexuality and the problems in defining it, and compare it to other sexual orientations.

4. Briefly outline and describe how attitudes toward homosexuality have evolved over time, beginning with Judeo-Christian tradition in the seventh century B.C.

5. List and describe four current positions toward homosexuality represented in contemporary Christianity.

6. Discuss some cross-cultural perspectives on homosexuality, citing specific examples.

7. Define homophobia, discuss various ways in which it may be expressed, and explain how homophobic attitudes can change.

8. Define what a hate crime is, how hate crime affect homosexuals, and legislative attempts to control hate crimes.

9. Making reference to relevant research, discuss the psychosocial and biological theories regarding how sexual orientation develops.

10. Discuss what research has revealed regarding the following:
    a. homosexual relationships
    b. homosexual family life

11. Define "coming out" and describe steps that may be involved in that process.

12. Discuss some of the significant events in the gay rights movement, beginning with the 1950s and continuing to the present time.

13. Discuss the goals of the gay right movement.

14. Making reference to specific films and television programs, discuss how the portrayal of homosexuality has changed over the last decade.

15. Citing specific Native American, Hispanic, African-American and Asian-American examples, discuss the impact of being an individual who is both gay and a member of an ethnic minority group.

16. Discuss the effectiveness of various conversion therapies.

Multiple Choice

1.
A
Answer: c
p. 261
Obj. #1

Which of the following is NOT true concerning the term "gay"?
a. This may refer to either men or women.
b. This was first used by homosexuals to refer to themselves.
c. This term is used to refer to homosexuals who have deliberately chosen this lifestyle.
d. This is often used by teens as a pejorative word, similar to faggot.

2.
A
Answer: b
pp. 261-262
Obj. #1

Which of the following statements about a person who is a homosexual is false?
a. A person may be homosexual despite having never had same-sex sexual contact.
b. Lesbians or gay males who refer to themselves as "queer" have a low self-concept.
c. A person may be in a heterosexual marriage, have children, and still be homosexual.
d. Most often, men who are in prison who have sex with other men are heterosexual.

3.
K
Answer: d
p. 262
Obj. #1
WWW

Sexual orientation is **best** evaluated by
a. A person's sexual behavior at a given point in time.
b. Analyzing the content of a person's sexual fantasies over a given length of time.
c. A description of a person's sexual self-identity at a given point in time.
d. Observing a person's patterns of sexual thoughts and behavior over a lifetime.

4.
K
Answer: a
p. 262
Obj. #2

Which of the following **best** describes Kinsey's continuum of sexual orientation?
a. a seven-point scale ranging from 0 (exclusive heterosexual contact and attraction) to 6 (exclusive homosexual contact and attraction).
b. a six-point scale ranging from 1 (exclusive homosexual contact and attraction) to 6 (exclusive heterosexual contact and attraction).
c. a ten-point scale ranging from 0 (exclusive homosexual contact and attraction) to 9 (exclusive heterosexual contact and attraction).
d. a five-point scale ranging from 1 (exclusive heterosexual contact and attraction) to 5 (exclusive homosexual contact and attraction).

5.
K
Answer: c
p. 262
Obj. #2

Which one is NOT true with respect to the incidence of homosexuality?
   a. More men than women identify themselves as homosexuals.
   b. About 1 in 20 of the NHSL survey reported feelings of attraction to someone of the same sex.
   c. More people now identify themselves as homosexual than in Kinsey's samples.
   d. How many are categorized as homosexual apparently depends on how you ask the question.

6.
K
Answer: a
p. 263
Obj. #3

Relatively speaking, bisexual people appear to have a _____ degree of general erotic interest.
   a. high
   b. moderate
   c. below average
   d. extremely low

7.
K
Answer: b
p. 263
Obj. #3

All of the following are types of bisexuality discussed in the text **except**
   a. bisexuality as a transitory orientation.
   b. bisexuality as a result of gender nonconformity.
   c. bisexuality as a transitional orientation.
   d. bisexuality as the result of homosexual denial.

8.
A
Answer: a
p. 263
Obj. #3

A man who has had sexual contact with and has fantasized about women all of his life is sent to prison where, for the duration of his sentence, he has sexual contact with men. Upon his release, he once again has exclusive sexual contact with women. According to information presented in the text, this man would **best** be described as
   a. a transitory bisexual.
   b. a transitional bisexual.
   c. a man experiencing homosexual denial.
   d. a true bisexual.

9.
A
Answer: d
pp. 263-264
Obj. #3
WWW

Casey is equally attracted to men and women, both sexually and emotionally. She is always involved in monogamous relationships that are usually heterosexual, primarily because she feels the social pressures of same sex relationships are difficult to manage. Casey would **best** be described as
   a. a transitory bisexual.
   b. a transitional bisexual.
   c. a woman experiencing homosexual denial.
   d. a true bisexual.

10.
A
Answer: a
p. 263
Obj. #3

Derek has had heterosexual relationships and fantasies about women throughout his adulthood, although he occasionally has sex with men for the money. Derek would **bes**t be described as
   a. a transitory bisexual.
   b. a transitional bisexual.
   c. a man experiencing homosexual denial.
   d. a true bisexual.

11.
A
Answer: b
p. 263
Obj. #3

Jason attended an all male boarding school for several years in which he engaged in sex with several schoolmates. Prior to attending boarding school, Jason had sexual and emotional relationships with women, and after he left the boarding school, he resumed having relationships with women. He would **best** be described as
   a. a true bisexual.
   b. a transitory bisexual.
   c. a transitional bisexual.
   d. a man experiencing homosexual denial.

12.
A
Answer: c
pp. 263-264
Obj. #3

Imelda is married and has two children, although she occasionally has sex with other women and fantasizes exclusively about other women. She admits to herself that she would rather be involved in a relationship with a woman, but the rejection she knows she would experience from her family and friends inhibits her pursuit of that lifestyle. She would **best** be described as
   a. a true bisexual.
   b. a transitional bisexual.
   c. a woman experiencing homosexual denial.
   d. a transitory bisexual.

13.
K
Answer: a
p. 264
Obj. #9

Which of the following is the **best** explanation of the "by default" theory of homosexual orientation?
   a. inability to attract partners of the other sex will sometimes result in a person becoming homosexual
   b. people become homosexual because they have been seduced by older homosexuals
   c. a distant relationship with his father and an overly close relationship with his mother might result in a man becoming homosexual
   d. a homosexual orientation may result from gender nonconforming play in childhood and subsequent attraction in adulthood to partners who differ from the preferred sex of our childhood playmates

14.
K
Answer: b
p. 264
Obj. #9
WWW

According to Bell's research, which of the following statements is true?
   a. During high school, homosexual people tend to date less frequently than heterosexual people.
   b. Most homosexual people have their first homosexual experience with someone close to their own age.
   c. It appears that sexual orientation is influenced primarily by childhood experiences and relationships with parents.
   d. During high school, homosexual people reported that they enjoyed dating to the same extent that heterosexual people did.

Chapter 10 Sexual Orientations 211

15.
K
Answer: c
p. 264
Obj. #9

Which of the following statements concerning lesbians is true?
a. In general, lesbians are less attractive than heterosexual women.
b. According to Bell's research, homosexual women dated less frequently during high school than heterosexual women.
c. The majority of lesbians have had sexual relationships with men.
d. Lesbianism is usually the result of distrust of men rather than attraction toward women.

16.
K
Answer: d
p. 265
Obj. #9

Research by Alan Bell and his colleagues on the family backgrounds of homosexuals has
a. found relationships for women but not men.
b. confirmed the pattern of a dominant, overprotective mother.
c. confirmed the pattern of an abusive, violent father.
d. found a few cases associated with father-son relationships but no strong overall relationship with family pattern.

17.
K
Answer: a
p. 265
Obj. #9

What have most contemporary sexologists concluded about the role of the family in the development of sexual orientation?
a. There are many variations in the family dynamics of homosexual men and women.
b. The relationship with the same sex parent is more critical than the relationship with the opposite sex parent.
c. The parents' relationship with each other is more critical than their relationship with each of their children.
d. The families of gay men are more disturbed than those of lesbians.

18.
K
Answer: c
p. 265
Obj. #9

According to Freud, which of the following statements is true?
a. If a boy has an overly close relationship with his father and a distant relationship with his mother he is likely to develop a homosexual orientation.
b. If a girl has an overly close relationship with her mother and a distant relationship with her father, she is likely to develop a homosexual orientation.
c. Passing through a "homoerotic" phase is a normal part of psychosexual development.
d. Having homosexual encounters for the first time as an adult may cause gender dysphoria.

19.
K
Answer: b
p. 265
Obj. #9

Which of the following **best** describes Bem's "exotic becomes erotic" theory of homosexual development?
a. A homosexual orientation may develop as the result of a classically conditioned fetish involving certain clothing of the other sex.
b. A homosexual orientation may result from gender nonconforming play in childhood and subsequent attraction in adulthood to partners who differ from the preferred sex of our childhood playmates.
c. A homosexual orientation may develop as a result of what begins as casual experimentation with same sex behavior.
d. A homosexual orientation may develop as the result of parents who inadvertently encourage gender nonconforming play in their children.

20.
K
Answer: b
pp. 265-266
Obj. #9
WWW

The occurrence of same-sex relationships
a. is a matter of choice for most individuals.
b. is more a matter of choice for women than men.
c. probably results from early seductions by someone older of the same sex.
d. is associated with circulating sex hormone levels.

21.
K
Answer: a
p. 266
Obj. #9

Animals who have been given other-sex hormones prenatally
a. exhibit other-sex mating behavior.
b. demonstrate a higher frequency of mating behavior than is typical.
c. demonstrate reduced interest in mating behavior.
d. exhibit no interest in mating behavior.

22.
K
Answer: c
p. 266
Obj. #9

Research on the relative length of index to ring finger
a. has primarily been done with young boys who are gender nonconforming.
b. has been used to suggest a genetic factor for homosexuality.
c. found lesbian finger lengths more like the typical male pattern than heterosexual females.
d. has been another dead end in the search for biological markers.

23.
K
Answer: c
pp. 266-267
Obj. #9

Investigations of homosexuality and handedness suggest
a. that there is no relationship.
b. that at least 39% of the left handed will become homosexual.
c. a prenatal influence for some homosexuality.
d. schools should try to change "lefties" to the predominant mode.

24.
K
Answer: a
p. 267
Obj. #9

In several research studies, the incidence of homosexual orientation was greater for those siblings of a homosexual male who were
a. an identical twin.
b. a fraternal twin.
c. an adoptive brother.
d. a half-brother.

25.
K
Answer: d
p. 267
Obj. #9

Which one is NOT true concerning concordance rates?
a. This refers to the similarity of identical twins on a particular trait.
b. This depends upon the particular sample used.
c. They provide clear evidence for a genetic component for some homosexual individuals an adoptive brother.
d. This is a measure of gender nonconformity.

26.
K
Answer: b
p. 268
Obj. #9

Research to find a genetic marker for homosexuality
a. is no longer being funded by the government.
b. has sometimes found a gene concordance and sometimes not.
c. has consistently found a "gay gene" for nontwin gay brothers.
d. is difficult to do because it is done with postmortem subjects.

27.
K
Answer: c
p. 268
Obj. #9

Gender nonconformity rates in childhood are
a. higher for female homosexuals than heterosexuals.
b. higher for male homosexuals than heterosexuals.
c. higher for both female and male homosexuals than heterosexuals.
d. approximately the same for both homosexuals and heterosexuals

28.
A
Answer: b
p. 268
Obj. #9

All of the following statements by men are examples of gender nonconformity **except**
a. "I hated physical education and sports."
b. "I liked hiking and being outdoors."
c. "I was fond of pretty things like ribbons and flowers and music."
d. "I was more emotional. Things upset me more than they did the other guys."

29.
K
Answer: c
p. 268
Obj. #9

Research has demonstrated that the cognitive patterns of homosexual men (spatial ability and verbal fluency)
a. are similar to those of heterosexual men.
b. are similar to those of heterosexual women.
c. fall between the patterns of heterosexual men and heterosexual women.
d. are more complex and refined than those of heterosexual men or heterosexual women.

30.
K
Answer: d
p. 269
Obj. #9
WWW

A homosexual orientation appears to be the result of
a. seduction during childhood or adolescence by an older homosexual.
b. a family background that includes a dominant mother and a passive, detached father.
c. a hormonal imbalance.
d. There are no definitive conclusions regarding what causes homosexual orientation at this time.

31.
K
Answer: c
pp. 268, 273
Obj. #9

Which of the following statements regarding homosexuals is true?
a. The American Psychiatric and Psychological Associations categorize homosexuality as a mental illness, although few counselors and therapists regard it as such.
b. Changing one's sexual orientation has been highly successful if a combination of cognitive, behavioral and psychodynamic therapy is used.
c. In working with homosexual clients, therapists often try to help them love and live in a society that still harbors considerable hostility toward them.
d. Eliminating gender nonconformity would go a long way to eliminating homosexuality.

32.
A
Answer: c
p. n/a
Obj. #9

An astronaut returning from an extended space voyage in the 25th century reports that on many distant planets there are homosexual groups within the population. This finding shows that homosexuality is
a. environmentally determined.
b. biologically determined.
c. widespread.
d. normal and healthy.

33.
K
Answer: b
p. 269
Obj. #4

Thomas Jefferson was among the political leaders who
a. was a closet homosexual.
b. suggested reducing the punishment from death to castration for men who committed homosexual acts.
c. first promoted a rudimentary conversion program for homosexual men who desired to change their sexual orientation.
d. suggested changing the punishment from incarceration to capital punishment for men who committed homosexual acts.

34.
K
Answer: b
p. 269
Obj. #4

In the seventh century B.C., Jewish religious leaders were able to establish the uniqueness of their religions by
a. glorifying religious rituals involving a range of sexual orientations and behavior.
b. rejecting religious rituals involving homosexual activities.
c. legitimizing sexual behaviors other than intercourse for sexual gratification and pleasure.
d. advocating multiple wives.

35.
K
Answer: d
p. 270
Obj. #6

One survey of 190 societies found that _____ of cultures considered homosexuality acceptable under certain circumstances.
a. one-sixth
b. one-third
c. one-half
d. two-thirds

36.
K
Answer: b
p. 270
Obj. #6
WWW

In ancient Greece, homosexual relationships between men
a. could result in the castration of both men if discovered.
b. were considered a superior intellectual and spiritual expression of love.
c. were required for adolescent males prior to making an exclusive heterosexual marital commitment.
d. could result in the death penalty for both men if discovered.

37.
K
Answer: a
p. 270
Obj. #5
WWW

The 1997 Southern Baptist boycott of Disney might be cited as an example of the theological position of
a. rejecting-punitive.
b. rejecting non-punitive.
c. qualified acceptance.
d. full acceptance.

38.
K
Answer: c
pp. 270-271
Obj. #5

The theological position known as _____ maintains that homosexuality is a sin but tolerates it, believing that it is largely insusceptible to change.
a. rejecting-punitive
b. rejecting non-punitive
c. qualified acceptance
d. full acceptance

39.
K
Answer: b
pp. 270-271
Obj. #5

The theological position known as _____ maintains that homosexuality itself is unnatural and must be condemned, but that the homosexual person's civil liberties should be supported.
a. rejecting-punitive
b. rejecting non-punitive
c. qualified acceptance
d. full acceptance

40.
K
Answer: c
pp. 270-271
Obj. #5

A pastor of a Baptist church in Texas believes homosexuality is a sin but opposed the expulsion of homosexuals from the church. His beliefs probably represent which of the following theological positions?
a. rejecting-punitive
b. qualified acceptance
c. rejecting non-punitive
d. full acceptance

41.
A
Answer: d
pp. 271-272
Obj. #4

Throughout history, which of the following has NOT been used in an attempt to "cure" homosexuality?
a. lobotomy
b. psychotherapy
c. castration
d. gender reassignment surgery

42.
K
Answer: d
p. 272
Obj. #4

The first major research to compare the adjustment of non-patient heterosexual and homosexual individuals found
a. significantly higher levels of adjustment in the heterosexual group.
b. somewhat higher levels of adjustment in the heterosexual group.
c. significantly higher levels of adjustment in the homosexual group.
d. no significant differences between the two groups.

43.
A
Answer: a
pp. 271-273
Obj. #4

Which of the following chronological sequences **best** describes historical attitudes toward homosexuality?
a. sin, illness, alternative sexual orientation
b. illness, sin, alternative sexual orientation
c. alternative sexual orientation, illness, sin
d. alternative sexual orientation, sin, illness

44.
K
Answer: d
p. 273
Obj. #7

All of the following are part of the definition of homophobia **except**
a. irrational fears of homosexuality in others.
b. the fear of homosexual feelings within oneself.
c. self-loathing because of one's homosexuality.
d. self-loathing because of one's gender dysphoria.

45.
K
Answer: d
pp. 272-273
Obj. #9

The majority of counselors and therapists working with homosexual clients typically
a. are being replaced by programs emphasizing will power and religious conversion.
b. provide hormone therapy in an attempt to change their sexual orientation.
c. use aversion therapy in an attempt to alter their sexual orientation.
d. try to help them to live satisfying, fulfilling lives in a society that is still considerably hostile toward them.

46.
K
Answer: d
p. 273
Obj. #7

Telling "queer" jokes and/or avoiding any behavior that might be interpreted as homosexual are manifestations of
a. xenophobia.
b. homoerotica.
c. heterophobia.
d. homophobia.

47.
A
Answer: b
p. 273
Obj. #7

Which of the following would be **least** indicative of homophobia?
a. verbally harassing someone on a bus who is suspected to be gay
b. being invited to attend a show put on by the Gay Men's Chorus, but attending a rock concert instead
c. enjoying telling "faggot" and "dyke" jokes
d. thinking that homosexual people shouldn't be allowed to teach in schools

Chapter 10 Sexual Orientations 217

48.
A
Answer: c
p. 273
Obj. #7

Which of the following would be **least** indicative of homophobia?
a. avoiding becoming friends with someone whose mannerisms look suspiciously gay
b. feeling repulsed by public displays of affection between lesbians or gay men, but accepting the same affectionate behavior between heterosexuals
c. being invited to hear a lesbian comedienne perform at a local theater, but accepting another invitation to go to a musical you have been wanting to see instead
d. looking at lesbians or gay men and automatically thinking about their sexuality rather than viewing them as whole persons

49.
A
Answer: a
p. 273
Obj. #7

Which of the following would be **least** indicative of homophobia?
a. interviewing two finalists for a job, and hiring the one with the most experience, knowing the other candidate is gay
b. not confronting a homophobic remark for fear of being identified with gay men or lesbians
c. wondering which one is the "man" or "woman" in a lesbian or gay couple
d. avoiding telling friends that you are involved with a woman's organization because you are afraid they will think you are a lesbian

50.
A
Answer: b
pp. 273-274
Obj. #8

Which of the following is NOT true concerning Hate Crimes?
a. The Hate Crime Statistics Act of 1990 provides money to document hate crimes in the United States.
b. Because of the federal laws, states do not need to pass hate-crimes laws.
c. 20% of lesbians and 25% of gay males have been victims of hate crimes.
d. Hate crimes are less likely to be reported to officials than are other crimes.

51.
K
Answer: c
p. 274
Obj. #9

Antigay hate-crime perpetrators are primarily motivated by
a. religious beliefs.
b. economic frustration.
c. threats to gender-role expectations.
d. Satanic possession.

52.
K
Answer: d
p. 274
Obj. #9

Negative attitudes toward homosexuality are associated with all but which one of the following?
a. authoritarian religious beliefs
b. traditional gender role beliefs
c. being male
d. being a college student

53.
K
Answer: c
p. 275
Obj. #9

A recent study examined arousal while watching videos of heterosexual, lesbian and gay male sexual interactions. Which one is true?
   a. Penile and reported arousal results were the same.
   b. Men were more aroused by lesbian sex than any other.
   c. Men with negative attitudes toward gay men were not aware of their penile arousal when viewing gay male sex.
   d. Your text suggested a version of this should be used to diagnose latent lesbianism.

54.
A
Answer: c
pp. 275-276
Obj. #7

All of the following are ways that homophobia might affect heterosexual behavior **except**
   a. a man may be reluctant to enjoy having his nipples stimulated by his female partner.
   b. a woman may be reluctant to identify herself as a feminist for fear of being called a lesbian.
   c. a married man who secretly cross-dresses on occasion because it is sexually arousing for him may be reluctant to seek help for this behavior.
   d. a man may not allow himself to have a deep emotional relationship with a male friend.

55.
A
Answer: c
p. 276
Obj. #7

Which of the following would be **least** likely to change homophobic attitudes?
   a. taking a human sexuality class
   b. finding out that your favorite professor is gay
   c. attending a theater performance in which the two lead male characters engage in cross-dressing
   d. attending a PFLAG meeting

56.
A
Answer: d
p. 276
Obj. #14

Which one is NOT an example of recent positive movie portrayal of homosexuality?
   a. My Best Friends' Wedding
   b. In and Out
   c. Philadelphia
   d. The Thomas Crown Affair

57.
A
Answer: c
p. 276
Obj. #7

An Olympic figure skater, a professional athlete and a high-profile fashion model publicly announce their homosexuality. They are probably doing this because they want to
   a. set the stage for "outing" someone else.
   b. make more money in endorsements.
   c. challenge the common stereotypes regarding homosexuals.
   d. attract others into a homosexual lifestyle.

Chapter 10 Sexual Orientations 219

58.
A
Answer: d
p. 277
Obj. #10

You see a man who wears tight, flashy clothing and has exaggerated, somewhat effeminate gestures. Which of the following statements concerning this man would be **most** accurate?
 a. He is gay.
 b. He is bisexual.
 c. He is a transvestite.
 d. There is no way of knowing the man's sexual orientation based on the above information.

59.
K
Answer: d
p. 277
Obj. #11

"Closeted" homosexual men and women may do all of the following **except**
 a. deny their homosexual orientation.
 b. get married.
 c. be sexually active with members of the other sex.
 d. become active in the gay community.

60.
K
Answer: a
pp. 277-278
Obj. #11
WWW

Which of the following is NOT part of the coming-out process?
 a. passing
 b. self-acceptance
 c. self-acknowledgment
 d. telling the family

61.
K
Answer: b
pp. 279-280
Obj. #11

The final step in the process of acknowledging and expressing one's homosexuality is
 a. telling the family.
 b. becoming involved in the gay community.
 c. disclosure.
 d. self-acceptance.

62.
K
Answer: a
p. 279
Obj. #11

A term used for maintaining the false image of heterosexuality is
 a. passing.
 b. coming out.
 c. masquerading.
 d. primary self-deception.

63.
K
Answer: a
p. 279
Obj. #7

Hostility and harassment of gay high school students
 a. is often contributed to by school staff.
 b. is forbidden by law in about half of the states.
 c. has resulted in higher rates of suicide for both lesbians and gay males.
 d. is probably desirable as it prepares them for the future.

64.
A
Answer: d
pp. 277-280
Obj. #11

When a lesbian tells her family that she is "coming out," what she means is that
a. she is making a commitment to be in a primary relationship with her lover.
b. she is going to become more active in the Metropolitan Community Church.
c. she has just had her first lesbian sexual experience.
d. she is accepting and openly acknowledging her homosexual identity.

65.
K
Answer: c
p. 280
Obj. #11

Which one is NOT true of "coming out" about ones sexual orientation?
a. This is more likely for those who live in cities than in small rural towns.
b. This should probably be preceded by mental practice of what you are going to say.
c. This should be done first with the most important people in your life e.g., family or best friend.
d. One should expect negative reactions and not respond with rudeness.

66.
K
Answer: a
p. 281
Obj. #10, 11

Which one is NOT true concerning homosexuals and their family?
a. It is more likely that homosexual will have told their mother than their father about their sexual orientation.
b. It can be expected coming out will be more easily accepted by family than casual people at work.
c. PFLAG is a group for the family of homosexuals.
d. More than half of homosexuals who have been married will have children.

67.
K
Answer: c
p. 282
Obj. #11

"Outing" refers to
a. maintaining the false image of heterosexuality.
b. openly acknowledging one's homosexual identity.
c. publicizing the homosexual orientation of someone who would otherwise not openly acknowledge it.
d. excluding a person with a homosexual orientation from a particular group or organization.

68.
A
Answer: d
p. 282
Obj. #11
WWW

Act-Up identifies a celebrity or public figure as homosexual in order to gain support and additional funding for AIDS research and treatment. This process is known as
a. coming out.
b. gay bashing.
c. hazing.
d. outing.

69.
K
Answer: b
pp. 282-283
Obj. #15

Which of the following ethnic groups tend to be **more** tolerant of homosexuality?
a. Asian American
b. Native American
c. African American
d. Hispanic American

Chapter 10 Sexual Orientations   221

70.
K
Answer: a
p. 282
Obj. #15

Placing a high value on women's subservience to men as well as their role in child bearing makes which of the following ethnic groups **least** accepting of lesbianism?
a. Hispanic and Asian
b. Native American and Hispanic
c. African-American and Asian
d. Asian and Native American

71.
K
Answer: b
p. 283
Obj. n/a

Which one is NOT true with respect to community for homosexuals?
a. The Metropolitan Community Church is a widespread religious organization for gay people.
b. Generally, homosexuals have avoided becoming too closely involved with community AIDS efforts because of possible negative stereotyping.
c. There are entire retirement communities for older gays and lesbians.
d. Gay and lesbian bars have served an important function for psychologically safe socializing.

72.
K
Answer: a
p. 284
Obj. #10a

According to one study, which of the following statements concerning gender roles in homosexual relationships was true?
a. Heterosexual couples were likely to adhere more closely to traditional gender-role expectations than were homosexual couples.
b. Homosexual couples were likely to adhere more closely to traditional gender-role expectations than were heterosexual couples.
c. Both homosexual and heterosexual couples were equally likely to adhere to traditional gender-role expectations.
d. No identifiable pattern was observed in either homosexual or heterosexual relationships.

73.
K
Answer: d
pp. 284-285
Obj. #10a

Which of the following statements concerning gay and lesbian relationships is false?
a. Lesbian couples are more likely than male couples to have monogamous relationships.
b. Gay men are likely to have had more sexual partners than lesbians.
c. Gay men with primary partners were much more likely to have sexual experiences with others than were lesbians.
d. Since the AIDS epidemic, the incidence of frequent casual sexual encounters among gay men has steadily decreased.

74.
K
Answer: b
p. 284
Obj. #10a

For both males and females, homosexual and heterosexual, the **most** important factor in a love relationship was
a. maintaining the passion and intensity.
b. talking about intimate feelings.
c. sharing common interests.
d. having a positive outlook on life.

75.
K
Answer: a
p. 284
Obj. #10a

When comparing gay and lesbian sexual relationships
a. lesbians are more likely to have monogamous relationships at all stages of their life.
b. there are no differences between lesbians and gays in the likelihood of being in a monogamous relationship.
c. lesbians wait longer than males before entering a committed relationship.
d. there are differences in the teen and twenties but not in later life.

76.
K
Answer: a
p. 285
Obj. #10b
WWW

Approximately _____ of lesbians are mothers.
a. one-third
b. one-half
c. two-thirds
d. three-fourths

77.
K
Answer: b
p. 285
Obj. #10b

Which one is NOT true concerning lesbians?
a. States differ as to whether they allow adoption by lesbian couples.
b. Most states do not allow lesbians to use a sperm bank for artificial insemination.
c. About 1/3 of lesbians are biological mothers.
d. There is a radical sex lesbian culture that involves such things as kinky sex and group sex.

78.
K
Answer: d
p. 286
Obj. #10b

Which of the following statements concerning lesbians and parenting is false?
a. Children of lesbian mothers are essentially no different from other children in terms of gender-related problems.
b. Lesbian mothers have been found to be similar to heterosexual mothers in maternal interests.
c. Lesbian mothers have been found to be similar to heterosexual mothers in parenting behavior.
d. Children of lesbian mothers tend to have a higher self-esteem than children of heterosexual mothers.

79.
K
Answer: c
p. 286
Obj. #12

Which of the following statements concerning the Stonewall incident is false?
a. It was the symbolic birth of gay activism.
b. It is named after a gay bar that was raided by the police.
c. It took place shortly after WWII ended.
d. It promoted the formation of various gay rights organizations.

80.
K
Answer: d
p. 287
Obj. #13

Which is NOT one of the goals of the Gay Rights Movement?
a. decriminalization
b. antidiscrimination
c. positive rights
d. proselytizaion

81.
K
Answer: d
pp. 287-288
Obj. #13

The military "Don't Ask, Don't Tell" policy has been followed by
   a. less gay bashing in the military.
   b. greater enlistment rates.
   c. lesser enlistment rates.
   d. more discharges on the basis of sexual orientation.

82.
K
Answer: d
p. 288
Obj. #13

About _____ of Americans believe that homosexuals should have equal rights in employment and housing.
   a. 40%
   b. 55%
   c. 70%
   d. 85%

83.
K
Answer: b
p. 288
Obj. #13

The federal Defense of Marriage Act
   a. made it illegal to perform civil marriages for same-sex people.
   b. gave states the right not to recognize same-sex marriages performed in other states.
   c. made it more difficult for lesbians and gays to adopt.
   d. will probably be overturned by the Supreme Court.

84.
K
Answer: d
p. 288
Obj. #13

Which one of the following was NOT reported concerning public opinion about rights for homosexuals?
   a. The vast majority believe that they should have equal housing rights.
   b. About 35% believe that same-sex couples should have legally sanctioned marriage.
   c. Less than half believe that same-sex couples should be able to adopt children.
   d. About 85% believe that the same health insurance benefits should be offered to same-sex partners as to married couples.

Multiple Choice from Study Guide

1.
K
Answer: d
p. 261
Obj. #1

A person with a homosexual orientation
   a. prefers to dress in the clothes of the other sex.
   b. has the gender identity of the other sex.
   c. has sex with a person of the same sex.
   d. has a primary erotic, psychological, emotional, and social orientation toward members of the same sex.

2.
K
Answer: b
p. 262
Obj. #2

The Kinsey continuum is best described as
   a. a 10 point scale where 1 = exclusively heterosexual and 10 = exclusively homosexual.
   b. a 7 point scale where 0 = exclusively heterosexual and 6 = exclusively homosexual.
   c. a 6 point scale where 1 = exclusively homosexual and 6 = exclusively heterosexual.
   d. a 6 point scale where 1= exclusively heterosexual and 6 = exclusively homosexual.

224 Test Bank to Accompany *Our Sexuality*

3.
K
Answer: a
p. 262
Obj. #2

The National Health and Social Life survey found that _____ percent of male and _____ percent of female respondents had sex with a same sex partner after age 18.
   a. 5; 4
   b. 6; 5.5
   c. 2.8; 1.4
   d. 2; 1

4.
K
Answer: b
pp. 263-264
Obj. #3

Sergio is a happily married, 36 year old father of three. When he visits his hometown in Mexico, Sergio occasionally has sex with men he meets at a gay bar, and in these encounters, Sergio is the insertive partner. Sergio's sexual orientation is **most** likely
   a. transitional bisexual.
   b. transitory bisexual.
   c. homosexual.
   d. homosexual denial.

5.
K
Answer: d
pp. 263-264
Obj. #3

Megan's first teenage crush was on another woman, and she has fantasized about other women and men as long as she can remember. Megan's first kiss was with a woman, and her first sexual encounter was with male. Megan is currently dating a woman after the breakup of a two-year relationship with a man. Megan's sexual orientation **most** likely is
   a. lesbian.
   b. transitory bisexuality.
   c. homosexual denial.
   d. bisexuality as a real orientation.

6.
K
Answer: c
p. 265
Obj. #9

What can be concluded from research examining Freud's theory of sexual orientation?
   a. gay men tended to come from families with a domineering other and absent father
   b. lesbians were more likely than heterosexual women to have identified with their father
   c. no particular family life pattern is associated with developing a heterosexual or homosexual orientation
   d. penis envy is typically found among lesbians with poor father-daughter relationships

7.
K
Answer: d
p. 266
Obj. #9

Research that compares hormone levels between heterosexuals and homosexuals has found that
   a. adult homosexual males have different levels of circulating estrogen than adult heterosexual males.
   b. adult lesbians have more circulating testosterone than adult heterosexual women.
   c. prenatal hormones have little influence on fetal brain development.
   d. lesbians' finger length patterns are more like heterosexual males due to prenatal androgens.

8.
K
Answer: c
p. 264
Obj. #9

Which of the following statements about the psychosocial origins of sexual orientation is true?
   a. Gay men dated less frequently than heterosexuals during high school.
   b. Most homosexuals have their first sexual experience with a homosexual that is considerably older.
   c. A majority of lesbians have had sexual experiences with men.
   d. Most gay and lesbian persons' childhood playmates were of the other sex.

9.
K
Answer: c
p. 267
Obj. #9

If a homosexual orientation has a genetic basis then
   a. identical twins should show a higher concordance rate than fraternal twins.
   b. fraternal twins should show a higher concordance rate than identical twins.
   c. other sex fraternal twins should show a higher concordance rate than same sex fraternal twins.
   d. homosexuality should run in families.

10.
K
Answer: c
p. 268
Obj. #9

Gender nonconformity rates in childhood are higher for
   a. lesbians than heterosexual women.
   b. gay men than heterosexual men.
   c. lesbians and gay men than heterosexuals of both sexes.
   d. homosexuals in all North, Central and South American countries except Guatemala and Brazil.

11.
K
Answer: d
pp. 269-270
Obj. #5

Which statement **best** reflects current Christian views on homosexuality?
   a. Homosexuality is a sin.
   b. Homosexuality is inherently unnatural.
   c. Homosexuality cannot be changed except through religious conversion.
   d. There is a great range of positions.

12.
K
Answer: b
p. 271
Obj. #8

All of the following countries have adopted national laws prohibiting discrimination against gays, lesbians, and bisexuals **except**
   a. Canada.
   b. United States.
   c. Israel.
   d. South Africa.

13.
K
Answer: b
pp. 272-273
Obj. n/a

Which statement is true regarding homosexuality and mental health?
   a. Homosexual adults show significantly higher levels of psychological distress than heterosexual adults.
   b. The American Psychiatric Association removed homosexuality from its list of mental disorders in 1973.
   c. Hooker's research found that adjustment was better for lesbians than gay men.
   d. Adjustment is better for gays and lesbians that are active in the gay community.

14.
K
Answer: c
p. 273
Obj. #7

Which of the following is the **best** example of homophobia?
a. Brad refuses to talk to his lesbian sister because she has not paid back the money he loaned her.
b. Jeff asks his gay coworker about how his life partner is doing with his new job.
c. Kyle is afraid of hugging his best friend because he's afraid others will think he is gay.
d. Sara refuses to listen to the lesbian folk-rock duo *Indigo Girls* because she doesn't like folk-rock music.

15.
K
Answer: d
pp. 274-275
Obj. #8

Research has revealed that hate crimes are related to
a. holding traditional gender role stereotypes.
b. having conservative and authoritarian religious views.
c. denying homoerotic arousal in oneself.
d. all of the above are true

16.
K
Answer: d
p. 276
Obj. #8

All of the following are ways that homophobia negatively impacts heterosexuals **except**
a. heterosexual men may feel uneasy about having their nipples stimulated.
b. a woman may be reluctant to identify herself as a feminist.
c. a man is unwilling to wear soft and silky shirts, even though he likes how they feel.
d. all of the above are true

17.
K
Answer: b
pp. 277-278
Obj. #11

The "coming out" process consists of all of the following phases **except**
a. self-acceptance.
b. passing.
c. disclosure.
d. Self-acknowledgement.

18.
K
Answer: c
p. 282
Obj. #6

Which group listed below is likely to have the **least** negative attitude toward homosexuality?
a. African Americans
b. Hispanic Americans
c. Native Americans
d. Asian Americans

19.
K
Answer: d
p. 284
Obj. #10a

Which statement is true regarding lesbian sexual expression?
a. Lesbians have fewer sex partners than gay men.
b. Lesbians are more likely to be monogamous.
c. Lesbians are more likely to wait to have sex until emotional intimacy is present.
d. all of the above are true

20.
K
Answer: a
p. 286
Obj. #10b

Current research shows that the children of gay and lesbian parents
a. grow up to be heterosexual.
b. show more problem behaviors if the child is raised by gay parents than lesbian parents.
c. are more likely to have confused gender identity than children of heterosexuals.
d. have reduced self-esteem compared to children of heterosexuals.

21.
K
Answer: c
p. 287
Obj. #13

Goals of the gay rights movement include all of the following **except**
a. decriminalization.
b. antidiscrimination.
c. government restitution.
d. positive rights.

True/False

Students may be asked to answer these questions using the traditional format of marking their answers either "true" or "false". Or, to encourage more active involvement, you may choose to use the following instructions:

If the statement is true, place a "T" on the line preceding it. If the statement is false, place an "F" on the line preceding it and then change the statement to make it true by deleting incorrect information and/or adding accurate information.

1.
Answer: T
p. 262
Obj. #1

___ Kinsey devised a 7 point (0 to 6) scale to assess sexual orientation.

2.
Answer: F
p. 263
Obj. #4

___ A prostitute who has both male and female clients but is involved only in heterosexual relationships in her personal life would be considered a transitional bisexual.

3.
Answer: F
p. 265
Obj. #9

___ There have been numerous studies that have indicated a typical family pattern among homosexual clients: most commonly, an authoritarian, domineering father and a passive and detached mother.

4.
Answer: F
p. 265
Obj. #9

___ Daryl Bern's "exotic becomes erotic" theory illustrates how particular fetish objects can influence the development of sexual orientation in some individuals.

5.
Answer: T
p. 267
Obj. #9

___ Recent research has demonstrated that homosexuals are more likely than heterosexuals to be left-handed.

6.
Answer: T
p. 268
Obj. #9

___ Those who believe that homosexuals are born that way are more likely to be accepting of homosexuality.

7.
Answer: T
p. 270
Obj. #6

___ In ancient Greece, homosexual relationships between men were considered superior to heterosexual relationships on an intellectual and spiritual level.

8.
Answer: T
p. 270
Obj. #6

___ The Sambia men in New Guinea engage in exclusively homosexual activities until they marry.

9.
Answer: F
p. 269-270
Obj. #5

___ The predominant Christian view of homosexuality throughout history is the rejecting non-punitive position.

10.
Answer: F
pp. 269-271
Obj. #4

___ Historically, homosexuality was first viewed as a sickness, then in more recent years as a sin, and finally a mental illness that could be treated by mental health professionals.

11.
Answer: T
p. 271
Obj. #5

___ The people who support a "full acceptance" theological position toward homosexuality are in the minority.

12.
Answer: F
p. 272
Obj. n/a

___ Gay conversion programs succeed with over half of all participants.

13.
Answer: T
p. 273
Obj. #4

___ The American Psychiatric Association no longer considers homosexuality to be a mental disorder.

14.
Answer: T
p. 274
Obj. #4

___ 20% of lesbians and 25% of gay males have been victims of hate crimes.

15.
Answer: F
p. 281
Obj. #11

___ PFLAG is an organization of gay men and women who are committed to civil rights legislation for gays.

16. Answer: F pp. 282-283 Obj. #15	___	Asian Americans tend to be more accepting of homosexuality than Native Americans.
17. Answer: T p. 286 Obj. #10b	___	Research has indicated that children of lesbian mothers are essentially no different from other children in terms of self-esteem, gender-related problems and general development.
18. Answer: T p. 286 Obj. #11	___	Lesbian teens are only slightly more likely to attempt suicide than straight girls, while gay male youths are 7 times more likely than heterosexual males to attempt suicide.
19. Answer: T p. 287 Obj. #12	___	The gay rights movement has been heavily invested in decriminalization, the elimination of laws making same-sex behavior illegal.
20. Answer: T pp. 288-289 Obj. #10a	___	In Vermont, gay and lesbian couples may form "civil unions" with the legal rights or married couples.

Short Answer Essay

1. What percentage of the population has a homosexual orientation? Back your conclusions with research, and indicate problems in interpreting data in this area. (Obj. #2)

2. If you were attempting to change people's attitude toward homosexuality would you use the following information: the percentage of the population; the causes of homosexuality; the names of well-known people who are homosexuality. Why, or why not? (Obj. n/a)

3. Discuss some of the problems in defining bisexuality, and then list, describe and give an example of four types of bisexuality. (Obj. #1, 3)

4. Trace the changes in attitudes toward homosexuality in the Western world, beginning with the period before Christ up until the present time. (Obj. #4)

5. Describe various cross-cultural perspectives on homosexuality, citing specific examples from cultures around the world and throughout history. (Obj. #6)

6. Describe four contemporary theological positions on homosexuality and give examples of each. (Obj. #5)

7. Use either your experience with churches, or your experience with family members, and categorize the views to which you have been exposed into the four positions used in your text to analyze various theological approaches. (Obj. #5)

8. Summarize the data on the mental health of gays and lesbians as compared to heterosexuals. Include information on suicide. What is your explanation for any differences? (Obj. n/a)

9. Describe the differences in the patterns of relationships between lesbians and male homosexuals, making reference to lifestyles and family life. (Obj. #10)

10. Discuss the evidence supporting a biological explanation for how a homosexual orientation develops. (Obj. #9)

11. Describe several psychosocial theories regarding how homosexuality develops. Consider data supporting or refuting this, including data on the ability to change orientation. (Obj. #9)

12. Define "coming out" and explain five different steps that may be involved in that process. (Obj. #11)

13. What are the factors that may be involved in the development or abatement of homophobia? Consider family, friendship, religion, and the media among others. (Obj. #7, 14)

14. Discuss the impact of being both gay and a member of an ethnic minority group, making specific references to Native American, Hispanic American and African American cultures. (Obj. #15)

15. Trace the development of the gay rights movement, discussing significant events that occurred in the 1950s up to the present time. What are the current goals of gay rights activists? (Obj. #12)

11

Contraception

Learning Objectives

After studying this Chapter, the student should be able to:

1. Explain when efforts to control conception first began and list various contraceptive methods that have been used throughout history.

2. From an historical and social perspective, briefly discuss each of the following:
   a. available methods of contraception throughout U.S. history
   b. obstacles to reliable contraceptive availability
   c. key people involved in promoting birth control
   d. key legislation related to contraceptive use

3. List some of the reasons why reliable contraception is a major worldwide concern today as well as what some of the objections are to contraceptive use.

4. Identify some of the ways in which couples can share responsibility for birth control.

5. List and describe several variables that influence the effectiveness of birth control.

6. Compare the effectiveness of various birth control methods.

7. For each of the following contraceptive methods, describe what it is and how it works, and list the advantages and disadvantages of each:
   a. "outercourse"
   b. oral contraceptives
   c. Norplant
   d. injectible contraceptives
   e. condoms
   f. diaphragms
   g. cervical caps
   h. vaginal spermicides
   i. intrauterine devices
   j. methods based on the menstrual cycle
   k. emergency contraception
   l. sterilization
   m. other methods such as nursing, withdrawal and douching

8. Discuss some of the future possibilities for contraceptive methods that may be available to men and women.

Multiple Choice

1.
K
Answer: c
p. 292
Obj. #1

In the eighteenth century, Italian adventurer _____ was noted for his animal membrane condoms tied with a ribbon at the base of his penis.
a. Christopher Columbus
b. Fredrick Condomini
c. Giovanni Casanova
d. Anthony Comstock

2.
K
Answer: d
p. 292
Obj. #1

Efforts to control contraception began
a. at the beginning of this century.
b. during the Renaissance.
c. in the Middle Ages.
d. at least as far back as recorded history.

3.
K
Answer: d
p. 292
Obj. #2c

Margaret Sanger was responsible for all of the following **except**
a. opening an illegal clinic for women to obtain diaphragms.
b. violating the Comstock Laws.
c. publishing birth control information.
d. establishing the first abortion clinic.

4.
K
Answer: d
p. 292
Obj. #2a

Birth control pills were first available in this country
a. at the turn of the century.
b. in 1920.
c. in 1945.
d. in 1960.

5.
K
Answer: b
p. 292
Obj. #2d
WWW

In 1972, the Supreme Court case _____ extended the right to privacy to unmarried individuals by decriminalizing the use of contraception by single people.
a. Griswold v. Connecticut
b. Eisenstadt v. Baird
c. Sanger v. Comstock
d. Roe v. Wade

6.
K
Answer: b
p. 293
Obj. #3

Research indicates that the rate of sexual activity _____ when condoms are available at no cost at school.
a. increases
b. remains stable
c. decreases
d. decreases dramatically

7.
K
Answer: c
p. 293
Obj. n/a

Which one did not occur following the introduction of the birth control pill in the 1970's?
a. Women married later in life.
b. Women entered professional programs in greater numbers.
c. The pill became a major expense for insurance companies.
d. Women entered business to a greater extent.

8.
K
Answer: d
p. 293
Obj. #3

Birth control was suggested to have all but which one of the following advantages?
   a. It results in better health for mothers.
   b. It results in better health for children.
   c. It may help avoid giving birth to children with hereditary diseases.
   d. It delays menopause.

9.
K
Answer: d
pp. 293-294
Obj. #3

Which statement **best** describes the relationship between the education of women and average number of children?
   a. There is no relationship world wide between women's education and family size.
   b. Educated women in third world countries have more living children as they can afford better health care.
   c. Only in the United States do women with more education have smaller families.
   d. World wide, women with more education have smaller families.

10.
K
Answer: c
p. 294
Obj. #3
WWW

According to one study, Catholic women are _____ to use birth control as non-Catholic women.
   a. three times as likely
   b. twice as likely
   c. as likely
   d. much less likely

11.
K
Answer: b
p. 294
Obj. #2

With respect to religion and contraception
   a. the official doctrine of the Roman Catholic Church is that any contraceptive means is immoral.
   b. some fundamental Muslims are opposed to artificial means of contraception.
   c. over 40% of nuns and priests in the United States do not believe that contraception by married people is a sin.
   d. about half of Catholic Women in the United States use artificial contraceptive devices.

12.
K
Answer: c
p. 295
Obj. #3, 4

Which one is the **best** summary of your texts position?
   a. Because women become pregnant they should assume major responsibility for birth control.
   b. Single women should assume major responsibility for birth control but married couples should share responsibility.
   c. Both single men and women need to be assertive about refusing to engage in intercourse without effective contraception.
   d. You should find someone from your own religious background so that you won't have major conflicts in making decisions about birth control.

13.
K
Answer: d
pp. 295-296
Obj. #5, 6

Which one is NOT true with respect to birth control?
a. Factors to consider when choosing a method include both the failure rate if used consistently and the typical number who become pregnant with that system.
b. About 85 of 100 sexually active women will become pregnant in a year if they use no method of birth control.
c. There is presently no ideal method of birth control.
d. When you find the birth control method that works for you, you should plan to stick with it for the rest of your reproductive years in an active sex life.

14.
K
Answer: c
p. 296
Obj. #4

Accompanying your partner to a medical exam for birth control is an example of
a. the buddy system.
b. participant modeling.
c. shared responsibility.
d. covert sensitization.

15.
K
Answer: a
pp. 296-297
Obj. #6

Which of the following is the **least** effective birth control method if used correctly and consistently?
a. diaphragm and spermicide
b. estrogen-progestin pills
c. male condom
d. Norplant

16.
K
Answer: c
pp. 296-297
Obj. #6

Which of the following is the **most** effective birth control method if used correctly?
a. male condoms
b. diaphragm and spermicide
c. Depo-Provera
d. cervical cap

17.
K
Answer: d
p. 298
Obj. #5

Research has indicated that individuals who _____ about sex are likely to use contraception ineffectively.
a. are apathetic
b. feel anxious
c. are phobic
d. feel guilty

18.
K
Answer: c
p. 298
Obj. n/a

Which one is NOT true concerning neonaticide?
a. This refers to killing an infant within 24 hours after birth.
b. This has occurred throughout history.
c. This is fortunately no longer a concern in the present world.
d. Moses is an example of a survivor of an infanticide attempt.

19.
K
Answer: c
p. 298
Obj. #5

With respect to contraceptive failure
a. this occurs more among married women.
b. this occurs less with persons who are anxious and guilty about having sex.
c. this occurs more with low-income women than the more affluent.
d. this is most often due to error on the part of the health care practitioner.

Chapter 11 Contraception 235

20.
K
Answer: d
pp. 298-299
Obj. n/a

Which one is NOT true concerning infanticide?
a. This decreased in the United States after the introduction of oral contraceptives.
b. This decreased in the United States after the introduction of legal abortion.
c. This occurs in the United Sates about 50 times a year.
d. This occurs primarily with uneducated girls, sometimes with mental problems.

21.
K
Answer: b
pp. 299-300
Obj. #5

Which one is NOT true concerning backup methods?
a. This refers to using more than one method of contraception simultaneously.
b. This will not be necessary if you are on the pill, except if you forget to take pills.
c. Foam and condom together are a common and effective combination.
d. This should be done in the first month or so after an IUD insertion

22.
K
Answer: d
p. 300
Obj. #7

You are a woman who smokes cigarettes, has high blood pressure, is somewhat forgetful and likes spontaneous sex. An unwanted pregnancy would be devastating for you. Which of the following contraceptive methods would be **best** for you?
a. combination pill
b. cervical cap
c. condom
d. Norplant

23.
K
Answer: c
p. 301
Obj. #7a

Which of the following statements regarding outercourse is false?
a. Oral sex is a form of it.
b. Anal intercourse is a form of it.
c. It is safe sex, in that you cannot contract or transmit a sexually transmitted disease.
d. It can be a viable form of birth control.

24.
A
Answer: a
p. 301
Obj. #7a

Sue and Randy enjoy oral sex and mutual masturbation but refrain from having penile-vaginal intercourse. The authors would consider these behaviors
a. "outercourse".
b. fondling.
c. vital preliminary sexual behaviors.
d. foreplay.

25.
K
Answer: c
p. 301
Obj. #7b
WWW

Hormone-based contraceptives can work in all of the following ways **except**
a. preventing the fertilized egg from implanting in the uterus.
b. inhibiting ovulation.
c. constricting the fallopian tubes to block passage of the fertilized egg.
d. altering cervical mucus so the passage of sperm is blocked.

26.
K
Answer: b
p. 302
Obj. #7b

The most commonly used oral contraceptive in the United States is the
a. multiphasic pill.
b. constant dose combination pill.
c. progestin-only pill.
d. "morning-after" pill.

27.
K
Answer: b
p. 302
Obj. #7b

_____ releases a constant dose of estrogen and progestin.
a. The multiphasic pill
b. The combination pill
c. The progestin-only pill
d. Depo-Provera

28.
K
Answer: a
p. 302
Obj. #7b

_____ provides fluctuations of estrogen and progesterone levels during the cycle.
a. The multiphasic pill
b. The combination pill
c. The progestin-only pill
d. Depo-Provera

29.
K
Answer: c
p. 302
Obj. #7b

The primary effect of the _____ pill is to alter the cervical mucus to a thick and tacky consistency that effectively blocks sperm.
a. multiphasic
b. combination
c. progestin-only
d. low estrin

30.
K
Answer: b
p. 302
Obj. #7b

Both the _____ and _____ pill prevent conception from occurring by inhibiting ovulation.
a. multiphasic; progestin-only
b. combination; multiphasic
c. progestin-only; combination
d. progestin-only; low estrin

31.
K
Answer: d
pp. 302-303
Obj. #7b

All of the following are advantages of taking birth control pills **except**
a. reduces menstrual cramps.
b. decreases the possibility of benign breast disease.
c. decreases acne.
d. reduces the possibility of hypertension.

32.
K
Answer: d
pp. 302-303
Obj. #7b

Oral contraceptives may do all of the following **except**
a. help relieve endometriosis.
b. decrease the incidence of benign breast disease.
c. reduce the risk of ovarian cancer.
d. reduce the incidence of liver tumors.

33.
K
Answer: a
p. 303
Obj. #7b

One danger sign for pill users, associated with the acronym ACHES, is
a. abdominal pain.
b. cervical discharge.
c. amenorrhea.
d. severe backache.

34.
K
Answer: d
pp. 303-304
Obj. #7b
WWW

All of the following problems may be associated with oral contraceptives **except**
a. blood clots.
b. liver tumors.
c. high blood pressure.
d. endometrial cancer.

35.
K
Answer: c
pp. 303-304
Obj. #7b

Using combination birth control pills may be associated with increased risk of all of the following **except**
a. heart attacks.
b. liver tumors.
c. ovarian cancer.
d. hypertension.

36.
K
Answer: b
pp. 303-304
Obj. #7b

Use of oral contraceptives may be associated with an increase in all of the following **except**
a. blood clots.
b. pain at ovulation.
c. depression.
d. gall bladder disease.

37.
K
Answer: d
p. 304
Obj. #7b

The progestin-only pill may be associated with
a. an increase in PMS symptoms.
b. endometrial cancer.
c. an increase in benign breast disease.
d. breakthrough bleeding.

38.
K
Answer: c
p. 304
Obj. #7b

Ectopic pregnancy is more likely among users of hormone-based contraceptives if they use
a. the constant-dose combination pill.
b. the multiphasic pill.
c. the progestin-only pill.
d. Norplant.

39.
K
Answer: c
p. 304
Obj. #7b

Which of the following statements regarding oral contraceptive use is false?
a. It may increase a woman's spontaneity and enjoyment.
b. It may change sexual motivation.
c. It often reduces reduce the incidence of migraine headaches and/or depression.
d. The risks associated with it are much lower than that of pregnancy.

40.
K
Answer: d
p. 305
Obj. #7c

Norplant is effective for
a. six months.
b. one year.
c. three years.
d. five years.

41.
K
Answer: a
p. 305
Obj. #7c

Which of the following statements regarding Norplant is true?
a. Menstrual irregularity is a common side effect.
b. After having Norplant removed, a woman is not able to become pregnant for two to three months.
c. Compared to using oral contraceptives over a five year period, Norplant is much more expensive.
d. It contains both estrogen and progestin.

42.
A
Answer: b
pp. 301, 305
Obj. #7b, 7c, 7d
WWW

What do the mini pill, Norplant and Depo-Provera have in common?
a. They are all barrier methods of contraception.
b. They are all progestin-only contraceptives.
c. The incidence of blood clots and hypertension are higher with all these methods.
d. They provide protection against STDs.

43.
K
Answer: a
p. 305
Obj. #7d

Depo-Provera
a. is an injectable contraceptive that needs to be given once every 12 weeks.
b. is implanted in a woman's arm and is effective for three years.
c. is taken orally on a daily basis.
d. is inserted into a woman's vagina.

44.
K
Answer: a
p. 306
Obj. #7e

The only temporary method of birth control for men is
a. condoms.
b. vasectomy.
c. sterilization.
d. male birth control pills.

45.
K
Answer: c
pp. 306-309
Obj. #7e

Which of the following statements regarding condoms is true?
a. Polyurethane condoms are more sensitive but not as strong as latex.
b. Natural membrane condoms are less expensive but interfere more with sensation than latex condoms do.
c. Polyurethane condoms are thinner, stronger and more heat sensitive than latex.
d. HIV can pass through latex condoms but not through natural membrane condoms.

46.
K
Answer: b
pp. 306-309
Obj. #7e
WWW

Which of the following statements regarding condoms is false?
a. For some men, the diminished sensation associated with condom use is preferred because it delays ejaculation.
b. They are the most commonly used contraceptive among college-age adults.
c. Nonlubricated condoms can be used for protection from infection during fellatio.
d. Some people are allergic to latex condoms.

47.
K
Answer: a
pp. 306-309
Obj. #7e

Which of the following statements is true?
- a. Natural-skin condoms interfere less with sensation than do latex ones.
- b. The concept of a penile sheath to prevent conception was first introduced at the turn of the century.
- c. The average shelf-life of condoms is about six months.
- d. Condoms should be stored in warm places to maintain their elasticity.

48.
K
Answer: c
p. 308
Obj. #7e

Women purchase _____% of condoms sold today.
- a. 10
- b. 25
- c. 50
- d. 75

49.
K
Answer: d
p. 308
Obj. #7e

Which of the following provide the most additional protection against sexually transmitted diseases?
- a. Lubricated condoms
- b. Condoms with Depo-Provera
- c. Natural membrane condoms
- d. Condoms with nonoxynol-9

50.
K
Answer: a
pp. 309-310
Obj. #7e

Which of the following statements regarding the female condom is false?
- a. It comes with spermicide on it.
- b. It is worn internally by the woman.
- c. It is made of latex or polyurethane.
- d. It may provide more protection from sexually transmitted disease than a male condom.

51.
K
Answer: d
p. 311
Obj. #7f

According to various sources, a woman may insert a diaphragm as long as _____ prior to intercourse and have it still be effective.
- a. one-half hour
- b. one hour
- c. three hours
- d. six hours

52.
K
Answer: d
p. 312
Obj. #7g

The diaphragm should remain in the vagina for at least _____ following intercourse, but not more than _____.
- a. one hour; eight hours
- b. two hours; ten hours
- c. four hours; fifteen hours
- d. six hours; twenty-four hours

53.
K
Answer: d
p. 312
Obj. #7f

Several cases of _____ have been associated with diaphragm use.
- a. ovarian cystitis
- b. chlamydia infection
- c. endometriosis
- d. toxic shock syndrome

54.
A
Answer: c
p. 312
Obj. #7f
WWW

A woman would probably have to be fitted for a new diaphragm in all of the following situations **except**
a. after a pregnancy.
b. after an abortion.
c. after being treated for a sexually transmitted disease.
d. after a weight change of 10 pounds or more.

55.
K
Answer: c
p. 312
Obj. #7f

All of the following may minimize the effectiveness of a diaphragm **except**
a. using an oil-based lubricant during intercourse.
b. gaining 15 pounds.
c. using antibiotics.
d. having an abortion.

56.
K
Answer: d
p. 313
Obj. #7g

The cervical cap resembles
a. a tampon.
b. an IUD.
c. a latex condom.
d. a miniature diaphragm.

57.
K
Answer: d
p. 314
Obj. #7g

All of the following are disadvantages of the cervical cap **except**
a. Women may have an allergic reaction to the rubber.
b. The cap may cause cervical damage.
c. It is usually more difficult to learn to use than the diaphragm.
d. It requires repeated applications of spermicide with additional intercourse.

58.
K
Answer: d
pp. 312-313
Obj. #7f, 7g

Both _____ and _____ , if used improperly, may cause toxic shock syndrome.
a. vaginal spermicides; Depo-Provera
b. cervical caps; vaginal spermicides
c. condoms; diaphragms
d. diaphragms; cervical caps

59.
K
Answer: a
pp. 314, 325
Obj. #7h

All of the following are presently available types of vaginal spermicides **except**
a. vaginal contraceptive ring
b. vaginal contraceptive film
c. vaginal suppositories
d. vaginal foam

60.
K
Answer: a
p. 315
Obj. #7h
WWW

_____ may increase the incidence of yeast infections and urinary tract infections.
a. Vaginal spermicides
b. Depo-Provera
c. Lubricated condoms
d. Norplant

Chapter 11 Contraception 241

61.
K
Answer: b
p. 316
Obj. #7i

All of the following contribute to the effectiveness of the IUD **except**
a. the copper in one type of IUD.
b. the barrier that is created when the IUD is inserted in the cervical os.
c. the progesterone in one type of IUD.
d. the irritation that occurs in the uterus, making implantation unlikely.

62.
K
Answer: c
pp. 296, 316
Obj. #7i

Which of the following statements regarding intrauterine devices is true?
a. Some types can reduce PID by clearing out the area.
b. It works by inhibiting ovulation.
c. It is more effective than using a diaphragm.
d. It increases the chances of ovarian cancer.

63.
K
Answer: c
p. 316
Obj. #7i

In order to confirm that the IUD is in place, the length of the _____ should be checked.
a. "T"
b. copper wire
c. string
d. plastic rim

64.
A
Answer: a
p. 316
Obj. #7i

If Sarah can't locate the string of her IUD, she should be advised to
a. see her health practitioner as soon as possible.
b. forget it; they slip around frequently.
c. wait until after her next period and check again.
d. immediately go to a hospital emergency room.

65.
K
Answer: d
p. 317
Obj. #7i

One danger sign for IUD users, associated with the acronym PAINS, is
a. stroke or high blood pressure.
b. severe headaches.
c. pain at ovulation.
d. nasty discharge.

66.
A
Answer: d
p. 317
Obj. #7i

Which of the following methods of birth control would a woman with a history of pelvic inflammatory disease definitely want to avoid?
a. diaphragm
b. birth control pill
c. cervical cap
d. IUD

67.
K
Answer: b
p. 318
Obj. #7k

One form of emergency contraceptive include giving doses of
a. androgens and estrogens.
b. estrogens or progestins.
c. prostaglandins.
d. antibiotics.

68.
A
Answer: c
p. 318
Obj. #7i

For which of the following conditions would a physician be **most** likely to discourage IUD use?
a. chronic yeast infections
b. an ovarian cyst
c. a history of ectopic pregnancy
d. chronic bladder infections

69.
K
Answer: c
pp. 318
Obj. #7k

All of the following are used as emergency contraceptives **except**
a. estrogens
b. progestins
c. androgens
d. copper IUDs

70.
A
Answer: a
p. 318
Obj. #7k

Rita is in need of emergency contraception. Although _____ would be most effective, because of her history of _____, she will need to use _____ instead.
a. a copper IUD; pelvic inflammatory disease; birth control pills
b. a copper IUD; blood clots; birth control pills
c. birth control pills; sexually transmitted diseases; antibiotics
d. estrogens; pelvic inflammatory disease; a copper IUD

71.
A
Answer: b
p. 318
Obj. #7k

A woman seeking emergency contraception has never given birth but has had one ectopic pregnancy. Her physician would probably recommend
a. a copper IUD.
b. high doses of estrogens or progestins.
c. a minilaparotomy.
d. a culpotomy.

72.
K
Answer: c
p. 319
Obj. #7j

Fertility awareness is also referred to as
a. ovulatory observation.
b. cyclic monitoring.
c. natural family planning.
d. menstrual monitoring.

73.
K
Answer: a
p. 319
Obj. #7j

The _____ method is based on cyclic changes of cervical mucus.
a. mucus
b. calendar
c. basal body-temperature
d. rhythm

74.
A
Answer: b
p. 319
Obj. #7j

Rosa has been using the ovulation method of birth control. She knows to avoid unprotected intercourse
a. when her basal body temperature rises slightly.
b. when a white or yellow sticky discharge begins.
c. 24 hours after a cloudy discharge begins.
d. three days before she begins to menstruate.

Chapter 11 Contraception 243

75.
A
Answer: d
p. 319
Obj. #7j

Stephanie and Brett are married and want a birth control method that has no side effects, is inexpensive and doesn't interrupt their spontaneity during sex. Although they are not really ready to have children yet, if they were to become pregnant that would be all right with them. Based on this information, the **best** method of birth control for them would be
    a. birth control pills.
    b. condom and spermicides.
    c. a diaphragm.
    d. the mucus method.

76.
K
Answer: b
p. 320
Obj. #7j

Immediately prior to ovulation, the basal body temperature
    a. rises slightly.
    b. drops slightly.
    c. rises significantly.
    d. drops significantly.

77.
K
Answer: c
p. 320
Obj. #7j

Which one is NOT true concerning the menstrual cycle methods?
    a. They restrict spontaneity.
    b. They are acceptable to some religious groups that oppose artificial methods.
    c. They are reliable when all three are used simultaneously.
    d. Because sperm can live for up to 72 hours the basal body temperature method may fail.

78.
K
Answer: b
p. 321
Obj. #7l
WWW

_____ is the **most** effective method of birth control except abstinence from coitus.
    a. The pill
    b. Sterilization
    c. The IUD
    d. The condom

79.
K
Answer: d
p. 321
Obj. #7l

All of the following are types of female sterilization **except**
    a. minilaparotomy.
    b. laparoscopy.
    c. culpotomy.
    d. salpingectomy.

80.
K
Answer: d
p. 321
Obj. #7l

_____ is (are) the leading method of birth control in the United States and around the world.
    a. Oral contraceptives
    b. The IUD
    c. Condom use
    d. Sterilization

81.
K
Answer: b
pp. 321-323
Obj. #7l

Sterilization
    a. is the third leading method of birth control in the United States.
    b. can be performed on both males and females.
    c. can be reversed easily and effectively.
    d. may have a detrimental effect on sexual satisfaction.

82.
K
Answer: b
p. 321
Obj. #7l

In this type of tubal sterilization, the incision is made through the back of the vaginal wall.
a. minilaparotomy
b. culpotomy
c. laparoscopy
d. recanalization

83.
K
Answer: c
p. 322
Obj. #7l

Vasectomy involves cutting and tying the
a. corpus cavernosum.
b. testes.
c. vas deferens.
d. fallopian tubes.

84.
K
Answer: c
p. 323
Obj. #7l

A man that has had a vasectomy
a. will not continue to produce sperm.
b. will notice that the amount of ejaculate decreases by about 25%.
c. can have a vasovasostomy at a later time if he desires.
d. will notice that ejaculation will usually be more delayed than it was prior to the surgery.

85.
A
Answer: d
p. 323
Obj. #7l
WWW

Ernest confides to Tim that he is scheduled to have a vasovasostomy. Ernest
a. is a volunteer participating in male contraceptive research.
b. should be advised of the side effects of this surgery related to potential birth defects.
c. is having a tube implanted in his scrotum to increase fertility.
d. is having a vasectomy reversed.

86.
K
Answer: b
p. 324
Obj. #7m

_____ usually occurs while nursing a baby.
a. Increased fertility
b. Amenorrhea
c. Dysmenorrhea
d. Increased PMS symptoms

87.
K
Answer: b
pp. 296, 324
Obj. #6

As a method of birth control
a. nursing will work if used only for the first three months after delivery.
b. douching may in fact help sperm reach the cervix.
c. those men who have good control of ejaculation can safely use this as a birth control method.
d. sterilization is more effective when done for women than men.

Chapter 11 Contraception 245

88.
K
Answer: a
p. 324
Obj. #8

Likely limitations on the future development of contraceptive methods include all but which of the following?
a. Growing consensus that there are more health hazards from manipulating the body than from multiple pregnancies.
b. The U.S. has cut fund for overseas clinical trials on contraceptive effectiveness.
c. Pharmaceutical company concerns about liability claims and insurance.
d. The expense of meeting clinical trial requirements of the FDS (Food and Drug Administration).

89.
K
Answer: c
p. 325
Obj. #8

With respect to future male contraceptives
a. women would rather trust themselves to take a pill than trust their partner to do this.
b. an effective male hormone is already being used in Europe.
c. it has proven difficult to find a contraceptive that reduces sperm level without interfering with sexual interest.
d. researchers have largely decided to focus on condoms rather than other reversible methods.

90.
K
Answer: d
p. 325
Obj. #8

Contraceptive methods under development for women include all but which one of the following?
a. microbiocides that stop STD transmission
b. Gynefix, a new IUD with fewer side effects
c. one size fits all diaphragms
d. testosterone based injections

Multiple Choice from Study Guide

1.
K
Answer: c
p. 292
Obj. #2c

Who is credited with making birth control available in the United States in the late 19th and early 20th centuries?
a. Anthony Comstock
b. Gloria Steinem
c. Margaret Sanger
d. Eleanor Roosevelt

2.
K
Answer: d
pp. 293-295
Obj. #3

Factors that affect contraceptive availability and choice in contemporary times include
a. gender role expectations.
b. insurance coverage.
c. religious mandates.
d. all of the above

3.
K
Answer: c
pp. 293-294
Obj. n/a

A recent cross cultural study showed that women who have fewer children have
a. happier marriages.
b. married at an early age.
c. more education.
d. European ancestry.

4.
K
Answer: e
p. 298
Obj. #5

Contraceptive failure is **more** likely among those who
a. feel guilty about their sexuality.
b. are under 30.
c. have lower incomes.
d. two of the above are true
e. all of the above are true

5.
K
Answer: c
p. 300
Obj. #7a

Outercourse is a form of sexual sharing that includes all of the following **except**
a. oral sex.
b. anal sex.
c. coitus.
d. mutual masturbation.
e. petting.

6.
K
Answer: b
pp. 296-297
Obj. #6

Of the following birth control methods, _____ is **least** effective when used correctly and consistently?
a. male condoms
b. sponge, with a woman who has never been pregnant
c. spermicides
d. Lunelle

7.
K
Answer: c
p. 301
Obj. n/a

The **most** common reversible birth control method among women in the United States is/are
a. Depo-Provera.
b. Norplant.
c. oral contraceptives.
d. spermicide.
e. condoms.

8.
K
Answer: d
p. 302
Obj. #7b

Multiphasic and constant-dose combination pills prevent pregnancy by releasing
a. gonadotropic releasing hormones (GnRH).
b. LH and FSH.
c. prostaglandins.
d. estrogen and progestin.

9.
K
Answer: a
p. 302
Obj. #7b

In order to maximize the effectiveness of oral contraceptives users should
a. take the pill at the same time each day.
b. take multiphasic pills.
c. take constant dose pills.
d. miss a pill occasionally in order to give the body a "rest".

10.
K
Answer: c
pp. 303-304
Obj. #7b

Users of birth control pills may experience all of the following **except**
a. reduced menstrual flow.
b. relief from endometriosis.
c. increased risk of ovarian cancer.
d. decreased PMS symptoms.
e. reduced menstrual cramps.

Chapter 11 Contraception 247

11.
K
Answer: a
p. 304
Obj. #7b

All of the following medications reduce the effectiveness of oral contraceptives **except**
a. ibuprofen.
b. antihistamines.
c. ampicillin.
d. tetracycline.

12.
K
Answer: c
p. 305
Obj. #7c

Norplant works by releasing _____ into the bloodstream.
a. relaxin
b. estrogen
c. progestin
d. inhibin
e. oxytocin

13.
K
Answer: c
pp. 304-305
Obj. #7c

Which of the following statements about Norplant is true?
a. Norplant is inserted below the skin of the shoulder blades.
b. Norplant lasts for a period of three years.
c. Norplant costs about the same as five years of birth control pills.
d. Menstrual irregularities are rare.

14.
K
Answer: c
p. 296
Obj. #7d

The failure rate of the injectable contraceptive Depo-Provera is
a. considerably higher than birth control pills when they are used correctly and consistently.
b. considerably lower than birth control pills when they are used correctly and consistently.
c. about the same as birth control pills when they are used correctly and consistently.
d. decreased if the user experiences side effects.

15.
K
Answer: d
pp. 303, 306
Obj. #7b, 7c, 7d

Hormone based contraceptives
a. have minimal side effects.
b. contain progestin and estrogen.
c. can be safely used by women who smoke.
d. fail to provide protection against STD's.
e. are less effective in women who have had children.

16.
K
Answer: b
pp. 307-308
Obj. #7e

There is less chance of a condom breaking if it is
a. made of polyurethane.
b. lubricated.
c. made of sheep membrane.
d. ribbed.

17.
K
Answer: c
p. 307
Obj. #7e

Which type of condom does NOT provide protection against STD's?
a. latex
b. polyurethane
c. sheep membrane
d. plain-end

18.
K
Answer: a
pp. 307-308
Obj. #7e

In order to correctly use condoms to prevent pregnancy
a. the condom must be used before the penis has contact with the vulva.
b. water-based lubricants should be used.
c. the condom must be held at the base of the penis as it is withdrawn from the vagina.
d. none of the above are true
e. all of the above are true

19.
K
Answer: d
p. 311
Obj. #7f

When a diaphragm is used contraceptive cream or jelly is
a. spread around inside of the rim.
b. squeezed into the cup.
c. spread around the outside of the rim.
d. spread around inside of the rim and squeezed into the cup.
e. spread on the outside of the cup.

20.
K
Answer: d
p. 310
Obj. #7f

A diaphragm must be left in place for at least _____ hours after intercourse.
a. two
b. three
c. five
d. six

21.
K
Answer: c
pp. 312, 314
Obj. #7f, 7g

Which disadvantage do the diaphragm and cervical cap have in common?
a. increased risk of cervical cell changes
b. headaches
c. high failure rate
d. repeated applications of spermicide are needed with additional acts of intercourse

22.
K
Answer: b
p. 314
Obj. #7h

The various types of vaginal spermicides include
a. foam, suppositories, ointment, jelly, and film.
b. foam, suppositories, cream, jelly, sponge, and film.
c. foam, cream, jelly, sponge, lotion, and film.
d. cream, jelly, suppositories, sponge, spray, and film.

23.
K
Answer: d
p. 315
Obj. #7h

Which of the following is NOT considered an advantage of vaginal spermicides?
a. The sponge is effective for repeated acts of intercourse
b. They do not require a visit to the doctor's office
c. There are no known dangerous side effects
d. Long term use is associated with reduced vaginal lubrication
e. Vaginal contraceptive film can be used by people allergic to other spermicides

Chapter 11   Contraception   249

24.
K
Answer: c
p. 316
Obj. #7i

While a woman is using an IUD she or her partner must
a. refrain from the woman-on-top intercourse position, to prevent dislodging the IUD.
b. avoid using tampons during menstruation.
c. check the length of the string after menstruation.
d. abstain from the "doggie" intercourse position, to avoid perforating the uterus.

25.
K
Answer: d
p. 317
Obj. #7i

Some women find an IUD a highly desirable form of contraception because
a. it is highly effective.
b. it does not interrupt spontaneity.
c. a woman doesn't have to remember to use it.
d. all of the above are true
e. two of the above are true

26.
K
Answer: d
p. 318
Obj. #7k

Which of the following represent methods of emergency contraception?
a. GnRH antagonists
b. copper IUDs
c. hormone pills
d. copper IUDs and hormone pills
e. misoprostol

27.
K
Answer: a
pp. 319-320
Obj. #7m

Fertility awareness methods include
a. mucus, calendar, and basal body temperature methods.
b. rhythm, calendar, and basal body temperature methods.
c. ovulation, mucus, and calendar methods.
d. ovu-quick, calendar, and rhythm methods.

28.
K
Answer: c
p. 321
Obj. #7l

Tubal sterilization involves
a. removing the fallopian tubes.
b. inserting gel into the fallopian tubes.
c. severing, cauterizing, typing, or placing a clip on the fallopian tubes.
d. removing a woman's ovaries and her fallopian tubes.

29.
K
Answer: d
p. 322
Obj. #7l

A vasectomy involves
a. removing one or more testicles.
b. placing a clip on the epididymis.
c. permanently closing the ejaculatory duct.
d. cutting and closing each vas deferens.

30.
K
Answer: a
p. 322
Obj. #7l

A vasectomy is as effective as _____ and has _____ complications than tubal sterilization.
a. tubal sterilization; fewer
b. tubal sterilization; more
c. oral contraceptives; fewer
d. oral contraceptives; more

31.
K
Answer: a
p. 324
Obj. #7m

All of the following are reasons why withdrawal is ineffective **except**
a. if ejaculation does not occur "blue balls" may result.
b. preejaculatory secretions may contain sperm.
c. it is difficult for a man to know when to withdraw.
d. if sperm settle on the labia they can swim into the vagina.

True/False

Students may be asked to answer these questions using the traditional format of marking their answers either "true" or "false". Or, to encourage more active involvement, you may choose to use the following instructions:

If the statement is true, place a "T" on the line preceding it. If the statement is false, place an "F" on the line preceding it and then change the statement to make it true by deleting incorrect information and/or adding accurate information.

1.
Answer: F
p. 292
Obj. #2a, 2c

___ In the early part of this century, Margaret Sanger opened an illegal clinic where women could obtain birth control pills.

2.
Answer: F
p. 294
Obj. #3

___ According to one study, Catholic women in the U.S. are much more likely to use birth control than non-Catholic women.

3.
Answer: T
pp. 296-297
Obj. #6

___ Both oral contraceptives and IUDs are very similar in terms of effectiveness.

4.
Answer: T
p. 298
Obj. #5

___ Research demonstrates that individuals who feel guilty about sex are more likely to use contraception ineffectively.

5.
Answer: T
p. 301
Obj. #7a

___ Oral and anal sex are types of "outercourse".

6.
Answer: F
p. 301
Obj. #7b

___ The most commonly used reversible method of birth control in the U.S. today is condom with foam.

7.
Answer: F
p. 302
Obj. #7b

___ The progestin-only birth control pill works by inhibiting ovulation.

8.
Answer: T
p. 303
Obj. #7b

___ Several of the major problems associated with oral contraceptive use are blood clots, heart attacks and non-cancerous liver tumors.

9.
Answer: T
p. 306
Obj. #7d

___ Because Depo-Provera only contains progestin, estrogen-related side effects do not occur.

10.
Answer: F
p. 306
Obj. #7f

___ Polyurethane condoms are thinner and less likely to break than are latex condoms.

11.
Answer: T
p. 307
Obj. #7f

___ Some sexually transmitted diseases, including HIV, can pass through natural membrane condoms.

12.
Answer: T
p. 312
Obj. #7d

___ Some cases of toxic shock syndrome have been reported in association with diaphragm use.

13.
Answer: T
p. 314
Obj. #7e

___ A major advantage of the cervical cap is the relative lack of side effects.

14.
Answer: T
p. 317
Obj. #7j

___ The most serious complication associated with IUD use is Pelvic Inflammatory Disease.

15.
Answer: F
p. 319
Obj. #7k

___ If a woman keeps a daily chart of changes in her vaginal secretions, she is probably practicing the rhythm method of birth control.

16.
Answer: T
p. 320
Obj. #7k

___ Immediately prior to ovulation, a woman's body temperature drops slightly.

17.
Answer: T
p. 321
Obj. #7k

___ Contraceptive methods based on the menstrual cycle are consistently less effective than most other methods.

18. ___ Sterilization is the leading method of birth control around the world.
Answer: T
p. 321
Obj. #7l

19. ___ If a woman undergoes tubal sterilization, it will most likely have a negative effect on her sexual motivation.
Answer: F
p. 322
Obj. #7l

20. ___ Female sterilization is sometimes successfully reversed.
Answer: T
p. 322
Obj. #7l

21. ___ In rare cases, the vas deferens will grow back together after a man has undergone a vasectomy.
Answer: T
p. 323
Obj. #7l

22. ___ After a vasectomy, while sexual functioning is not usually diminished, a man will experience a significant decrease in the amount of ejaculate after orgasm.
Answer: F
p. 323
Obj. #7l

Short Answer Essay

1. Discuss the history of contraceptive use in the United States, making specific reference to methods available, obstacles to contraceptive availability, significant people involved in promoting birth control legislation and key legislation related to contraceptive use. (Obj. #2)

2. What are some reasons that people do not use effective birth control? Consider both voluntary decisions and involuntary behaviors. (Obj. n/a)

3. Discuss the comparative effectiveness of at least three methods of birth control and describe several factors that influence contraceptive effectiveness. (Obj. #5, 6)

4. Describe what birth control method you find most desirable at the present time. Consider what methods you might use at various stages in your future life. (Obj. #5, 6)

5. Describe three different types of oral contraceptives and explain some of the advantages and disadvantages of using this method of birth control. (Obj. #7b)

6. Taking the point of view of a male, describe how one could involve ones partner in making shared birth control decisions, considering at least three different kinds of birth control. (Obj. #4)

7. Taking the point of view of a female, describe how one could involve ones partner in making shared birth control decisions, considering at least three different kinds of birth control. (Obj. #4)

8. Discuss how Norplant and Depo-Provera are similar and different as methods of contraception. (Obj. #7c, 7d)

9. Briefly discuss three methods of birth control based on the menstrual cycle, outlining how they work and the advantages and disadvantages of each. (Obj. #7k)

10. Describe some of the sterilization procedures available to men and their advantages and disadvantages. (Obj. #7l)

11. Describe some of the sterilization procedures available to women and their advantages and disadvantages. (Obj. #7l)

12. Describe the barrier methods of contraception and the advantages and disadvantages of each. Include a brief consideration of barrier methods that were reported to have occurred historically. (Obj. #7e, 7f, 7g)

13. What methods are used for emergency contraception? How available do you believe these should be for teens? Unmarried adults? Married adults? (Obj. #7k)

14. Assume that a friend comes to you and says that they have decided to become sexually active and they would like you to help them decide what birth control method to use. What questions would you ask to help them decide? (Obj. # 5, 6)

15. Why are there so few new birth control methods? If you had the financial resources, in what area would you concentrate your research and development efforts? Why? (Obj. #8)

12

Conceiving Children: Process and Choice

Learning Objectives

After studying this chapter, the student should be able to:

1. Discuss each of the following in relationship to becoming a parent:
    a. advantages and disadvantages of becoming a parent
    b. how common remaining childless is
    c. how women who voluntarily remain childless feel about the decision
    d. how common adoption is
    e. why people choose to adopt children

2. List several factors that will increase the possibility of conception.

3. Cite statistics that indicate how common infertility is, how successful treatment is, and then describe some of the factors that contribute to both female and male infertility.

4. Explain how problems with fertility may affect a couple's emotional and sexual relationship.

5. List and describe options for conception available to couples with infertility problems.

6. Identify the initial signs of pregnancy a woman may experience and how these may be confirmed.

7. Discuss the incidence of and issues, including the emotional experience, involved in spontaneous abortion (miscarriage).

8. Cite statistics that indicate how common elective abortion is among women from various age groups and discuss the characteristics that women who seek elective abortions have in common.

9. Describe surgical and medical procedures that may be used in having an abortion.

10. Discuss research data related to the following:
    a. effects of first-trimester abortion on subsequent fertility
    b. effects of having two or more abortions
    c. number of women that have abortions who have had a previous abortion
    d. what factors can contribute to repeat abortions
    e. percentage of women who have abortions as a result of contraceptive failure
    f. how often late abortions occur

11. Describe how a woman's partner might share the responsibility of an unwanted pregnancy.

12. Make reference to research that addresses the emotional effects of legal abortion on both women and men.

13. Explain why some women may risk an unwanted pregnancy by not using contraceptives reliably.

14. Outline and elaborate upon some of the reasons why elective abortion is such a controversial social and political issue.

15. Compare the beliefs of individuals who hold strong pro-choice values with those individuals who are anti-abortion.

16. Discuss some of the following aspects of a healthy pregnancy:
    a. fetal development
    b. prenatal care
    c. detection of birth defects
    d. pregnancy after age 35

17. Compare the different emotional and physical reactions to pregnancy from both a female and male perspective.

18. Discuss how sexual interaction may be affected during pregnancy.

19. List and describe the three stages in the process of childbirth.

20. Outline and briefly explain some contemporary philosophies regarding childbirth.

21. List and briefly describe three birthplace alternatives and under what circumstances each is appropriate.

22. Discuss the advantages and disadvantages of various medical procedures used during childbirth, making reference to appropriate research studies that support each position.

23. Describe the physical and psychological adjustments that family members experience during the postpartum period.

24. Explain the physiological changes that accompany nursing and list the advantages and disadvantages of it.

25. Describe some of the considerations a couple may need to make in resuming sexual interaction after childbirth.

26. Discuss current techniques that are being used to predetermine the sex of a child, and the impact this has had in various countries in which there is a strong preference for having sons.

27. Discuss new reproductive technologies, including those available for postmenopausal women, and some of the controversies surrounding these technologies.

28. Discuss prenatal care guidelines for pregnant women.

Multiple Choice

1.
K
Answer: c
p. 329
Obj. #1a

Some studies show that marriages without children
   a. are not as fulfilling and satisfying as marriages with children.
   b. are more stressful than marriages with children.
   c. are happier and more satisfying than marriages with children.
   d. tend to last longer than marriages with children.

2.
K
Answer: d
p. 329
Obj. #1b

Which one is NOT true with respect to remaining childless?
   a. In 1997 more than 15% of women aged 40 did not have children.
   b. This leaves more time for intimacy in an adult relationship.
   c. This often leaves more opportunity for fulfillment in a professional life.
   d. This often is a reason for stress in a marriage.

3.
K
Answer: b
pp. 329-330
Obj. #1a

All of the following are potential advantages to having children **except**
   a. can build self-esteem of parents
   b. less stress on marital relationship
   c. parents experience tremendous personal growth
   d. being able to give and receive love from children

4.
A
Answer: b
p. 330
Obj. #2

Matt and Sandra want very much to have a baby. To maximize the possibility of pregnancy they should have intercourse
   a. once a day for several days following ovulation.
   b. once a day for several days prior to ovulation.
   c. once a day for several days beginning the third day of the menstrual cycle.
   d. at least seven days a month in the morning.

5.
K
Answer: d
p. 330
Obj. #2

All of the following methods could help a couple increase the probability of conception by predicting the time of ovulation **except**
   a. mucus.
   b. body-temperature.
   c. calendar.
   d. withdrawal.

6.
K
Answer: b
p. 330
Obj. #2

The _____ measures the rise in LH in urine prior to ovulation.
   a. mucus method test
   b. ovulation-predictor test
   c. rhythm method
   d. body-temperature method

7.
K
Answer: b
p. 330
Obj. #3

Approximately one in _____ U.S. couples experience fertility problems.
   a. three
   b. six
   c. ten
   d. fifteen

8.
K
Answer: a
p. 330
Obj. #3

Sixty percent of couples that attempt it become pregnant within _____.
a. three months
b. six months
c. nine months
d. one year

9.
K
Answer: b
p. 330
Obj. #3
WWW

Which of the following statements regarding infertility is false?
a. Infertility is a result of male factors, female factors, or a combination of both.
b. Once a couple is able to conceive a child the first time, it is highly unlikely they will have fertility problems the second time.
c. Approximately half the couples seeking help for infertility will ultimately be unsuccessful.
d. Despite medical and scientific advances, the causes of infertility may be difficult to determine.

10.
K
Answer: c
p. 330
Obj. #3

Approximately _____% of infertility cases involve male factors.
a. 15
b. 25
c. 50
d. 75

11.
A
Answer: a
p. 330
Obj. #2

Monique and Hassan purchase an over-the-counter test kit to determine when she is ovulating. This is accomplished by Monique measuring _____ with the test kit.
a. the level of LH (luteinizing hormone) in her urine prior to ovulation
b. the level of acidity in her vaginal secretions prior to ovulation
c. the level of follicle stimulating hormone produced by her ovaries
d. her basal body temperature

12.
K
Answer: d
p. 331
Obj. #3

Which of the following would be **least** likely to cause female fertility problems?
a. being under emotional stress
b. smoking cigarettes
c. severe vitamin deficiencies
d. being overweight

13.
K
Answer: d
p. 331
Obj. #3

Which of the following statements is true?
a. Being 10–15% above normal weight may inhibit ovulation.
b. Women who smoke are more likely to have a varicocele than women who don't smoke.
c. Endometriosis may reduce fertility by inhibiting ovulation.
d. Douching reduces fertility.

14.
K
Answer: b
p. 331
Obj. #3

Most causes of male infertility are related to abnormalities in sperm _____ and number.
a. size
b. motility
c. shape
d. viscosity

Chapter 12 Conceiving Children: Process and Choice 259

15.
K
Answer: b
pp. 331-332
Obj. #3

All of the following affects male fertility **except**
   a. smoking.
   b. low percentage of body fat.
   c. alcohol abuse.
   d. environmental toxins.

16.
A
Answer: d
p. 331
Obj. #5

Caitlin is unable to conceive due to a history of endometriosis. This means that
   a. her body produces antibodies that reduce sperm motility.
   b. her fallopian tubes are twisted and scarred.
   c. she has a sexually transmitted disease.
   d. uterine-like tissues has grown in the pelvic cavity.

17.
K
Answer: b
p. 332
Obj. #3

Which of the following would be **least** likely to cause male infertility?
   a. the presence of a varicocele
   b. undescended testes
   c. sexually transmitted diseases
   d. contracting mumps during adulthood

18.
K
Answer: c
p. 332
Obj. #3
WWW

Which of the following statements regarding a varicocele is true?
   a. It may be treated with hormone therapy.
   b. It most commonly occurs during puberty.
   c. It is a major cause of infertility in men.
   d. It may inhibit ovulation in women.

19.
K
Answer: c
pp. 332-333
Obj. #4

All of the following are common reactions couples may have regarding their inability to conceive **except**
   a. They may deny their desire to have children.
   b. They may feel isolated from other couples who have children.
   c. They may experience more intense periods of sexual satisfaction resulting from the increased frequency of sexual interaction.
   d. They may feel guilty about their inability to conceive.

20.
K
Answer: a
p. 333
Obj. #26

The **most** successful technique for sex preselection is based on
   a. a laboratory procedure which separates X- from Y-bearing sperm.
   b. using an alkaline douche to conceive a boy and an acidic douche to conceive a girl.
   c. eating sodium and potassium foods for a boy and eating calcium and magnesium foods for a girl.
   d. altering hormone ratios prior to attempts at conception.

21.
K
Answer: c
p. 333
Obj. #26

Selective abortion of female fetuses is illegal but common in all of the following countries **except**
   a. China.
   b. South Korea.
   c. Croatia.
   d. India.

22.
K
Answer: d
p. 333
Obj. #26

Which is NOT true concerning laboratory techniques to separate X- from Y-bearing sperm?
a. This is now in widespread clinical usage.
b. This requires artificial insemination.
c. This is of benefit to couples with X-linked disease risks.
d. Success rates are better for male babies than female babies.

23.
K
Answer: d
pp. 333-334
Obj. #5

Semen from a woman's partner is mechanically introduced into her vagina, cervix or uterus in order to facilitate conception. This procedure is called
a. IVF (in vitro fertilization).
b. GIFT (gamete intrafallopian transfer).
c. ZIFT (zygote intrafallopian transfer).
d. artificial insemination.

24.
K
Answer: c
p. 334
Obj. #5

A woman who is willing to be artificially inseminated by the male partner of a childless couple, carry the pregnancy to term, deliver the child, and give it to the couple for adoption is called a/an
a. implantation host.
b. in vivo host.
c. surrogate mother.
d. substitute mother.

25.
K
Answer: b
p. 334
Obj. #5

For in vitro fertilization (IVF),
a. semen is mechanically introduced into a woman's vagina.
b. a woman's eggs are removed and fertilized in the laboratory by her partner's sperm and then introduced into her uterus.
c. semen is introduced into a woman's fallopian tube.
d. the sperm and ova are placed directly into the fallopian tube.

26.
K
Answer: a
p. 334
Obj. #5

A method called _____ attempts to facilitate implantation by placing the fertilized egg in the fallopian tube.
a. ZIFT (zygote intrafallopian transfer)
b. IVF (in vitro fertilization)
c. artificial insemination
d. GIFT (gamete intrafallopian transfer)

27.
K
Answer: a
p. 334
Obj. #5

The procedure called ZIFT involves
a. fertilizing an ovum in vitro and then placing the zygote in a woman's fallopian tube.
b. stimulating the ovaries with fertility drugs to provide multiple mature ova.
c. injecting a sperm into an egg.
d. placing donated sperm and ova into the fallopian tube.

28.
K
Answer: c
pp. 334-335
Obj. #5

Assisted reproductive techniques are
a. inexpensive.
b. used with low risk to the mother of serious problems.
c. not usually successful.
d. increasingly less expensive with each subsequent attempt.

29.
K
Answer: c
pp. 335-336
Obj. #5

Which one is NOT true concerning the multiple births that frequently accompany Assisted Reproductive Techniques?
   a. The frequency of such births is about 30%.
   b. Multiple births increase the likelihood of pregnancy and birth problems for the mother.
   c. This has been recommended by some professional organizations as a way of completing ones family rapidly.
   d. Multiple births increase the likelihood of dangerous conditions for the babies.

30.
K
Answer: d
p. 336
Obj. #3

One of the side effects of medications used to stimulate ovulation is
   a. increased incidence of birth defects.
   b. an allergic reaction that causes nausea and vomiting.
   c. increased incidence of uterine infection.
   d. multiple births.

31.
K
Answer: c
p. 336
Obj. #3

Which one is NOT true concerning moral or legal disputes over ART issues?
   a. Some have requested the use of sperm from deceased men.
   b. Of the 150,000 frozen embryos, 20,000 are in dispute.
   c. Many states have laws regulating the storage and usage (including possible adoption) of frozen embryos.
   d. There have been legal battles between divorcing couples over the disposition of frozen embryos.

32.
K
Answer: d
pp. 337-338
Obj. #6

All of the following may indicate a woman is pregnant **except**
   a. breast tenderness.
   b. nausea and vomiting.
   c. human chorionic gonadotropin in blood test.
   d. follicle-stimulating hormone in blood test.

33.
K
Answer: a
p. 337
Obj. #6

The first indication of pregnancy is usually
   a. the absence of the menstrual period.
   b. nausea.
   c. breast tenderness.
   d. increased sexual desire.

34.
K
Answer: b
p. 337
Obj. #6

Some tests for pregnancy are based on the fact that the blood and urine of a pregnant woman contain
   a. trophoblast hormone.
   b. human chorionic gonadotropin.
   c. follicle-stimulating hormone.
   d. prostaglandins.

35.
K
Answer: d
p. 337
Obj. #3

Which one is NOT true concerning reproductive technology issues?
   a. Reproductive technology in the U.S. is market drive with few legal restraints.
   b. The Internet has often been used to solicit or sell "eggs".
   c. An artificial womb has been developed that has kept fetal animals alive for weeks.
   d. Attitudes are about equally negative toward males or females who become parents over the age of 60.

36.
K
Answer: a
p. 338
Obj. #7

Which one is NOT true with respect to miscarriage?
a. The best way to cope with an early miscarriage is to become pregnant again right away.
b. Emotional shock is one possible factor that can cause a miscarriage.
c. An underactive thyroid gland has been suspected of causing miscarriages.
d. Following miscarriage some parents have found it helpful to have a memorial service.

37.
K
Answer: c
p. 338
Obj. #6

Sensitive blood tests for HCG can detect pregnancy as early as _____ after conception.
a. 24 hours
b. 2 days
c. 1 week
d. 3 weeks

38.
K
Answer: d
p. 338
Obj. #7

Which of the following statements regarding miscarriage is false?
a. The majority of miscarriages occur within the first trimester of pregnancy.
b. About 10–20% of pregnancies end in miscarriage.
c. Early miscarriages may appear as a heavier than usual menstrual flow.
d. A miscarriage is usually indicative of unsuccessful future pregnancies.

39.
K
Answer: a
p. 339
Obj. #9

The **most** common type of elective abortion is
a. suction curettage.
b. dilation and evacuation.
c. prostaglandin induction.
d. aspiration and evacuation.

40.
A
Answer: c
p. 339
Obj. #9
WWW

Lynn misses one menstrual period and three weeks later confirms the fact that she is pregnant. She decides to have an abortion and she schedules the procedure to occur in two weeks. The type of abortion procedure that will be used at this stage of her pregnancy is
a. prostaglandin induction.
b. aspiration and evacuation.
c. suction curettage.
d. dilation and evacuation.

41.
A
Answer: c
p. 349
Obj. #8, 29

Which of the following sets of variables would **most** increase the likelihood of a woman having an abortion?
a. African-American woman, age 37, single, high income
b. white woman, age 25, married with two children
c. African-American woman, age 23, four children, single
d. Hispanic woman, age 29, married with three children living in suburbs

Chapter 12 Conceiving Children: Process and Choice 263

42.
K
Answer: c
p. 339
Obj. #8

According to research, Catholic women are
a. more likely to obtain abortions than other women.
b. less likely to obtain abortions than other women.
c. as likely to obtain abortions as other women.
d. less likely to obtain abortions than other women, with the exception of Asian-American women and Hispanic women.

43.
A
Answer: d
p. 339
Obj. #9

Which of the following groups of words belong together?
a. prostaglandins, first trimester, dilation and evacuation
b. third trimester, dilation and evacuation, methotrexate
c. second trimester, suction curettage, prostaglandins
d. first trimester, suction curettage, laminaria

44.
K
Answer: b
p. 339
Obj. #9

The safest and most widely used technique for pregnancy termination between 13 and 21 weeks is
a. suction curettage.
b. dilation and evacuation.
c. prostaglandin induction.
d. laminaria insertion.

45.
K
Answer: a
p. 339
Obj. #9

The majority of abortions are performed
a. during the first trimester.
b. during the second trimester.
c. during the third trimester.
d. Roughly an equal number of abortions are performed each trimester.

46.
K
Answer: b
p. 340
Obj. #10b

Research has indicated that having two or more abortions
a. may lead to a higher incidence of birth defects in subsequent pregnancies.
b. may lead to a higher incidence of miscarriages in subsequent pregnancies.
c. may lead to a higher incidence of fertility problems in subsequent pregnancies.
d. has little effect on subsequent fertility or pregnancy.

47.
K
Answer: d
p. 340
Obj. #10a

Research has indicated that having one first-trimester abortion
a. may lead to a higher incidence of birth defects in subsequent pregnancies.
b. may lead to a higher incidence of miscarriages in subsequent pregnancies.
c. may lead to a higher incidence of fertility problems in subsequent pregnancies.
d. has little effect on subsequent fertility or pregnancy.

48.
K
Answer: a
p. 340
Obj. #10f

About _____% of abortions occur after 20 weeks.
a. 1
b. 5
c. 9
d. 15

49.
K
Answer: d
p. 341
Obj. n/a

Worldwide, about _____ unsafe abortions are performed each year and at least _____ women die each year as a result.
a. 5 million, 5,000
b. 50 million, 25,000
c. 100 million, 50,000
d. 200 million, 75,000

50.
K
Answer: c
pp. 341-342
Obj. #11

With respect to the extent of involvement in his partner's abortion, the male partner
a. has a legal right to demand an abortion.
b. has a legal right to deny an abortion.
c. can help pay medical expenses as a way to support his partner.
d. rarely experiences much emotional distress.

51.
K
Answer: d
pp. 341-342
Obj. #11

All of the following are ways in which a man might share in his partner's decision to have an abortion **except**
a. help her clarify her feelings about the procedure.
b. share the medical expenses.
c. accompany her to the clinic.
d. refrain from having intercourse for at least three days.

52.
A
Answer: d
p. 342
Obj. #13

If Karen experiences a high degree of guilt about sex, then research findings would predict all of the following **except**
a. she may be less likely to use contraception effectively.
b. she may think obtaining birth control information acknowledges her intent to engage in nonmarital intercourse.
c. she may avoid using contraception altogether.
d. she may be more likely to use birth control pills than barrier methods.

53.
K
Answer: c
p. 342
Obj. #10e

Almost _____% of women who have an abortion were using contraception the month they became pregnant.
a. 20
b. 40
c. 60
d. 80

54.
K
Answer: a
p. 342
Obj. #13

According to research findings, all of the following increase contraceptive risk-taking **except**
a. not feeling guilty about sex.
b. using drugs and alcohol.
c. a history of abuse.
d. fear of alienating partner by asking for his cooperation in using birth control.

55.
K
Answer: d
p. 342
Obj. #13

According to research findings, a woman may take contraceptive risks for all of the following reasons **except**
a. the high social value associated with pregnancy.
b. to test a man's commitment to the relationship.
c. to prevent an impending break-up with a man.
d. because she has very little guilt about being sexually active.

Chapter 12 Conceiving Children: Process and Choice   265

56.
K
Answer: d
p. 343
Obj. #14

_____ outlined the Catholic Church's view that the fetus developed a soul: 40 days after conception for males and 90 days for females.
   a. Pope Pius IX
   b. Pope John Paul II
   c. Martin Luther
   d. St. Thomas Aquinas

57.
K
Answer: c
p. 343
Obj. #n/a

Viability is a term used to describe
   a. the health of the infant in the first six months.
   b. the health of the mother postpartum.
   c. the ability of the fetus to survive independently of the woman's body.
   d. the integrity of the sperm upon ejaculation.

58.
K
Answer: b
p. 343
Obj. #n/a

Which one is NOT true concerning Supreme Court decisions concerning abortion?
   a. Roe v. Wade occurred in 1973.
   b. Roe v. Wade allowed women to decide for themselves if they wish to have an abortion up until the time of quickening.
   c. The Supreme Court has ruled that states may require minors to notify parents prior to an abortion.
   d. The Supreme Court has upheld Federal legislation barring federally funded clinics for poor women from discussing the option of abortion.

59.
K
Answer: a
p. 343
Obj. #12

The Hyde Amendment
   a. prohibited federal Medicaid funds for abortion.
   b. established that states are required to provide Medicaid funds for abortion.
   c. defined viability at six months of pregnancy.
   d. gave state legislatures the right to impose limitations on abortions.

60.
K
Answer: c
p. 344
Obj. #14

What percentage of American believe that women should have access to legal abortion?
   a. about 1/3
   b. about 45%
   c. between 55 and 65%
   d. over 75%

61.
K
Answer: b
p. 344
Obj. n/a

Mandatory parental consent for abortion
   a. was primarily opposed by the Clintons.
   b. has been initiated in about 30 states.
   c. is recommended by the American Academy of Pediatrics.
   d. is necessary because most adolescents do not discuss pregnancy options with their parents.

62.
K
Answer: c
p. 345
Obj. #14

When comparing attitudes toward legal abortion
a. there are no race differences, but sex differences.
b. there are no sex differences but race differences.
c. older white women have the strongest positive prochoice attitudes.
d. older African American women have the strongest prochoice attitudes.

63.
K
Answer: c
p. 345
Obj. #14

Which one is NOT true concerning antiabortion advocates?
a. They are often called "prolife".
b. Prolife extremists have resorted to killing physicians and other associated personnel who provide legal abortions.
c. They have decided to work more with changing individual attitudes than changing laws.
d. They picket and try to block clinic entrances where abortions occur.

64.
A
Answer: c
p. 346
Obj. #15
WWW

John claims his position is pro-choice. John **most** likely
a. is involved in the "right to life" movement.
b. is concerned with protecting the unborn fetus.
c. supports the woman's right to choose to terminate her pregnancy.
d. has strong fundamentalist affiliations.

65.
A
Answer: c
pp. 346-347
Obj. #15

Joan would never have an abortion, but she believes all women should have the right to make that decision for themselves. Her position would **best** be described as
a. pro-life.
b. anti-abortion.
c. pro-choice.
d. pro-abortion.

66.
K
Answer: a
pp. 346-347
Obj. #15

According to research, people who disapprove of legal abortion are **more** likely to
a. have disapproving attitudes toward government spending.
b. have few ties to formal religion.
c. be college-educated.
d. support civil liberties.

67.
K
Answer: b
pp. 346-347
Obj. #15

According to one study, which of the following are **most** likely to disapprove of legal abortion?
a. People who disapprove of homosexuality and government spending and who have few ties to formal religion.
b. People who have traditional attitudes about the female role and who disapprove of nonmarital sex and homosexuality.
c. People who support government spending, have strong Catholic or fundamentalist Protestant affiliations and disapprove of homosexuality.
d. People who have traditional attitudes about the female role, disapprove of nonmarital sex and are politically liberal.

68.
K
Answer: a
p. 347
Obj. #15

According to research, women who are antiabortion activists are **more** likely to
a. have low-paying or no employment outside the home.
b. believe that intimacy is the most important purpose of sexuality.
c. be college-educated.
d. have few ties to formal religion.

69.
K
Answer: c
p. 348
Obj. #15

According to research, women who actively support a woman's right to legal abortion are **more** likely to
a. base their self-esteem on their maternal roles.
b. have low-paying jobs or no employment outside the home.
c. believe that intimacy is the most important purpose of sexuality.
d. be politically conservative.

70.
K
Answer: c
p. 348
Obj. #n/a

Which of the following **best** describes colostrum?
a. a thin, yellowish vaginal fluid that is secreted during the first trimester of pregnancy
b. the fluid surrounding the fetus
c. a thin, yellowish fluid secreted by the breasts during late pregnancy
d. a waxy, protective substance on the skin of the fetus

71.
K
Answer: d
p. 348
Obj. #17

All of the following are listed as common experiences during the first trimester of pregnancy **except**
a. breast enlargement.
b. nausea.
c. fatigue.
d. colostrum secretion.

72.
K
Answer: c
p. 349
Obj. #17
WWW

One study of expectant fathers found that when men shared their feelings with their partners,
a. the men felt vulnerable and exposed, resulting in a negative effect on the relationship.
b. the women responded by becoming depressed and irrational due to their hormonal fluctuations.
c. the relationships expanded in depth and intimacy.
d. the relationships deteriorated because the women felt overburdened by the men's concerns.

73.
K
Answer: a
p. 350
Obj. #18

Most research shows that there is
a. a progressive decline in sexual interest and activity over the nine months of pregnancy.
b. a progressive increase in sexual interest and activity over the nine months of pregnancy.
c. a progressive decline in sexual interest and activity until the third trimester, at which time there is a dramatic increase.
d. no change in sexual interest or activity over the nine months of pregnancy.

74.
K
Answer: d
p. 350
Obj. #18

In pregnancies with no risk factors, sexual activity and orgasm may continue
a. through the sixth month of pregnancy.
b. through the seventh month of pregnancy.
c. through the eighth month of pregnancy.
d. as desired until labor begins.

75.
K
Answer: c
p. 351
Obj. #16a

A united sperm cell and ovum is called a/an
a. blastocyst.
b. varicocele.
c. zygote.
d. embryo.

76.
K
Answer: a
p. 351
Obj. #16a

By the end of the _____, the internal organs of the fetus begin limited functioning.
a. first trimester
b. second trimester
c. third trimester
d. first month

77.
K
Answer: b
p. 351
Obj. #16a

The sex of the fetus can be distinguished during the
a. first trimester.
b. second trimester.
c. third trimester.
d. first month.

78.
K
Answer: a
p. 351
Obj. #16a

The vernix caseosa
a. is a protective, waxy substance that covers the fetus.
b. implants on the wall of the uterus one week after fertilization.
c. is a reddish uterine discharge that is expelled after childbirth.
d. is a thick, yellowish fluid secreted by the breasts in late pregnancy.

79.
K
Answer: d
p. 352
Obj. #16b

All of the following substances pass through the placenta to the fetus **except**
a. nutrients.
b. oxygen.
c. waste products.
d. maternal blood.

80.
A
Answer: a
p. 352
Obj. #16a, 16b
WWW

Mehera has a very bad cold and is concerned that the cold virus might pass to her developing fetus. Typically, the virus will
a. not pass though the placenta.
b. infect the amniotic fluid, but not the fetus.
c. have run its course before there is adequate time to pass to the fetus.
d. not affect the fetus because of its hardy immune system.

Chapter 12 Conceiving Children: Process and Choice   269

81.
A
Answer: c
pp. 352-353
Obj. #16a, 16b

Which of the following would be **least** likely to pass into the fetal blood system?
a. the HIV virus
b. alcohol
c. bacteria
d. nicotine

82.
K
Answer: c
p. 353
Obj. #16b
WWW

_____ is the leading cause of developmental disabilities and birth defects in the United States.
a. Taking thalidomide during pregnancy
b. Maternal smoking during pregnancy
c. Fetal alcohol syndrome
d. Taking tetracycline during pregnancy

83.
K
Answer: d
p. 353
Obj. #16b

Cigarette smoking during pregnancy
a. can cause fetal deformities.
b. accelerates fetal growth.
c. increases the probability of sensory and motor defects in infants.
d. is related to low birthweight and breathing irregularities in infants.

84.
K
Answer: d
p. 353
Obj. #16b

Children of mothers who smoked during pregnancy may experience all of the following **except**
a. weigh less than other infants.
b. have significantly lower developmental scores.
c. have increased incidence of reading disorders.
d. have impaired motor development.

85.
K
Answer: d
p. 354
Obj. #16c

Amniocentesis
a. is a procedure in which chorionic villi are removed for analysis.
b. is also called ultrasound.
c. is routinely administered for first pregnancies.
d. is a procedure in which fluid surrounding the fetus is removed to check for birth defects.

86.
K
Answer: c
p. 354
Obj. #16b

Pregnant women who drink more than one cup of coffee per day may put their infants at risk for
a. genital tract abnormalities.
b. stunted bone growth.
c. lower birth weight.
d. impaired motor development.

87.
K
Answer: b
p. 354
Obj. #16c

Chorionic villus sampling may be a beneficial procedure for women with a
a. history of drug and alcohol abuse.
b. previous child with Down syndrome.
c. mental disorder.
d. severe vitamin deficiency.

88.
K
Answer: b
p. 355
Obj. #16d
WWW

Which of the following is the most accurate statement regarding pregnancy after age 35?
a. Women over 35 demonstrate more anxiety and depression during pregnancy than first time mothers in their mid-20s.
b. Women over 35 may have higher rates of pregnancy and delivery complications than younger women.
c. There is an increase in perinatal mortality in women over 35.
d. Women over 35 have no higher risk than younger women of having a child with birth defects due to chromosomal abnormalities.

89.
K
Answer: c
p. 355
Obj. #16d

Which one is NOT true with respect to pregnancy after age 35?
a. 20% of U.S. women have their first baby after age 35.
b. Most find that pregnancy for healthy women after 35 is safe.
c. There is no change in fertility as women get older until a year or so before menopause.
d. Fatal defects due to chromosome abnormalities increase with maternal age.

90.
K
Answer: a
p. 356
Obj. #20

Prepared childbirth centers around the philosophy that
a. by learning to relax and reduce their anxiety, women can have a more positive experience with childbirth.
b. by giving birth in a quiet, softly lit room, the trauma of birth for the infant can be minimized.
c. by taking advantage of appropriate medical interventions, women can have a positive birth experience while being physically comfortable during labor and delivery.
d. too much knowledge concerning the birthing process can increase anxiety, so it is best to just relax and let the physician make the decisions.

91.
K
Answer: c
p. 356
Obj. #21

Most hospitals today
a. provide water-birthing experiences.
b. insist on the use of medication at delivery.
c. offer birthing-room experiences.
d. will send medical personnel to private homes to facilitate home births on request.

92.
K
Answer: d
pp. 357-358
Obj. #19

Which of the following was NOT discussed as an indicator of the first stage of labor?
a. "bloody show"
b. uterine contractions
c. a ruptured amniotic sac
d. complete cervical dilation

93.
K
Answer: b
pp. 357-358
Obj. #19

The first stage of labor is characterized by all of the following **except**
a. effacement of the cervix.
b. separation of placenta from uterine wall.
c. dilation of the cervix.
d. more intense uterine contractions.

Chapter 12 Conceiving Children: Process and Choice 271

94.
A
Answer: c
p. 357
Obj. #16b

Halfway through her pregnancy, Nicole discovers that she has very high blood pressure and is swelling from excessive fluid retention. She should consult with her physician because of the potential danger of
  a. HIV infection.
  b. Down syndrome.
  c. toxemia.
  d. fetal alcohol syndrome.

95.
K
Answer: d
p. 357
Obj. #21

All of the following are conditions related to delivery risk **except**
  a. toxemia.
  b. placenta previa.
  c. multiple births.
  d. fetal alcohol syndrome.

96.
K
Answer: a
p. 358
Obj. #19

The second stage of labor involves
  a. the birth of the infant.
  b. the delivery of the afterbirth.
  c. passing through the transition phase.
  d. the discharge of the mucus plug.

97.
K
Answer: a
p. 359
Obj. #22
WWW

All of the following were given as reasons for performing a cesarean section **except**
  a. mother's preference.
  b. fetal distress during labor.
  c. feet or bottom coming out of the uterus first.
  d. large fetal head.

98.
A
Answer: b
p. 359
Obj. #22

Rachel is ready to deliver her first baby, which is in the breech fetal position in her uterus. Which of the following medical procedures will **most** likely be used in the course of her delivery?
  a. dilation and evacuation
  b. cesarean section
  c. episiotomy
  d. a VBAC

99.
K
Answer: b
p. 359
Obj. #22

Which of the following statements regarding cesarean section is true?
  a. Once a woman has a cesarian, subsequent births must be c-sections as well.
  b. It is one of the most common hospital surgical procedures in the U.S. today.
  c. Most women who have cesarians are just as satisfied with the experience as women who have vaginal births.
  d. A cesarian can be performed using prepared childbirth techniques.

100.
K
Answer: a
p. 360
Obj. #23

The first several weeks following birth are referred to as the
  a. postpartum period.
  b. afterbirth.
  c. postfetal period.
  d. postnatal adjustment.

101.
K
Answer: c
p. 360
Obj. #24

The yellowish liquid produced by the breasts after delivery is called
a. preliminary breast milk.
b. lactation fluid.
c. colostrum.
d. lochia.

102.
K
Answer: b
p. 361
Obj. #24
WWW

How does cigarette smoking affect breastfeeding?
a. It leeches nutrients from the milk.
b. It reduces the amount of milk produced.
c. Women who smoke tend to nurse for longer periods of time than mothers who do not smoke.
d. It subtly changes the taste of the milk, making it less appetizing to the newborn.

103.
K
Answer: b
p. 361
Obj. #24

All of the following are advantages of nursing **except**
a. provides the infant with antibodies.
b. inhibits ovulation, so it can be used as a temporary method of birth control.
c. an emotional and sensual experience for the mother.
d. helps uterus return to prepregnancy size.

104.
K
Answer: b
p. 361
Obj. #25

After childbirth, most couples resume intercourse
a. after the lochia has stopped.
b. 6 to 8 weeks following the delivery.
c. after the placenta has been discharged.
d. when colostrum begins being produced.

105.
K
Answer: d
p. 362
Obj. #25

There is evidence that for many women sexual desire and frequency _____ for several months following the birth of a baby.
a. increase significantly
b. increase slightly
c. return to the same level they were prior to pregnancy
d. decrease

106.
K
Answer: c
p. 362
Obj. #25

Which one was found in a study of sexual problems and pregnancy?
a. About 18% had problems prior to pregnancy.
b. In the first three months about half of new mothers reported one or more sexual problems.
c. At six months post delivery almost 2/3 were having sexual difficulties.
d. Most problems came about because husbands were turned off by breast-feeding wives.

Multiple Choice from Study Guide

1.
K
Answer: a
p. 329
Obj. #1c

Having childless marriage is associated with all of the following **except**
a. less marital satisfaction.
b. greater spontaneity in work and leisure.
c. more financial resources.
d. less stress.

Chapter 12 Conceiving Children: Process and Choice   273

2.
K
Answer: b
p. 329
Obj. #1a

Choosing to have children may bring all of the following **except**
   a. a sense of accomplishment.
   b. saving a troubled marriage.
   c. discovering untapped dimensions in oneself.
   d. increased personal growth.

3.
K
Answer: c
p. 330
Obj. #2

Conception is **most** likely to occur
   a. during the three days after ovulation.
   b. during the five day period after ovulation.
   c. during the six day period ending with ovulation.
   d. during the three day period ending with ovulation.

4.
K
Answer: d
p. 330
Obj. #3

Male factors account for _____ percent of infertility.
   a. 14
   b. 28
   c. 31
   d. 50

5.
K
Answer: a
pp. 331-2
Obj. #3

Which of the following is NOT a cause of low sperm count and motility?
   a. childhood measles
   b. a varicocele
   c. smoking
   d. marijuana use

6.
K
Answer: e
p. 331
Obj. #3

Ovulation may be adversely affected by
   a. poor nutrition.
   b. smoking.
   c. emotional stress.
   d. below normal levels of body fat.
   e. all of the above

7.
K
Answer: b
p. 331
Obj. #3

Problems with fallopian tubes are frequently caused by
   a. tubes that are too thin.
   b. tubes that are scarred from past STDs.
   c. being on birth control pills for many years.
   d. using an IUD.

8.
K
Answer: c
p. 332
Obj. #4

Which of the following statements **best** reflects responses to infertility?
   a. Intercourse becomes more pleasurable because it on a schedule.
   b. Performance anxiety is typically lower.
   c. Partners often feel grief, anxiety, and depression.
   d. Couples feel a sense of connection with others discussing child rearing.

9.
K
Answer: d
p. 333
Obj. #5

Artificial insemination involves introducing sperm into the
   a. vagina.
   b. cervix.
   c. uterus.
   d. all of the above

10. K
Answer: c
p. 334
Obj. #5

Which technique involves placing a fertilized egg into a woman's fallopian tubes?
a. IVF (in vitro fertilization)
b. GIFT (gamete intrafallopian transfer)
c. ZIFT (zygote intrafallopian transfer)
d. ICSI (intra cytoplasmic sperm injection)

11. K
Answer: a
p. 335
Obj. #5

Success rates for assisted reproductive technologies are no higher than
a. 28%.
b. 33%.
c. 51%.
d. 64%.

12. K
Answer: d
pp. 337-338
Obj. #6

Pregnancy tests are designed to detect _____, which is present in the blood or urine of pregnant women.
a. Estrogen
b. Progesterone
c. lutenizing hormone
d. human chorionic gonadotropin

13. K
Answer: a
p. 338
Obj. #7

Which of the following statements about spontaneous abortion (miscarriage) is true?
a. Early miscarriages may appear as a heavier than normal menstrual period.
b. One miscarriage increases the risk that subsequent pregnancies will be unsuccessful.
c. Miscarriages are most commonly experienced during the second trimester.
d. Miscarriages are seldom perceived as a loss.

14. K
Answer: c
p. 339
Obj. #8

Which of the following women is **most** likely to have an elective abortion?
a. Sallie, a 39 year old married woman with two children
b. Beth, a 27 year old affluent lawyer
c. Shawn, an 18 year old single college student
d. Barbara, a 30 year old Catholic living in a rural area

15. K
Answer: b
p. 339
Obj. #9

Most elective abortions are performed
a. before 8 weeks.
b. before 12 weeks.
c. between 13-16 weeks.
d. between 14-26 weeks.

16. K
Answer: a
p. 339
Obj. #9

A medical abortion using RU486 can be done
a. before 7 weeks.
b. between 6-9 weeks.
c. any time prior to the 13th week.
d. only on women who have already given birth to one child.

Chapter 12 Conceiving Children: Process and Choice 275

17.
K
Answer: b
pp. 339-40
Obj. #9

All of the following are methods of elective abortion **except**
a. prostaglandin induction.
b. suction curettage.
c. dilation and evacuation.
d. laminaria evacuation.

18.
K
Answer: b
p. 342
Obj. #13

Which of the following women is **most** likely to engage in contraceptive risk taking leading to unwanted pregnancy?
a. Tanika, who has a low degree of guilt about sex.
b. Mai, who frequently gets drunk with her boyfriend before having intercourse.
c. Maisol, who has a strong sense of self-esteem.
d. Sarah, who does not care if her partner thinks she is a "that kind of girl".

19.
K
Answer: c
p. 343
Obj. #n/a

Which Supreme Court decision made abortion legal as long as it was done before the fetus was viable?
a. Rust vs. Sullivan
b. Planned Parenthood vs. Casey
c. Roe vs. Wade
d. Griswold vs. Connecticut

20.
K
Answer: a
pp. 346-7
Obj. #15

Studies of attitudes toward elective abortion have shown that those
a. opposed to abortion are more likely to oppose government spending.
b. opposed to abortion tend to have smaller families.
c. who approve of abortion have larger families.
d. who approve of abortion are more likely to be politically conservative.

21.
K
Answer: b
p. 348
Obj. #16

Early pregnancy is characterized by all of the following **except**
a. increased fatigue.
b. decreased urination.
c. increased breast size.
d. nausea.

22.
K
Answer: d
p. 348
Obj. #16a

Fetal movements may first be noticed
a. during the third month.
b. during the last three months.
c. at the six month.
d. during the fourth or fifth month.

23.
K
Answer: d
p. 349
Obj. #17

Research involving expectant fathers has shown that
a. fathers' involvement during pregnancy does not predict positive interaction between fathers and newborns.
b. few fathers feel frightened about the upcoming birth.
c. few fathers fear loosing their wife's affection to the baby.
d. fathers who shared their feelings with their partner had their relationships deepen.

24. K
Answer: c
p. 350
Obj. #18

In pregnancies with no risk factors sexual activity and orgasm can continue until
a. Braxton-Hicks contractions begin.
b. colostrum secretions are noted.
c. as desired until the beginning of labor.
d. until the start of the 3rd trimester.

25. K
Answer: b
p. 351
Obj. #16a

When a sperm and egg are united the developing organism is called a(n)
a. gamete.
b. zygote.
c. blastocyst.
d. embryo.

26. K
Answer: d
p. 351
Obj. #16a

The waxy, protective coating called *vernix caseosa* appears during the
a. first trimester.
b. fourth month of pregnancy.
c. six month of pregnancy.
d. third trimester.

27. K
Answer: c
p. 352
Obj. #16a

Nutrients, oxygen, and waste products pass between the fetus and mother using the
a. chorionic villus.
b. amniotic sac.
c. placenta.
d. intestinal transfuser

28. K
Answer: d
p. 353
Obj. #n/a

Infants of mothers who smoke are **more** likely to
a. be born with cleft lip or palate.
b. have lower birth weight.
c. have lower developmental scores.
d. all of the above
e. two of the above

29. K
Answer: a
p. 355
Obj. #16b

Which of the following statements is false regarding pregnancy after age 35?
a. One of every three women has her first baby after 35.
b. Birth defects due to abnormal chromosomes are more common.
c. A woman's ability to conceive may diminish.
d. Women 35 and over feel less anxiety during pregnancy than women in their mid 20's.

30. K
Answer: d
p. 357
Obj. #19

Which is the correct sequence of events in childbirth?
a. bloody show, expulsion of the afterbirth, infant descends into birth canal
b. pushing, expulsion of the afterbirth, bloody show
c. effacement, dilation, expulsion of the afterbirth, infant is born
d. full dilation of the cervix, infant descends into birth canal, expulsion of the afterbirth

Chapter 12 Conceiving Children: Process and Choice   277

31.
K
Answer: a
p. 357-359
Obj. #19

Which stage of labor is the longest?
a. first
b. second
c. third
d. delivering the placenta

32.
K
Answer: b
p. 358
Obj. #19

The baby is born during the _____ stage of labor.
a. first
b. second
c. third
d. transition

33.
K
Answer: d
p. 359
Obj. #22

Routine, normal births without complications do NOT include
a. use of forceps.
b. episiotomy.
c. medications.
d. two of the above
e. all of the above

34.
K
Answer: c
p. 356
Obj. #n/a

What do Lamaze and Dick-Read have in common?
a. They are both medical doctors.
b. They are both certified nurse-midwives.
c. They developed methods of prepared childbirth.
d. They were both advocates of water births.

35.
K
Answer: a
p. 360
Obj. #23

The postpartum period
a. is a time of intensified emotional highs and lows.
b. lasts during the year following the baby's birth.
c. is characterized by the routine presence of postpartum depression.
d. is shorter for women who have had a cesarean birth.

36.
K
Answer: d
p. 361
Obj. #24

Advantages of breast-feeding include all of the following **except**
a. providing the infant with antibodies.
b. speeding the return of the uterus to pregnant size.
c. close physical contact with the baby.
d. reduced levels of estrogen.

37.
K
Answer: d
p. 361
Obj. #25

Which of the following is true regarding sexual interaction after pregnancy?
a. Intercourse may begin when lochia appears.
b. A majority of mothers continue to experience sexual problems as long as six months after birth.
c. Decreased sexual interest is common in women only.
d. Most women discussed sexual concerns with their health care provider.

True/False

Students may be asked to answer these questions using the traditional format of marking their answers either "true" or "false". Or, to encourage more active involvement, you may choose to use the following instructions:

If the statement is true, place a "T" on the line preceding it. If the statement is false, place an "F" on the line preceding it and then change the statement to make it true by deleting incorrect information and/or adding accurate information.

1.
Answer: T
p. 329
Obj. #1a

___ Studies show that marriages without children are happier and more satisfying than are marriages with children, especially in the years following a first child's birth.

2.
Answer: T
p. 330
Obj. #2

___ The mucus method, body-temperature and calendar methods can all be used to determine when a woman is ovulating.

3.
Answer: T
p. 331
Obj. #3

___ The majority of people seeking help for fertility problems will ultimately be unsuccessful in their efforts to conceive.

4.
Answer: F
p. 332
Obj. #3

___ One of the most common causes of male infertility is undescended testes.

5.
Answer: F
p. 334
Obj. #5

___ For in vitro fertilization, the sperm and ova are placed directly into the fallopian tube.

6.
Answer: T
p. 334
Obj. #5

___ Zygote intrafallopian transfer and gamete intrafallopian cost over $6,000 per attempt.

7.
Answer: T
p. 339
Obj. #8

___ The majority of women who obtain abortions are white, unmarried and under 25 years of age, although Hispanic and black women receive a higher number of abortions relative to their proportion of the population.

8.
Answer: F
p. 339
Obj. #9

___ The most commonly used abortion procedure is dilation and evacuation.

9.
Answer: F
pp. 339-340
Obj. #9

___ The dilation and evacuation method of abortion results in uterine contractions that expel the fetus and placenta from the vagina.

10.
Answer: F
p. 348
Obj. #10b

___ Having two or more abortions may result in birth defects in future pregnancies.

11.
Answer: T
p. 344
Obj. #14, 15

___ A majority of Americans believe that abortion should remain legal.

12.
Answer: T
p. 347
Obj. #15

___ Women who are antiabortion activists tend to be Catholic, to have large families, to have no or low-paying employment outside the home and to base their self-esteem on maternal roles.

13.
Answer: T
p. 350
Obj. #18

___ Sexual desire typically diminishes throughout a woman's pregnancy, although there may be an increase in desire during the second trimester for some women.

14.
Answer: F
p. 351
Obj. #30

___ The vernix caseosa develops into a multicelled blastocyst and implants on the uterine wall.

15.
Answer: T
p. 351
Obj. #16a

___ By the end of the second trimester, fetal movements can be felt and the fetus has opened its eyes.

16.
Answer: T
p. 354
Obj. #16c, 30

___ Both chorionic villus sampling and amniocentesis can help detect some fetal abnormalities.

17.
Answer: F
p. 358
Obj. #19

___ Cervical effacement usually begins in second stage labor.

18.
Answer: T
p. 358
Obj. #19

___ Second stage labor ends when the baby is born.

19.
Answer: T
p. 359
Obj. #22

___ Routine episiotomy presents greater risks than benefits.

20. ___ Postpartum depression affects only about 1% of new mothers.
Answer: F
p. 360
Obj. #23

Short Answer Essay

1. Discuss the advantages and the disadvantages of becoming a parent. Indicate what is known about the frequency and consequences of the childfree life. (Obj. #1)

2. What is your present view as to whether or not you wish to become a parent? What factors have influenced your decision or would you consider in the future if you do not now have a decision made? (Obj. #2)

3. Discuss the topic of infertility in men and women, making specific reference to the following: a. how common it is; b. how successful treatment interventions are for infertility; c. specific fertility problems men and women experience. (Obj. #3)

4. If you wanted to become pregnant and this had not happened after 6 months, what would you do? What about after 12 months? What about after 2 years? (Obj. #2, 3)

5. Describe at least five alternatives available to individuals with infertility problems. (Obj. #5)

6. Discuss the issue of abortion from a historical, social and political perspective, and speculate on future directions this issue will be taking based on the current social and political climate. (Obj. #14, 15)

7. Discuss each of the following: a. effects of first trimester abortion on subsequent fertility; b. effects of having two or more abortions; c. factors that can contribute to repeat abortions; d. the emotional effects of legal abortion on women. (Obj. #10a, 10b, 10d; 12)

8. Explain why some women may risk unwanted pregnancy by not using contraceptives reliably, citing relevant research. (Obj. #13)

9. Assume that you were to become pregnant. What changes would you make in your behavior because of this? What other important choices would you makes, e.g., when would you first see a doctor, where would you delivery and who would be present, would you have amniocentesis, would you want to know the sex of your child prior to delivery, etc.? (Obj. #16)

10. Discuss the various components of optimum prenatal care. (Obj. #16b, 16c, 16d)

11. Describe fetal development during each trimester and discuss how the mother typically responds sexually, physically and emotionally during each trimester. (Obj. #16a, 17)

12. Discuss options and guidelines for sexual interaction during pregnancy and after birth. (Obj. #18, 25)

13. Compare the advantages and disadvantages of home birth, birthing centers, and hospital birth. (Obj. #21)

14. List and describe the three stages in the process of childbirth. (Obj. #19)

15. If a postmenopausal woman wanted to get pregnant by her husband, describe the method might she use to accomplish that. Discuss the controversy surrounding assisted reproductive technology for postmenopausal women. (Obj. #28)

13

Sexuality During Childhood and Adolescence

Learning Objectives

After studying this chapter, the student should be able to:

1. Discuss examples that demonstrate how infants of both sexes are born with the capacity for sexual pleasure and response.

2. Discuss common features of sexual development that occur during childhood and cite research that supports these various phases.

3. Define adolescence, and explain how childhood and adolescent sexuality in Western society compares to that of other cultures.

4. Define puberty and explain what happens during this period of development for males and females.

5. Describe the changes that occur in adolescent friendships during puberty.

6. Discuss the double standard as it affects adolescent social and sexual behavior, and make specific reference to what research suggests regarding the current status of the sexual double standard among adolescents.

7. Describe the incidence and frequency of masturbation among male and female adolescents.

8. Define petting and discuss how common it is among adolescent females and males.

9. Explain how likely ongoing sexual relationships are among adolescents.

10. Discuss why the term "premarital sex" may be misleading and then summarize what the research reveals regarding the following:
    a. incidence of intercourse among adolescents and reasons for engaging in this behavior
    b. percentage of men and women who abstain from adolescent intercourse
    c. the effect of AIDS education on teenage sexual behavior

11. Discuss how common same-sex contact may be during adolescence and explain how this may reflect a transitory, experimental phase of sexual development or how it may be indicative of a homosexual orientation.

12. Summarize available research and statistical data regarding various aspects of adolescent pregnancy, including strategies for how to reduce it.

13. Discuss how an adolescent mother's decision to keep her child may affect her education, financial status, and the life of her child.

14. Explain how prevalent contraceptive use is among adolescents and what factors affect contraceptive use on a regular basis.

15. Summarize the result of comparative studies of adolescent pregnancy and discuss factors that may contribute to the difference in pregnancy rates.

16. Summarize the authors' list of four suggestions for reducing the teenage pregnancy rate.

17. Making reference to relevant research, describe some general guidelines that the authors suggest in talking to children about sex.

18. Discuss the nature of sex education programs in schools, and what the research says regarding the effects of sex education on behavior.

19. Describe differences in the onset of puberty and menarche between African-American and white girls.

20. Discuss American ethnic diversity in adolescent coitus among African-American, Hispanic and white adolescents.

21. Discuss normative sexual behavior in young children and maternal correlates of sexual behavior.

Multiple Choice

1.
K
Answer: d
p. 366
Obj. n/a

In infancy and childhood
a. sexuality does not exist for most in a normal upbringing.
b. sexuality exists but in a form that is not predictive of the future.
c. sexuality can best be described as dormant.
d. many experiences of this time have great impact on future expression of adult sexuality.

2.
K
Answer: c
pp. 366-367
Obj. #1

Which of the following statements is false?
a. Male infants have been observed experiencing what appears to be an orgasm.
b. Female infants have been observed experiencing what appears to be an orgasm.
c. Some male infants have been observed ejaculating after stimulating themselves.
d. Bathing or breastfeeding a child may stimulate a genital or sexual response in the child.

3.
K
Answer: a
p. 367
Obj. #2

Most of what we know about childhood sexual behavior is based on
a. research done outside of America.
b. observations of children at home and at school.
c. interviews of adolescents and their parents.
d. recollections of adults who are asked to recall childhood experiences.

Chapter 13 Sexuality During Childhood and Adolescence 285

4.
K
Answer: b
p. 367
Obj. n/a

There is a scarcity of data on childhood sexuality for all but which one of the following reasons.
   a. People are concerned about introducing sexual ideas to children.
   b. The data would have little practical application.
   c. It is difficult to obtain financial support for basic research in this area.
   d. Federal guidelines make such research impossible or difficult.

5.
A
Answer: d
p. 368
Obj. #2
WWW

Based on research, if a child is rarely touched and held during the first few months and years of life, how would this be **most** likely to affect his or her behavior as an adult?
   a. The person would be more likely to engage in sadistic behavior with animals.
   b. The person would be more likely to engage in masochistic behavior.
   c. The person would be more likely to want to touch and be touched than the average person.
   d. The person would be more likely to have difficulty establishing intimate relationships.

6.
K
Answer: a
p. 368
Obj. #2

Psychologists emphasize the importance of being touched and held in early childhood. This is commonly referred to as
   a. contact comfort.
   b. sensate focus.
   c. affectional conditioning.
   d. tactile grounding.

7.
K
Answer: a
p. 368
Obj. #2

In one study of 49 societies, in cultures where children were nurtured with physical affection
   a. there were few instances of adult violence.
   b. there were higher rates of childhood and adolescent masturbation.
   c. men and women exhibited more androgynous behavior as adults.
   d. there were higher rates of child abuse and molestation than in other cultures.

8.
K
Answer: b
p. 368
Obj. #2

The rhythmic manipulation of the genitals associated with adult masturbation generally does not occur until
   a. six months of age.
   b. a child is two to three years old.
   c. a child is five to six years old.
   d. preadolescence — ages nine to eleven.

9.
K
Answer: d
pp. 368-369
Obj. #2

Which one was NOT true for the study of normative sexual behavior in children, as reported by their mothers?
   a. Observed sexual behaviors peaked at age 5.
   b. There were no ethnic differences.
   c. Mothers who had more years of education reported observing more sexual behavior in their children.
   d. A five-year-old boy who touches his genitals on and off should be watched for possible sexual abuse.

10.
K
Answer: c
p. 369
Obj. #2

According to research, approximately _____ of women and _____ of men reported having masturbated prior to adolescence.
a. 50%; 50%
b. 10%; 80%
c. 33%; 66%
d. 25%; 75%

11.
K
Answer: b
p. 369
Obj. #2

Most boys learn about masturbation _____; **most** girls learn about masturbation _____.
a. through self-discovery; through self-discovery
b. from friends; by accident
c. from friends; from friends
d. by accident; through self-discovery

12.
A
Answer: c
pp. 370-371
Obj. #2

Based on their discussion, which of the following responses to a child masturbating would the authors be **most** likely to advocate?
a. Slap the hands of a young child, and give time out for older ones.
b. Ignore the activity and distract the child by engaging their interest in something else.
c. "I know that it feels good, but this is something that you should do when you are alone".
d. Gently inform the child that this kind of touch is inappropriate and could cause sexual or psychological problems if continued.

13.
K
Answer: d
pp. 369, 371
Obj. #2

Which of the following statements is false?
a. Sex play with friends of the same sex or other sex is a common part of growing up for many children.
b. By the age of eight or nine most, generally boys and girls begin to play separately.
c. Most young boys learn about masturbation from their friends.
d. In the childhood years, an approximately equal number of boys and girls engage in masturbation.

14.
K
Answer: d
p. 370
Obj. #2

Young girls are **most** likely to learn about masturbation
a. from other young girls.
b. from other young boys.
c. from hearing about it in sex education classes.
d. accidentally.

15.
K
Answer: c
p. 371
Obj. #2

Which one is NOT true of childhood sex play?
a. It is most likely to take place between the ages of four and seven.
b. Curiosity about the forbidden probably encourages early sexual exploration.
c. Those who are brighter engage in this less.
d. This may normally occur with either the same or the other sex.

Chapter 13 Sexuality During Childhood and Adolescence   287

16.
A
Answer: a
p. 372
Obj. #2

Which of the following statements regarding sex play with same sex friends during childhood is false?
   a. Parents are advised to discourage this behavior as it may "set the stage" for a homosexual orientation.
   b. It is common during the late childhood years.
   c. It is usually transitory.
   d. In a small percentage of cases, this behavior may be indicative of a homosexual orientation.

17.
K
Answer: c
p. 372
Obj. #3

In Western societies, adolescence typically spans the period from _____ to _____ years of age.
   a. 10; 15
   b. 11; 16
   c. 12; 20
   d. 13; 18

18.
K
Answer: b
p. 372
Obj. #3
WWW

By cross-cultural standards,
   a. adult roles in Western society are assumed at an early age.
   b. adolescence in Western society is rather extended.
   c. adolescents in Western society are very sexually permissive compared to adolescents in Mangaia.
   d. adolescents in Western society are very sexually repressed compared to the African Ashanti or the Kwoma society of New Guinea.

19.
K
Answer: a
p. 372
Obj. #4

Puberty is a term used to describe the period of rapid _____ changes in early adolescence.
   a. physical
   b. emotional
   c. social
   d. physical, social and emotional

20.
K
Answer: b
p. 372
Obj. #4

During puberty, the hypothalamus causes the pituitary to secrete _____ into the bloodstream.
   a. libido
   b. gonadotropins
   c. androgens and estrogens
   d. adrenalin

21.
K
Answer: d
p. 373
Obj. #4

The onset of puberty is approximately
   a. the same for girls and boys.
   b. one year earlier for girls than for boys.
   c. one year later for girls than for boys.
   d. two years earlier for girls than for boys.

22.
K
Answer: c
p. 373
Obj. #4

The best example of a secondary sexual characteristic is
   a. growth of the penis.
   b. growth of the uterus.
   c. growth of pubic hair.
   d. growth of the scrotum.

23.
K
Answer: b
p. 373
Obj. #4

The earliest signs of puberty for a girl are
a. a growth spurt and increase in vaginal secretions.
b. breast budding and growth of pubic hair.
c. an increase in vaginal secretions and menarche.
d. menarche and breast budding.

24.
K
Answer: b
p. 373
Obj. #4

The first menstrual period is called
a. menstruation.
b. menarche.
c. prima privea.
d. pubertal discharge.

25.
K
Answer: d
pp. 373-374
Obj. #4

Which of the following statements is false?
a. Initial menstrual periods may occur without ovulation.
b. Initial menstrual periods may be irregular.
c. A recent study has indicated that many girls may be starting to reach puberty by age eight.
d. Adolescent women may experience delayed menarche if they are overweight.

26.
K
Answer: b
p. 374
Obj. #4

A recent study revealed that girls are starting to reach puberty as early as age eight. The authors suggest that one reason for this might be
a. increased exposure to sexually explicit materials on television and elsewhere.
b. increased exposure to environmental estrogens.
c. sex education programs that are being taught starting in kindergarten.
d. dietary changes over the last twenty years.

27.
K
Answer: b
p. 374
Obj. #4

The first ejaculation in boys
a. occurs around age 10.
b. occurs when the prostate and seminal vesicles begin functioning.
c. occurs when the testicles have fully descended.
d. occurs when the vas deferens is fully functioning.

28.
K
Answer: c
p. 374
Obj. #4

The initial appearance of sperm in the ejaculate typically occurs at about age
a. 10.
b. 12.
c. 14.
d. 16.

29.
A
Answer: c
p. 375
Obj. #6

An adolescent girl wears her boyfriend's letterman's jacket and gains status as a result, but if he were to wear her cheerleader's cardigan, he would be teased. This may be an example of
a. cheap thrills.
b. transvestism.
c. the double standard.
d. androgynous behavior.

Chapter 13 Sexuality During Childhood and Adolescence   289

30.
K
Answer: d
p. 375
Obj. #6
WWW

Which one is NOT true of the sexual double standard?
a. It was originally defined as allowing coitus prior to marriage for men but not women.
b. It refers to the belief that women, but not men, are to have sexual relations only within committed love relationships.
c. It is decreasing among adolescents and adults in North America.
d. It is best explained by an innate tendency, resulting from evolutionary success.

31.
K
Answer: c
p. 375
Obj. #6

The sexual double standard was originally defined as
a. men did not have to be as physically attractive as women.
b. men but not women were allowed to commit adultery.
c. men but not women were allowed coitus prior to marriage.
d. women were assumed to be responsible when infertility occurred.

32.
K
Answer: c
p. 375
Obj. #6

What percent of Canadian female students recently reported that it was considered more acceptable for a man to have more sexual partners than a woman?
a. 25%
b. 55%
c. 75%
d. 95%

33.
K
Answer: d
p. 376
Obj. #3

All of the following are true of many island societies of the South Pacific **except**
a. Children may engage in group masturbation.
b. Children may engage in oral-genital contacts.
c. Children may be allowed to observe adult sexual activity.
d. Children may experience sexual activity with parents or other adult caretakers as a form of "sexual mentoring".

34.
K
Answer: b
p. 376
Obj. #3

Cultural variation in early sexuality
a. may be assumed largely to remain as originally reported by anthropological investigations after 1950.
b. includes some societies in which coitus is encouraged among young unmarried males and females.
c. should be studied so we can decide which society to emulate.
d. occurs primarily for masturbation.

35.
K
Answer: b
p. 377
Obj. #7

Which of the following statements regarding masturbation during adolescence is true?
a. It increases in frequency in both sexes, but more girls engage in it than boys.
b. It increases in frequency in both sexes, but more boys engage in it than girls.
c. It increases in frequency in both sexes, and approximately the same number of boys and girls engage in it.
d. Available research is dated so there is no current information at this time.

36.
A
Answer: d
p. 378
Obj. #7
WWW

Sex therapists would be **most** likely to disagree with which of the following statements regarding adolescent masturbation?
a. It is a good way to relieve sexual tension.
b. Adolescents who do not engage in it may be missing an important part of their sexual development.
c. It is a healthy way to learn about your body and what feels good.
d. It may inhibit eventual sexual expression with a partner, because of the self-focused nature of the behavior.

37.
K
Answer: d
p. 378
Obj. #8

All of the following would be considered petting **except**
a. oral-genital stimulation.
b. kissing.
c. manual stimulation.
d. coitus.

38.
K
Answer: d
p. 378
Obj. #8

Recent studies indicate that the incidence of oral sex among teenagers has
a. decreased slightly.
b. remained similar to the statistics Kinsey reported.
c. increased slightly.
d. increased significantly.

39.
K
Answer: a
p. 378
Obj. #8

_____ is more frequently reported than _____ by adolescents of both sexes.
a. Cunnilingus; fellatio
b. Fellatio; cunnilingus
c. Intercourse; masturbation
d. Intercourse; petting

40.
K
Answer: d
p. 379
Obj. #9

Contemporary adolescent males are **more** likely to have sex _____ than males surveyed several decades ago.
a. with an older, sexually experienced woman
b. with a stranger
c. with a casual acquaintance
d. with someone they love or feel affection for

41.
K
Answer: b
p. 379
Obj. #9

Contemporary adolescents have indicated that _____ is important in their intimate relationships.
a. good sex
b. emotional attachment
c. gaining peer approval
d. similarity in family background

42.
A
Answer: d
p. 379
Obj. #10a

Rudy and Elaine are involved in a relationship and are both seniors in high school. They engage in kissing, petting, oral sex and mutual masturbation. They have not engaged in penile-vaginal intercourse and do not intend to until the point at which they make a permanent commitment — to each other, or someone else. Based on the authors' discussion, how would they describe the couple's behavior?
   a. They have chosen to be sexually active in ways that do not put them at risk for contracting sexually transmitted diseases.
   b. They have chosen to refrain from having premarital sex.
   c. They have chosen to be celibate prior to marriage.
   d. They have chosen to refrain from adolescent coitus.

43.
K
Answer: a
p. 379
Obj. #10a

The incidence of adolescent intercourse among very young teenagers
   a. is increasing.
   b. has leveled off.
   c. has decreased slightly.
   d. has decreased dramatically.

44.
A
Answer: c
pp. 379-381
Obj. #10a
WWW

Which of the following statements **best** summarizes the rate of adolescent coital activity over the last five decades?
   a. It has been slowly increasing over time.
   b. It slowly increased until it peaked in the mid-1970s, at which point it decreased for several years and then leveled off.
   c. It has increased over time, leveled off within the past decade, but has increased among very young teenagers.
   d. It has increased steadily until the mid-1980s, at which point it began a slow but steady decrease.

45.
K
Answer: a
p. 381
Obj. #20

In regard to ethnic variation in the incidence of adolescent coitus, _____ were the most likely to have experienced intercourse by their senior year in high school and _____ were the **least** likely to have experienced it.
   a. African-Americans; whites
   b. whites; Hispanic-Americans
   c. African-Americans; Hispanic-Americans
   d. whites; African-Americans

46.
K
Answer: d
p. 381
Obj. #20

Which of the following statements is true?
   a. By 12th grade, more white males and females report having had sexual intercourse than African-American or Hispanic males and females.
   b. White girls tend to begin menstruating 1–1½ years earlier than African-American girls do.
   c. Comparable numbers of white males and white females have had sexual intercourse by 12th grade.
   d. African-American girls tend to enter puberty 1–1½ years earlier than white girls.

47.
K
Answer: d
p. 381
Obj. #20

Differences in adolescent coital experiences among African-Americans, Hispanic-Americans and whites may be related to
a. religious differences.
b. ethnic customs.
c. racial differences.
d. economic status.

48.
A
Answer: d
p. 381
Obj. #20

Which of the following individuals would be **most** likely to experience coitus at an early age?
a. an upper-middle class Hispanic-American
b. an upper-middle class African-American
c. a lower class white
d. a lower class African-American

49.
K
Answer: b
p. 381
Obj. #20

_____ adolescents are several times **more** likely to initiate sexual intercourse before age 13 than _____ adolescents.
a. Hispanic-American; African-American
b. African-American; white and Hispanic-American
c. White; Hispanic-American and African-American
d. Both Hispanic-American and African American; white

50.
K
Answer: a
p. 382
Obj. #10b

In the NHSLS study, what percentage of men and women had their first intercourse experience on their wedding night?
a. 7% of men; 21% of women
b. 5% of men; 8% of women
c. 14% of men; 18% of women
d. 29% of men; 10% of women

51.
K
Answer: a
p. 382
Obj. #10a

According to the NHSLS study, approximately _____% of women reported being forced into first intercourse.
a. 4
b. 8
c. 12
d. 16

52.
K
Answer: c
p. 382
Obj. #10a

According to the NHSLS study, _____ was the most common reason reported by women for having first intercourse and _____ was the most common reason reported by men.
a. peer pressure and curiosity; readiness for sex
b. curiosity and readiness for sex; curiosity and readiness for sex
c. affection for partner; curiosity and readiness for sex
d. affection for partner; affection for partner

53.
K
Answer: d
p. 382
Obj. #10a

All but which one of the following factors has been empirically found to be associated with early onset of coitus?
a. poverty
b. low educational expectations
c. a history of sexual abuse
d. unusually good looks

Chapter 13 Sexuality During Childhood and Adolescence   293

54.
K
Answer: c
p. 382
Obj. #10a

All but which one of the following factors has been empirically found to be associated with later onset of coitus?
- a. strong religious beliefs
- b. parental disapproval of teenage intercourse
- c. poor athletic ability
- d. good school performance

55.
K
Answer: b
p. 383
Obj. #10c

Which of the following statements is true?
- a. Most adolescents are inadequately informed about AIDS and as a result continue to engage in high-risk behavior.
- b. Most adolescents are adequately informed about AIDS but continue to engage in high-risk behavior because they don't believe it will affect them.
- c. Most adolescents are adequately informed about AIDS and as a result have decreased the extent to which they engage in high-risk behavior.
- d. Most adolescents are somewhat informed about AIDS to the extent they have decreased the degree to which they engage in intercourse, but participation in other high-risk behaviors has increased.

56.
K
Answer: c
p. 383
Obj. #10c

Which of the following statements is NOT true concerning AIDS?
- a. Multiple sex partners increase the risk of HIV infection.
- b. 20% of all reported cases are for persons in their 20's.
- c. Those who have learned the facts about AIDS in school are apparently less likely to engage in risky behaviors.
- d. The average age of HIV infection has been steadily decreasing over the past 20 years.

57.
K
Answer: c
p. 384
Obj. #10c

In one study of teenage women who had received prescriptions for oral contraceptives, it was found that condoms
- a. were used by 76% of the women to protect against HIV infection.
- b. were used by 47% of the women to protect against HIV infection.
- c. were used by 16% of the women to protect against HIV infection.
- d. were never used, even if the women were considered to be at risk for HIV infection.

58.
K
Answer: d
p. 384
Obj. #11
WWW

Which of the following statements concerning same-sex contact during adolescence is false?
- a. It may be experimental and not indicative of a homosexual orientation.
- b. More men tend to experience it than women.
- c. It may be indicative of a homosexual orientation.
- d. The majority of same-sex contact occurs between an adolescent and an older adult.

59.
K
Answer: d
p. 384
Obj. #11

The majority of homosexual contact that takes place during adolescence
a. is experienced by roughly equal numbers of men and women.
b. is most often indicative of a homosexual orientation.
c. occurs with older adults.
d. occurs between peers.

60.
K
Answer: b
p. 384
Obj. #11

Several studies indicate that _____% of girls and _____% of boys report having experienced same-sex contact during adolescence.
a. 2–5; 15–19
b. 6–11; 11–14
c. 4–7; 7–10
d. 10–13; 12–18

61.
K
Answer: d
p. 385
Obj. n/a

Which one is NOT true of high school Gay-Straight Alliances (GSAs)?
a. There about 700 of these.
b. They are trying to change antigay attitudes among classmates.
c. They are trying to change antigay attitudes among teachers and parents.
d. Some states have declared these illegal.

62.
K
Answer: c
p. 385
Obj. n/a

Which of the following has NOT been suggested as likely to make life easier for adolescents with homosexual orientations?
a. the Internet
b. positive media portrayals
c. recent reports that this orientation can sometimes be changed
d. openly gay sports celebrities

63.
K
Answer: a
p. 386
Obj. #12

When comparing adolescent pregnancy rates across 33 developed countries
a. adolescent birthrate is decreasing in a majority of these countries.
b. adolescent birthrate is increasing in a majority of these countries.
c. adolescent birthrate has gone up notably in some countries and down notably in others.
d. in most countries, teen mothers are married.

64.
K
Answer: a
p. 386
Obj. #12

The rate of teen pregnancy in the United States
a. is the highest in the western world.
b. has steadily decreased over the last 20 years and is now the second highest in the western world.
c. has steadily increased in the last twenty years.
d. is probably unknown as so many girls lie about this.

65.
K
Answer: d
p. 387
Obj. #12

Which ethnic group in the United States has the highest reported adolescent pregnancy rate?
a. white Americans
b. Asian Americans
c. African Americans
d. Hispanic Americans

Chapter 13 Sexuality During Childhood and Adolescence   295

66. Of the teenage pregnancies each year in the United States how many
K end in live births?
Answer: b a. one-quarter
p. 387 b. one-half
Obj. #12 c. three-quarters
  d. we don't have these data

67. Approximately _____ unmarried American adolescents
K become pregnant each year.
Answer: c a. 250,000
p. 387 b. 500,000
Obj. #12 c. 1,000,000
  d. 2,000,000

68. Approximately _____ abortions would be eliminated each year
A if we could eliminate teenage pregnancy.
Answer: d a. 50,000
p. 387 b. 100,000
Obj. #12 c. 150,000
  d. 300,000

69. Which of the following statements regarding children born to
K adolescent mothers is **least** accurate?
Answer: c a. They are more likely to die as infants.
p. 388 b. They are more likely to demonstrate deficits in intellectual
Obj. #13 ability.
  c. They are more likely to have birth defects.
  d. They are more likely to have physical and emotional problems.

70. Which one is NOT true for pregnant teenagers as compared to
K mothers in their 20's or older?
Answer: d a. They are more likely to hemorrhage when delivering.
p. 396 b. They are more likely to miscarry.
Obj. #13 c. They are more likely to get inadequate prenatal care.
  d. They are more likely to be in good health.

71. A study of condom failure in adolescents showed a one year failure
K rate
Answer: c a. of about 1%.
p. 388 b. over 5%.
Obj. #14 c. over 15%.
  d. over 25%.

72. A minority of teenagers
K a. are sexually active.
Answer: c b. who become pregnant go on to deliver.
p. 388 c. use reliable birth control.
Obj. #14 d. who become pregnant are eventually dependent on welfare
  services.

73.
K
Answer: c
pp. 388-389
Obj. #14
WWW

Which of the following statements regarding contraceptive use among teenagers is true?
   a. While contraceptive use is unreliable, the majority use contraceptives the first few times they have intercourse.
   b. While contraceptive use is generally reliable, the majority do not use contraceptives the first few times they have intercourse.
   c. The majority of teenagers lack knowledge about effective birth control.
   d. Teenagers in established relationships tend to not use contraceptives.

74.
K
Answer: c
p. 389
Obj. #14

Ineffective or nonusage of contraception has been associated with all but which one of the following?
   a. opposition to abortion
   b. early age of intercourse
   c. long-term relationships
   d. teenage women with older male partners

75.
K
Answer: c
p. 389
Obj. #14

Youth who use contraception are **more** likely to come from families
   a. where they were highly religious.
   b. that stress personal responsibility.
   c. where fathers do at least half of the sex education.
   d. that have resulted from accidental pregnancies.

76.
K
Answer: d
p. 390
Obj. #16
WWW

All of the following are suggestions given by the authors to reduce teenage pregnancies **except**
   a. Provide compulsory sex education curriculum at all grade levels.
   b. Provide free or low-cost contraceptives to all adolescents who want them.
   c. Educate males to assume at least partial responsibility for birth control.
   d. Emphasize abstinence from intercourse until the early twenties to minimize risk of pregnancy as well as the risk of contracting AIDS.

77.
K
Answer: b
p. 391
Obj. #17

Research indicates that most children begin asking questions regarding how babies are made by about age
   a. three.
   b. four.
   c. six.
   d. seven.

78.
K
Answer: d
p. 392
Obj. #17

The authors suggest that parents should take the initiative in sexual discussions
   a. very rarely.
   b. most of the time.
   c. with children of their same sex.
   d. for menstruation and ejaculation.

79.
K
Answer: c
p. 393
Obj. #17

Most young people prefer that their _____ be the primary source of sex information.
a. friends
b. siblings
c. parents
d. teachers

80.
K
Answer: a
p. 393
Obj. #17

Most young people prefer that their _____ be the primary source of sex education. In reality, their _____ are the primary source of information.
a. parents; friends
b. friends; parents
c. teachers; friends
d. teachers; siblings

81.
K
Answer: c
p. 393
Obj. #17
WWW

Research indicates that adolescents who talk openly with their parents regarding sex and contraception are _____ than adolescents who do not talk to their parents.
a. more likely to engage in sexual activity at an earlier age
b. less likely to engage in nonmarital intercourse
c. more likely to use birth control consistently
d. more likely to have had multiple sexual partners by age 17

82.
K
Answer: b
pp. 393-394
Obj. #18
WWW

Which of the following statements regarding sex education in the schools is **most** accurate?
a. The majority of parents do not support the idea of sex education in schools.
b. Only a minority of American schools offer comprehensive sex education courses.
c. Research indicates that sex education promotes sexual experimentation.
d. Research indicates that sex education promotes sexual restraint.

83.
K
Answer: c
p. 394
Obj. #18

Abstinence-only programs
a. change adolescents' attitudes but not behavior.
b. delay the onset of sexual intercourse.
c. have been heavily funded by the U. S. Congress.
d. are effective only when combined with religious education.

84.
K
Answer: b
p. 394
Obj. #18

A survey of U.S. public school districts concerning sexuality education found that
a. over 90% of schools have a district wide policy to teach some sexuality education.
b. about 1/3 teach abstinence-only in order to prevent STDs and adolescent pregnancies.
c. there were no regional differences in approaches to sex education.
d. the school personnel themselves often did not understand what the questions were about.

Multiple Choice from Study Guide

1. K
Answer: a
pp. 366-368
Obj. #1

Which of the followings statements **best** reflects current understanding about infant sexuality?
a. Vaginal lubrication, penile erection, and masturbation have been observed.
b. Infant males have displayed erections, but infant girls have yet to develop the capacity for vaginal lubrication.
c. Infant females have shown vaginal lubrication and what appears to be orgasm, but infant boys do not develop erectile function until puberty.
d. Sexuality remains latent until puberty, as Freud theorized.

2. K
Answer: c
pp. 366-368
Obj. #2

During childhood
a. self-pleasuring is primarily observed in sexually abused children.
b. ethnicity strongly predicts the types of sexual behaviors observed in children.
c. responses to the child's expressions of affection help shape the way sexuality is expressed later in life.
d. most girls learn about masturbation from childhood friends.

3. K
Answer: d
p. 369
Obj. #2

Masturbation is practiced **more** frequently by _____ children than _____ children.
a. African-American male children; White male
b. Hispanic-American male children; African-American male
c. female; male
d. male; female

4. K
Answer: c
p. 370
Obj. #2

According to the authors, which of the following is the **best** response for a parent to give to their child who was discovered masturbating?
a. "Stop doing that!"
b. Ignore the behavior, in order to discourage excess masturbation in the future.
c. "I bet that feels good."
d. Cast a stern look at the child and announce that you're taking away a privilege.

5. K
Answer: d
p. 369
Obj. #2

Friedrich and colleagues' interview study of mothers identified _____ as behaviors that occurred most frequently among children.
a. talking about sex acts, self-stimulation, exhibitionism
b. touches breasts, self-stimulation, exhibitionism
c. self-stimulation, touches others' sex parts, tries to have coitus
d. exhibitionism, self-stimulation, rubbing against another person

Chapter 13 Sexuality During Childhood and Adolescence   299

6.
K
Answer: a
p. 371
Obj. #2

Which statement **most** accurately summarizes research on childhood sex play?
   a. The majority of children experience sex play, and same-sex play in and of itself is not necessarily indicative of a homosexual orientation.
   b. The majority of children experience sex play, and same-sex play is associated with a homosexual orientation in adulthood.
   c. The majority of children do NOT experience sex play, and same-sex play in and of itself is not necessarily indicative of a homosexual orientation.
   d. The majority of children do NOT experience sex play, and same-sex play is associated with a homosexual orientation in adulthood.

7.
K
Answer: c
p. 373
Obj. #4

Which of the following **best** represents a secondary sex characteristic?
   a. external genitalia
   b. gonads
   c. underarm hair
   d. increase in height

8.
K
Answer: b
p. 373
Obj. #4

A growing body of research data suggests that menarche is triggered by
   a. secretion of prostaglandins.
   b. the presence of a minimum percentage of body fat.
   c. reaching a threshold of breast development.
   d. a decline in the excretion of growth hormone from the pituitary gland.

9.
K
Answer: c
p. 374
Obj. #4

The seminal vesicles and prostate gland must function with sufficient testosterone before _____ can occur.
   a. orgasm
   b. erection
   c. ejaculation
   d. epididymal aptosis

10.
K
Answer: a
p. 375
Obj. #6

Which statement below **best** illustrates the effect of the sexual double standard on adolescents?
   a. Steve brags to his male friends about the kind of sex he and his girlfriend have; Emily tells her friends little about sex with Steve, fearing they'll think she's a slut.
   b. Jose is proud of being a virgin and doesn't care what his friends think about it; Lora is determined to have intercourse so she'll feel like a real woman.
   c. Carmen wishes that her boyfriend would wear the earring she bought for him; Dave is worried that his classmates will think he's a sissy since he seldom dates.
   d. Sierra feels proud of her body and enjoys wearing sexy clothes; Kyle loves to "catch" a girl and then drop her as soon as she falls for him.

11.
K
Answer: c
p. 377
Obj. #6

Current research shows that the sexual double standard
a. shows no signs of eroding.
b. has decreased, especially among men.
c. has decreased, especially among women.
d. decreased during the early 90's, and is beginning to increase.

12.
K
Answer: b
p. 376
Obj. #3

Which society openly encourages children to masturbate and have homosexual contacts during childhood?
a. The Truk
b. The Ashanti
c. The Kwoma
d. The Marquesans

13.
K
Answer: a
p. 378
Obj. #8

Petting is an important form of sexual expression among teenagers for all of the following reasons **except**
a. Petting is less emotionally involving than other forms of sexual expression.
b. A set of sexual behaviors can be learned that do not carry the risk of pregnancy.
c. Within the boundaries of an intimate relationship, teens can learn about their own sexual responses.
d. Sexual intimacy may be experienced while technically remaining a virgin.

14.
K
Answer: b
p. 379
Obj. #10a

Teenagers are **most** likely to be sexually intimate with
a. casual acquaintances.
b. someone for whom they feel affection.
c. a somewhat older adult.
d. strangers that have been met for the first time.

15.
K
Answer: a
p. 379
Obj. #10a

Recent studies have revealed that the age of first adolescent coitus
a. is occurring earlier.
b. was at its lowest in the 70's.
c. has begun to rise.
d. is dropping, but only for Hispanic Americans.

16.
K
Answer: b
p. 381
Obj. #10a

Ethnic differences in the age of first intercourse are **best** explained by
a. differences between rural and urban youth.
b. economic status.
c. religious beliefs among ethnic groups.
d. differing sexual mores among ethnic groups.

17.
K
Answer: b
p. 382
Obj. #10a

According to the National Health and Social Life Survey the most common reason reported for first intercourse was
a. "it was my wedding night" – reported by women.
b. curiosity/readiness for sex – reported by men.
c. affection for partner – reported by men.
d. curiosity/readiness for sex – reported by women.

Chapter 13 Sexuality During Childhood and Adolescence 301

18.
K
Answer: e
p. 382
Obj. #10a, 12

Who is **most** likely to delay the onset of adolescent intercourse?
a. Tyrone, who gets good grades in school
b. Shoshanna, whose friends share the same spiritual beliefs
c. Trinh, who feels she can talk openly with her parents
d. two of the above are true
e. all of the above are true

19.
K
Answer: c
p. 383
Obj. #10c

Which of the following **decreases** a teenager's risk for contracting HIV infection?
a. the personal fable
b. using alcohol or other drugs
c. delaying first intercourse until after age 15
d. believing that condoms are a hassle because you or your partner uses birth control pills

20.
K
Answer: c
p. 384-385
Obj. #11

All of the following are reasons why sexual contact with a member of the same sex during adolescence does NOT reflect sexual orientation later in life except
a. Many heterosexual persons have had early homosexual experiences.
b. Same sex contact may be experimental.
c. Same sex contact with peers does not predict adult sexual orientation, but same sex contact with adults does.
d. Persons with a homosexual orientation may not act on those feelings until they are adults.

21.
K
Answer: d
p. 386
Obj. #15

Which country has the highest rate of teenage pregnancy?
a. the Netherlands
b. Sweden
c. England
d. the United States

22.
K
Answer: a
p. 387
Obj. #15

Teen birth rates have begun to decline for all ethnic groups **except**
a. Hispanic Americans.
b. African Americans.
c. White Americans.
d. Native Americans.

23.
K
Answer: b
p. 387
Obj. n/a

Of the one million teenage pregnancies in the United States each year, how many result in a live birth?
a. 17 percent
b. 50 percent
c. 66 percent
d. 73 percent

24.
K
Answer: c
p. 388
Obj. #13

Which of the following is true regarding the consequences of teenage pregnancy?
a. Teenage mothers have a lower prenatal mortality rate than older women.
b. Pregnant teenagers may be legally prevented from attending public school.
c. Teenage mothers provide parenting that is of lower quality than adult mothers.
d. Children of teenage mothers are no more likely than other children to have problems with school performance.

25.
K
Answer: b
p. 388-389
Obj. #14

Of the persons below, who is **most** likely to correctly and consistently use contraception?
a. Adam, who had first intercourse at age 12
b. Alex, who has frequently talked with his mother about birth control
c. Brianna, whose boyfriend is six years older than her
d. Betse, who has intercourse infrequently

26.
K
Answer: a
p. 389
Obj. #14

Research has revealed that _____ adolescents use effective contraception consistently after they have been sexually active for a long period of time.
a. a minority of
b. two-thirds of
c. 71% of
d. most female

27.
K
Answer: c
p. 390
Obj. #16

The authors suggest all of the following to reduce adolescent pregnancy **except**
a. establishing compulsory sex education at all grade levels.
b. stressing that males must share responsibility for birth control as well as females.
c. implementing abstinence-only sex education programs on a wider basis.
d. removing restrictions on advertising nonprescription contraceptives.

28.
K
Answer: b
p. 391-392
Obj. #17

One strategy the authors suggest for providing sex education with one's own children is
a. wait to have "the talk" until puberty is imminent.
b. integrate information about sex into everyday conversations, where appropriate.
c. avoid expression the idea that sex is pleasurable.
d. be sure to provide detailed responses every chance you get, even though the child may not want a thorough reply.

29.
K
Answer: d
p. 394
Obj. #18

Numerous research studies have demonstrated that comprehensive sex education programs
a. increase the frequency of sexual intercourse.
b. lead teens to have intercourse at an earlier age.
c. increase the number of a teen's sexual partners.
d. none of the above are true
e. all of the above are true

30.
K
Answer: b
p. 393
Obj. n/a

Studies have revealed that teenagers get **most** of their sexuality information from _____ yet they would prefer to get such information from _____.
a. television; friends
b. friends; parents
c. parents; friends
d. friends; magazines

True/False

Students may be asked to answer these questions using the traditional format of marking their answers either "true" or "false". Or, to encourage more active involvement, you may choose to use the following instructions:

If the statement is true, place a "T" on the line preceding it. If the statement is false, place an "F" on the line preceding it and then change the statement to make it true by deleting incorrect information and/or adding accurate information.

1.
Answer: T
pp. 367-368
Obj. #2

___ The tendency we have as adults toward giving and receiving affection seems to be related to our early experiences regarding this with significant others, especially our parents.

2.
Answer: T
p. 369
Obj. #7

___ About 1/3 of females and 2/3 of males report having masturbated prior to adolescence.

3.
Answer: T
p. 371
Obj. #2

___ A majority of adults report having engaged in some form of sex play, with same or other sex friends or siblings, by the age of 12.

4.
Answer: T
p. 372
Obj. #3

___ Compared to many other cultures, adolescence in our society lasts much longer than others.

5.
Answer: T
p. 374
Obj. #4

___ Recent research suggests that girls are reaching puberty earlier, perhaps because of environmental estrogens.

6.
Answer: F
p. 375
Obj. #6

___ Recent research suggests that the sexual double standard among American adolescents may be on the increase.

7.
Answer: F
p. 378
Obj. #8

___ Fellatio is more common among adolescents than cunnilingus.

8.
Answer: T
p. 379
Obj. #9

___ Adolescent males are more inclined to have sex with someone they care about than with a casual acquaintance or stranger.

9.
Answer: T
p. 381
Obj. #10a

___ Affluent adolescents are more likely to abstain from sexual intercourse than those who are poor.

10.
Answer: F
p. 383
Obj. #10c

___ Current research suggests that teenagers are not familiar with basic information regarding AIDS and HIV transmission.

11.
Answer: F
p. 384
Obj. #11

___ When same-sex contact occurs during adolescence it is usually between an adolescent and an older enticing adult.

12.
Answer: T
p. 387
Obj. #12

___ Of all the teenagers that become pregnant each year, approximately 30% of those have abortions.

13.
Answer: T
p. 387
Obj. #12

___ About one million unmarried adolescents in America become pregnant each year.

14.
Answer: F
p. 388
Obj. #12

___ Recent research has demonstrated that the negative health consequences associated with adolescent pregnancy are due to biological immaturity.

15.
Answer: F
p. 388
Obj. #18

___ Adolescents experience a condom failure rate over 15% each year.

16.
Answer: F
p. 389
Obj. #14

___ Sexually active adolescents who have conservative religious beliefs and oppose abortion are more likely to use birth control, and to do it effectively.

17
Answer: F
p. 390
Obj. n/a

___ Condom availability in schools has been shown to contribute to increased sexual activity.

18.
Answer: F
p. 392
Obj. #17

___ Parents should not initiate conversation about sex unless their children ask questions.

19.
Answer: F
p. 393
Obj. #17

___ Most young people over the age of 12 prefer teachers as their primary source of sex education.

20.
Answer: T
p. 393
Obj. #18

___ A majority of parents support having sex education in schools.

21.
Answer: F
p. 394
Obj. #18

___ Abstinence-only sex education in schools has been proven the best way to delay sexual intercourse in adolescents.

Short Answer Essay

1. Discuss normative sexual development through childhood, citing relevant research as appropriate. (Obj. #2)

2. Describe some of the physical and social changes that occur for most children between the ages of ten and fifteen. (Obj. #4, 5, 6)

3. What does data say about self stimulation in children? About sex play with other children? What would you do if you were a parent and this occurred with your children? (Obj. #1, 2)

4. Describe your sexual education at home and school with respect to information about menstruation, nocturnal emission, and same-sex contact. What do you believe should occur at home and school with respect to these topics? (Obj. n/a)

5. Describe the incidence of same-sex contact during childhood and adolescence? How does this compare to the rate of homosexuality? What school support systems are available concerning homosexuality? What systems do you believe should be available? (Obj. #11)

6. Define, discuss the incidence of, and issues associated with petting, intercourse, and virginity among adolescents. (Obj. #7, 8, 9, 10, 11)

7. Describe some of the shortcomings of the term "premarital sex" and discuss the incidence of adolescent coitus among teenagers, taking into account age, gender and ethnic background. (Obj. #10, 21)

8. Explain how prevalent contraceptive use is among adolescents and what factors affect contraceptive use on a regular basis. (Obj. #14)

9. Discuss adolescent pregnancy, including how common it is, roughly what percentage of women choose to have an abortion or give birth, and of those who give birth, how many choose to keep their babies, and how an adolescent mother's decision to keep her baby affects her and the life of her unborn child. (Obj. #12, 13)

10. Outline some specific strategies for reducing the teenage pregnancy rate. (Obj. #16)

11. Making reference to appropriate research, discuss how the adolescent pregnancy rate in the United States compares to that of other countries and explain some of the possible reasons for why the discrepancies exist. (Obj. #15)

12. Discuss cultural variations in childhood and adolescent sexuality, making reference to specific cultures and how the sexual norms vary behaviorally from one culture to another. (Obj. #3)

13. What is the sexual double standard? Describe how it exists making use of both research and you own observations. (Obj. #6)

14. Outline a research study in the area of childhood (i.e., preadolescent) sexuality. What arguments would you make to a funding agency as to why it would be desirable to fund this? What would you say to parents to encourage them to cooperate? (Obj. n/a)

15. Outline a research study in the area of adolescent sexuality. What arguments would you make to a funding agency as to why it would be desirable to fund this? What would you say to parents to encourage them to cooperate? (Obj. n/a)

14

Sexuality and the Adult Years

Learning Objectives

After studying this chapter, the students should be able to:

1. Discuss single living, making specific reference to the following:
   a. what factors account for the increasing number of single people and what forms being single take
   b. sexual activity among single people as opposed to married people

2. Discuss cohabitation, making specific reference to the following:
   a. social attitudes toward it over time
   b. how prevalent it is in our society
   c. advantages and disadvantages of cohabitation
   d. how cohabitation may affect a subsequent marital relationship
   e. domestic partners

3. Discuss the institution of marriage, making specific reference to the following:
   a. statistically how common it is and what marital trends indicate
   b. the functions it serves
   c. the various forms it takes
   d. changing expectations and marital patterns
   e. factors that contribute to marital satisfaction as well as factors that are indicative of marital discord
   f. sexual behavior patterns within marriage

4. Describe consensual and nonconsensual extramarital relationships, noting the motivations for, the prevalence and the effects of.

5. Discuss divorce, making specific reference to the following:
   a. what divorce statistics reveal
   b. factors that account for high and low divorce rates
   c. how covenant marriage is attempting to lower divorce rates
   d. adjustments a person must make as the result of a divorce
   e. sexual behavior of divorced people

6. Discuss some of the reasons why aging in our society is associated with sexlessness.

7. Explain how the double standard relates to male and female sexual expression throughout the aging process.

8. Discuss three factors that affect sexual activity in later years.

9. Describe the nature of sexual expression and relationships in the later years for both heterosexual and homosexual individuals.

10. Explain why people tend to become more androgynous when they age and how that may be expressed.

11. Discuss widowhood, making specific reference to the following:
    a. Describe how the ratio of widows to widowers has changed since the turn of the century.
    b. Compare and contrast the adjustments of widowhood to those of divorce.

12. Discuss how attitudes toward extramarital sex vary cross-culturally.

13. Distinguish between miscegenation and interracial marriage. Discuss how incidence of interracial marriage has changed over time and how this may affect census categories.

14. Discuss some of the controversial issues related to extramarital affairs in cyberspace.

Multiple Choice

1.
K
Answer: d
p. 398
Obj. #1a

Which of the following is **least** likely to be a contributing factor to the increase in the number of single adults?
a. greater emphasis on more education
b. an increase in the number of women who no longer depend on marriage for economic stability
c. an increase in the number of people choosing to not marry at all
d. an increase in the practice of serial monogamy

2.
K
Answer: d
p. 398
Obj. #1a

Which of the following is **least** likely to be a contributing factor to the increase in the number of single adults?
a. tendency of more women to place career goals ahead of marriage
b. rising divorce rates
c. an increase in number of people who live together outside of marriage
d. an increase in the influence of religion

3.
A
Answer: c
p. 398
Obj. #1b
WWW

Which of the following is the **best** example of serial monogamy?
a. a married person who has a succession of extramarital affairs, but is never involved in more than one affair at a time
b. a married person who has concurrent extramarital affairs
c. a single person who has a succession of sexually exclusive relationships
d. a single person who has concurrent sexual relationships with a number of different partners

4.
K
Answer: c
p. 399
Obj. #2a

Current social attitudes toward cohabitation can **best** be described as
a. tolerant.
b. negative.
c. increasingly accepting.
d. indifferent.

Chapter 14 Sexuality and the Adult Years 309

5.
K
Answer: d
p. 399
Obj. #2c

All of the following were mentioned in the text as reasons for living together **except**
a. informality of living together.
b. less pressure to take on roles of wife or husband.
c. stigma of failure is less severe than that of divorce if relationship ends.
d. dissatisfaction with prior living conditions.

6.
A
Answer: a
p. 399
Obj. #2e

Laurie and Andy live together as lovers in a committed relationship but are not married. This type of relationship is referred to as
a. a domestic partnership.
b. serial monogamy.
c. an open marriage.
d. polyandry.

7.
K
Answer: d
p. 399
Obj. #2

Which one is NOT true of cohabitation?
a. This was first included in the census in 1990.
b. Cohabiting women are more likely than married women to have as much education as their partners.
c. There are in the U. S. about 4 million couples unmarried but living together.
d. Many cohabiting couples are waiting to marry until after they have a child.

8.
K
Answer: a
p. 400
Obj. #2c
WWW

One of the major problems many cohabiting couples experience is
a. disapproval of parents or other family members.
b. sexual boredom.
c. the nature of the relationship is usually not as egalitarian as a marital relationship.
d. more pressure to assume traditional gender roles than in marital relationships.

9.
K
Answer: c
p. 400
Obj. #2b

About how many of today's newlyweds have lived together prior to marriage?
a. about 7%
b. about one-quarter
c. more than half
d. about three-quarters

10.
K
Answer: c
p. 400
Obj. #3a

Statistics demonstrate that approximately _____ percent of adults in the United States marry.
a. about 80%
b. about 85%
c. about 90%
d. about 95%

11.
K
Answer: c
p. 400
Obj. #3

Which one is NOT true of marriage?
a. It is found in about 80% of societies.
b. It serves both personal and societal functions.
c. It is an economic partnership.
d. It defines inheritance rights for family property.

12.
K
Answer: c
p. 400
Obj. #3b

Traditionally, a primary function of marriage has been to
a. reproduce until there are enough children to take care of the parents.
b. provide emotional security for women.
c. provide a stable economic unit in which to raise children.
d. provide emotional security for men.

13.
K
Answer: a
p. 401
Obj. #3

All of the following are traditional elements of most Western marriages **except**
a. polyandry.
b. heterosexuality.
c. legality.
d. sexual exclusivity.

14.
K
Answer: c
p. 401
Obj. #3c

Polygyny is a form of marriage
a. in the Polynesian Islands.
b. between one woman and several men.
c. between one man and several women.
d. that is legal in Utah.

15.
K
Answer: c
p. 401
Obj. #3c

The term that most specifically describes a form of marriage between one woman and several men simultaneously is called
a. cuckoldry.
b. polygyny.
c. polyandry.
d. serial monogamy.

16.
K
Answer: b
p. 402
Obj. #3d

People's expectations for marriage have _____ and our supportive network for marriage has _____.
a. declined; expanded
b. expanded; declined
c. shrunk; increased
d. expanded; increased

17.
K
Answer: b
p. 402
Obj. #13

Which one is NOT true with respect to interracial marriages?
a. About 30% of white Americans oppose black-white marriages.
b. About 1/3 of young adults have dated someone of another race.
c. Miscegenation refers to sex between members of different races, whether married or not.
d. One out of 19 children born today is of mixed race.

18.
K
Answer: c
p. 402
Obj. #13
WWW

Interracial marriage
a. is more frequent in New York than any other state.
b. is banned in more than a dozen states.
c. is increasing dramatically.
d. is forbidden by the Catholic Church.

Chapter 14 Sexuality and the Adult Years   311

19.
K
Answer: d
p. 403
Obj. #3e

According to the authors, a good marriage
- a. will have great sex.
- b. will be largely problem free.
- c. will occur in about 1 out of 5 marriages.
- d. means a commitment to working on problems.

20.
K
Answer: c
p. 403
Obj. #3e
WWW

When Gottman's team videotaped married couples resolving conflict, they identified all of the following patterns as predictors of marital dissatisfaction and separation **except**
- a. facial expressions of disgust or fear.
- b. defensiveness.
- c. verbal expressions of anger.
- d. verbal expressions of contempt.

21.
A
Answer: b
p. 403
Obj. #3e

According to Gottman's research, which of the following patterns would be **least** likely to predict eventual marriage separation?
- a. a man showing no response when his partner expresses her concerns
- b. a man expressing his anger using "I" language regarding his partner's dependence and lack of initiative
- c. a woman constantly making excuses for her behavior and not accepting responsibility for her role in creating problems in the relationship
- d. a woman verbally expressing contempt for her partner's behavior

22.
A
Answer: d
p. 403
Obj. #3e

Which of the following behaviors, if frequently demonstrated in a relationship, would be **least** likely to predict eventual marital separation?
- a. a husband showing no response when his wife expresses her concerns
- b. making excuses for one's behavior and not taking responsibility for one's contribution to the problem
- c. a wife showing contempt for her husband
- d. a wife verbally expressing her boredom and lack of interest in the relationship

23.
K
Answer: d
p. 404
Obj. #3e

Gottman's research team has found that lasting and happy marriages are characterized by a _____ to _____ ratio of positive to negative emotional interactions.
- a. 2; 1
- b. 3; 1
- c. 4; 1
- d. 5; 1

24.
K
Answer: c
p. 404
Obj. #3e

Which of the following statements regarding Gottman's research on predicting marital satisfaction is true?
a. Validating couples are the most healthy.
b. Volatile couples are at the highest risk for maintaining marital satisfaction.
c. Showing contempt or disgust for one's partner is one pattern that can predict eventual marital dissatisfaction or separation.
d. Avoiding conflict with one's partner is one pattern that can predict eventual marital dissatisfaction or separation.

25.
K
Answer: a
p. 404
Obj. #3e

Which of the following is the **best** predictor of marital satisfaction?
a. moments of support, kindness, passion and mutual pleasure that far outweigh moments of disgust, criticism, defensiveness and anger
b. having a validating relationship style
c. sharing similar goals and interests
d. sharing compatible views on money and money management

26.
A
Answer: c
p. 404
Obj. #3e

Which of the following couples would be **most** likely to maintain a happy, stable relationship?
a. They share a validating relationship style.
b. They demonstrate a 2 to 1 ratio of positive to negative interactions in the relationship.
c. He listens to his wife's requests and concerns and accepts her influence; she initiates discussions with him in a soft and diplomatic manner.
d. They share similar short-term and long-term goals and "choose their battles" by agreeing to avoid conflict in most instances.

27.
K
Answer: a
p. 404
Obj. #3e

PREPARE, a premarital assessment, evaluates relationship strengths and weaknesses in all of the following areas **except**
a. political views.
b. personality issues.
c. money management.
d. conflict resolution.

28.
K
Answer: d
p. 404
Obj. #3e

PREPARE, a premarital assessment, evaluates relationship strengths and weaknesses in all of the following areas **except**
a. conflict resolution and communication skills
b. children and marriage; family and friends
c. money management; leisure activities
d. political views; substance use and abuse

29.
K
Answer: b
p. 405
Obj. #3f

As compared with Kinsey's research, contemporary American married men and women appear to be
a. engaging in intercourse with about the same frequency.
b. experiencing a wider repertoire of sexual behavior.
c. experiencing a decrease in the duration of precoital activity.
d. experiencing an increase in fellatio and a decrease in cunnilingus.

Chapter 14 Sexuality and the Adult Years 313

30.
K
Answer: b
p. 406
Obj. #3f

According to several researchers, all of the following were associated with marital sexual satisfaction **except**
a. frequency of sexual interaction.
b. willingness to experiment sexually.
c. mutuality in initiating sex.
d. frequency of orgasm among women.

31.
A
Answer: c
p. 406
Obj. #3f

Ken reports that sex is the "bread and butter" of his relationship. He probably is
a. single.
b. newly married.
c. in a satisfying long-term relationship.
d. experiencing a mid-life crisis.

32.
A
Answer: c
pp. 405-406
Obj. #3d, 3f

Craig and Lisa are a married couple in their mid-20s. Drawing from available research, if you were to compare their relationship to that of their parents, which of the following statements would **most** likely be accurate?
a. Craig and Lisa do not expect as much from marriage as their parents did.
b. Craig and Lisa have more social and familial support for their marriage than their parents did.
c. Craig and Lisa probably have sex more often than their parents did at their age.
d. When Craig and Lisa have intercourse, it probably lasts as long as it did when their parents had intercourse at their age.

33.
A
Answer: a
p. 406
Obj. #3f

Which one is NOT true about the relationships with sexuality in marriage?
a. None of those who reported sex less than once a month were satisfied with their marriage.
b. When both partners are willing to initiate sex this contributes to sexual satisfaction in marriage.
c. Sex is more exciting at the outset of marriage and less so later.
d. Of those couples who had sex three or more times a week, 90% were satisfied with their sex lives.

34.
A
Answer: d
p. 406
Obj. #3e

Gottman's research found that the most important factor in marital satisfaction is
a. being satisfied with ones sexual activity level, whatever the frequency.
b. mutuality of values.
c. spending lots of time together.
d. the quality of their friendship.

35.
A
Answer: c
p. 407
Obj. #3b

Which of the following is NOT one of the tasks of a happy marriage, according to Wallerstein and Blakeslee?
a. sharing laughter
b. sustaining memories of courtship and early marriage
c. finding and economically successful life
d. detaching emotionally from the families of childhood

36.
A
Answer: d
pp. 407, 412
Obj. #4

Sharon is married and has promised fidelity to her husband, but engages in a one-night stand. Sharon has experienced all of the following **except**
a. an extramarital relationship.
b. nonconsensual extramarital sex.
c. adultery.
d. open marriage.

37.
K
Answer: d
pp. 408-409
Obj. #4

All of the following were cited by the authors as reasons for engaging in nonconsensual extramarital sex **except**
a. wanting to expand emotionally or sexually.
b. unavailability of sex within the marriage.
c. a way to begin ending a marriage that is no longer satisfying.
d. a manifestation of sexual addiction.

38.
K
Answer: c
p. 409
Obj. #4

With respect to extramarital sex
a. Women report that they would do this more than men if they could be sure of not getting pregnant.
b. Men are programmed to do this more than women.
c. There are no sex differences when men and women are matched for sexual attitudes and interest.
d. Men and women tend not to do this until after they have children.

39.
K
Answer: a
p. 409
Obj. #4

Factors increasing the likelihood of extramarital sex include all but which one of the following?
a. being at the age of midlife crisis
b. out of town travel
c. higher interest in sex
d. permissive sexual attitudes

40.
K
Answer: d
pp. 408-409
Obj. #14
WWW

Your text suggested that Cybersex
a. is just like other harmless fantasies.
b. may help some people learn how to develop relationships.
c. occurs so rarely that we know little about it.
d. and Cybercheating have ramifications like that of traditional infidelity.

41.
K
Answer: a
p. 410
Obj. #4

The prevalence of extramarital involvements
a. is difficult to estimate.
b. is higher than the *Playboy* and *Cosmopolitan* surveys indicate.
c. is as high as 75 percent in men and 60 percent in women.
d. is related to socioeconomic factors.

42.
K
Answer: d
p. 422
Obj. #4

According to the National Health and Social Life Survey in 1994, compared to Kinsey's research, the number of men and women participating in extramarital affairs has
a. stayed about the same.
b. increased dramatically, and is now leveling off.
c. increased.
d. decreased.

Chapter 14 Sexuality and the Adult Years 315

43.
K
Answer: d
p. 410
Obj. #4

According to research, the impact of extramarital sex on the primary couple
a. is positive, motivating a couple to deal with their problems.
b. is negative, often resulting in the dissolution of the marriage.
c. is usually traumatic, often resulting in severe guilt and betrayal of trust.
d. is difficult to determine; it may involve all of the above.

44.
K
Answer: d
p. 422
Obj. #4

According to the National Health and Social Life Survey, _____% of the married subjects reported that during the past year they had been monogamous.
a. 67
b. 75
c. 86
d. 94

45.
A
Answer: d
p. 422
Obj. #4
WWW

Which of the following statements regarding extramarital affairs is **most** accurate?
a. Extramarital affairs are the major cause of divorce.
b. Extramarital affairs are most always symptoms of a troubled marital relationship.
c. Monogamous couples have similar divorce rates as compared to couples in which one or both partners have participated in extramarital affairs.
d. The impact of extramarital affairs on both the individual and the couple varies considerably.

46.
K
Answer: a
p. 410
Obj. #4

Which of the following statements regarding extramarital affairs is false?
a. Research indicates that monogamous couples had higher divorce rates than couples in which one or both partners had participated in extramarital affairs.
b. Extramarital affairs may have serious consequences for both the participant and his or her spouse.
c. Extramarital affairs may be a symptom of a disintegrating marriage.
d. Extramarital affairs may cause marital breakups.

47.
K
Answer: d
p. 411
Obj. #13

Which of the following statements is true?
a. In most societies around the world, women are allowed greater access to extramarital coitus than men are.
b. Next to fellatio and/or cunnilingus, marital coitus is the most common form of adult sexual activity in all societies around the world.
c. In the Polynesian Mangaians, married women are allowed to take lovers but married men are not.
d. Many societies impose fewer restrictions on extramarital sex than does our own.

48.
K
Answer: a
p. 411
Obj. #4

Which of the following is an example of a consensual extramarital relationship?
a. swinging
b. infidelity
c. polygyny
d. polyandry

49.
K
Answer: c
p. 411
Obj. #4

Which of the following statements is false?
a. Swinging appears to have been most popular in the 1970s and early 1980s.
b. Another term for swinging is comarital sex.
c. Most couples who have an open marriage are swingers.
d. Swinging is a type of consensual extramarital relationship.

50.
K
Answer: b
p. 411
Obj. #4

Swinging is
a. also called wife swapping.
b. something that about 5% reported having done in the 70's and 80's.
c. dangerous if your swings aren't firmly anchored in the ceiling.
d. enjoying a renewed interest among couples after almost a decade of relative apathy.

51.
K
Answer: c
p. 412
Obj. #4

Open marriages
a. are an example of polyandry.
b. are a form of nonconsensual extramarital sex.
c. are based on the assumption that one relationship is unlikely to fulfill a person's intimacy needs.
d. were popularized through the work of Masters and Johnson.

52.
K
Answer: a
p. 412
Obj. #4

Participants in an open marriage
a. encourage each other to have close, meaningful relationships with others.
b. discourage each other from having emotional relationships outside the marriage, but encourage sexual encounters.
c. often evolve into "swingers".
d. are committing a felony in most states.

53.
K
Answer: a
p. 412
Obj. #5a, 5b

In regard to divorce statistics, which of the following statements is false?
a. The fact that about half of all marriages will end in divorce is a sign of the societal rejection of the institution of marriage.
b. A significant percentage of divorces involve people who have been married and divorced more than once.
c. The proportion of marriages ending in divorce has increased dramatically since the 1950s.
d. Recent statistics reveal that the divorce rate has leveled off and is even declining slightly.

54.
K
Answer: a
pp. 413-414
Obj. #5b

All of the following were given as reasons for the high divorce rate in the United States **except**
a. decreasing expectations for marriage to provide sexual and emotional fulfillment.
b. the reduction in the social stigma attached to divorce.
c. increased economic independence of women.
d. the liberalization of divorce laws.

55.
K
Answer: b
pp. 413-414
Obj. #5c

All of the following statements regarding covenant marriage are accurate **except**
a. Louisiana was the first state to implement this practice.
b. This practice may put victims of domestic violence at risk because of the protracted length of time to finalize a divorce.
c. This practice is optional, not mandatory.
d. Premarital counseling is required as part of this practice.

56.
A
Answer: d
p. 414
Obj. #5b

Which of the following individuals would be **least** likely to get a divorce?
a. a woman who marries at age 18
b. a man who marries at age 24
c. a woman who marries at age 26
d. a man who marries at age 32

57.
K
Answer: c
p. 415
Obj. #5b

One study of over 600 divorced men and women revealed that the most frequently cited reason for divorce for men was _____, and for women was _____.
a. sexual incompatibility; money problems
b. money problems; communication difficulties
c. communication difficulties; communication difficulties
d. sexual incompatibility; sexual incompatibility

58.
K
Answer: c
p. 414
Obj. #5b
WWW

Which of the following individuals would be **most** likely to get a divorce?
a. a woman with a baccalaureate degree who marries at age 25
b. a man with a baccalaureate degree who marries at age 25
c. a woman with a postbaccalaureate degree who marries at age 35
d. a man with a postbaccalaureate degree who marries at age 35

59.
K
Answer: c
p. 415
Obj. #5b

According to anthropologist Helen Fisher, the reason that humans have a natural inclination to want to end a relationship after four years is
a. because they naturally crave sexual variety, and most relationships are sexually stagnant after four years.
b. because they are biologically driven to mate with as many people as possible.
c. because that is approximately enough time for a child to be weaned from total dependence.
d. by that time, the qualities that initially attracted them to their partners are now a source of irritation and frustration.

60.
K
Answer: b
p. 416
Obj. #5b, 5c

Many people who remarry claim that their second marriage is _____ than the first. _____ marriages are **more** likely to end in divorce.
a. better; First
b. better; Second
c. worse; First
d. worse; Second

61.
K
Answer: a
p. 416
Obj. #5c

High divorce rates with second marriages may be attributed to
a. less willingness to stick around when things get rough.
b. diminishing tolerance of partner's children.
c. meddling ex-spouses.
d. sexual problems.

62.
K
Answer: a
p. 416
Obj. #5e

After a divorce, when do the **majority** of people become sexually active?
a. within one year
b. within two years
c. within three years
d. within four years

63.
K
Answer: b
p. 416
Obj. #5e

Approximately _____ of divorced persons remarry, most within _____ year(s) of the divorce.
a. 90%; two
b. 80%; three
c. 70%; four
d. 65%; three

64.
K
Answer: d
p. 417
Obj. #6

Aging is our society is often associated with sexlessness for all of the following reasons **except**
a. many people still equate sex with procreation.
b. there is a disproportionate focus on youth in this culture.
c. there is an unspoken attitude that it is not acceptable for older people to have sexual needs.
d. the majority of older people no longer want or enjoy sexual contact.

65.
A
Answer: b
p. 417
Obj. #6, 7

Use of the expression "dirty old man" reflects the fact that
a. when older men are interested in sex it is usually because they are pedophiles.
b. there is a cultural bias against older people who are interested in sex.
c. it is acceptable for older women to be interested in sex, but that is not the case for men.
d. older people are generally not interested in sex.

Chapter 14 Sexuality and the Adult Years 319

66.
A
Answer: c
p. 416
Obj. #6, 7

Some cartoons that have appeared in *Playboy* magazine depict an old wrinkled woman who is constantly attempting to contrive situations with various men that will enable her to have sex with them. Many people find this amusing because
  a. women over 70 are not capable of enjoying sexual activity.
  b. older women rarely find younger men attractive.
  c. older women in our culture are not supposed to be interested in sex and even when they are, because of their age, no one supposedly would be interested in having sex with them.
  d. women over 70 have stronger sexual desires than ever before.

67.
K
Answer: c
p. 417
Obj. #7
WWW

The double standard of aging is reflected in the pairing of
  a. rich, older women and young, penniless men.
  b. aging female sex educators with young male students.
  c. powerful, older men and young, beautiful women.
  d. prestigious, older women and young, athletic men.

68.
A
Answer: d
p. 417
Obj. #7

In the film "Harold and Maude," a 60-year-old woman and a 20-year-old man have a love affair. Relating this to what you have read in the text, which of the following statements is true?
  a. This film supports the double standard of aging.
  b. This film conflicts with research that indicates the percentage of women who marry younger men is increasing.
  c. This film supports the cultural notion that aging is associated with sexlessness.
  d. This film confronts us with our double standard of sex and aging by portraying the opposite of what we might expect.

69.
K
Answer: a
p. 418
Obj. #7

According to one study, aspects of sexuality that contributed to a feeling of well-being were _____ in women and _____ in men.
  a. feeling sexually attractive to the other sex; sexual performance and attractiveness to the other sex
  b. being able to orgasm consistently; being able to orgasm consistently
  c. being able to orgasm consistently; being able to achieve an erection consistently
  d. having intercourse regularly; having intercourse regularly

70.
K
Answer: b
p. 418
Obj. #7

Susan Sontag's advice to women as they grow older is
  a. to exercise regularly and eat well.
  b. to age naturally without embarrassment.
  c. to seek plastic surgery in order to maintain a youthful appearance.
  d. to cultivate their youthfulness for as long as possible.

71.
K
Answer: b
p. 419
Obj. #8
WWW

All of the following were discussed as factors influencing sexual activity in later years **except**
  a. physical health.
  b. religious background.
  c. regularity of sexual expression.
  d. sexual activity levels in early adulthood.

72.
K
Answer: a
p. 419
Obj. #9

Which of the following statements regarding sexuality and aging is false?
a. While the majority of older people do not approve of masturbation, they still engage in it.
b. According to one survey, a majority of older men and women fantasize about sex.
c. The incidence of masturbation among men and women usually declines with age.
d. More older men engage in masturbation than older women.

73.
K
Answer: c
p. 420
Obj. #9

Which of the following statements regarding sexuality and aging is false?
a. Lower socioeconomic men are likely to stop all sexual activity when they become older and unable to have intercourse.
b. Married women 50 and older have sexual satisfaction most closely related to overall marital satisfaction.
c. The older generation rarely uses such things as vibrators, or sexually explicit materials.
d. For older adults genital contact may become less frequent but nonintercourse activities remain stable or increase.

74.
K
Answer: a
p. 420
Obj. #9

Which of the following statements regarding socioeconomic factors and aging is true?
a. Middle class older adults are more likely to include options beyond intercourse than those in lower socioeconomic groups.
b. Middle class older adults are more likely to avoid oral stimulation than those in lower socioeconomic groups.
c. There are social class differences for women but not for men.
d. There are social class differences for men but not for women.

75.
K
Answer: c
p. 421
Obj. #9
WWW

The majority of older gay men
a. were sexually active with younger men.
b. indicated that they experienced more sexual variety than ever before.
c. indicated that their current sex lives were satisfying.
d. reported that sex was more frequent than when they were younger.

76.
K
Answer: a
p. 421
Obj. #9

Which of the following statements regarding sexuality and aging is false?
a. It is extremely rare for new sexual relationships to begin in later adulthood, i.e., over 65.
b. It is possible that homosexuals may be better able to deal with losses with aging because of the adversity that they have already experienced.
c. It is useful for the older to redefine their affectional relationships.
d. Sex therapy may be useful even for older individuals and couples.

Chapter 14 Sexuality and the Adult Years 321

77.
K
Answer: c
p. 422
Obj. #9

Older lesbians may have all of the following advantages over older heterosexual women **except**
a. a lesbian is less likely to be left alone because statistically her partner is not likely to die at a younger age.
b. if a lesbian is left alone, she will have more potentially available partners.
c. lesbians are less likely to be affected by the physiological aspects of aging.
d. the double standard is not an issue for lesbians, as most older lesbians prefer partners of similar ages.

78.
K
Answer: c
p. 422
Obj. #10

Which of the following is an example of how androgyny expresses itself in later years?
a. Women become more nurturant and men become more assertive.
b. Orgasm becomes important for both men and women.
c. Women become more assertive while men become more expressive.
d. Women focus more on relationships and men focus more on genital sex.

79.
K
Answer: a
p. 423
Obj. #11a

The ratio of widows to widowers
a. has increased.
b. has decreased.
c. has stayed the same.
d. increased until 1985 then reached a plateau.

80.
K
Answer: d
p. 423
Obj. #9

One survey revealed that in healthy people over 80 years old, _____ of the men and _____ of the women fantasized about sex.
a. the majority; less than half
b. less than half; the majority
c. less than half; less than half
d. the majority; the majority

81.
K
Answer: d
p. 424
Obj. #11b

Which of the following statements regarding postmarital adjustment to widowhood is false?
a. Widowed people do not usually feel that they have failed at marriage in the way that many divorced people do.
b. Widowed people may experience more intense grief than divorced people.
c. More divorced women than widows remarry.
d. Over half of widowed men and women remarry.

82.
K
Answer: a
p. 424
Obj. #9

One study indicated that women between the ages of 60 and 91 are becoming **more** accepting of _____ as a means of sexual expression.
a. masturbation
b. fellatio
c. cunnilingus
d. tribadism

Multiple Choice from Study Guide

1.
K
Answer: c
p. 398
Obj. #1

Which of the following statements is true regarding single living?
a. The number of adults who choose not to marry at all has remained relatively the same since 1970.
b. Single people have higher levels of sexual activity than married persons.
c. Larger numbers of couples living together outside of marriage has helped increase the number of single adults.
d. Choosing to be celibate is the most common reason reported for living single.

2.
A
Answer: c
pp. 394-400
Obj.#2

Given research on cohabitation, what will **most** likely happen to Susheela and Raj, who have been living together for the past 14 months?
a. If they marry, they have a lower risk of divorce than couples who did not cohabitate.
b. If they marry, they have the same risk of divorce as couples who did not cohabitate.
c. If they marry, they have a greater risk of divorce than couples who did not cohabitate.
d. Research has shown there is no relationship between cohabitation and divorce, so nothing about this couple can be predicted.

3.
K
Answer: b
p. 399
Obj. #2c

People choose to cohabitate for all of the following reasons **except**
a. They do not wish to feel the pressure of assuming marital roles.
b. They wish to reduce the chance that their partner will engage in infidelity.
c. They do not wish to have the binding legal contract associated with marriage.
d. They wish to avoid the stigma associated with divorce.

4.
K
Answer: d
pp. 400-401
Obj. #3b

Marriage has served all of the following functions **except**
a. defining inheritance rights.
b. providing a structured economic partnership.
c. regulating sexual behavior.
d. providing a place to ensure happiness.

5.
K
Answer: d
p. 403
Obj. # 3e

Gottman and colleague's study of marital interaction patterns demonstrated that all of the following predict marital discord with the exception of
a. high levels of heart rate.
b. defensive behaviors.
c. stonewalling.
d. husbands' verbal expressions of contempt.

6.
K
Answer: a
p. 404
Obj. # 3e

A ratio of _____ positive to _____ negative interaction(s) was found in couples with satisfying marriages.
a. 5:1
b. 3:2
c. 4:1
d. 6:2

7.
K
Answer: c
pp. 404-405
Obj. n/a

Studies with the PREPARE premarital inventory show _____ percent accuracy in predicting which couples would divorce.
a. 55
b. 62
c. 80
d. 90

8.
K
Answer: a
pp. 405-406
Obj. n/a

Compared with Kinsey's study, newer studies of sexual activity during marriage show
a. a wider array of sexual activities among couples.
b. couples spending more time having coitus.
c. a reduction in cunnilingus.
d. more frequent masturbation.

9.
K
Answer: b
pp. 406-407
Obj. #3b

Recent studies by Gottman and Wallerstein & Blakeslee identified _____ as important influences on marital satisfaction.
a. low frequency of arguments and expression of anger
b. quality of friendship and respect
c. the validating and conflict-avoiding marital styles
d. a predictable routine and feelings of security

10.
K
Answer: c
p. 408
Obj. #4

According to a recent study using the NHSLS sample, those **most** likely to engage in extramarital sex are people who
a. are over 50.
b. have a desire for revenge.
c. have more permissive sexual attitudes.
d. are more thrilled by secrecy than others.

11.
K
Answer: d
pp. 408-409
Obj. #14

Which statement regarding extramarital affairs in cyberspace is true?
a. If the online lover is never met in person, no harm is done to the relationship.
b. If sex with the online lover never occurs, many therapists believe there is no infidelity.
c. A person is considered faithful if they have only engaged in masturbation while communicating with the on line lover.
d. Extramarital affairs in cyberspace have similar consequences for a relationship as traditional infidelity.

12.
K
Answer: a
p. 410
Obj. #4

What can be concluded about the effect of extramarital sex on marriage?
a. Discovering infidelity can prompt a couple to solve problems that improve the marriage.
b. Infidelity inevitably leads to divorce.
c. If the participating partner feels guilty, there is hope of saving the marriage.
d. The betrayed spouse should suppress feelings of jealousy and anger in order for counseling to be effective.

13.
K
Answer: c
p. 411
Obj. #12

Which cultural group has the **least** restrictive norms regarding extramarital sexuality?
a. Jordanians
b. The Truk
c. Aborigines of Australia's Arnhem Land
d. The Irish of Ines Beag

14.
K
Answer: b
p. 412
Obj. #5a

Of the persons described below, who is **most** likely to divorce?
a. Rick, who gets married at age 32.
b. Kristina, who gets married at age 19.
c. Thich, who has a bachelor's degree.
d. Letitica, who has a bachelor's degree.

15.
K
Answer: c
pp. 413-414
Obj. #5b

Which of the following was NOT mentioned as a possible explanation for high divorce rates?
a. liberalization of divorce laws
b. increased economic independence of women
c. the demise of covenant marriage
d. changing expectations for marital fulfillment

16.
K
Answer: c
pp. 415-416
Obj. #5d

All of the following are reactions commonly experienced by people adjusting to divorce **except**
a. shock.
b. loneliness.
c. unwavering interest in establishing intimacy or sexual relationships.
d. a sense of relief and acceptance several months to a year later.

17.
K
Answer: b
p. 418
Obj. #7

An older woman's sense of well being is **most** strongly influenced by
a. her sexual performance.
b. feeling she is attractive to the other sex.
c. the type of hormone replacement therapy she receives.
d. frequency of sexual activity

18.
A
Answer: a
p. 419
Obj. #8

Who is **most** likely to maintain sexual activity in their later years?
a. Susan, who had frequent sexual activity during early adulthood and middle age.
b. Stan, who belongs to an organized religion.
c. Nina, who seldom masturbated in earlier adulthood.
d. Nestor, who has diabetes and heart disease.

19.
K
Answer: d
p. 420
Obj. #9

Which of the following is true regarding sexual expression in older adulthood?
a. Older women masturbate as frequently as older men.
b. Men do not experience an age-related decline in frequency of masturbation.
c. Lower income adults are somewhat more likely to explore noncoital forms of lovemaking.
d. Greater opportunities often exist for relaxed and prolonged lovemaking.

20.
K
Answer: b
p. 422
Obj. n/a

Older lesbians may have which of the following advantages over heterosexual women?
a. Lesbians experience fewer of the physical effects of aging.
b. She is less likely to be living without her life partner than a heterosexual woman.
c. If her life partner dies, a lesbian has numerous cultural rituals and supports to assist with the grieving process.
d. The stigma associated with a non-heterosexual orientation declines with age.

21.
K
Answer: a
p. 423
Obj. #10

A man who becomes **more** androgynous in his later years is likely to experience
a. greater emotional expression and interest in non-genital forms of sex.
b. greater declines in sexual performance than non-androgynous males.
c. a somewhat more fragmented sense of self.
d. a greater interest in achieving orgasm than was present in earlier adulthood.

True/False

Students may be asked to answer these questions using the traditional format of marking their answers either "true" or "false". Or, to encourage more active involvement, you may choose to use the following instructions:

If the statement is true, place a "T" on the line preceding it. If the statement is false, place an "F" on the line preceding it and then change the statement to make it true by deleting incorrect information and/or adding accurate information.

1.
Answer: T
p. 398
Obj. #1b

___ Recent research indicates that married people experience higher levels of sexual activity and satisfaction than singles.

2.
Answer: T
p. 398
Obj. #1b

___ Jennifer has had several sexually exclusive relationships with men in her adult life, and yet she has never married and lives alone. She is engaging in serial monogamy.

3.
Answer: T
p. 399
Obj. #2e

___ Both homosexual and heterosexual couples may participate in a domestic partnership.

4.
Answer: F
p. 400
Obj. #2d

___ Although somewhat contradictory, the majority of available data suggest that cohabitation has a positive effect on subsequent marriage.

5.
Answer: F
p. 400
Obj. #2d

___ The number of unmarried couples living together has increased to such a degree that it appears that the trend is to substitute cohabitation for marriage.

6.
Answer: T
p. 401
Obj. #3c

___ A society with marriages involving one woman and several men is said to practice polyandry.

7.
Answer: T
p. 401
Obj. #3b

___ On the average, married people are healthier physically and psychologically happier than single people.

8.
Answer: T
p. 404
Obj. #3e

___ According to Gottman, men who accept influence from their wives end up in long-term good marriages.

9.
Answer: F
p. 404
Obj. #3e

___ Of the three marital styles Gottman has identified, the conflict-avoiding couple is at the highest level of risk for marital dissatisfaction and separation.

10.
Answer: F
p. 404
Obj. #4e

___ Gottman's research suggests that a 3 to 1 ratio of positive to negative interactions is necessary and sufficient to maintain marital satisfaction.

11.
Answer: T
p. 406
Obj. #3f

___ Research indicates that frequency of sexual interaction as well as mutuality in initiating sex appear to be linked with the sexual satisfaction of both partners.

12.
Answer: F
p. 411
Obj. #12

___ From a cross-cultural perspective, our culture places fewer restrictions on extramarital sex than most cultures.

13. Answer: T p. 412 Obj. #5a	___	Second marriages are more likely to end in divorce than first marriages.
14. Answer: T p. 412 Obj. #5a	___	Estimates suggest that 50% or more of all first marriages in the United States will end in separation or divorce.
15. Answer: T p. 412 Obj. #5a	___	In the last several years the divorce rate has leveled off and even declined slightly.
16. Answer: T p. 414 Obj. #5b	___	The younger a person is when he/she marries, the greater the possibility of divorce.
17. Answer: T p. 415 Obj. #5b	___	One study of 600 divorced men and women found that having communication difficulties was the most frequently cited cause for divorce for both men and women.
18. Answer: T p. 415 Obj. #5b	___	Generally speaking, the lower the education level, the higher the divorce rate.
19. Answer: F p. 415 Obj. #5b	___	Helen Fisher contends that humans are biologically programmed for serial pair bonding with a natural tendency to move on after seven years (the "seven year itch").
20. Answer: T p. 419 Obj. #9	___	There is a close correlation between sexual activity levels in early adulthood and sexual activity in later years.
21. Answer: F p. 423 Obj. #11a	___	The ratio of widows to widowers increased dramatically until the middle of this century, and has been slowly declining since then.

Short Answer Essay

1. Discuss factors that have contributed to the increase in the number of single people. (Obj. #1a)

2. Compare sexual behavior and activity among single, married and divorced people. (Obj. #1b, 3f, 5d)

3. Define cohabitation. Making reference to the text, list possible advantages and disadvantages of cohabitation. (Obj. #2c)

4. Define cohabitation and briefly indicate how frequently this occurs. Would you yourself be willing to cohabit? Why, or why not? (Obj. #2)

5. Describe the changing patterns and expectations in marriage. Offer some explanation(s) as to why these have come about. (Obj. #3d)

6. Summarize the findings of Gottman's research on predicting marital satisfaction. Be sure to include information about behavioral patterns predicting discord as well as the predictors of marital satisfaction and longevity. (Obj. #5e)

7. Discuss options available for couples who would like to help prepare themselves for marriage. Why might these be useful? (Obj. #3e)

8. Describe factors that may contribute to marital satisfaction, as well as factors that may be predictive of marital discord. (Obj. #3e)

9. Define "nonconsensual extramarital relationship". How common are these? What are some the reasons that a person might become involved in this type of relationship. (Obj. #4)

10. Define "consensual extramarital relationship" and describe two types of consensual extramarital relationships. (Obj. #4)

11. Discuss some of the controversial issues related to extramarital affairs in cyberspace. (Obj. #13)

12. Discuss the frequency of divorce in the past few decades. What are some of the major reasons why people divorce or separate? (Obj. #5a, 5b)

13. Give some examples of the double standard of aging with respect to American men and women? Do you believe this double standard is understandable? Is it likely to continue? (Obj. #7)

14. Discuss three factors that will affect sexual activity in later years. (Obj. #8)

15. Citing relevant research, discuss how patterns of sexual expression change, if at all, as women and men age. What can individuals do to maximize their sexual functioning as they grow older? (Obj. #8, 9, 10)

15

The Nature and Origin of Sexual Difficulties

Learning Objectives

After studying this chapter, the student should be able to:

1. Discuss how common various sexual problems are among men and women, making reference to the National Health and Social Life Survey.

2. Discuss some of the physiological factors that may contribute to sexual problems, making specific reference to the effects of some abused and/or illicit drugs.

3. Explain how chronic illness may affect sexual function and expression, making specific reference to each of the following:
   a. diabetes
   b. arthritis
   c. cancer
   d. multiple sclerosis
   e. cerebrovascular accidents (CVA)

4. Explain how major disabilities may affect sexual function and expression, making specific reference to each of the following:
   a. spinal cord injury
   b. cerebral palsy
   c. blindness and deafness

5. Discuss how each of the following may affect sexual desire, arousal and orgasm:
   a. psychiatric medications
   b. antihypertensive medications
   c. miscellaneous medications

6. Describe how various cultural influences may contribute to sexual problems, making specific reference to each of the following:
   a. negative childhood learning
   b. the sexual double standard
   c. a narrow definition of sexuality
   d. performance anxiety

7. Describe how various individual factors may contribute to sexual problems, making specific reference to each of the following:
   a. sexual knowledge and attributes
   b. self-concept
   c. emotional difficulties
   d. sexual abuse and assault

8. Describe how various relationship factors may contribute to sexual difficulties, making specific reference to each of the following:
   a. unresolved relationship problems
   b. ineffective communication
   c. fears about pregnancy or sexually transmitted diseases
   d. sexual orientation

9. Distinguish between generalized and situational sexual problems.

10. Describe each of the following desire phase difficulties and some of the factors that may contribute to or be associated with each:
    a. hypoactive sexual desire
    b. dissatisfaction with frequency of sexual activity
    c. sexual aversion disorder

11. Define each of the following excitement phase difficulties and discuss some of the factors that might contribute to or be associated with each:
    a. female sexual arousal disorder
    b. male erectile disorder

12. Define each of the following orgasm phase difficulties and discuss some of the factors that might contribute to or be associated with each:
    a. female orgasmic disorder
    b. male orgasmic disorder
    c. premature ejaculation
    d. faking orgasms

13. Define dyspareunia, and discuss some of the reasons why men and women may experience it.

14. Define vaginismus, and explain how common it is and under what circumstances it may occur.

Multiple Choice

1.
K
Answer: a
p. 427
Obj. #1

Sexual problems
   a. are common.
   b. primarily occur with those who have had some traumatic experience either in childhood or adulthood.
   c. are overdiagnosed because of our societies emphasis on sexuality.
   d. occur more in people who have taken human sexuality courses in college.

Chapter 15 The Nature and Origin of Sexual Difficulties 331

2.
K
Answer: b
p. 427
Obj. #1

The National Health and Social Life survey found all but which one of the following?
a. Women are more likely than men to have lack of interest in sex.
b. Women are more likely to have pain during sex as they grow older.
c. The less education, the more reported sexual problems.
d. Not only the unmarried but also the married report frequent sexual problems.

3.
K
Answer: d
p. 428
Obj. n/a

Sexual satisfaction is **best** determined by
a. consulting a therapist specializing in this area.
b. a conversation with one's sexual partner or partners.
c. taking a test and finding out one's categorization.
d. the individual's own subjective perception.

4.
K
Answer: b
p. 428
Obj. n/a

Which one is true concerning the origins of sexual difficulty?
a. It is best to figure out the specific cause so that one can do the right intervention.
b. Experiences that help bring about sexual difficulty in one person may not affect another.
c. They are most often caused initially by physiological variables.
d. They are most often psychological in origin.

5.
K
Answer: c
p. 429
Obj. #2

With which of the following sexual problems has cigarette smoking been associated?
a. anorgasmia
b. ejaculatory inhibition
c. erectile inhibition
d. vaginismus

6.
K
Answer: a
p. 429
Obj. #2

_____ is the problem **most** likely to have an organic component.
a. Erectile dysfunction
b. Anorgasmia
c. Ejaculatory inhibition
d. Vaginismus

7.
K
Answer: a
p. 430
Obj. #3a

Diabetes is a disease of the _____ system.
a. endocrine
b. neurological
c. hormonal
d. muscular

8.
A
Answer: b
p. 430
Obj. #3a

Which of the following diseases would be **most** likely to directly impair erectile functioning?
a. heart attack
b. diabetes
c. cerebrovascular accidents
d. arthritis

9.
K
Answer: c
p. 430
Obj. #4a

Which of the following was mentioned as a sexual problem experienced by diabetic men?
a. hypoactive sexual desire
b. ejaculatory inhibition
c. erectile problems
d. premature ejaculation

10.
A
Answer: c
p. 430
Obj. #3d

Jack has _____, which results in erectile difficulties, and occasionally he will also experience retrograde ejaculation.
a. cerebral palsy
b. multiple sclerosis
c. diabetes
d. heart disease

11.
K
Answer: d
p. 430
Obj. #3d

All of the following are affected in the person who has multiple sclerosis **except**
a. vision
b. voluntary movement
c. sensation
d. cognitive functioning

12.
K
Answer: d
p. 430
Obj. #3d
WWW

Which of the following statements concerning multiple sclerosis is true?
a. It impairs verbal communication.
b. Approximately twenty percent of MS patients experience a sexual problem.
c. Lack of desire is the primary sexual difficulty that MS patients experience; arousal and orgasm abilities remain intact.
d. It is a very common disabling neurological condition in young adults.

13.
K
Answer: a
p. 430
Obj. #4a

Which of the following is **most** likely to increase the chances of sexual problems in diabetic men?
a. heavy alcohol use
b. cigarette smoking
c. marijuana use
d. high salt and caffeine intake

14.
K
Answer: b
p. 430
Obj. #3b
WWW

Which of the following would **least** likely be an effect of arthritis?
a. body image problems
b. erectile inhibition
c. chronic pain
d. decrease in sexual desire

15.
A
Answer: d
p. 430
Obj. #3d

As a result of her illness, Cathy's vision, sensation, and voluntary movement have become worse over time. She is not as interested in sex as she used to be, and when she does interact sexually with her partner, her genitals are often hypersensitive to stimulation. Cathy probably has which of the following conditions?
 a. diabetes
 b. cerebral palsy
 c. arthritis
 d. multiple sclerosis

16.
K
Answer: d
p. 431
Obj. #4a

Which of the following statements is **most** accurate?
 a. A person with SCI has loss of desire.
 b. A person with SCI has arousal difficulties.
 c. A person with SCI has orgasm difficulties.
 d. There is great individual variation in sexual desire and behavior among people with SCI.

17.
K
Answer: c
p. 431
Obj. #4a

Which of the following statements concerning SCI men is true?
 a. The majority are able to ejaculate.
 b. The majority are able to experience orgasm.
 c. The majority are able to experience erection.
 d. The majority are able to produce children.

18.
K
Answer: b
p. 431
Obj. #4a

The act of thinking about a physical stimulus and amplifying the sensation in one's mind for purposes of arousal and/or orgasm is called
 a. mental imaging.
 b. sensory amplification.
 c. stimulus expansion.
 d. sensory augmentation.

19.
K
Answer: c
p. 431
Obj. #4b

_____ is caused by damage to the brain before or during birth or during early childhood, and it is characterized by mild to severe lack of muscular control.
 a. Spinal cord injury (SCI)
 b. Multiple sclerosis (MS)
 c. Cerebral palsy (CP)
 d. Diabetes

20.
K
Answer: c
p. 431
Obj. #4b

Which of the following statements concerning cerebral palsy is true?
 a. Most people with CP are mentally disabled.
 b. Genital sensation is lost as the result of CP.
 c. CP may disrupt speech and facial expressions.
 d. CP most commonly occurs in adolescence.

21.
K
Answer: c
p. 432
Obj. #4b

Which of the following would probably be **most** helpful in the sexual adjustment of the person with CP?
 a. use of moist heat to alleviate pain
 b. lubricants to help with vaginal dryness
 c. assistance from someone in preparing and positioning for sex
 d. sensory amplification technique

22.
K
Answer: b
p. 432
Obj. #5
WWW

Which one is NOT true about medication effects on sexual functioning?
a. More is known about the impact of medication on men than on women.
b. Health care professionals almost always inform patients about potential sexual side effects of medications.
c. At least 200 medications, either prescription or nonprescription, have negative effects of sexuality.
d. There are often alternative medications for those with negative side effects.

23.
K
Answer: d
p. 433
Obj. #2

All of the following medications may cause sexual problems **except**
a. drugs used to treat high blood pressure.
b. some medications used to treat depression.
c. barbiturates and narcotics.
d. acetaminophen and papaverine.

24.
K
Answer: d
p. 433
Obj. #6a

One researcher found that the more rigidly orthodox that married members of _____ churches were, the less sexual interest, response, frequency and pleasure they reported in marital sex.
a. Jewish
b. Protestant
c. Catholic
d. Jewish, Protestant and Catholic

25.
K
Answer: b
p. 434
Obj. #6a

Research has found that women with low sexual desire
a. did not remember how their parents touched or felt about one another.
b. perceived their parents to be more negative about sex and in affectionate interactions than did those with normal desire.
c. perceived their parents as being inappropriately publicly sexual.
d. were less likely to agree to participate in research studies about sexual matters.

26.
K
Answer: a
p. 434
Obj. #6b
WWW

According to Masters and Johnson, many of women's sexual problems are a result of
a. sociocultural influences.
b. excessive pressure from the women's movement for women to be more sexually active.
c. toilet-training practices that focus exclusively on hygiene.
d. lack of exposure to sensate focus exercises at an early age.

27.
K
Answer: a
pp. 434-435
Obj. #6b

The sexual double standard
a. seems to less a problem for same-sex couples.
b. primarily influences men.
c. primarily influences women.
d. is no longer of much influence in our society.

28.
K
Answer: c
p. 435
Obj. #6c

Your authors believe that coitus
a. is the ultimate avenue for exploring sexual pleasure.
b. has been overemphasized but this has primarily had negative effects for those with disability, or the aging.
c. has been overemphasized and this may contribute to inadequate stimulation for women.
d. is a term that should be dropped and the phrase penile-vaginal intercourse be substituted.

29.
K
Answer: c
p. 436
Obj. #6d

Performance anxiety
a. primarily affects men.
b. primarily affects women.
c. can turn a transitory problem into a serious one.
d. oftentimes helps increase the pleasure by first increasing the overall arousal level.

30.
K
Answer: a
p. 436
Obj. #7

Negative attitudes toward sexuality
a. contribute to poor sexual responsiveness.
b. emerge without the individuals having any control.
c. will disappear when you meet the right person.
d. appear to develop as a result of watching media images.

31.
K
Answer: b
p. 437
Obj. #7b

Research has found that women who are **least** self-conscious about their bodies as compared to similarly shaped women
a. were more often lesbian.
b. were more assertive with their partners.
c. had a lower sex drive.
d. tended to be unusually thin.

32.
K
Answer: d
p. 437
Obj. n/a

Which one is NOT true concerning media images?
a. In the 1980's the average model weighted 8% less than the average American woman.
b. Presently, the average model weights 23% less than the average American woman.
c. Media images help shape perceptions of attractiveness and desirability.
d. College women are too smart to be affected by media images.

33.
K
Answer: c
p. 438
Obj. n/a

Media images of men
a. primarily contribute to women's ideas, but not those of men.
b. have not changed in the last few decades although they have for women.
c. may be related to the finding that most men prefer bodies with 30 pounds more muscle than their own.
d. have been shown by research to negatively affect sexual expression for many.

34.
K
Answer: c
p. 438
Obj. #7c

The NHSLS found concerning life unhappiness and sexual problems that
a. unhappiness causes sexual problems.
b. sexual problems cause life unhappiness.
c. they are correlated.
d. they are related for men but not women.

35.
K
Answer: a
p. 439
Obj. #7d
WWW

Which of the following difficulties are **most** likely to be associated with a history of childhood sexual abuse in women?
a. depression, anxiety, low self-esteem, sexual aversion
b. depression, hypochondriasis, amenorrhea, low self-esteem
c. anxiety, dyspareunia, Peyronie's disease, sexual aversion
d. anxiety, low self-esteem, endometriosis, vascular disorder

36.
K
Answer: d
p. 439
Obj. #7d

The childhood experience that has the **greatest** negative impact on sexual functioning is
a. parental divorce.
b. parental death.
c. lack of masturbation.
d. sexual abuse.

37.
K
Answer: d
p. 439
Obj. #7d

Which is NOT a reported consequence for females following adult sexual assault?
a. fear of sex
b. lack of desire
c. compensatory overassertiveness in sexual encounters
d. sexual problems for more than three years for a majority

38.
K
Answer: d
pp. 439-441
Obj. #8
WWW

All of the following are relationship factors that might contribute to sexual difficulties **except**
a. ineffective communication.
b. sexual orientation.
c. fears about getting pregnant.
d. self-concept.

39.
K
Answer: d
pp. 439-440
Obj. #8

Which one is NOT true concerning sexual problems?
a. Emotional reactions to infertility can cause such difficulties.
b. Fear of pregnancy can interfere with enjoyment.
c. It is a myth that sexual assertiveness in women is unfeminine.
d. There are fewer problems when one of the partners is dependent and the other is independent.

40.
K
Answer: b
p. 441
Obj. #3

Many categories and labels for diagnosing sexual dysfunctions come from the
a. Physicians Desk Reference.
b. Diagnostic and Statistical Manual (DSM IV).
c. NHSLS Diagnostic Index.
d. Kinsey Reports.

Chapter 15 The Nature and Origin of Sexual Difficulties   337

41.
A
Answer: b
p. 441
Obj. #9, 10a

Which of the following statements concerning HSD is false?
  a. Generalized, lifelong HSD is rare.
  b. If a person has HSD, he/she will typically have excitement and orgasm difficulties as well.
  c. HSD has been described as "lack of sexual appetite".
  d. HSD would be an adaptive response if a person's partner practiced poor hygiene.

42.
A
Answer: c
p. 441
Obj. #10a

Maria rarely thinks or fantasizes about sex. When not in a relationship, she rarely masturbates. When in a relationship, she never initiates sex, but if her partner does, she is able to lubricate and be orgasmic. Her problem would **best** be described as
  a. dyspareunia.
  b. female sexual arousal disorder.
  c. hypoactive sexual desire.
  d. sexual aversion disorder.

43.
A
Answer: c
p. 442
Obj. #10b

A woman prefers early morning sex two to three times a week and her partner prefers late night sex once a week. How would you define their problem?
  a. He is experiencing nocturnal penile tumescence (NPT).
  b. The couple is experiencing sexual aversion.
  c. The couple has dissatisfaction with the amount and timing of their sexual activity.
  d. The couple is experiencing hypoactive sexual desire.

44.
A
Answer: b
pp. 442-443
Obj. #10c

Whenever a man makes a sexually suggestive remark to her, Susan begins trembling, sweating, and feels dizzy and nauseated. She is probably experiencing
  a. hypoactive sexual desire.
  b. sexual aversion disorder.
  c. female sexual arousal disorder.
  d. anorgasmia.

45.
K
Answer: d
pp. 441-443
Obj. #10a, 10c

Which of the following is NOT a desire phase difficulty?
  a. HSD
  b. sexual aversion disorder
  c. dissatisfaction with frequency of sexual activity
  d. female sexual arousal disorder

46.
K
Answer: b
p. 442
Obj. #10a

In one study, lack of sexual desire was associated with all of the following relationship problems **except**
  a. the woman's partner did not behave affectionately except when intercourse was expected to follow.
  b. the woman experienced lubrication inhibition.
  c. communication and conflict resolution were unsatisfactory.
  d. the couple did not maintain love, romance and emotional closeness.

47.
K
Answer: d
p. 442
Obj. #10a

Which of the following difficulties would be **most** likely to occur in homosexual men or women who have not fully accepted their sexual orientation?
a. dissatisfaction with frequency of sexual activity
b. anorgasmia or male orgasmic disorder
c. premature ejaculation or female sexual arousal disorder
d. hypoactive sexual desire

48.
K
Answer: c
p. 442
Obj. #10a

One study found that women with _____ reported more dissatisfaction with relationship issues then women with other sexual problems.
a. dyspareunia
b. anorgasmia
c. hypoactive sexual desire
d. female sexual arousal disorder

49.
K
Answer: a
p. 442
Obj. #10c

Sexual aversion disorder is **best** defined as
a. a fear of sex combined with a desire to avoid sexual situations.
b. a woman's irrational fear of men based on a rape or incest experience.
c. inability to lubricate or to have an erection in response to sexual stimuli.
d. lack of interest in initiating and participating in sexual activity.

50.
A
Answer: a
p. 443
Obj. #10c
WWW

Neil cringes every time his partner becomes affectionate with him. If his partner persists, Neil becomes nauseated and highly anxious, and his feelings of sexual repulsion escalate. Neil is experiencing
a. sexual aversion disorder.
b. hypoactive sexual desire.
c. male arousal disorder.
d. male orgasmic disorder.

51.
K
Answer: a
p. 443
Obj. #10c

Which of the following statements concerning sexual aversion disorder is false?
a. It is an excitement phase difficulty.
b. Physiological symptoms include nausea, sweating, and diarrhea.
c. People who experience sexual aversion may feel irrationally fearful of sexual activity.
d. People who experience sexual aversion may feel disgusted or repulsed regarding sexual activity.

52.
K
Answer: d
p. 443
Obj. #11a

The first physiological sign of sexual arousal in women is
a. nipple erection.
b. vaginal expansion.
c. clitoral retraction.
d. vaginal lubrication.

53.
K
Answer: c
p. 443
Obj. #11a

Female sexual arousal disorder may be result of
a. high androgen levels.
b. a plateau phase that is too brief.
c. feelings of anger or apathy.
d. coitus that lasts only briefly due to premature ejaculation.

54.
K
Answer: b
p. 443
Obj. #11b

The word "impotent"
a. is used to refer to men who have HSD.
b. is a term opposed by the authors.
c. is the Greek word for "spilling of seed".
d. can be used to refer to both male and female sexual problems.

55.
A
Answer: c
pp. 443-444
Obj. #10–12

Which of the following is an excitement phase problem?
a. HSD
b. premature ejaculation
c. erectile disorder
d. sexual aversion disorder

56.
K
Answer: a
p. 444
Obj. #11b

Which of the following statements regarding male erectile dysfunction is true?
a. Age itself does not cause this problem.
b. Approximately 40% of these disorders involve organic impairment.
c. Approximately 30% of men in the United States have this problem.
d. There are five different types of this problem.

57.
K
Answer: c
p. 444
Obj. #11b

Which one is NOT true of erectile dysfunction (ED)?
a. As many as 25% of cases are related to medication side effects.
b. Tobacco appears to be one causative factor.
c. About 10 million U.S. men have ED.
d. A man in his 50's is twice as likely to experience ED as a man in his 20's.

58.
K
Answer: d
p. 444
Obj. #12a

Which of the following statements concerning anorgasmia is false?
a. Women with this problem may still maintain sexual desire.
b. Women may feel highly disappointed or distressed by this condition.
c. Women may enjoy sex very much despite this problem.
d. Women who experience generalized lifelong anorgasmia have orgasms in some situations but not in others.

59.
K
Answer: c
p. 444
Obj. #12a

A woman with situational anorgasmia
a. has never experienced orgasm by masturbation or with a partner.
b. can have orgasm through manual or oral stimulation, but not with intercourse.
c. experiences orgasm in some situations but not in others.
d. experiences clitoral, but not vaginal, orgasm.

60.
K
Answer: a
p. 444
Obj. #12a

Approximately _____ percent of adult women in the United States have generalized, lifelong anorgasmia.
a. 5–10
b. 10–15
c. 15–20
d. 20–25

61.
K
Answer: d
p. 445
Obj. #12a

The number of women with generalized, lifelong anorgasmia is
a. increasing significantly.
b. increasing slightly.
c. staying the same.
d. decreasing.

62.
A
Answer: d
p. 445
Obj. #12a

Nicole makes an appointment to see a sex therapist because, although she is orgasmic with manual stimulation, she is unable to experience orgasm with intercourse. The sex therapist would **most** probably
a. tell her that, while this is a somewhat difficult problem to treat, if she has the help and support of her partner, substantial progress can be made.
b. recommend a physical exam to ensure that there are no genital adhesions that interfere with her response.
c. recommend Kegel exercises combined with partner exercises to focus on vaginal sensitivity and response to stimulation.
d. explain that her response is typical and that she does not have a sexual problem, but recommend direct manual clitoral stimulation during intercourse to better facilitate orgasmic response.

63.
K
Answer: b
p. 445
Obj. #12b

Which of the following statements regarding female orgasmic disorder is true?
a. Physiological causes are most common.
b. The number of women with generalized, lifelong anorgasmia has decreased.
c. A woman who can have orgasm through masturbation but not with her partner has generalized orgasmic disorder.
d. More married than unmarried women have this.

64.
K
Answer: a
p. 445
Obj. #12b
WWW

Which of the following statements concerning male orgasmic disorder is false?
a. Approximately 20 percent of men experience this problem.
b. Most men with this problem can usually reach orgasm through masturbation or manual stimulation from a partner.
c. This might also be called partner anorgasmia.
d. Some men with this disorder have been unable to ejaculate through any means of sexual stimulation.

65.
K
Answer: c
p. 446
Obj. #12c

Premature ejaculation is defined
a. as that occurring in less than 3 minutes.
b. Differently depending upon the age of the male.
c. On the basis of the satisfaction of the male or his partner.
d. Most accurately by laboratory instrumentation.

66.
K
Answer: c
p. 446
Obj. #12c

Research into men with premature ejaculation has found that compared to those with less rapid ejaculation
  a. they enjoy orgasm more and are eager to get to it.
  b. they require more stimulation to get aroused originally and have run out of steam.
  c. they ejaculate before reaching full sexual arousal.
  d. they primarily learned rapid ejaculation in the back seat of cars.

67.
K
Answer: d
p. 446
Obj. #12c

In the authors' human sexuality classes, over _____ percent of the men have consistently reported that premature ejaculation was at least sometimes a problem.
  a. 20
  b. 35
  c. 60
  d. 75

68.
K
Answer: a
p. 446
Obj. #12d

Which one is NOT true about the faking of orgasms?
  a. This is not possible for gay males.
  b. Lesbians do this as much or more as female heterosexuals.
  c. This is a conscious decision.
  d. This is often motivated by performance pressure.

69.
K
Answer: a
p. 447
Obj. #12d

Which one is NOT true if you have been faking orgasms?
  a. Your partner likely doesn't know.
  b. This has probably helped create emotional closeness.
  c. One may well decide to discontinue this without telling your partner.
  d. It may be necessary to use a counselor to help honest communication about this and the future.

70.
K
Answer: b
p. 447
Obj. #13

Peyronie's disease refers to
  a. accumulation of smegma under the foreskin of a man's penis.
  b. fibrous tissue and calcium deposits that develop in the space between the cavernous bodies of the penis.
  c. a severe penile urethral infection.
  d. a condition in which the foreskin of the penis is abnormally tight.

71.
K
Answer: c
p. 447
Obj. #13

The medical term for painful intercourse is
  a. pelvic inflammatory disease.
  b. vaginismus.
  c. dyspareunia.
  d. vulvar vestibulitis.

72.
K
Answer: a
p. 448
Obj. #13
WWW

Which of the following would be **most** likely to cause deep pelvic pain as opposed to pain at the vaginal opening?
  a. endometriosis
  b. inadequate stimulation
  c. insufficient lubrication
  d. vulvar vestibulitis syndrome

73.
K
Answer: b
p. 448
Obj. #13

Occasionally _____ collects under the clitoral hood and may cause discomfort when the hood is moved during sexual stimulation.
a. yeast
b. smegma
c. Cowper's glands secretions
d. endometrial tissue

74.
K
Answer: a
p. 448
Obj. #14

Approximately _____ percent of women experience vaginismus.
a. 2
b. 6
c. 10
d. 15

75.
A
Answer: c
p. 448
Obj. #13

Which of the following would be **least** likely to cause deep pelvic pain during intercourse?
a. jarring of the ovaries
b. stretching of the uterine ligaments
c. vulvar vestibulitis syndrome
d. endometriosis

76.
K
Answer: a
p. 448
Obj. #14

_____ is characterized by strong involuntary contractions of the muscles in the outer third of the vagina.
a. Vaginismus
b. Vulvar vestibulitis syndrome
c. Vaginitis
d. Peyronie's disease

77.
K
Answer: d
p. 449
Obj. #14

Which of the following problems would **least** likely be associated with vaginismus?
a. a homosexual orientation
b. erectile difficulties of a woman's partner
c. past physical or sexual assault
d. premature ejaculation of a woman's partner

78.
K
Answer: b
p. 449
Obj. #14

Which one was suggested by your text?
a. Women should expect that intercourse will intermittently be uncomfortable.
b. Tampon usage should not be painful for a woman.
c. Women should expect that pelvic exams will be painful although this will be very brief if done correctly.
d. If you suspect vaginismus first try some herbal relaxation remedies.

79.
K
Answer: d
p. 449
Obj. #14

Which one is NOT true about vaginismus?
a. These are conditioned and involuntary responses.
b. This is often deliberately used by women to avoid intercourse.
c. This may be occurring in a heterosexual encounter because of a homosexual orientation.
d. This may be associated with feelings of fear or hostility toward the partner.

Chapter 15 The Nature and Origin of Sexual Difficulties 343

80.
K
Answer: c
p. 449
Obj. #14
WWW

Which of the following statements regarding vaginismus is false?
a. Very few women experience this problem.
b. A woman with vaginismus may be orgasmic with manual stimulation.
c. A woman with vaginismus consciously contracts her vaginal muscles to protect herself against potential pain.
d. A woman with vaginismus may be orgasmic with oral stimulation.

Multiple Choice from Study Guide

1.
K
Answer: b
p. 429
Obj. #2

Which of the following "recreational" drugs may impair erectile functioning?
a. alcohol
b. tobacco
c. marijuana
d. LSD

2.
K
Answer: d
p. 430
Obj. #3a

Diabetes may adversely affect sexual expression by
a. promoting erectile dysfunction.
b. reducing vaginal lubrication.
c. increasing the risk of Peyronie's disease.
d. a and b
e. all of the above

3.
K
Answer: c
p. 430
Obj. #3b

Which of the following would **most** likely occur in someone with arthritis?
a. reduced genital sensation
b. involuntary spasms of the outer third of the vagina
c. difficulty with certain intercourse positions
d. erectile dysfunction

4.
K
Answer: a
p. 430
Obj. #3e

A cerebrovascular accident or _____ may result in _____.
a. stroke; depression
b. heart attack; impaired communication
c. epilepsy; limited mobility
d. aneurysm; altered sensation

5.
K
Answer: c
p. 430
Obj. #3d

Multiple sclerosis (MS) alters sexuality because of damage to the
a. prostate gland.
b. vulva.
c. brain and spinal cord.
d. musculoskeletal system.

6.
K
Answer: d
p. 431
Obj. #3e

Spinal cord injury does NOT adversely affect
a. sexual arousal
b. orgasm
c. sensation
d. sexual desire

7.
K
Answer: a
p. 431
Obj. #3e

Many men with spinal cord injury are able to have erections, yet **most** are unable to
a. ejaculate
b. stop having retrograde ejaculation
c. utilize sensory amplification
d. utilize sensate focus exercises

8.
K
Answer: b
p. 431
Obj. #3e

One study demonstrated that about 50% of women with spinal cord injury who experienced _____ before their injury could do so after their injury.
a. vaginal intercourse
b. orgasm
c. the sex flush
d. the G-spot reflex

9.
K
Answer: c
p. 433
Obj. #5

All of the following medications may have undesirable effects on sexual functioning **except**
a. antidepressants
b. tranquilizers
c. ginko biloba
d. antihistamines

10.
K
Answer: b
pp. 433-436
Obj. #6

Which of the following would NOT be considered a cultural factor that contributes to difficulties in sexual functioning?
a. negative childhood learning
b. emotional difficulties
c. narrow definition of sexuality
d. sexual double standard
e. performance anxiety

11.
K
Answer: c
p. 437
Obj. #7b

Which of the following is true regarding the impact of body image on sexuality?
a. Newer studies suggest that men's desire for a body with a more muscular appearance has decreased.
b. A woman may avoid positions that allow her lover to look at body parts she thinks are too fat.
c. Women's concerns about body image do not tend to surface until adolescence.
d. Self-consciousness during lovemaking was reported primarily by older women and men.

12.
K
Answer: d
p. 438
Obj. #7c

Emotional difficulties that can negatively affect sexuality include all of the following **except**
a. depression.
b. extreme work stress.
c. fear of intimacy.
d. satyriasis.

13.
A
Answer: a
p. 439
Obj. #8a

Which of the following is the **best** example of an unresolved relationship difficulty that affects sexuality?
   a. Steve, who expresses his resentment toward his partner by showing disinterest in sex.
   b. Soraya, who believes that intercourse is the only acceptable form of sexual activity.
   c. Cau, whose fear of contracting AIDS results in erectile dysfunction.
   d. Carol, who will not have intercourse with her husband since she was raped while walking home from the bus stop.

14.
A
Answer: d
pp. 439-440
Obj. #8b

Gina won't tell her boyfriend that she needs clitoral stimulation to reach orgasm because she believes that if her boyfriend really loved her, he would know what to do. Gina is showing the impact of which relationship factor on sexuality?
   a. fear of pregnancy
   b. unresolved relationship problems
   c. emotional difficulties
   d. ineffective communication

15.
K
Answer: d
pp. 441-442
Obj. #10A

Hypoactive sexual desire disorder (HSD) is **more** common among
   a. gays or lesbians who have not fully accepted their sexual orientation.
   b. women.
   c. people with unresolved relationship problems.
   d. All of the above

16.
K
Answer: d
pp. 441-442
Obj. #10a

Someone who has generalized, lifelong HSD
   a. masturbates, but does not have sex with a partner.
   b. engages in sexual fantasy, but will not masturbate or have sex with a partner.
   c. had sexual experiences earlier in prior relationship, but has low desire in the current relationship.
   d. does not engage in fantasy, masturbation, or other sexual activity.

17.
A
Answer: c
p. 443
Obj. n/a

For the last 8 months, Miguel has been unable to have an erection of sufficient quality to penetrate his partner. During this time Miguel and his partner have been enjoying sensual massage, kissing, caressing, and don't mind if he cannot have an erection. What can be concluded about this couple?
   a. Miguel has erectile problems stemming from diabetes.
   b. Miguel has dyspareunia.
   c. The couple does not have a problem, as they are content with the situation.
   d. The couple has unresolved relationship difficulties and should seek sex therapy.

18.
K
Answer: a
p. 444
Obj. #12a

A woman with situational anorgasmia
a. may have orgasm during masturbation, but not when her partner orally stimulates her.
b. does not experience lubrication.
c. experiences lubrication, but does not experience psychological arousal.
d. is at greater risk of developing HSD.

19.
A
Answer: b
p. 445
Obj. n/a

What would **most** sex therapists conclude about woman who enjoys sex, but does not experience orgasm during intercourse without clitoral stimulation?
a. She is emotionally immature.
b. She is showing a normal and common pattern.
c. She has lifelong anorgasmia.
d. She is showing early signs of sexual aversion disorder.

20.
K
Answer: c
p. 445
Obj. #12b

A man can ejaculate when he masturbates, yet when he has vaginal intercourse, he is unable to ejaculate. He **most** likely be diagnosed with
a. priapism.
b. phismosis.
c. male orgasmic disorder.
d. retrograde ejaculation.

21.
K
Answer: b
p. 446
Obj. #12c

In surveys of the authors' sexuality classes, over _____ percent of male students reported that premature ejaculation was sometimes a problem.
a. 82
b. 75
c. 61
d. 29

22.
K
Answer: a
p. 447
Obj. #13

Dyspareunia refers to
a. painful intercourse.
b. involuntary contractions of the vaginal muscles.
c. involuntary contractions of the scrotal muscles.
d. accumulations of smegma under the clitoral or penile glans.

23.
K
Answer: c
pp. 447-448
Obj. # 13

Which of the following is NOT a possible cause of dyspareunia?
a. untreated infections of the reproductive tract
b. Peyronie's disease
c. oral contraceptive use
d. endometriosis

24.
K
Answer: d
p. 449
Obj. #14

Vaginismus may be related to
a. religious taboos about sex.
b. use of high absorbency tampons.
c. past sexual assault.
d. a and c
e. all of the above

Chapter 15 The Nature and Origin of Sexual Difficulties

True/False

Students may be asked to answer these questions using the traditional format of marking their answers either "true" or "false". Or, to encourage more active involvement, you may choose to use the following instructions:

If the statement is true, place a "T" on the line preceding it. If the statement is false, place an "F" on the line preceding it and then change the statement to make it true by deleting incorrect information and/or adding accurate information.

1. ___ According to data from the NHSL survey, the incidence of sexual problems decreases as educational level increases.
Answer: T
p. 427
Obj. #6a

2. ___ Smoking cigarettes can reduce the frequency and duration of erections.
Answer: T
p. 429
Obj. #2

3. ___ Diabetes is a leading organic cause of erection difficulties in men.
Answer: T
p. 430
Obj. #3a

4. ___ The most common disabling neurological condition for young adults in the United States is multiple sclerosis.
Answer: T
p. 430
Obj. #3d

5. ___ Genital sensation is unaffected by multiple sclerosis.
Answer: F
p. 430
Obj. #3d

6. ___ Arthritis is a neurological disease that directly affects sexual excitement and response.
Answer: F
p. 430
Obj. #3b

7. ___ A spinal cord injury almost always affects sexual desire.
Answer: F
p. 431
Obj. #4a

8. ___ The majority of men with spinal cord injuries are able to experience erections.
Answer: T
p. 431
Obj. #4a

9. ___ Genital sensation is unaffected by cerebral palsy.
Answer: T
p. 431
Obj. #4b

10.
Answer: F
p. 443
Obj. #10a
___ Julie rarely fantasizes about or initiates sex with her partner, but when her partner initiates sex with her, she lubricates adequately and is orgasmic. Julie is experiencing female sexual arousal disorder.

11.
Answer: T
p. 443
Obj. #11b
___ Men with lifelong erectile disorder have never been able to maintain an erection sufficiently rigid for penetrative intercourse.

12.
Answer: T
p. 443
Obj. #11a
___ It is normal for women to experience a decrease in vaginal lubrication while breastfeeding.

13.
Answer: T
p. 443
Obj. #11a
___ Feeling angry or apathetic can decrease vaginal lubrication in women.

14.
Answer: F
p. 443
Obj. #11b
___ Erectile disorder is defined as a man being unable to have an erection in half or more of his sexual experiences.

15.
Answer: F
p. 444
Obj. #12a
___ Sex therapists and educators use the term "frigid" to describe a woman who does not achieve orgasm.

16.
Answer: F
p. 444
Obj. #12a
___ A woman who is orgasmic when she masturbates but not when she is with her partner has generalized, lifelong anorgasmia.

17.
Answer: T
p. 444
Obj. #12a
___ Approximately 5–10 percent of adult American women experience generalized, lifelong anorgasmia.

18.
Answer: T
p. 445
Obj. #12a
___ Most sex therapists believe that women who enjoy intercourse even if they are not orgasmic during coitus do not have a sexual problem.

19.
Answer: T
p. 446
Obj. #12c
___ The majority of men experience problems with premature ejaculation at least occasionally.

20. ___ Both men and women report having faked orgasms.
Answer: T
p. 446
Obj. #12d

21. ___ One type of dyspareunia that men may experience is Peyronie's disease.
Answer: F
p. 447
Obj. #13

22. ___ Vaginismus is a fairly common problem that women experience.
Answer: F
p. 448
Obj. #14

Short Answer Essay

1. Your book discusses the following chronic conditions and their possible effect upon sexual expression: diabetes, arthritis, cancer, M.S., CVA's, CP, blindness or deafness. Choose four and outline the likely ramifications of these for sexual functioning. (Obj. #3)

2. Discuss the effects of spinal cord injury on men's and women's sexual abilities and expression. What coping strategies may individuals use to enhance sexual sharing? (Obj. #4a)

3. Discuss the possible effects of abused and/or illicit drugs upon sexual functioning. (Obj. #2)

4. What is HSD? When is it considered a problem? Discuss common physiological and psychological factors associated with it. (Obj. #10a)

5. How is erectile difficulty defined, how common is it, and what factors may contribute to it? (Obj. #11b)

6. Discuss the symptoms and causes of dyspareunia in women. (Obj. #13)

7. Define vaginismus, and explain how common it is and under what circumstances it may occur. (Obj. #14)

8. How is premature ejaculation defined, how common is it, and what factors may contribute to it? (Obj. #12c)

9. Discuss anorgasmia in both females and males. (Obj. #12a, 12b)

10. What is known about the effects of sexual abuse or assault on later sexual functioning? (Obj. #7d)

11. If a person suddenly has problems with sexual functioning, what medically prescribed medications might be involved? (Obj. #5)

12. How does the sexual double standard as well as our self-image lead to difficulties in sexual functioning? (Obj. #6b, 7b)

13. Discuss how performance anxiety or narrow definitions of sexuality may lead to difficulties in sexual functioning. (Obj. #8c, 8d)

14. What are some of the childrearing or parental factors that may lead to difficulties in sexual functioning? (Obj. #6a)

15. Describe how relationship factors may lead to difficulties in sexual functioning. (Obj. #8)

16

Sex Therapy and Enhancement

Learning Objectives

After studying this chapter, the student should be able to:

1. Discuss each of the following and how they can improve body awareness and enhance a relationship with a partner:
   a. self-awareness
   b. communication
   c. sensate focus
   d. masturbation with a partner present

2. Explain some of the procedures involved for women who are learning to become orgasmic, both alone and with a partner.

3. Describe what treatment procedures are available for dealing with vaginismus and under what conditions vaginismus may be difficult to treat.

4. Outline at least six specific strategies used to cope with premature ejaculation.

5. Describe various treatment alternatives that are available for men who experience erectile difficulties and how successful they typically are.

6. Outline some of the strategies used to treat men who experience ejaculatory disorder.

7. Discuss some of the dynamics and specific treatment strategies involved in dealing with people who experience hypoactive sexual desire.

8. List and describe the four levels of treatment involved in the PLISSIT model of sex therapy.

9. Discuss the following in regard to seeking help for sexual difficulties:
   a. how sessions with a therapist might be structured
   b. the differences among psychosexual therapy, systems therapy and eye movement desensitization and reprocessing (EMDR)
   c. criteria to consider in selecting a therapist

10. Citing specific examples, explain how modern sex therapy may clash with the values of other cultures.

Multiple Choice

1.
K
Answer: c
p. 452
Obj. n/a

Your text suggests all but which one of the following?
a. Self-awareness may involve becoming familiar with ones own genitals.
b. We need to be aware of our own body responses in part to share this information with a partner.
c. We should be careful of sharing too much emotionally as this will take away some of the necessary mystery in sex.
d. All of us have the potential for self-help.

2.
K
Answer: c
p. 453
Obj. n/a

Modern sex therapy is our culture is based on all but which one of the following values and goal?
a. open communication
b. emotional intimacy
c. keeping parents in one house
d. physical pleasure for both partners

3.
K
Answer: d
p. 453
Obj. #1a

The major purpose of doing masturbation exercises is to
a. experience orgasmic release.
b. relax and relieve tension.
c. increase the possibility of having multiple orgasms.
d. learn and experience sexual response.

4.
A
Answer: a
p. 453
Obj. #10
WWW

In a culture where male superiority predominates, which of the following would be **most** likely to be perceived as a problem?
a. vaginismus
b. situational anorgasmia
c. female hypoactive sexual desire
d. generalized, lifelong anorgasmia

5.
A
Answer: d
p. 453
Obj. #10

According to a study done in Saudi Arabia, for which of the following sexual problems would men and women be **most** likely to seek help?
a. female hypoactive desire and premature ejaculation
b. situational anorgasmia and male hypoactive sexual desire
c. female arousal disorder and premature ejaculation
d. dyspareunia and erectile disorder

6.
K
Answer: c
p. 454
Obj. #1b

One of the primary benefits of sex therapy is
a. learning to masturbate with a partner present.
b. exposure to a variety of new sexual techniques.
c. developing more effective communications skills.
d. learning to have simultaneous orgasms.

7.
K
Answer: b
p. 454
Obj. #1b

Schnarch believes that that a couple who wants a high level of self-expression and sexual intimacy in their relationship should
a. have a high frequency of sexual interaction.
b. realize that intimacy means knowing and being known by one's partner.
c. work for simultaneous orgasm.
d. demonstrate effective conflict resolution skills.

Chapter 16 Sex Therapy and Enhancement 353

8.
K
Answer: b
p. 455
Obj. # 1c
WWW

Sensate focus is **best** described as
- a. a series of self-pleasuring exercises that an individual does alone and then with a partner.
- b. a series of touching exercises experienced with a partner.
- c. a technique for reducing premature ejaculation.
- d. a series of active listening and feedback exercises.

9.
K
Answer: d
p. 469-470
Obj. #1c

Which of the following statements concerning sensate focus is true?
- a. The bridge maneuver is one of the techniques used.
- b. Having intercourse during the first sensate focus experience is encouraged because the sexual problem(s) will be identified immediately.
- c. The stop and start technique is part of the sensate focus format.
- d. This technique is useful in sex therapy as well as in relationships in general.

10.
K
Answer: c
pp. 455-456
Obj. #1c

Which of the following statements concerning sensate focus is false?
- a. One partner takes an active role and the other a passive role.
- b. It encourages communication between partners.
- c. The goal is to find the best way to produce orgasm in the partner.
- d. One partner is encouraged to tell the other preferences in location and intensity of touching.

11.
K
Answer: d
p. 456
Obj. #1d

Masturbating with a partner present
- a. is kinky.
- b. is generally not recommended as this is better done in private.
- c. should be done only as a remedy for differential desire.
- d. may be a good way to inform your partner what kind of touch you find arousing.

12.
A
Answer: c
pp. 456-457
Obj. #2

The use of masturbation exercises in the treatment of anorgasmic women
- a. was widely promoted at one time, but has recently been found to detract from the ability to have orgasm with a partner.
- b. is effective only when suggested in a group setting with the knowledge that other women will be doing the same exercises.
- c. is an effective way for women to learn what produces erotic responses and orgasm in themselves.
- d. can result in compulsive masturbatory habits if proper guidelines are not established.

13.
K
Answer: b
p. 457
Obj. #2

Therapy programs for anorgasmia begin with
- a. learning to masturbate with a partner present.
- b. progressive self-awareness exercises.
- c. learning to integrate the bridge maneuver into sexual sharing.
- d. improving sexual communication skills between a woman and her partner.

14.
K
Answer: b
p. 457
Obj. #2

For women who are learning to become orgasmic for the first time,
a. sometimes vibrators are recommended because they facilitate orgasm quickly and can then be incorporated into sexual sharing with a partner.
b. sometimes vibrators are recommended so a woman knows she can have this response, but then manual stimulation is recommended.
c. vibrators are not recommended because the stimulation they provide is unable to be replicated by self or partner.
d. vibrators are not recommended because they can cause nerve damage in the genital area.

15.
K
Answer: d
p. 457
Obj. #2

A sexological exam is **best** described as
a. a medical exam that evaluates possible physiological factors that may be contributing to a sexual problem.
b. a series of touching exercises developed by Masters and Johnson.
c. a series of self-stimulation exercises that an individual is encouraged to do in learning to become orgasmic.
d. an exercise in which a couple takes turns first visually exploring and then touching each other's genitals.

16.
A
Answer: d
p. 457
Obj. #2
WWW

Which of the following is **least** likely to be used in the treatment of a woman who has generalized, lifelong anorgasmia?
a. Kegel exercises
b. masturbation exercises
c. use of a vibrator
d. rapid pelvic thrusting during intercourse

17.
K
Answer: c
p. 457
Obj. #2

A _____ can help anorgasmic women experience sexual climax for the first time.
a. ribbed dildo
b. kitten mitten
c. vibrator
d. cock ring

18.
K
Answer: b
pp. 458-460
Obj. #2

All of the following are suggested as ways to increase the possibility of orgasm during intercourse for a woman **except**
a. direct manual stimulation of the clitoris during intercourse.
b. the man-above intercourse position.
c. female-initiated movements.
d. use of the bridge maneuver.

19.
K
Answer: d
pp. 458-459
Obj. #2

Which one is NOT true about stimulation of the clitoris during orgasm?
a. This can be done manually by the woman.
b. A male can comfortably do this with his thumb.
c. This may be done making use of a vibrator.
d. One of the goals of therapy is to eliminate the need to do this.

Chapter 16 Sex Therapy and Enhancement 355

20.
K
Answer: b
p. 459
Obj. #2

The back-to-chest position is recommended for
a. delaying ejaculation.
b. genital sensate focus.
c. the bridge maneuver.
d. the squeeze technique.

21.
K
Answer: d
p. 460
Obj. #3
WWW

Dilators of graduated sizes are used to treat
a. erectile inhibition.
b. anorgasmia.
c. premature ejaculation.
d. vaginismus.

22.
K
Answer: c
p. 460
Obj. n/a

Routinely orgasmic women reported facilitating orgasm in all but which one of the following ways?
a. Paying attention to their own sensations.
b. Positioning their body to get the stimulation they needed.
c. Shutting their eyes and imagining another partner.
d. Tightening and relaxing pelvic muscles.

23.
K
Answer: a
p. 460
Obj. #2

In _____, manual stimulation during intercourse is employed until the woman is close to orgasm. Then manual stimulation is stopped and she actively moves her pelvis to provide sufficient stimulation to induce orgasm.
a. the bridge maneuver
b. sensate transfer
c. the stop-start technique
d. the squeeze technique

24.
K
Answer: a
p. 461
Obj. #4

When working with a man who experiences premature ejaculation, most sex therapists use a multiphase program that focuses on
a. the stop-start technique.
b. the squeeze technique.
c. Kegel exercises.
d. sensate focus.

25.
K
Answer: b
p. 461
Obj. #4

Which of the following **increases** the possibility of premature ejaculation?
a. ejaculating more frequently
b. using the man-above intercourse position
c. starting and stopping stimulation
d. communicating during coitus

26.
K
Answer: a
p. 461
Obj. #4

Which of the following is suggested for a man who has problems with premature ejaculation?
a. If a man ejaculates rapidly, continue sexual interaction until his erection returns.
b. Have a "small orgasm".
c. Use the bridge maneuver.
d. Practice sensate focus exercises.

27.
K
Answer: c
p. 461
Obj. #4

The squeeze technique is when a man's partner
a. applies pressure to the base of his penis in order to delay ejaculation.
b. practices her Kegel exercises during intercourse.
c. applies pressure to the glans of the penis in order to delay ejaculation.
d. applies pressure to the shaft of his penis in order to delay ejaculation.

28.
A
Answer: c
p. 461
Obj. #4

If a man finds that he is ejaculating more rapidly when he first experiences the woman-above position with his partner, it may be due to
a. the increase in muscle tension.
b. reduced pelvic thrusting.
c. increased arousal due to the novelty of a new position.
d. the effects of the bridge maneuver.

29.
K
Answer: d
pp. 461-162
Obj. #4

Which of the following statements regarding the stop-start technique is false?
a. A man can benefit from using this technique on himself during masturbation.
b. A man can benefit from using this technique with his partner.
c. A urologist developed this technique.
d. Masters and Johnson reported a 60% success rate in treating this problem.

30.
K
Answer: c
pp. 461-462
Obj. #4

Which of the following statements concerning the stop-start technique is false?
a. It was developed by James Semans.
b. It is more commonly used than the squeeze technique.
c. This technique is used primarily for treating ejaculatory inhibition.
d. It can be used both alone or with a partner.

31.
K
Answer: a
p. 462
Obj. #4

It appears that small doses of medication used to treat _____ may also help men who wish to delay ejaculation.
a. depression
b. hypogonadism
c. anxiety
d. Peyronie's disease

32.
K
Answer: c
p. 462
Obj. #5

A man is experiencing difficulty maintaining an erection, and organic causes have been ruled out. Which of the following is **most** likely the cause of his problem?
a. anger
b. depression
c. anxiety
d. guilt

33.
A
Answer: a
p. 462
Obj. #4
WWW

A man who is able to have intercourse with his partner for 20-30 minutes before ejaculating is put on Prozac in order to deal with depression. Which of the following side effects would be **most** common?
    a. ejaculatory inhibition
    b. premature ejaculation
    c. Peyronie's disease
    d. priapism

34.
K
Answer: a
pp. 462-463
Obj. #5

Which of the following is part of the therapy program for dealing with erectile dysfunction?
    a. sensate focus exercises
    b. vaginal penetration as soon as the man is able to sustain an erection
    c. intercourse in the man-above position
    d. use of the stop-start technique

35.
K
Answer: d
p. 462
Obj. #4

Which of the following would be **least** likely to facilitate erection in men?
    a. Viagra
    b. yohimbe
    c. devices that suction blood into the penis and hold it there during intercourse
    d. anti-depressant medication

36.
K
Answer: a
p. 462
Obj. #6

In the final phase of treatment for ejaculatory disorder, which intercourse position is used?
    a. woman-above
    b. man-above
    c. side position, face-to-face
    d. None of the above; intercourse is not the final phase of treatment for ejaculatory inhibition.

37.
A
Answer: c
p. 462
Obj. #5
WWW

Jack is having problems maintaining an erection and it has been determined that there is no physiological basis for this problem. His partner may be most helpful to him if she
    a. persuades him to have intercourse with her as soon as he begins to have an erection.
    b. is able to increase his blood pressure and thus the vascular flow to his penis.
    c. can help reduce his anxiety over sexual performance.
    d. shares with him specific ways in which he can stimulate her and bring her to an orgasm.

38.
A
Answer: a
p. 463
Obj. #5

George is experiencing erectile difficulties, so he and his partner have been following the steps outlined in the text to deal with this problem. They progress through several phases of the program, but then George "fails" to respond during one of the exercises. According to the text, George and his partner should
a. return to an earlier phase of the program.
b. continue repeating the current exercise until success is achieved.
c. proceed to the following step.
d. stop the program and immediately seek the help of a professional.

39.
K
Answer: d
p. 463
Obj. #6

Which one is NOT true concerning Viagra?
a. Four million Americans are taking it.
b. It was originally developed for cardiovascular disease.
c. It takes effect in ½ to 2 hours with physical stimulation.
d. It has no known side effects.

40.
K
Answer: b
p. 463
Obj. #6
WWW

When doing therapy for erectile dysfunction it is important that
a. the partner concentrate on repeating whatever actions finally get the man aroused.
b. the man learn that he can lose an erection and regain it.
c. the man think about the woman's pleasure as much as his own.
d. he be heterosexual.

41.
K
Answer: d
p. 464
Obj. #6

Which one is NOT true of Viagra?
a. It is available on the Internet.
b. It has been used recreationally by some without ED.
c. It allows erections to continue after ejaculation.
d. It is not recommended for men over 65.

42.
K
Answer: b
p. 465
Obj. #6

External vacuum constriction devices
a. are used over a woman's clitoris.
b. are used in combination with an elastic band at the base of the penis.
c. have been found to result in tissue damage.
d. are the treatment of choice for vascular impairment.

43.
K
Answer: a
p. 465
Obj. #5

_____ is a penile support sleeve that can help facilitate the erectile support needed for penetration.
a. Rejoyn
b. Spontane
c. Vasomax
d. Viagra

Chapter 16 Sex Therapy and Enhancement 359

44.
K
Answer: a
pp. 465-466
Obj. #5

Which of the following statements regarding penile implants is true?
a. In general, men tend to be more satisfied with the inflatable prosthetic device than the semi-rigid rods.
b. Implants allow men to experience genital sensation which had been lost due to medical problems.
c. Implants allow men to ejaculate who had previously been unable to do so as a result of medical problems.
d. Although men report a high degree of sexual satisfaction with the implants, the residual scarring makes some men feel self-conscious about the appearance of their genitals.

45.
K
Answer: a
p. 466
Obj. #5

Which of the following is an advantage of having a penile implant?
a. restoring the ability to have an erection
b. restoring genital sensation
c. restoring the ability to ejaculate
d. all of the above

46.
K
Answer: d
p. 466
Obj. #5

Surgical solutions for erectile difficulties include all but which of the following:
a. a penile prosthesis
b. microsurgical vascular repair
c. nerve grafts for damaged nerves
d. nerve regeneration stimulated by yohimbe

47.
K
Answer: b
pp. 466-467
Obj. #6

Which of the following is a recommended sequence of events in treating for male orgasmic disorder?
a. sensate focus; self stimulation with partner present; squeeze technique; ejaculation during intercourse
b. sensate focus; self-stimulation with partner present; manual or oral stimulation by partner to orgasm; ejaculation during intercourse
c. papaverine injections; sensate focus; stop-start techniques; ejaculation during intercourse
d. sensate focus; self-stimulation with partner absent; stop-start technique; ejaculation during intercourse

48.
K
Answer: a
p. 467
Obj. #7

Many therapists consider _____ the most difficult sexual problem to treat.
a. hypoactive sexual desire
b. anorgasmia
c. ejaculatory inhibition
d. premature ejaculation

49.
A
Answer: b
p. 467
Obj. #4-7

Which of the following sexual problems is typically the **most** difficult to treat?
a. hypoactive sexual desire
b. premature ejaculation
c. erectile disorder
d. male orgasmic disorder

50.
K
Answer: b
p. 467
Obj. #7

Which of the following problems would require more intensive therapy than the others?
a. vaginismus
b. hypoactive sexual desire
c. anorgasmia
d. premature ejaculation

51.
K
Answer: c
p. 467
Obj. #7
WWW

The goal for treatment of HSD is
a. to resume intercourse on a regular basis.
b. to provide appropriate medical intervention in order to alleviate the problem.
c. to modify the person's pattern of inhibiting his or her erotic impulses.
d. to follow a six-step, behaviorally-based program that focuses on the couple assuming responsibility for each other's pleasure.

52.
K
Answer: d
p. 467
Obj. #7

All of the following problems may be associated with HSD **except**
a. fears about vulnerability and closeness.
b. power imbalance in the relationship.
c. poor sexual skills.
d. elevated levels of androgen in the bloodstream.

53.
K
Answer: b
p. 468
Obj. #8

All of the following are levels of the PLISSIT model **except**
a. limited information.
b. self-stimulation.
c. permission.
d. intensive therapy.

54.
K
Answer: c
p. 468
Obj. #8

Giving a client exercises or activities to do at home would be part of the _____ level of the PLISSIT model of sex therapy.
a. permission
b. limited information
c. specific suggestions
d. intensive therapy

55.
K
Answer: d
p. 468
Obj. #8

Providing interpretations to help clients better understand the unconscious thoughts and feelings that have been contributing to their sexual problems is called _____ therapy.
a. supportive
b. Gestalt
c. systems
d. psychosexual

56.
K
Answer: a
p. 468
Obj. #8

The therapeutic approach that makes the assumption that a particular sexual problem a person is experiencing serves a certain function in the relationship is called _____ therapy.
a. systems
b. PLISSIT
c. psychosexual
d. functional

Chapter 16 Sex Therapy and Enhancement   361

57.
A
Answer: c
p. 468
Obj. #8

Riccardo and Estelle are seeing a sex therapist. Part of the program involves doing sensate focus exercises at home. According to the PLISSIT model, what level of treatment is this?
a. permission
b. limited information
c. specific suggestions
d. self-stimulation

58.
A
Answer: b
p. 468
Obj. #8
WWW

Katie and Jack are seeing a sex therapist. At this point in treatment, the therapist is describing some of the differences between male and female sexual response as well as explaining the effects of a medication Katie is taking on her sexual desire. According to the PLISSIT model, what level of treatment is this?
a. specific suggestions
b. limited information
c. permission
d. intensive therapy

59.
A
Answer: d
p. 468
Obj. #8

Tran and Linh are seeing a sex therapist. At this point in treatment, they are being encouraged to read a book that supports people in their desire to have a good, healthy sexual relationship. It also provides case examples of couples who are experiencing similar problems to theirs, as well as outlining some behavioral exercises to practice at home. According to the PLISSIT model, what level of treatment is this?
a. specific suggestions
b. limited information
c. permission
d. all of the above

60.
K
Answer: d
p. 468
Obj. #8

Which one is NOT true with respect to EMDR?
a. This stand for Eye Movement Desensitization and Reprocessing.
b. This is a treatment for symptoms resulting from past trauma.
c. This is something that might be used for sexual compulsions.
d. This is often done during REM sleep using tape recorded messages.

61.
K
Answer: b
p. 469
Obj. #9a
WWW

Which of the following is NOT true about sex therapy?
a. A first session usually identifies the problem and sets goals.
b. Sex therapy is usually done several times a week.
c. Therapy clients will usually be given homework assignments to do between sessions.
d. A medical history will usually be taken.

62.
K
Answer: c
p. 469
Obj. #9c

Which one is NOT true about sex therapists?
a. They should have at least a master's degree.
b. Good ones will help you improve the marital communication and satisfaction.
c. You should choose one who is of the opposite sex.
d. Many will be certified by AASECT (the American Association of Sex Educators, Counselors, and Therapists).

63
K
Answer: d
p. 469
Obj. n/a

A sexual relationship between therapist and client
a. is sometimes therapeutic.
b. has been admitted by 1 or 2% of therapists.
c. is never considered acceptable by the American Association for Marriage and Family Therapy.
d. will likely result in negative effects – e.g., anxiety and depression – for the client.

64.
K
Answer: c
p. 470
Obj. #9d

In regard to cost of therapy, _____ are usually on the upper end of the fee scale, _____ are in the middle, and _____ are on the lower end.
a. psychologists; psychiatrists; social workers
b. psychologists; social workers; psychiatrists
c. psychiatrists; psychologists; social workers
d. psychiatrists; social workers; psychologists

Multiple Choice from Study Guide

1.
K
Answer: b
p. n/a
Obj. n/a

All of the following are parts of basic sex therapy **except**
a. masturbation exercises.
b. the squeeze technique.
c. sensate focus.
d. genital self-exam.

2.
K
Answer: c
p. 453
Obj. n/a

Which cultural group would be **least** likely to discuss sexual matters with a therapist?
a. Orthodox Jews
b. Wiccans
c. Asians
d. Native Americans

3.
K
Answer: a
pp. 455-456
Obj. #1c

Which of the following is false regarding sensate focus exercises?
a. Early sessions focus on bringing the partners to orgasm.
b. Partners switch roles.
c. The toucher explores for their own pleasure, not their partner's.
d. The recipient of touch remains quiet, except when touch is uncomfortable.

4.
K
Answer: d
p. 457
Obj. #2

For a woman who has never experienced orgasm what would be **most** helpful?
a. the bridge maneuver
b. the man-on-top coital position
c. Viagra
d. masturbation

Chapter 16 Sex Therapy and Enhancement   363

5.
K
Answer: c
pp. 457-460
Obj. #2

Couples who wish to increase the possibility of a woman's orgasm during intercourse would be advised to all of the following **except**
a. begin intercourse when she feels ready, instead of when she is adequately lubricated.
b. use the bridge maneuver.
c. avoid use of water-soluble lubricants like K-Y jelly.
d. use an intercourse position that allows for direct clitoral stimulation.

6.
K
Answer: b
p. 460
Obj. #2

The bridge maneuver is **best** described as
a. a variation of sensate focus exercises.
b. manual stimulation of the clitoris during intercourse until climax is near, followed by active pelvic movements.
c. the rear-entry or "doggie" intercourse position, where the woman keeps her back flat like a tabletop.
d. using a vibrator to approach climax during masturbation, then switching to manual stimulation of the clitoris.

7.
K
Answer: a
p. 460
Obj. #3

Which of the following would NOT be included in a treatment program for vaginismus?
a. using SS-cream
b. relaxation exercises
c. manual stimulation
d. insertion of fingers or dilators

8.
K
Answer: c
p.461
Obj. #4

All of the following techniques may delay ejaculation **except**
a. having more frequent orgasms.
b. continuing sexual activity after a first ejaculation.
c. using energetic pelvic movements.
d. using the woman-above position during intercourse.

9.
K
Answer: d
p. 461
Obj. #4

The stop-start technique involves
a. communicating the level of stimulation one is experiencing to the partner.
b. applying the technique using oral or manual stimulation first.
c. stopping stimulation until pre-ejaculatory sensations are reduced.
d. all of the above
e. two of the above

10.
K
Answer: b
p. 461
Obj. #4

Of the following statements, which is true regarding the squeeze technique?
a. Urologist James Semans developed the technique.
b. Pressure is applied to the frenulum and glans of the penis to delay ejaculation.
c. The base of the penis is grasped firmly and given three quick squeezes.
d. The squeeze technique is used to treat retrograde ejaculation.

11.
K
Answer: a
p. 462
Obj. #5

A treatment program to deal with erectile dysfunction would include
a. sensate focus exercises.
b. viewing erotic films.
c. using manual or genital stimulation to first cause an erection, then beginning penetration immediately to prevent loss of an erection.
d. using the EROS treatment device to produce an erection.

12.
K
Answer: e
pp. 463-464
Obj. # 5

Which of the following statements is true about Viagra?
a. It allows erections to continue after ejaculation.
b. It promotes blood flow to the penis.
c. Flushing and headaches are common side effects.
d. b and c are true
e. all of the above are true

13.
K
Answer: d
pp. 465-466
Obj. #5

Erections may be produced by all of the following methods **except**
a. penile implants.
b. vacuum suction.
c. injections.
d. gossypol.

14.
K
Answer: c
p. 462
Obj. #5

A **major** goal of treatment approaches for erectile dysfunction that does not have an organic basis is
a. getting the client stabilized on a proper dose of Viagra.
b. encouraging a man to attempt intercourse as often as possible.
c. reducing anxiety.
d. using EMDR to increase arousal.

15.
K
Answer: d
p. 466
Obj. #6

Treatment of male orgasmic disorder involves
a. asking the couple to express affection at times other than intercourse.
b. using antidepressants to increase orgasmic response.
c. using anti-anxiety agents to promote relaxation.
d. using behavioral approaches and psychotherapy to reduce resentment.

16.
K
Answer: b
p. 467
Obj. #7

Hypoactive sexual desire
a. can often be treated through therapy that is less intensive than that used for other problems.
b. is often a symptom of unresolved relationship problems.
c. is uncomplicated to treat.
d. is most often caused by hormonal imbalances.

Chapter 16 Sex Therapy and Enhancement 365

17. The acronym PLISSIT refers to a model of sex therapy that
K emphasizes
Answer: d
p. 468
Obj. #8
a. Playfulness, Love, Integration, Specific Suggestions, Information, and Therapy.
b. Permission, Love, Information, Specific Suggestions, Integration, and Therapy.
c. Passion, Limited Information, Specific Suggestions, Integration Therapy.
d. Permission, Limited Information, Specific Suggestions, Intensive Therapy.

18. Leila and Irene are seeing a sex therapist that is helping them gain
A awareness of unconscious feelings regarding their early relationships
Answer: c with their parents. This couple is experiencing _____ therapy.
p. 468
Obj. #9b
a. postmodern
b. systems
c. psychosexual
d. EMDR

19. All of the following may happening in sex therapy **except**
K
Answer: c
p. 469
Obj. #9
a. a medical history will be taken.
b. screening for major psychological problems.
c. sexual relations with the therapist may occur.
d. homework assignments may be given.

True/False

Students may be asked to answer these questions using the traditional format of marking their answers either "true" or "false". Or, to encourage more active involvement, you may choose to use the following instructions:

If the statement is true, place a "T" on the line preceding it. If the statement is false, place an "F" on the line preceding it and then change the statement to make it true by deleting incorrect information and/or adding accurate information.

1. ___ Sensate focus is a series of self-awareness and communication
Answer: F exercises developed by Helen Singer Kaplan.
p. 455
Obj. #1c

2. ___ In sensate focus exercises, the goal is for the person who is
Answer: F doing the touching to discover what gives the recipient pleasure.
pp. 455-456
Obj. #1c

3. ___ Using a vibrator is recommended as an option for self-stimulation
Answer: T for women who are becoming orgasmic.
p. 457
Obj. #2

4.
Answer: T
p. 459
Obj. #2

___ The back-to-chest position is recommended for genital sensate focus.

5.
Answer: F
p. 460
Obj. #3

___ The first step in treatment for vaginismus is to practice vaginal penetration with a fingertip, using a lubricant such as K-Y jelly.

6.
Answer: T
p. 460
Obj. #3

___ In treating vaginismus, the woman is instructed to do various exercises on her own, and then eventually her partner participates in the exercises with her.

7.
Answer: T
p. 460
Obj. #3

___ Vaginismus can sometimes be difficult to treat successfully, especially if a couple has never experienced penile-vaginal intercourse.

8.
Answer: T
p. 461
Obj. #4

___ Although many men report problems with premature ejaculation, there is a high probability for positive change with various treatment strategies available.

9.
Answer: F
pp. 460-461
Obj. #2, 4

___ The bridge maneuver, stop-start and squeeze techniques are all used to treat premature ejaculation.

10.
Answer: T
p. 461
Obj. #4

___ The best intercourse position for a man who would like to delay ejaculation is woman-above.

11.
Answer: F
p. 461
Obj. #4

___ The squeeze technique is the most commonly used technique for premature ejaculation.

12.
Answer: F
p. 462
Obj. #5

___ Physical problems aside, deep-seated resentment is the most common reason a man would have erectile difficulties.

13.
Answer: T
p. 464
Obj. #5

___ Viagra has been readily obtained through the Internet even by people who do not erectile dysfunction.

14. ___ Men who have penile implants in order to restore their ability to
Answer: T   have erections are unable to ejaculate if that ability was already
p. 466   lost as a result of their medical condition.
Obj. #5

15. ___ The most difficult sexual problem to treat is ejaculatory disorder.
Answer: F
p. 467
Obj. #6, 7

16. ___ HSD is usually successfully treated with a behavioral approach.
Answer: F
p. 467
Obj. #7

17. ___ PLISSIT stands for Permission, Limited Information, Self-
Answer: F   Stimulation, and Intensive Therapy.
p. 468
Obj. #8

18. ___ Insight-oriented therapy is another term for systems therapy.
Answer: F
p. 468
Obj. #8

19. ___ When the focus of the therapy is on the functions the problems
Answer: T   serve in the relationship, systems therapy is being used.
p. 468
Obj. #8

20. ___ Sex therapy that integrates systems, psychosexual and
Answer: F   behavioral approaches is called progressive therapy.
p. 468
Obj. #8

Short Answer Essay

1. Specify the three assumptions on which modern sex therapy is based and then indicate to what extent these match your values. (Obj. #10)

2. Describe the process of sensate focus and give two examples of how it might be used therapeutically. (Obj. #1c)

3. Outline the steps used in the treatment of anorgasmic women. (Obj. #2)

4. Describe what couples may do to help a woman learn to experience orgasm with a partner. (Obj. #1d, 2)

5. Define vaginismus, and discuss how it is treated. Comment on its incidence and how successful the treatment is. (Obj. #3)

6. Your book describes six ways in which a man might delay ejaculation. List at least four of them, with a notation about how well these might work. (Obj. #4)

7. What is the basic procedure for treating men with ejaculatory disorder? (Obj. #6)

8. Describe some of the options available to men who have impaired erectile functioning as the result of a medical problem. (Obj. #5)

9. If you or your partner were to develop an inability to have an erection, what would your preference be for dealing with this? That is, which if any of the various treatment options would you choose? Why? (Obj. #5)

10. Have you ever known anyone who used Viagra? If so, what was your understanding of why they used it? What was your reaction to this usage? If you have not in fact known anyone then report your reaction to the possible usage of this by someone with ED, and by someone for recreational usage? (Obj. #5)

11. How does the treatment of HSD differ from that of other sexual problems? Give specific examples. (Obj. #7)

12. Name the four levels of the PLISSIT model of sexual therapy. For the last level, specify the various kinds of therapy, giving specific examples to illustrate. (Obj. #8, 9b)

13. Explain what the acronym PLISSIT represents and give an example of each phase of treatment. (Obj. #8)

14. If you were to consider seeing a sex therapist for you and your partner, which of the various therapy options do you think you would prefer? What criteria would you use in selecting your therapist? (Obj. #9)

15. If a friend called and asked for information that might be helpful in deciding whether and how to contact a sex therapist, what information would you give her/him? (Obj. #9c)

17

Sexually Transmitted Diseases

Learning Objectives

After studying Chapter 17, students will be able to:

1. Cite statistics that indicate in what age groups sexually transmitted diseases will most commonly occur.

2. Discuss some of the factors that give rise to the incidence of sexually transmitted diseases.

3. Describe the cause, incidence and transmission, symptoms and complications and treatment alternatives for the following bacterial infections: chlamydia infection; gonorrhea; nongonococcal urethritis; syphilis chancroid.

4. Describe the cause, incidence and transmission, symptoms and complications and treatment alternatives for the following viral infections: herpes; genital warts; viral hepatitis.

5. Describe the cause, incidence and transmission, symptoms and complications and treatment alternatives for the following vaginal infections: bacterial vaginosis; candidiasis; trichomoniasis.

6. Describe the cause, incidence and transmission, symptoms and complications and treatment alternatives for the following ectoparasitic infections: pubic lice; scabies

7. Describe each of the following in reference to acquired immunodeficiency syndrome (AIDS):
    a. what causes it and how it is diagnosed
    b. when it was first recognized in the U.S. and around the world
    c. some of the serious diseases to which AIDS patients are vulnerable
    d. incidence and transmission in the U.S. and worldwide
    e. symptoms and complications
    f. HIV antibody tests
    g. development of AIDS
    h. treatment
    i. prevention
    j. HIV/AIDS issues and the law
    k. the development of vaccines for AIDS
    l. new drug treatments for age, particularly the HAART regime

8. Outline and describe strategies that can help reduce the likelihood of contracting a sexually transmitted disease.

9. Describe developing research on vaginal microbicides.

10. Describe cross-cultural difficulties in AIDS prevention and treatment citing differences between China and Africa's resources and approaches.

Multiple Choice

1.
K
Answer: d
p. 474
Obj. #1

Approximately 50 percent of the U.S. population will acquire one or more STDs by age
 a. 15-20.
 b. 20-25.
 c. 25-30.
 d. 30-35.

2.
K
Answer: a
p. 474
Obj. #1

Which age group has highest rate of STDs of any sexually active age group?
 a. 15-25
 b. 26-35
 c. 36-45
 d. 46-55

3.
K
Answer: c
p. 474
Obj. #1

_____ have the highest rates of gonorrhea of any age group in the U.S.
 a. Male adults age 20-25
 b. Male adolescents age 12-16
 c. Female adolescents age 15-19
 d. Female adults age 21-26

4.
K
Answer: c
p. 474
Obj. #1
WWW

The **largest** proportion of AIDS cases in the U.S. are
 a. gay men in their 50s and 60s who were infected in their 40s and 50s.
 b. lesbians in their 40s and 50s who were infected in their 30s and 40s.
 c. people in their 20s and 30s who were infected in their teens or 20s.
 d. people in their 40s and 50s who were infected in their 30s and 40s.

5.
K
Answer: b
p. 474
Obj. #2
WWW

All of the following were cited as factors contributing to the high incidence of STDs **except**
 a. increasing sexual activity among young people.
 b. unreliability of latex condoms.
 c. increasing tendency to have multiple sexual partners.
 d. use of birth control pills.

6.
K
Answer: a
p. 475
Obj. n/a

In a nationally representative survey of adults ____ responded that they were asked about STDs during routine medical checkups.
 a. 28%
 b. 43%
 c. 58%
 d. 73%

Chapter 17 Sexually Transmitted Diseases   371

7.
K
Answer: b
p. 475
Obj. n/a

Factors you should consider when deciding whether to tell a lover that you have and STD include
   a. that they'll probably find out anyway and then be angry.
   b. that even if you are cured you could get it back from them.
   c. that it's often illegal not to do so.
   d. whether or not you were considering breaking up with them.

8.
K
Answer: c
p. 478
Obj. #3

_____ is the **most** common bacterial STD in the United States.
   a. Trichomoniasis
   b. Candidiasis
   c. Chlamydia
   d. Gonorrhea

9.
K
Answer: a
p. 478
Obj. #5

Chlamydia infection, if left untreated, may result in all of the following **except**
   a. condylomata acuminata.
   b. cervicitis.
   c. pelvic inflammatory disease.
   d. urethritis.

10.
K
Answer: b
pp. 478-479
Obj. #3

Which of the following statements concerning chlamydia infection is false?
   a. The majority of women with lower reproductive tract chlamydia infection have few or no symptoms.
   b. It is associated with penile cancer in men if left untreated.
   c. The infection is transmitted primarily through sexual contact.
   d. It is usually treated with doxycycline or ofloxacin.

11.
K
Answer: b
p. 479
Obj. #3

_____ causes _____, the world's leading cause of preventable blindness.
   a. Viral hepatitis; conjunctivitis
   b. Chlamydia; trachoma
   c. Syphilis; conjunctivitis
   d. Trichomoniasis; trachoma

12.
K
Answer: c
p. 479
Obj. #3

_____ and _____ in men are commonly caused by chlamydia infections.
   a. Nongonococcal urethritis; herpes keratitis
   b. Viral hepatitis; epididymitis
   c. Nongonococcal urethritis; epididymitis
   d. Trichomoniasis; epididymitis

13.
K
Answer: b
p. 479
Obj. #3

A woman with a history of pelvic inflammatory disease would probably be advised to avoid which of the following birth control methods?
   a. diaphragm
   b. IUD
   c. birth control pills
   d. spermicides and condoms

14.
K
Answer: d
p. 479
Obj. #3
WWW

The dramatic increase of ectopic pregnancies in the U.S. over the past twenty years has been largely attributed to the increased incidence of
a. genital warts.
b. herpes.
c. trichomoniasis.
d. chlamydia.

15.
K
Answer: d
p. 480
Obj. #3

Approximately _____ percent of women who are infected with gonorrhea will be asymptomatic until the disease has progressed considerably.
a. 20
b. 40
c. 60
d. 80

16.
K
Answer: a
p. 480
Obj. #3
WWW

There is a marked tendency for _____ to coexist with gonorrhea.
a. a chlamydia infection
b. trichomoniasis
c. candidiasis
d. syphilis

17.
K
Answer: a
p. 480
Obj. #3

The **most** common symptom(s) of gonorrhea in men is/are
a. bad-smelling, cloudy penile discharge and burning sensations during urination.
b. white, cheesy penile discharge and ticklish sensation during urination.
c. inflammation of the penile glans and foreskin.
d. thick, greenish penile discharge.

18.
K
Answer: a
p. 480
Obj. #6

Which of the following STDs can infect the throat and the anus as well as the genitals?
a. gonorrhea
b. bacterial vaginosis
c. trichomoniasis
d. chlamydia infection

19.
A
Answer: d
p. 480
Obj. #3

Five days after sexual contact with a new partner, Gary experiences burning during urination and a bad-smelling, cloudy discharge from his penis. Assuming he does not have NGU, the suspected disease would **most** likely be
a. candidiasis.
b. syphilis.
c. trichomoniasis.
d. gonorrhea.

Chapter 17 Sexually Transmitted Diseases 373

20.
K
Answer: b
p. 481
Obj. #10

Ten million Chinese had an STD when Mao Zedong came to power. STDs were virtually eradicated by all but which one of the following:
a. closing brothels
b. criminal penalties for sexual activity if you had an untreated STD
c. mass screening
d. free treatment for those infected

21.
K
Answer: d
p. 481
Obj. #10

China, the world's largest country, has an emerging STD problem. Which one has NOT been suggested as a factor contributing to this?
a. wider availability of pornography
b. emerging commercial sex workers
c. increasing freedom of movement
d. government silence about the problem

22.
K
Answer: b
pp. 482-483
Obj. #3b

The use of silver nitrate eye drops immediately after birth averts what potential complication in the infant of an infected mother?
a. herpes lesions
b. gonococcal eye infection
c. genital warts
d. sudden infant death syndrome

23.
K
Answer: d
pp. 482-483
Obj. #3

Which of the following statements regarding gonorrhea is true?
a. It is a viral infection.
b. It is usually treated with penicillin.
c. If left untreated, complication include cervical and penile cancer.
d. Gonorrhea may infect the throat and rectum.

24.
K
Answer: b
p. 483
Obj. #3
WWW

_____ and _____ often coexist together.
a. Herpes; genital warts
b. Chlamydia; gonorrhea
c. Viral hepatitis; chlamydia
d. Genital warts; gonorrhea

25.
K
Answer: d
pp. 483-484
Obj. #3

Which of the following statements regarding NGU is false?
a. In women, there are usually no symptoms.
b. In men, the symptoms are similar to those of gonorrhea.
c. It may result in PID if left untreated in women.
d. There are no known consequences if left untreated in men.

26.
K
Answer: d
p. 484
Obj. #3, 4

All of the following are viral infections **except**
a. hepatitis A
b. genital warts
c. herpes
d. syphilis

27.
K
Answer: d
p. 484
Obj. #3

_____ is caused by a thin, corkscrew-like bacterium commonly called a spirochete.
a. Chlamydia
b. Candidiasis
c. Gonorrhea
d. Syphilis

28.
K
Answer: b
p. 484
Obj. #3

All of the following are phases of syphilitic development **except**
a. tertiary.
b. prodromal.
c. latent.
d. primary.

29.
K
Answer: c
p. 484
Obj. #3

Which of the following is characteristic of the initial phase of syphilis?
a. penile discharge in men; no symptoms in women
b. a skin rash all over the body
c. a chancre at the site where the organism enters the body
d. painful blister-like lesions on the genitals

30.
K
Answer: b
p. 485
Obj. #3

The second stage of syphilis is characterized by
a. painful, blister-like lesions on the genitals.
b. a skin rash.
c. high fever, genital inflammation, and night sweats.
d. no observable symptoms.

31.
K
Answer: d
pp. 484-486
Obj. #3

Which of the following statements concerning syphilis is false?
a. A latent stage can last for several years.
b. A pregnant woman with syphilis in any stage can pass the infection to the fetus.
c. It can result in death.
d. The incidence of syphilis has been steadily increasing since the mid-1970s.

32.
K
Answer: a
pp. 484-486
Obj. #3

Which of the following **best** describes the progression of syphilis over time if left untreated?
a. painless sore; skin rash; no symptoms; death or blindness
b. painful blister; no symptoms; eye infection; sterility
c. vaginal or penile discharge; epididymitis or PID; penile or cervical cancer
d. painless sore; no symptoms; PID or epididymitis; sterility

33.
K
Answer: c
pp. 484-486
Obj. #3

Which of the following statements concerning syphilis is true?
a. It can be effectively treated with metronidazole at any stage.
b. It is a viral infection that is asymptomatic in the primary phase.
c. A pregnant woman with syphilis can pass the infection to her fetus.
d. It is asymptomatic in women.

34.
K
Answer: b
p. 486
Obj. #3

If left untreated, _____ can result in severe mental disturbances and even death.
a. gonorrhea
b. syphilis
c. chlamydia
d. herpes

35.
K
Answer: a
p. 486
Obj. #3

Chancroid is
a. a bacterial infection.
b. a viral infection.
c. a fungus.
d. a parasitic insect.

36.
K
Answer: d
p. 486
Obj. #3

Which of the following statements about chancroid is false?
a. It is prevalent in Africa.
b. The incidence of chancroid has increased in the U.S. in recent years.
c. It is associated with an increased incidence of HIV infections.
d. It is usually without visible symptoms

37.
K
Answer: a
p. 487
Obj. #4

_____ is usually manifested as cold sores on the mouth or lips, and _____, generally as lesions on and around the genital areas.
a. HSV-1; HSV-2
b. HSV-2; HSV-1
c. HPV-1; HPV-2
d. HPV-2; HPV-1

38.
K
Answer: d
p. 487
Obj. #4

When is a person who has herpes the **least** contagious?
a. when the person experiences prodromal symptoms
b. when the papules develop into blisters
c. after the blisters form a crust
d. during asymptomatic periods

39.
K
Answer: d
pp. 487-488
Obj. #4
WWW

Which of the following statements concerning herpes is false?
a. Oral herpes may be transmitted by kissing.
b. Herpes may be transmitted during asymptomatic periods.
c. Herpes will not pass through latex condoms.
d. Herpes incidence is decreasing.

40.
K
Answer: c
p. 488
Obj. #4

At what point is a woman able to resume coitus after a herpes outbreak with a significantly reduced likelihood of transmitting the virus to her partner?
a. when the blister begins to form a crust
b. when the sores on the labia have completely healed
c. ten days after the sores on the labia have completely healed
d. one month after the sores on the labia have completely healed

41.
K
Answer: a
p. 489
Obj. #4

All of the following are mentioned as factors that may trigger a herpes outbreak **except**
a. a diet high in complex carbohydrates.
b. emotional stress.
c. menstruation.
d. being overtired.

42.
K
Answer: c
p. 489
Obj. #4

Which of the following is a prodromal symptom of herpes?
a. the appearance of a papule
b. the rupture of the blisters
c. an itching or burning sensation
d. a feeling of depression

43.
K
Answer: d
p. 489
Obj. #4

Which of the following statements concerning the recurrence of genital herpes is true?
a. Everyone infected with herpes will experience a recurrence because the virus does not go away.
b. The more extensive the primary attack, the lesser the chance of recurrence.
c. Symptoms associated with recurrent attacks tend to become more severe over time.
d. The majority of people prone to recurrent outbreaks experience prodromal symptoms.

44.
K
Answer: d
p. 490
Obj. #4

Possible complications of a herpes infection in women include all of the following **except**
a. cervical cancer.
b. infection of the newborn.
c. severe eye infection.
d. ectopic pregnancy.

45.
A
Answer: b
p. 490
Obj. #4

While advisable for all women, regular Pap smears would be **most** recommended for women with
a. chlamydia.
b. genital herpes.
c. viral hepatitis.
d. candidiasis.

46.
K
Answer: b
p. 490
Obj. #4

Which one is NOT true concerning pregnant women with herpes and their children?
a. A newborn may be infected with genital herpes while passing through the birth canal.
b. Everyone agrees that cesarean deliveries should be done with women who have herpes.
c. If newborns infected with herpes are not treated about 60% of them will die or be severely damaged.
d. Skin sores on newborns of mothers with herpes can be cultured to confirm a herpes diagnosis.

Chapter 17 Sexually Transmitted Diseases 377

47.
K
Answer: c
p. 491
Obj. #4

Which of the following is the **most** accurate statement regarding the treatment of herpes?
   a. Adequate rest, relaxation and fluid intake can eliminate the virus over time.
   b. AZT is effective in the treatment of herpes.
   c. There is no cure for herpes at this time, although Zovirax is helpful in managing it.
   d. There is no cure for herpes at this time, although research with alpha interferon looks promising.

48.
A
Answer: c
p. 491
Obj. #4

Janet experiences recurrent herpes outbreaks fairly frequently. Which of the following suggestions would be **least** helpful to her in minimizing the discomfort associated with these outbreaks?
   a. avoid drinking liquids that would make her urine more acidic
   b. use a local topical anesthetic
   c. wear nylon underwear
   d. learn relaxation techniques

49.
K
Answer: a
pp. 492-493
Obj. #4
WWW

Genital warts
   a. are associated with various cancers.
   b. are caused by a bacterial microorganism.
   c. are usually treated with antibiotics.
   d. have decreased in incidence in recent years.

50.
K
Answer: c
pp. 492-493
Obj. #4

Which of the following statements concerning genital warts is true?
   a. The incubation period is seven to ten days.
   b. Genital warts are unattractive and a nuisance, but there are few serious complications associated with having them.
   c. The incidence of genital warts has reached epidemic proportions.
   d. In women, genital warts appear on the external, but not the internal genitals.

51.
K
Answer: d
p. 492
Obj. #1

Which of the following is **most** prevalent in the United States?
   a. AIDS
   b. gonorrhea
   c. viral hepatitis
   d. genital warts

52.
K
Answer: d
p. 492
Obj. #3

All of the following are bacterial infections **except**
   a. gonorrhea.
   b. chancroid.
   c. chlamydia.
   d. genital warts.

53.
K
Answer: a
pp. 492-493
Obj. #4

Which of the following statements regarding genital warts is false?
a. In women, they most commonly appear on the labia majora.
b. The average incubation period is three months.
c. There is a strong association between genital warts and cervical and penile cancer.
d. Cryotherapy and topical applications of podofilox are commonly used to treat them.

54.
K
Answer: a
p. 493
Obj. #4

All of the following may be used to treat genital warts **except**
a. Zovirax.
b. vaporization by carbon dioxide laser.
c. topical applications of podofilox.
d. freezing with liquid nitrogen.

55.
K
Answer: c
pp. 493-494
Obj. #4

Which of the following statements concerning viral hepatitis is true?
a. It is a disease in which bladder function is impaired by a viral infection.
b. The three major types of viral hepatitis are commonly sexually transmitted.
c. Treatment consists of bed rest and adequate fluid intake.
d. Hepatitis B is the most common type.

56.
K
Answer: d
p. 494
Obj. #4

All of the following are symptoms of viral hepatitis **except**
a. high fever.
b. yellowing of the whites of the eyes.
c. fatigue.
d. burning with urination.

57.
K
Answer: a
p. 494
Obj. #4

The most common type of viral hepatitis is
a. hepatitis A.
b. hepatitis B.
c. hepatitis C.
d. hepatitis non-A, non-B.

58.
K
Answer: b
p. 495
Obj. #5

Which of the following statements concerning common vaginal infections is false?
a. Bacterial vaginosis is the most common type.
b. The vaginal environment is typically alkaline in nature.
c. The lactobacilli usually help maintain a healthy vaginal environment.
d. Antibiotic therapy may increase the likelihood of vaginal infection.

59.
A
Answer: d
p. 495
Obj. #5

Selena has problems with chronic vaginitis. Which of the following might be a factor in this?
a. She takes multiple vitamins on a regular basis.
b. She wears all cotton underwear.
c. She is masturbating.
d. She is on birth control pills.

60.
A
Answer: d
p. 495
Obj. #5

All of the following changes would **most** likely increase Lucy's susceptibility to chronic vaginal infections **except**
a. douching more frequently to keep her body free of harmful lactobacilli.
b. taking antibiotics.
c. wearing pantyhose more often.
d. changing her method of contraception from birth control pills to condom and spermicides.

61.
K
Answer: d
p. 496
Obj. #5

The **most** common cause of vaginitis in women is
a. lactobacilli.
b. *Candida albicans*.
c. *Trichomonas vaginalis*.
d. *Gardnerella vaginalis*.

62.
K
Answer: b
p. 496
Obj. #5

Recent evidence suggests a link between _____ and premature rupture of the amniotic sac and preterm labor during pregnancy.
a. candidiasis
b. bacterial vaginosis
c. trichomoniasis
d. chlamydia

63.
K
Answer: b
p. 496
Obj. #5

Which of the following statements concerning bacterial vaginosis is false?
a. It is unclear whether there is any benefit to treating both a woman and her partner for this.
b. There are no known serious complications.
c. Metronidazole (Flagyl) is typically the prescribed medication.
d. The discharge usually smells musty or fishy.

64.
K
Answer: c
p. 496
Obj. #5

A "yeast infection" is caused by
a. a protozoan parasite called *Trichomonas vaginalis*.
b. a bacterium known as *Gardnerella vaginalis*.
c. a fungus called *Candida albicans*.
d. a bacterial microorganism called *Chlamydia trachomatis*.

65.
K
Answer: a
p. 496
Obj. #5

Sugar stored in vaginal cells appears to increase susceptibility to
a. yeast infections.
b. trichomoniasis.
c. bacterial vaginosis.
d. chlamydia infection.

66.
K
Answer: c
p. 497
Obj. #5

Which of the following is a symptom of candidiasis?
a. a thin, gray discharge with a flour paste consistency
b. a frothy, yellow or white discharge with a bad odor
c. a white, clumpy discharge that resembles cottage cheese
d. painful, blister-like bumps on the labia

67.
K
Answer: b
p. 497
Obj. #5

Which of the following infections can be passed from a partner's mouth to a woman's vagina during oral sex?
a. bacterial vaginosis
b. candidiasis
c. trichomonias
d. chlamydia

68.
K
Answer: a
pp. 497-498
Obj. #4

Which of the following statements concerning trichomoniasis is true?
a. Both men and women may carry this infection, but men often have no symptoms.
b. The most common symptom in women is a watery gray discharge that smells like burning rubber.
c. Treatment consists of vaginal suppositories such as clotrimazole.
d. There are no long-term effects of trichomonal infection.

69.
K
Answer: c
p. 498
Obj. #5
WWW

Some health specialists believe that trichomoniasis that is left untreated may increase susceptibility to
a. penile cancer.
b. ovarian cancer.
c. cervical cancer.
d. endometriosis.

70.
K
Answer: d
p. 498
Obj. #6

Which of the following statements concerning pubic lice is false?
a. They may be found in the armpits or scalp.
b. They may be found in the pubic hair.
c. They may be transmitted nonsexually.
d. They are treated with tetracycline.

71.
K
Answer: c
p. 498
Obj. #6
WWW

The primary symptom of pubic lice is
a. tiny red spots on the genitals.
b. smooth, rounded, waxy-looking bumps on the genitals that are painless.
c. itching in the pubic area.
d. painful genital chancres.

72.
A
Answer: d
pp. 480, 498
Obj. #3, 6

Chris has the "clap" and Janelle has "crabs". In clinical terminology, Chris has _____ and Janelle has _____.
a. chlamydia; syphilis
b. pubic lice; gonorrhea
c. herpes; chlamydia
d. gonorrhea; pubic lice

73.
K
Answer: b
p. 499
Obj. #6

All clothes and sheets used prior to treatment must be washed when infected with
a. pubic lice and chancroid.
b. pubic lice and scabies.
c. scabies and trichomoniasis.
d. scabies and chancroid.

Chapter 17 Sexually Transmitted Diseases 381

74.
K
Answer: c
p. 499
Obj. #6

Which of the following would **most** likely be found among nursing home residents and the indigent, in addition to people who are sexually active?
 a. syphilis
 b. chancroid
 c. scabies
 d. pubic lice

75.
K
Answer: b
p. 499
Obj. #6

Small, pimple-like bumps, a rash surrounding the primary lesion, and intense itching are all symptoms of
 a. pubic lice.
 b. scabies.
 c. chancroid.
 d. trichomoniasis.

76.
K
Answer: c
pp. 499-508
Obj. #7d, 7e

Which of the following statements regarding HIV is false?
 a. HIV has been found in the vaginal secretions, blood, semen, saliva, urine and breast milk of infected individuals.
 b. Reported cases of heterosexually transmitted HIV have been increasing in recent years.
 c. The incidence of AIDS is increasing more rapidly among men than women in the United States.
 d. Symptoms of HIV infection are commonly associated with other types of illnesses.

77.
K
Answer: d
p. 500
Obj. #7b

AIDS originated in
 a. Africa.
 b. Haiti.
 c. southern Europe.
 d. The origin of AIDS is unknown at this time.

78.
K
Answer: c
p. 500
Obj. #7a

Currently, HIV infection is diagnosed as AIDS when
 a. a person tests positive for HIV antibodies.
 b. the immune system becomes so impaired that the person develops a severe, life-threatening disease.
 c. a person has a CD4 count of 200 cells per cubic millimeter of blood or less.
 d. a person has a CD4 count of 800 cells per cubic millimeter of blood or less.

79.
K
Answer: b
p. 501
Obj. #7d

The majority of all reported AIDS cases in the U. S. since 1981
 a. are women.
 b. are from ethnic/racial minorities.
 c. are drug users.
 d. are heterosexual.

80.
K
Answer: d
p. 501
Obj. #7d

Which one is NOT given as a reason for the growing problem of HIV infection among adolescents?
a. The high rate of other STDs in the teen population.
b. Sexual activity without condoms.
c. Many teenagers have multiple sexual partners.
d. Teens have not been given the information as to how to avoid HIV infections.

81.
K
Answer: d
pp. 501-502
Obj. #7d

Over the past decade, the overall incidence of AIDS has _____ among men and _____ among women.
a. increased; increased
b. decreased; decreased
c. increased; decreased
d. decreased; increased

82.
K
Answer: b
p. 502
Obj. #7d

Which of the following statements is true?
a. There is a higher concentration of HIV in vaginal fluids than in semen.
b. Adolescent women are more biologically vulnerable to HIV infection than adult women because the immature cervix is more easily infected.
c. Both penile-vaginal intercourse and oral sex are equally high risk behaviors for HIV transmission.
d. There is growing documented evidence that saliva is a source of HIV transmission.

83.
K
Answer: c
p. 503
Obj. #7d

Which one is NOT true concerning viral load?
a. This refers to how much virus is present in an infected person's blood.
b. The greater the viral load the greater the chance of transmitting HIV infection.
c. Viral load is lowest at the time of initial infection and only gradually increases.
d. There is a period of time between viral load occurrence and the development of antibodies.

84.
K
Answer: c
p. 504
Obj. #7d

Which one is NOT true concerning HIV infection in Africa?
a. More than 1/10 of the 15 to 49 year old population of sub-Saharan countries is infected.
b. African men's dislike of barrier contraceptives is contributing to the problem.
c. This is a problem, in part, because there have been few other STDs and the countries have had no need to deal with this.
d. Thirteen million children have lost a mother or both parents to AIDS.

Chapter 17 Sexually Transmitted Diseases 383

85.
K
Answer: d
p. 504
Obj. #7d

Of the 20 million worldwide deaths from AIDS to date ____ have occurred in Africa.
a. 35%
b. 50%
c. 70%
d. 85%

86.
K
Answer: a
p. 504
Obj. #7d

The primary mode of HIV transmission in Africa is
a. heterosexual contact.
b. homosexual contact.
c. intravenous drug use.
d. blood transfusions.

87.
K
Answer: c
p. 505
Obj. #7d

Which one is NOT true with respect to HIV transmission?
a. A small percentage of people appear to be resistant to HIV infection.
b. There is no evidence that hugging, shaking hands, or eating with an infected person will transmit the virus.
c. The world's blood supply is now largely safe from HIV.
d. There is no risk of getting HIV from being a blood donor.

88.
K
Answer: a
p. 506
Obj. #7e

Which of the following **most** accurately describes symptoms of HIV infection?
a. fever, skin rashes, loss of appetite, swollen lymph glands
b. headaches, high blood pressure, constipation, bloating
c. chronic fatigue, night sweats, low blood pressure, hair loss
d. swollen lymph glands, migraines, nausea, vomiting

89.
K
Answer: b
p. 506
Obj. #7e

All of the following are symptoms of HIV infection **except**
a. night sweats.
b. high blood pressure.
c. skin rash.
d. severe headaches.

90.
K
Answer: a
p. 506
Obj. #7f

Which of the following blood tests are used to detect the presence of antibodies to HIV?
a. Western blot and ELISA
b. HAART and STD
c. HPV and AIDS
d. HIV and CDC

91.
K
Answer: c
p. 506
Obj. #7g

Most people develop antibodies to HIV _____ after the initial infection.
a. two weeks
b. one month
c. within a few months
d. one year

92.
K
Answer: a
p. 507
Obj. #7e

The **most** common cancer affecting people with AIDS is
   a. Kaposi's sarcoma.
   b. lymphomas.
   c. lung cancer.
   d. colon cancer.

93.
K
Answer: c
p. 507
Obj. #7g

The average time between HIV infection and the onset of a disease associated with impairment of the immune system is between
   a. six months and one year.
   b. one and five years.
   c. eight and eleven years.
   d. twelve and fifteen years.

94.
K
Answer: a
p. 508
Obj. #7i

With respect to AIDS in the U. S.,
   a. the majority of those who have developed AIDS have already died.
   b. deaths due to AIDS have steadily increased.
   c. deaths due to AIDS have precipitously dropped each years since 1996 with the new drug therapies.
   d. the most common cause of death is encephalitis.

95.
K
Answer: d
p. 508
Obj. #7

In 1999, the number of worldwide deaths from AIDS was
   a. unknown.
   b. about 1 million.
   c. about 2 million.
   d. about 3 million.

96.
K
Answer: d
pp. 508-509
Obj. #7h

Which of the following statements regarding HIV/AIDS is false?
   a. Zidovudine and other early antiretroviral drugs provided only limited clinical benefits to HIV infected adults.
   b. Taken during pregnancy, zidovudine can dramatically reduce the risk of HIV transmission from an infected woman to her fetus.
   c. HAART therapy refers to the use of three protease inhibitors such as ritonavir, indinavir and saquinavir to treat AIDS.
   d. There are several problems with HAART therapy that make its real-world use highly impractical for many HIV-infected people.

97.
K
Answer: b
pp. 509-510
Obj. #7h

Which one is NOT true concerning HAART therapy?
   a. This regimen may reduce transmission of HIV.
   b. When on HSSRT the virus is eliminated from the body.
   c. HAART treatment failure has occurred even for people who have correctly adhered to the regimen.
   d. Some people cannot use HAAART because of toxicity reactions.

98.
K
Answer: c
p. 511
Obj. #7d

Mother to child transmission of HIV can be reduced ____ by the administration of zidovudine to the infected mother and newborn child.
   a. about ¼
   b. by half
   c. by 2/3
   almost completely

Chapter 17 Sexually Transmitted Diseases 385

99.
K
Answer: b
p. 512
Obj. #7g

Each year an estimated ____ infants throughout the world contract HIV via mother to child transmission.
a. 310,000
b. 590,000
c. 800,000
d. over one million

100.
K
Answer: a
p. 513
Obj. #7i

Which one is true concerning an HIV vaccine?
a. A prophylactic vaccine may never be developed.
b. A prophylactic vaccine is likely to be developed but seems a decade or so away.
c. Vaccines have yet to be tested although they are still being developed.
d. It appears that it would be most cost effective to depend on drug therapies rather than vaccines.

101.
K
Answer: c
p. 513
Obj. #8

Suggestions for avoiding HIV infection include all but which one of the following?
a. Avoid anal intercourse
b. Avoid sexual intercourse during menstruation.
c. Use oral-genital contact instead of penile-vaginal.
d. Avoid sexual contact with either male or female prostitutes.

102.
K
Answer: c
p. 513
Obj. #8

Suggestions for avoiding HIV infection include all but which one of the following?
a. Do not share needles if you use injected drugs.
b. Do not share a toothbrush.
c. Use manual (finger) stimulation of the anus instead of inserting the penis.
d. Avoid prolonged open mouth kissing.

103.
K
Answer: a
p. 513
Obj. #7i

The risk of contracting HIV is **highest** in people infected with which of the following?
a. herpes
b. chlamydia infection
c. trichomoniasis
d. gonorrhea

104.
K
Answer: c
p. 514
Obj. #8

Recently gay males
a. have overall reduced their dangerous sexual practices.
b. who are young have reduced their dangerous practices while older ones continue them.
c. who are young have lapsed into dangerous practices.
d. have refused to be subjects of research into dangerous sexual practices.

105.
K
Answer: d
pp. 515-520
Obj. #8
WWW

The authors suggest all of the following guidelines for preventing sexually transmitted diseases **except**
a. obtain a medical examination prior to engaging in genital sexual activity.
b. inspect your partner's genitals.
c. wash both your genitals and your partner's before and after sexual contact.
d. engage in "outercourse only" for the first six months before proceeding to have intercourse.

106.
K
Answer: c
p. 515
Obj. #8

What do some experts suggest as the single **most** important message to convey to people who want to minimize the possibility of contracting an STD?
a. Wear latex condoms before engaging in genital sex with a partner.
b. Obtain routine medical examinations.
c. Get to know prospective sexual partners for several months before engaging in genital sex.
d. Discreetly inspect your partner's genitals before engaging in genital sex.

107.
K
Answer: b
p. 515
Obj. #8

In one survey of 400 college students, _____% of men and _____% of women said they had lied about pregnancy risk and other sexual involvements in order to have sex.
a. 20; 5
b. 35; 10
c. 50; 25
d. 15; 25

108.
K
Answer: b
p. 515
Obj. #8

In one survey of 400 college students, approximately _____% of the men and women said they would report fewer previous sexual partners than they really had.
a. 5-10 %
b. one-quarter
c. 40–50%
d. almost 90%

109.
K
Answer: a
p. 516
Obj. #8

Which of the following is **most** effective in helping to prevent STDs?
a. a latex condom with Nonoxynol-9
b. a latex condom with clotrimazole
c. a latex condom with K-Y jelly
d. a natural membrane condom

110.
K
Answer: c
p. 517
Obj. #8

Vaginal microbides
a. are being tested in Africa.
b. are products that kill sperm.
c. ideally would protect against STDs.
d. could protect women by giving men another sexual outlet.

Chapter 17 Sexually Transmitted Diseases 387

111.
K
Answer: c
p. 517
Obj. #8

Condoms help protect against the transmission of all but which one of the following?
a. candidiasis
b. chlamydia
c. scabies
d. syphilis

112.
K
Answer: c
p. 517-518
Obj. #8

Which of the following statements about condom use is false?
a. Unroll the condom directly onto the erect penis; do not unroll it first and then put it on.
b. Store condoms in a cool, dry place.
c. Use an oil-based lubricant if additional lubrication is preferred.
d. While using a condom, withdraw the penis after ejaculation while it is still erect, holding the base of the condom in order to prevent slippage.

113.
K
Answer: c
p. 518
Obj. #8

Condom usage rules include all but which one of the following?
a. Never reuse a condom.
b. If it breaks, replace it immediately.
c. You may wish to fill a condom with water to test for leaks.
d. Use only water-based lubricants with condoms.

114.
K
Answer: b
p. 518
Obj. #8

Which one is NOT true of condoms?
a. They are about 90% effective at preventing pregnancy.
b. They reduce the risk of HIV infection by about 90%.
c. They were reported to have broken at least once in the past year by 23% of a representative user sample.
d. Condom problems include both breakage and slippage.

115.
K
Answer: d
pp. 518-519
Obj. #8

Which one is NOT true about condoms?
a. Condoms manufactured in the U. S. are labeled for vaginal use only.
b. Condoms, to be effective, must be used correctly on every instance of a sexual encounter.
c. Sex workers report less condom breakage and slippage rate than the general population.
d. Condoms break or slip in slightly less than 5% of the times they are used.

116.
K
Answer: b
p. 519
Obj. #8

Which of the following is the **best** description of a "short-arm inspection?"
a. discreetly examining your partner's genitals prior to genital sexual contact
b. "milking" the penis for a suspicious discharge
c. examining the vulva for the presence of an unusual discharge, unpleasant odor, sores, blisters, etc.
d. genital self-exam

117.
K
Answer: c
p. 520
Obj. n/a

Your book recommended medical evaluations for STDs if you have multiple partners
a. as soon as you have any suspicious symptom.
b. once a year.
c. preferably every three months.
d. shortly after you add a new partner.

118.
K
Answer: c
p. 520
Obj. n/a

Which one is true about those diagnosed with STD's?
a. HPV is disclosed to new partners by a majority of those infected.
b. Medical personnel will often volunteer to notify past partners for a diagnosed person.
c. Very few past partners of those diagnosed with HIV are informed by the infected partner or anyone else.
d. Both primary and other and other sexual contacts are usually informed if the STD is one of the more serious ones.

119.
A
Answer: c
p. 521
Obj. #7j

Which one is **most** accurate with respect to consequences for someone who knows they have HIV and engages in sexual contact without telling the partner?
a. Some states have tried to make this a crime but federal courts have overturned these laws.
b. Many states have made this illegal bur the laws are in abeyance while the Supreme Court considers appeals.
c. Civil litigation against the perpetrator is possible and has been successful.
d. These people will answer only to their own conscience or any afterlife judgment.

Multiple Choice from Study Guide

1.
K
Answer: d
p. 474
Obj. #1

Which of the following age groups is **most** likely to contract a sexually transmitted disease?
a. adolescents
b. young adults
c. people 35 and over
d. a and b
e. b and c

2.
K
Answer: b
p. 478
Obj. #3

Of the STDs listed below, which one is the **most** prevalent?
a. syphilis
b. chlamydia
c. HIV
d. gonorrhea

3.
K
Answer: a
p. 479
Obj. #3

If chlamydia infection is left untreated in a female, what will result?
a. pelvic inflammatory disease
b. chancroid
c. blindness
d. liver damage

Chapter 17 Sexually Transmitted Diseases 389

4.
K
Answer: d
p. 479
Obj. #3

Most women and men with chlamydia
   a. will become infertile.
   b. will have a foul smelling discharge from the vagina or penis.
   c. display a rash on the scrotum or labia.
   d. show few or no symptoms.

5.
K
Answer: c
p. 482
Obj. #3

All of the following complications may result if gonorrhea infection if a male is untreated **except**
   a. abscesses on the prostate.
   b. epididymitis.
   c. adhesions in the spongy bodies of the penis.
   d. Infertility.

6.
K
Answer: d
p. 482
Obj. #3

Complications of untreated gonorrhea in women include
   a. vulvar vestibultitis.
   b. adenocarcinoma of the cervix.
   c. inflamed Skene's glands.
   d. infertility.

7.
K
Answer: b
pp. 483-484
Obj. #3

The symptoms of nongoncoccal urethritis (NGU) in males are similar to those of
   a. syphilis.
   b. gonorrhea.
   c. AIDS.
   d. viral hepatitis.

8.
K
Answer: a
p. 484
Obj. #3

About three weeks after syphilis infection, which symptom is typically manifested?
   a. a chancre
   b. a rash on the palms of hands or the soles of the feet
   c. a flu-like illness
   d. a watery vaginal discharge

9.
K
Answer: c
p. 486
Obj. #3

During the tertiary stage of syphilis
   a. observable symptoms disappear.
   b. weight loss begins.
   c. complications may result in death.
   d. lymph glands reduce in size.

10.
K
Answer: d
pp. 487-488
Obj. #4

The herpes simplex virus may be spread
   a. when lesions are present.
   b. during the incubation period.
   c. if Zovirax treatment is stopped.
   d. even if no symptoms are present.

11.
K
Answer: a
p. 487
Obj. #4

Which of the following is true regarding oral herpes?
   a. Oral herpes may spread to the genitals through oral sex.
   b. It is caused by HSV-2.
   c. It is caused by HSV-8.
   d. Unlike genital herpes, recurrence is not likely.

12.
K
Answer: c
p. 491
Obj. #4

The discomfort of herpes blisters can be minimized by
a. douching with plain yogurt.
b. applying aloe lotion.
c. keeping sores clean and dry.
d. exposing the blisters to sunlight.

13.
K
Answer: d
p. 490
Obj. #4

Studies indicate that _____ are more likely to experience major herpes complications than _____.
a. younger women; older women
b. heterosexuals; homosexuals
c. older men; younger men
d. women; men

14.
K
Answer: a
p. 491
Obj. #4

The preferred medication for managing herpes is
a. acyclovir (Zovirax).
b. metronidazole (Flagyl).
c. zidovudine.
d. doxycycline.

15.
K
Answer: c
p. 492
Obj. #4

A serious complication of genital warts (HPV) is
a. cervical erosion.
b. prostatitis.
c. cancer.
d. nephritis.

16.
K
Answer: b
p. 493
Obj. #4

Which of the following is true regarding genital warts (HPV)?
a. In moist areas, warts have a hard, yellow-gray appearance.
b. No known treatment exists that will completely eradicate HPV.
c. If no warts are visible, the individual is considered cured.
d. In dry areas, the warts have cauliflower-like appearance

17.
K
Answer: a
p. 494
Obj. #4

The **most** common form of hepatitis in the United States is
a. hepatitis A.
b. hepatitis B.
c. hepatitis C.
d. non-A/non-B hepatitis.

18.
K
Answer: c
p. 494
Obj. #4

Hepatitis A is transmitted by
a. semen.
b. vaginal fluid.
c. oral-anal sexual activity.
d. shared, contaminated needles.

19.
K
Answer: d
p. 494
Obj. #4

A key symptom of viral hepatitis is
a. swelling of the testicles.
b. vulva irritation.
c. intense itching of the lower abdomen.
d. yellow of the whites of the eyes.

Chapter 17 Sexually Transmitted Diseases

20.
A
Answer: b
p. 496
Obj. #5

After she had intercourse, Sierra noticed a fishy odor and a foul-smelling vaginal discharge. Sierra's symptoms are characteristic of
  a. candidiasis.
  b. bacterial vaginosis.
  c. Vulvodynia.
  d. Trichomoniasis.

21.
A
Answer: c
p. 497
Obj. #5

Griselda has intense itching and soreness in her vulva, and a white, clumpy discharge on her panties. Griselda's experiences are consistent with
  a. gardnerella vaginalis infection.
  b. genital herpes.
  c. a yeast infection.
  d. cystitis.

22.
K
Answer: c
p. 495
Obj. #5

All of the following increase a woman's chance of contracting a vaginal infection **except**
  a. wearing nylon panties.
  b. taking antibiotics.
  c. using Norplant.
  d. pregnancy.

23.
K
Answer: a
p. 498
Obj. #5

In order to prevent passing trichomoniasis back and forth between male and female sex partners, it is necessary to
  a. treat the male partner even if he has no symptoms.
  b. avoid sexual intercourse for six weeks.
  c. give the woman ampicillin in addition to Flagyl.
  d. apply gentian violet to the penis and scrotum.

24.
K
Answer: c
p. 498
Obj. #6

Pubic lice may be transmitted through
  a. urine.
  b. blood.
  c. eggs deposited on clothing or bedsheets.
  d. poor genital hygiene.

25.
K
Answer: d
p. 501
Obj. #7d

Which of the following statements is false regarding AIDS in the United States?
  a. AIDS is the second leading cause of death for people aged 25-44.
  b. The proportion of AIDS cases among men having sex with men has declined.
  c. Higher rates of AIDS are found among ethnic/minority groups.
  d. HIV infection rates for women have been reduced.

26.
K
Answer: c
p. 502
Obj. #7d

HIV has been found in all of the following **except**
  a. blood.
  b. semen.
  c. skin.
  d. saliva.

27.
K
Answer: a
p. 503
Obj. #7

The viral load for HIV is highest
a. during the period of primary infection.
b. when AIDS is in its late stages.
c. when flu-like symptoms first appear.
d. at all stages. It remains relatively the same once a person is infected.

28.
K
Answer: c
p. 503
Obj. #7d

Which activity makes HIV transmission **least** likely?
a. receptive oral sex
b. penis-vagina intercourse
c. open mouth kissing
d. sharing injection drug equipment

29.
K
Answer: b
pp. 504-505
Obj. # 10

All of the following factors play a role in spreading HIV infection in Africa **except**
a. low status of women.
b. "kept-boy" syndrome.
c. lack of medical care.
d. "dry" sex.

30.
K
Answer: b
p. 506
Obj. #7e

Which of the following is a symptom of HIV infection?
a. jaundice
b. oral Candidiasis
c. itchy skin
d. weight gain

31.
K
Answer: d
pp. 507-508
Obj. #7e

Complications associated with full-blown AIDS include
a. pneumonia.
b. Kaposi's sarcoma.
c. cervical cancer.
d. all of the above

32.
K
Answer: a
p. 510
Obj. #3h

Although HAART is the preferred treatment for AIDS, the treatment is **less** than optimal because
a. it is difficult to consistently and correctly follow this complicated treatment regimen.
b. physicians are reluctant to prescribe HAART, due to FDA regulations.
c. the Food and Drug Administrations (FDA) has restricted its use.
d. HAART is more effective in women than men.

33.
K
Answer: d
p. 512
Obj. #7i

The **best** way to avoid contracting HIV sexually is to
a. take the AIDS vaccine.
b. use latex condoms and a spermicide with nonoxynol-9 during every act of sex.
c. avoid getting too "run down" so that your immune system remains strong.
d. avoid any form of sexual contact that places one at risk for infection.

Chapter 17 Sexually Transmitted Diseases 393

34.
K
Answer: c
p. 515
Obj. n/a

Which statement is true regarding studies that have examined people's honesty about past sexual and drug use histories?
a. Women were more likely than men to lie about past sexual involvements than men.
b. Most HIV infected persons disclosed their status to their prior sex partners.
c. Over 40% of college students would report fewer sex partners than they actually had.
d. IV drug users were the least likely to disclose their HIV status.

35.
K
Answer: c
p. 517
Obj. n/a

All of the following describe proper condom use **except**
a. wear a condom before any genital contact.
b. withdraw the condom clad penis while it is still erect.
c. store condoms in a warm, moist place.
d. lubricate the condom with K-Y jelly if needed.

True/False

Students may be asked to answer these questions using the traditional format of marking their answers either "true" or "false". Or, to encourage more active involvement, you may choose to use the following instructions:

If the statement is true, place a "T" on the line preceding it. If the statement is false, place an "F" on the line preceding it and then change the statement to make it true by deleting incorrect information and/or adding accurate information.

1.
Answer: T
p. 474
Obj. #2

___ One reason for the rising incidence of STDs is the increased use of birth control pills.

2.
Answer: T
pp. 478-479
Obj. #3a

___ Generally speaking, lower reproductive tract infections that are the result of chlamydia infection produce few or no symptoms, while upper reproductive tract infections often produce a variety of symptoms.

3.
Answer: F
p. 479
Obj. #3a

___ Left untreated, trichomoniasis can cause trachoma, the world's leading cause of preventable blindness.

4.
Answer: F
p. 480
Obj. #3b

___ The majority of women who are infected with gonorrhea will have noticeable symptoms.

5.
Answer: F
p. 482
Obj. #3a, 3b

___ Regular Pap smears will indicate whether or not a woman has been infected with gonorrhea.

6.
Answer: T
p. 482
Obj. #3b

____ If gonorrhea is left untreated in women, it may result in sterility, although that is rarely the case for men.

7.
Answer: T
p. 483
Obj. #3c

____ Both men and women can contract nongonococcal urethritis.

8.
Answer: F
p. 486
Obj. #3d

____ Once a person progresses to the tertiary stage of syphilis, treatment is not effective.

9.
Answer: T
p. 488
Obj. #6c

____ Even with condom use, a man may contract herpes from a female partner because vaginal secretions containing the virus may wash over his scrotal area.

10.
Answer: F
p. 489
Obj. #4a

____ The prodromal phase is the point at which herpes blisters rupture to form wet, painful sores.

11.
Answer: T
p. 492
Obj. #4b

____ The incidence of genital and anal warts has reached epidemic proportions, and this virus can be associated with serious complications.

12.
Answer: F
p. 494
Obj. #4c

____ The most common treatment for viral hepatitis is antibiotic therapy.

13.
Answer: T
p. 495
Obj. #5

____ Douching and taking antibiotics may increase the likelihood of vaginal infections in some women.

14.
Answer: T
p. 496
Obj. #5a

____ Some physicians recommend that male partners of women diagnosed with recurrent bacterial vaginosis may also harbor the organism and need to be treated for it.

15.
Answer: T
p. 497
Obj. #5b

____ Yeast infections may be transmitted from a partner's mouth to a woman's vagina during oral sex.

16. ____ The symptoms of trichomoniasis are a white, clumpy discharge accompanied by vaginal itching and soreness.
Answer: F
p. 497
Obj. #5c

17. ____ It is possible to get pubic lice by sleeping in the bed or wearing the clothes of a person who is infected with them.
Answer: T
p. 498
Obj. #6a

18. ____ Men are at higher risk than women are for becoming HIV infected through penile-vaginal intercourse.
Answer: F
p. 502
Obj. #7d

19. ____ Unless blood banks fail to use sterilized equipment and disposable needles, there is no danger of becoming HIV infected as a result of donating blood.
Answer: T
pp. 504-505
Obj. #7d

20. ____ In most, but not all cases, an individual will develop antibodies to HIV within several months of being infected.
Answer: T
p. 506
Obj. #7d

Short Answer Essay

1. Discuss some of the factors that may have contributed to the rising incidence of sexually transmitted diseases. (Obj. #2)

2. Indicate the frequency of chlamydia. Describe some of the complications for men, women and children if chlamydia infection is left untreated. (Obj. #3)

3. Describe some of the factors that may increase the likelihood of vaginal infections. Discuss common vaginal infections, including what causes them, their symptoms, how they might be transmitted, and treatment alternatives. (Obj. #5)

4. List and describe the four stages of a syphilis infection. (Obj. #3)

5. Describe the two most common types of herpes. How may the virus be transmitted? (Obj. #4)

6. Discuss medical treatment for herpes, and suggestions for minimizing personal discomfort associated with a herpes outbreak. (Obj. #4)

7. Discuss current information regarding the incidence and transmission, symptoms, and possible complications of genital warts. What options are available for treating genital warts? (Obj. #4)

8. Distinguish between the two most common forms of viral hepatitis, including how common they are, how they are transmitted, symptoms and possible complications, and treatment alternatives. (Obj. #4)

9. Your book discussed techniques for telling a partner that you have a sexually transmitted disease. Outline some of these suggestions. Consider also whether or not you believe there should be legal requirements or sanctions if someone does not tell a former or present partner about their disease status. (Obj. n/a)

10. When is HIV infection diagnosed as AIDS? Describe the incidence and transmission of HIV infection from a worldwide perspective. (Obj. #7a, 7d)

11. Discuss how HIV may be transmitted as well as factors that may affect the likelihood of its transmission, making specific reference to the following: modes of transmission; routes of HIV exposure during sexual contact; viral dose; differences in transmission between the sexes. (Obj. #7d)

12. Discuss the issues and problems surrounding HAART therapy for HIV/AIDS. (Obj. #7h)

13. Describe difficulties in prevention and treatment of AIDS in African countries. Contrast this with the approach of China and the United States. (Obj. #10)

14. List and describe suggestions for reducing your risk of HIV infection. (Obj. #7i)

15. List and describe guidelines for reducing the risk of contracting sexually transmitted diseases in general. (Obj. #8)

18

Atypical Sexual Behavior

Learning Objectives

After studying Chapter 18, students will be able to:

1. Define atypical sexual behavior and paraphilia and distinguish it from other labels such as deviant, perverted, abnormal, etc.

2. Explain each of the following considerations in discussing atypical sexual behavior:
   a. how these behaviors exist on a continuum
   b. what our knowledge base is regarding these various behaviors
   c. to what extent paraphilias may exist in clusters and the implications of that
   d. the impact of atypical sexual behavior both on the person exhibiting the behavior and on the recipient of the behavior

3. Distinguish between noncoercive and coercive paraphilias.

4. Describe fetishism, making specific reference to the following:
   a. problems in defining it
   b. common fetish objects
   c. how it develops
   d. other offenses that may be associated with fetishism

5. Discuss each of the following in regard to transvestic fetishism:
   a. the range of behaviors that may comprise it
   b. who is most likely to engage in this behavior, citing relevant statistics
   c. what studies reveal regarding partner response to this behavior

6. Define sadomasochistic behavior, sexual sadism and sexual masochism and discuss each of the following in reference to these behaviors:
   a. the complexity involved in labeling these behaviors
   b. available statistics that indicate how common these behaviors may be
   c. the behavioral and psychological dynamics involved
   d. social views regarding these behaviors
   e. reasons why people may choose to engage in these behaviors

7. Describe each of the following noncoercive paraphilias:
   a. autoerotic asphyxiation
   b. klismaphilia
   c. coprophilia and urophilia

8. Define exhibitionism and discuss each of the following in regard to it:
   a. variations on this behavior
   b. what we know about the type of person who exhibits this behavior, and what some of the problems are with the available data
   c. theories regarding what influences the development of this behavior
   d. how likely exhibitionists are to engage in other illegal behaviors
   e. how to respond to exhibitionistic behavior

9. Explain what we know about the person who makes obscene phone calls, and the likelihood that this person will engage in other illegal sexual behaviors.

10. Outline several strategies for dealing with obscene phone calls.

11. Define voyeurism and discuss the problems in attempting to determine what qualifies as voyeuristic behavior.

12. Discuss common characteristics of voyeurs, the likelihood of voyeurs engaging in other serious offenses, and explain what factors may trigger voyeuristic behavior.

13. Briefly describe each of the following coercive paraphilias:
    a. frotteurism
    b. zoophilia
    c. necrophilia

14. Describe each of the following treatment alternatives for coercive paraphilias:
    a. psychotherapy
    b. behavior therapy
    c. aversive conditioning
    d. systematic desensitizing
    e. orgasmic reconditioning
    f. satiation therapy
    g. drug treatment
    h. social skills training

15. Discuss the controversy surrounding sexual addiction—what it is, how to categorize it and how to treat it.

Multiple Choice

1.
K
Answer: c
p. 526
Obj. #1

From the authors' perspective, which of the following terms would be **least** acceptable in labeling uncommon sexual behaviors?
a. paraphilia
b. atypical
c. deviant
d. variant

2.
K
Answer: a
p. 526
Obj. #1

Which one did your book NOT suggest concerning urinating on a sexual partner who then drinks it?
a. This should never be done.
b. This should only be done if you know the partner's HIV status.
c. This is called urophilia.
d. This has been called "golden showers."

3.
K
Answer: d
pp. 526-527
Obj. #2, 3

Which of the following statements regarding atypical sexual behavior is false?
a. Atypical behaviors often occur in clusters.
b. They are also called paraphilias.
c. Some atypical sexual behaviors are illegal.
d. With the proper reporting it appears that women engage in this about as often as men.

4.
K
Answer: b
p. 545
Obj. #2b

John Money has suggested that atypical sexual behavior may be **more** prevalent among men because
a. men are socially conditioned to be freer regarding their range of sexual expression than women.
b. male erotosexual differentiation is more complex than that of the female.
c. men are much more likely than women to have dysfunctional relationships with their mothers, which may result in atypical sexual behavior.
d. men are under the influence of greater amounts of testosterone than women are.

5.
K
Answer: d
p. 527
Obj. #2b, 2d
WWW

Which of the following statements concerning atypical sexual behavior is false?
a. Men tend to be more likely to engage in atypical sexual behavior than women.
b. People who are unwilling recipients of atypical sexual behavior may be psychologically traumatized.
c. People who are unwilling recipients of atypical sexual behavior are not necessarily negatively affected.
d. Individuals who engage in atypical sexual behavior find that it usually enhances their sexual/intimate relationship with a partner.

6.
K
Answer: b
p. 528
Obj. #4

Obtaining sexual excitement primarily or exclusively from an inanimate object or a particular part of the body is called
a. transvestism.
b. fetishism.
c. klismaphilia.
d. frotteurism.

7.
A
Answer: a
p. 528
Obj. #4

Which of the following would **most** likely be a fetish object?
a. leather boots
b. a German shepherd
c. a peacock feather
d. a person of the same sex as the fetishist

8.
K
Answer: c
p. 528
Obj. #4

Symbolic transformation is one explanation for how _____ develops.
a. zoophilia
b. coprophilia
c. fetishism
d. exhibitionism

9.
K
Answer: a
p. 528
Obj. #4c

Classical conditioning is one explanation for how _____ develops.
a. fetishism
b. autoerotic asphyxia
c. transsexualism
d. zoophilia

10.
A
Answer: d
p. 528
Obj. #4
WWW

Which of the following individuals would **most** likely be described as a fetishist?
a. a man who likes to wear white lacy lingerie when he has sex with his wife
b. a man who uses partial asphyxiation as a way to enhance orgasm
c. a man who becomes sexually aroused whenever he sees a woman with large breasts
d. a man who cannot reach orgasm unless he is masturbating with a woman's high-heeled shoe

11.
K
Answer: c
p. 529
Obj. #4d

Which of the following offenses is **most** frequently associated with fetishism?
a. assault
b. murder
c. burglary
d. forgery

12.
K
Answer: c
p. 529
Obj. #5

Some writers have speculated that there may be a link between _____ and _____.
a. exhibitionism; coprophilia
b. transvestism; transsexualism
c. fetishism; transvestism
d. fetishism; transsexualism

13.
K
Answer: d
p. 529
Obj. #5

A person who obtains sexual arousal by putting on clothing of the other sex is engaging in
a. transsexualism.
b. gender dysphoric experimentation.
c. fetishism.
d. transvestism.

14.
K
Answer: c
p. 529
Obj. #5

A person who cross-dresses for purposes of sexual arousal is
a. a transsexual.
b. a drag queen.
c. a transvestite.
d. androgynous.

Chapter 18 Atypical Sexual Behavior   401

15.
K
Answer: b
p. 529
Obj. #5
WWW

A man who wears women's clothing because doing so makes his appearance more consistent with his identity is called a _____, while a man who cross-dresses for sexual titillation is called a _____.
a. transvestite; transsexual
b. transsexual ; transvestite
c. transvestite; homosexual
d. homosexual; fetishist

16.
K
Answer: c
p. 530
Obj. #5c

Data reveal that **most** wives _____ their husbands' cross-dressing.
a. are sexually aroused by
b. support
c. tolerate
d. resent

17.
K
Answer: a
p. 530
Obj. #5b

Transvestism occurs primarily among
a. married men with predominantly heterosexual orientations.
b. unmarried men with predominantly heterosexual orientations.
c. married men with predominantly homosexual orientations.
d. unmarried men with predominantly homosexual orientations.

18.
A
Answer: c
pp. 530-531
Obj. #5

All of the following may be possible explanations for the development of transvestism **except**
a. a young boy becomes fascinated by pictures of women modeling undergarments, and then later learns to masturbate while wearing his mother's lingerie
b. a mother repeatedly dresses her son as a girl and then cuddles and adores him
c. a man, whose gender identity has been female for as long as he can remember, finally begins to dress and act in ways that are consistent with his identity
d. parents repeatedly dress their son as a girl in order to punish him when they feel he has behaved inappropriately

19.
K
Answer: b
p. 531
Obj. #6a

In Kinsey's survey, approximately _____ percent of both sexes reported erotic response to receiving love bites during sexual interaction.
a. 10
b. 25
c. 40
d. 65

20.
K
Answer: a
p. 531
Obj. #6

Which of the following statements concerning sadomasochism is false?
a. A person who engages in sadism most always exhibits masochistic behavior as well.
b. Although sadomasochistic behaviors can be physically dangerous, most people who engage in sadomasochism have agreed-upon limits.
c. It appears that people with masochistic tendencies may be more common than people with sadistic tendencies.
d. It is defined as obtaining sexual arousal through giving or receiving physical or mental pain.

21.
K
Answer: d
pp. 531-532
Obj. #6

People with masochistic tendencies may be sexually aroused by
a. something soiled or filthy, such as dirty underwear.
b. having intercourse with a corpse.
c. inflicting physical or mental pain.
d. being spanked, whipped, or humiliated.

22.
K
Answer: c
p. 532
Obj. #6c

Which of the following statements regarding bondage is false?
a. This is a form of masochistic behavior.
b. It has been suggested that autoerotic asphyxia is a rare and dangerous form of bondage.
c. Research reveals a relatively small percentage (less than 10%) of men and women engage in this practice.
d. This practice involves being tied up, spanked or whipped.

23.
K
Answer: d
p. 532
Obj. #6c, 6e

Weinberg's research (1984) revealed that most of the individuals they interviewed who practiced sadomasochism
a. engaged in sexual behaviors involving severe physical pain and suffering.
b. engaged in sexual behaviors involving severe mental degradation and humiliation where the victims were often unwilling participants.
c. had personality disorders or severe emotional problems.
d. viewed it as a form of sexual enhancement that involved elements of dominance and submission.

24.
K
Answer: d
p. 532
Obj. #6c, 6e

According to Weinberg's research, all of the following were social features of sadomasochism **except**
a. consensuality.
b. dominance and submission.
c. role playing.
d. forced participation.

25.
K
Answer: c
p. 532
Obj. #6c

According to Weinberg's research, **most** people who engage in sadomasochistic activities are usually motivated by
a. a need to experience power and control.
b. a need to experience pain and guilt.
c. a need to experience dominance and submission.
d. hyperactive sexual desire.

Chapter 18 Atypical Sexual Behavior 403

26.
A
Answer: b
p. 533
Obj. #6c, 6e

Which of the following experiences would be **least** likely to result in a subsequent desire to engage in sadomasochistic activity?
a. getting a spanking for being caught masturbating
b. being discovered while cross-dressing by a partner who ends the relationship as a result
c. receiving a spanking when one's pants are pulled down and becoming sexually aroused as a result of the physiological stimulation
d. being caught "playing doctor" as a child and being verbally embarrassed and humiliated for doing so

27.
K
Answer: d
p. 533
Obj. #6c, 6e
WWW

Which of the following reasons would be **least** likely to explain why people may engage in sadomasochistic behavior?
a. Masochistic behavior may provide a guilt-relieving mechanism for people who believe sex is sinful and immoral.
b. Sadistic behavior may temporarily alleviate feelings of inferiority.
c. Sadistic or masochistic behavior may heighten physiological arousal.
d. Sadomasochism may help individuals overcome hyperactive sexual desire or sexual aversion.

28.
K
Answer: b
p. 533
Obj. #6

When engaging in SM activities
a. men are more likely to play masochistic roles than are women.
b. women are more likely to play masochistic roles than are men.
c. there are no sex differences in who plays masochistic roles.
d. the only reason a man would play a masochistic role is if he had been abused when he was a child.

29.
K
Answer: d
p. 534
Obj. #7a, 7c
WWW

Which of the following pairs of paraphilias are noncoercive?
a. exhibitionism; zoophilia
b. obscene phone calls; frotteurism
c. necrophilia; voyeurism
d. autoerotic asphyxia; urophilia

30.
K
Answer: c
p. 534
Obj. #8a

Which of the following paraphilias would be **most** likely to result in death?
a. fetishism
b. coprophilia
c. autoerotic asphyxia
d. transvestism

31.
K
Answer: d
p. 534
Obj. #7a

Which of the following may be a variant of sexual masochism?
a. frotteurism
b. voyeurism
c. fetishism
d. autoerotic asphyxia

32.
K
Answer: c
p. 534
Obj. #7b

Klismaphilia refers to a variation in sexual behavior in which
a. a person may become primarily or exclusively aroused by having sex with a much older person.
b. a person obtains sexual arousal from contact with feces.
c. an individual becomes sexually excited from receiving enemas.
d. a person becomes sexually aroused by something soiled or filthy.

33.
K
Answer: c
p. 534
Obj. #7c

Becoming sexually aroused by watching someone defecate or by defecating on someone is an example of
a. frotteurism.
b. klismaphilia.
c. coprophilia.
d. urophilia.

34.
K
Answer: a
p. 534
Obj. #7c

The clinical term for sexual expression that involves "water sports" or "golden showers" is
a. urophilia.
b. coprophilia.
c. frotteurism.
d. necrophilia.

35.
K
Answer: b
p. 535
Obj. #8
WWW

An exhibitionist obtains sexual gratification from
a. cross-dressing.
b. exposing his genitals to an involuntary observer.
c. secretly observing other people who are naked.
d. inflicting pain upon another person.

36.
K
Answer: d
p. 535
Obj. #8

Based on the available data, which of the following would **least** characterize an exhibitionist?
a. adult male in 20s or 30s
b. feelings of inadequacy
c. raised in oppressive sexual atmosphere
d. single or never married

37.
K
Answer: c
pp. 535-536
Obj. #8

Which of the following is an exhibitionist **least** likely to do?
a. masturbate while exhibiting himself
b. masturbate later to the mental image of the observer's reaction to his exposure
c. physically assault the woman to whom he is exposing himself
d. expose himself in a subway

38.
K
Answer: d
pp. 535-536
Obj. #8b, 8c

Which of the following would be **least** likely to explain what may motivate exhibitionistic behavior?
a. a man looking for affirmation of his masculinity
b. a man seeking attention
c. a man who has hostile feelings toward women
d. a man who was raised in a family or in a culture where public nudity was the social norm

39.
K
Answer: c
p. 536
Obj. #8

Which is the **most** accurate statement concerning the future behavior of an exhibitionist?
    a. Most of them will spontaneously stop this behavior by about age 40.
    b. None of them will engage in any more threatening behavior.
    c. A few of them will escalate to more dangerous behavior.
    d. This behavior will continue unless the perpetrator has the shock of being incarcerated.

40.
A
Answer: c
p. 537
Obj. #8e

Joanne is going out to her car after taking a night class, and just as she is about to open the car door, a man appears who has his pants down to his knees and is masturbating. According to the text, Joanne's **best** immediate response prior to notifying campus security would be to
    a. scream loudly.
    b. stand still and watch for a while.
    c. calmly ignore the man.
    d. start laughing and tell him to put the silly thing away.

41.
A
Answer: c
pp. 535, 538
Obj. #8, 11

Exhibitionism is to exposing as voyeurism is to
    a. "flashing".
    b. inflicting pain.
    c. peeping.
    d. cross-dressing.

42.
K
Answer: b
p. 537
Obj. #9

One study indicated that people who make obscene phones calls are male and
    a. can be potentially violent and aggressive.
    b. have strong feelings of inadequacy and insecurity.
    c. tend to have a homosexual orientation.
    d. have a history of being arrested for other illegal behaviors.

43.
A
Answer: b
p. 537
Obj. #10

If you receive an obscene phone call, it is suggested that you
    a. slam down the phone.
    b. set the phone down gently and proceed with what you were doing.
    c. blow in the mouthpiece with a police whistle.
    d. tell the caller he is a disgusting pervert.

44.
A
Answer: a
p. 538
Obj. #10
WWW

All of the following were suggested as effective ways to respond to obscene phone calls **except**
    a. use a police whistle to blow in the caller's ear.
    b. pretend you are deaf and cannot hear the caller.
    c. quietly hang up the telephone.
    d. screen via answering machine.

45.
K
Answer: d
p. 538
Obj. #11

Which of the following is a voyeur **least** likely to do?
a. peer in someone's bedroom window at night
b. stand outside the door of a women's restroom
c. drill a hole through the walls of a public women's dressing room
d. go to a nude beach

46.
K
Answer: a
p. 538
Obj. #12

The characteristics of people with voyeuristic tendencies are similar to those who engage in
a. exhibitionism.
b. fetishism.
c. transvestism.
d. sadomasochism.

47.
K
Answer: c
p. 538
Obj. #12

Most individuals who engage in voyeuristic behavior
a. almost always engage in other kinds of antisocial behavior.
b. go on to more serious offenses.
c. prefer to maintain distance between themselves and their "victims".
d. tend to be men in their 40s and 50s.

48.
K
Answer: a
p. 538
Obj. #12

Which of the following statements regarding voyeurs is true?
a. They tend to be men in their early 20s.
b. They usually "peep" at someone they know.
c. They tend to engage in other antisocial behavior.
d. They like to frequent nudist camps.

49.
A
Answer: d
p. 538
Obj. #12

Which of the following **best** describes the point at which voyeurism qualifies as an atypical behavior?
a. when the experience culminates in orgasm
b. when a person is arrested for doing it
c. when it is practiced with some risk and/or when it is practiced once a week or more
d. when it is preferred to having sex with a partner and/or when it is practiced with some risk

50.
K
Answer: c
p. 539
Obj. n/a

Video voyeurism
a. refers to a preference for renting pornographic videos over real life activity.
b. may actually involve the use of either videos or DVD.
c. refers to high tech, small and difficult to spot video cameras.
d. are seen in some selected store windows in large cities.

51.
K
Answer: c
p. 539
Obj. n/a

Video voyeurism
a. is a federal offense.
b. is illegal in most states.
c. is illegal in a few states.
d. is illegal only if it involves a minor.

Chapter 18 Atypical Sexual Behavior   407

52.
K
Answer: d
p. 540
Obj. #13a

_____ involves a person, usually male, who becomes aroused by pressing or rubbing against a fully clothed female in a crowded elevator or bus.
a. Exhibitionism
b. Klismaphilia
c. Asphyxia
d. Frotteurism

53.
K
Answer: a
p. 540
Obj. #7, 13

All of the following are noncoercive paraphilias **except**
a. frotteurism.
b. coprophilia.
c. klismaphilia.
d. fetishism.

54.
K
Answer: b
p. 540
Obj. #13b
WWW

According to Kinsey's survey, _____ percent of men and _____ percent of women reported having had sexual experience with animals at some point in their lives.
a. 4; 1
b. 8; 4
c. 15; 3
d. 20; 5

55.
K
Answer: b
p. 540
Obj. #13b

Which of the following statements concerning zoophilia is false?
a. It is sometimes called bestiality.
b. According to Kinsey, the frequency of such behaviors was highest among men who had worked in a zoo or in a veterinary setting.
c. It is commonly a transitory experience of young people to whom a human sexual partner is inaccessible or forbidden.
d. Typically more men experience this than women.

56.
A
Answer: a
p. 540
Obj. #13b

Which of the following is the **best** example of true zoophilia?
a. A man is dating and having sex with a woman who is attracted to him, but he prefers to have sex with his dog.
b. A woman whose partner is overseas has her vulva orally stimulated by her dog.
c. A teenage boy who lives on a farm and has not yet been sexually active with women has sex with a variety of animals.
d. A teenage boy agrees to have sex with a sheep on a dare.

57.
K
Answer: a
p. 540
Obj. #13c

A sexual variation in which a person obtains sexual gratification by having intercourse with a corpse is called
a. necrophilia.
b. klismaphilia.
c. coprophilia.
d. mortuphilia.

58.
K
Answer: c
p. 541
Obj. #13c

Which of the following is **least** descriptive of a person who engages in necrophilia?
a. severely emotionally disordered
b. socially and sexually inept
c. sexually aroused by receiving enemas
d. hates and fears women

59.
K
Answer: a
p. 541
Obj. #14

Which of the following approaches, used alone, is **least** effective in treating coercive paraphilias?
a. psychotherapy
b. aversive conditioning
c. systematic desensitization
d. orgasmic reconditioning

60.
A
Answer: d
pp. 541-542
Obj. #14
WWW

Which of the following is out of place?
a. aversive conditioning
b. systematic desensitization
c. orgasmic reconditioning
d. psychotherapy

61.
A
Answer: b
p. 542
Obj. #14c

A convicted sex offender is participating in a treatment program in which he is instructed to inhale smelling salts every time he feels compelled to expose himself. This type of treatment is called
a. systematic desensitization.
b. aversive conditioning.
c. exhibitionist restructuring.
d. orgasmic reconditioning.

62.
A
Answer: c
p. 542
Obj. #14b

Behavior therapy
a. does not work well with the paraphilias.
b. assumes that we must understand atypical behavior in different ways than we do the usual behavior.
c. assumes that maladaptive behavior has been learned and can be unlearned.
d. is another term for cognitive therapy.

63.
K
Answer: a
p. 543
Obj. #14

A treatment approach for coercive paraphilias that is based on the premise that people cannot be both anxious and relaxed at the same time is
a. systematic desensitization.
b. satiation therapy.
c. aversive conditioning.
d. psychotherapy.

64.
K
Answer: b
p. 543
Obj. #14g

Drug treatment of coercive paraphilias
a. is often used by courts.
b. is most effective when combined with other therapies.
c. has some dangerous long-term physical effects.
d. involves the use of rohypnol to help them forget.

65.
K
Answer: c
p. 544
Obj. #15

The traditional term for men who have insatiable sexual needs is
a. nymphomania.
b. hypogonadism.
c. satyriasis.
d. hypoactive sexual desire.

66.
K
Answer: d
p. 544
Obj. #15

All of the following are phases of sexual addiction described by Carnes **except**
a. despair.
b. preoccupation.
c. ritualistic behaviors.
d. denial.

67.
K
Answer: c
pp. 544-545
Obj. #15
WWW

According to Patrick Carnes, a person who cruises specific neighborhood playgrounds where he has made contact with children who are potential victims of his sexual molestation is in what phase of the addiction cycle?
a. preoccupation
b. sexual trance
c. ritualistic behaviors
d. obsession

68.
K
Answer: d
pp. 544-545
Obj. #15

Which of the following statements is true?
a. The clinical term for sexual addiction that can be found in the DSM-IV is hypersexuality.
b. The first phase of Carnes' addiction cycle is engaging in ritualistic behavior.
c. The last phase of Carnes' addiction cycle is the behavioral expression of the sexual act.
d. Most treatment programs for sexually addictive behavior are modeled after AA's twelve-step program.

Multiple Choice from Study Guide

1.
K
Answer: c
p. 526
Obj. #1

Paraphilias are _____ sexual behaviors.
a. deviant
b. perverted
c. atypical
d. illegal

2.
K
Answer: b
p. 527
Obj. #2b

Most persons who disclose that they have engaged in a paraphilia are
a. psychologically disordered.
b. male.
c. adults with histories of childhood maltreatment.
d. erotosexually undifferentiated.

3.
K
Answer: d
p. 529
Obj. #5

A person who dresses in the clothes of the other sex in order to obtain sexual arousal is referred to as a
a. homosexual.
b. transsexual.
c. transgendered person.
d. transvestite.

4.
K
Answer: a
p. 531
Obj. #6

Obtaining sexual pleasure by receiving physical or psychological pain is called
a. sexual masochism.
b. sexual sadism.
c. bondage.
d. domination.

5.
K
Answer: d
p. 540
Obj. #13a

Rubbing or pressing one's genitals against an unwilling or unaware person while in a public place is **best** described as
a. klismaphilia.
b. coprophilia.
c. exhibitionism.
d. frotteurism.

6.
K
Answer: c
p. 534
Obj. #7c

Urophilia describes the act of experiencing sexual arousal due to contact with _____.
a. diapers
b. rubber
c. urine
d. feces

7.
K
Answer: a
p. 528
Obj. #4

Someone who engages in fetishism becomes sexually aroused by
a. inanimate objects or particular parts of the body.
b. violent or degrading pornographic films.
c. engaging in ritualized stroking of housecats.
d. viewing childhood pornography.

8.
K
Answer: b
p. 534
Obj. #7a

Which paraphilia listed below may result in death for the person engaging in it?
a. necrophilia
b. autoerotic asphyxiation
c. frotteurism
d. telephone scatalogia

9.
K
Answer: a
p. 535
Obj. #8

Seeking sexual gratification by exposing one's genitals to an unwilling observer is termed
a. exhibitionism.
b. sadism.
c. voyeurism.
d. nudism.

10.
K
Answer: c
p. 528
Obj. #4c

Fetishism is thought to develop through
a. abusive childhood discipline.
b. aversion conditioning.
c. classical conditioning.
d. instrumental conditioning.

11.
K
Answer: a
p. 530
Obj. #5b

The majority of persons who engage in transvestic fetishism are
a. heterosexual.
b. bisexual.
c. homosexual.
d. celibate.

12.
K
Answer: c
p. 531
Obj. #5b

Anthropologists have noted that transvestic fetishism is more common in societies where
a. gender roles are fluid.
b. participation in organized religion is low.
c. males have more economic responsibility than women.
d. homosexuality is sanctioned.

13.
K
Answer: a
p. 532
Obj. #6

A study of SM participants in a nonclinical environment found that SM activities involve
a. consensuality.
b. the expression of both sadism and masochism within the same encounter.
c. coercion.
d. severe physical pain.

14.
K
Answer: d
p. 531
Obj. #6b

A large study of 975 persons found that _____ of the respondents reported at least occasionally engaging in some form of SM.
a. 5%
b. 10%
c. 15%
d. 25%

15.
K
Answer: c
p. 533
Obj. #6c

Some theorists have suggested that SM allows participants to
a. increase self-awareness
b. relinquish ego control
c. escape from restrictive roles they occupy in everyday life
d. express thanatological urges

16.
K
Answer: b
p. 535
Obj. #8b

All of the following are characteristics of persons who engage in exhibitionism **except**
a. They often feel inadequate.
b. Most go on to physically assault the victim.
c. Most exhibitionists are married men.
d. They have difficulty with intimacy.

17.
K
Answer: a
pp. 537-538
Obj. #10

All of the following are strategies suggested to deal with obscene phone calls **except**
a. slamming down the phone.
b. pretending to be hard-of-hearing.
c. calmly hanging up the phone.
d. ignoring the phone if it rings again.

18.
K
Answer: c
p. 538
Obj. #12

People who engage in voyeurism are similar to
a. rapists.
b. sexual sadists.
c. exhibitionists.
d. Pedophiles.

19.
K
Answer: a
p. 540
Obj. #13b

Which statement regarding zoophilia is true?
a. It is commonly transitory experience.
b. The National Health and Social Life Survey found a decrease in this behavior since Kinsey's time.
c. Zoophilia is considered a noncoercive paraphilia.
d. Females typically have contact with farm animals.

20.
K
Answer: c
p. 541
Obj. #14

Treating coercive paraphilias is difficult because
a. few treatment modalities are available.
b. malpractice suits are more likely to be brought against a therapist by this client type.
c. people with coercive paraphilias often do not believe they need treatment.
d. rates of depression and suicide are high.

21.
K
Answer: a
pp. 541-542
Obj. #14

All of the following are methods of treating coercive paraphilias **except**
a. psychoanalysis.
b. cognitive therapy.
c. orgasmic reconditioning.
d. aversive conditioning.

22.
K
Answer: b
p. 543
Obj. #14g

Antiandrogen drugs work to reduce compulsive, paraphiliac urges by
a. stimulating estrogen production.
b. reducing testosterone levels.
c. prompting the prostate gland to release prostate-specific-antigen.
d. temporarily stopping sperm production.

23.
K
Answer: a
pp. 544-545
Obj. #15

Sexologists disagree about the existence of sexual addiction because
a. there are no clear criteria about what normal levels of sexual activity are.
b. the disorder is not distinguishable from other compulsive disorders.
c. the disorder negates individual responsibility.
d. all of the above

True/False

Students may be asked to answer these questions using the traditional format of marking their answers either "true" or "false". Or, to encourage more active involvement, you may choose to use the following instructions:

If the statement is true, place a "T" on the line preceding it. If the statement is false, place an "F" on the line preceding it and then change the statement to make it true by deleting incorrect information and/or adding accurate information.

1. ____ The term "paraphilia" is currently used to describe sexual behavior that is uncommon.
Answer: T
p. 526
Obj. #1

2. ____ According to John Money, atypical sexual behavior is more prevalent among men than women because men are influenced by greater amounts of androgen than women are.
Answer: F
p. 526
Obj. #2b

3. ____ Many of the coercive paraphilias discussed in the text are illegal.
Answer: T
p. 527
Obj. #2d, 3

4. ____ People who are involuntary recipients of atypical sexual expression may be psychologically traumatized.
Answer: T
p. 527
Obj. #2d, 3

5. ____ Fetishism usually develops as a result of operant conditioning.
Answer: F
p. 528
Obj. #4

6. ____ The most common serious offense to be associated with fetishistic behavior is burglary.
Answer: T
p. 528
Obj. #4

7. ____ Although male transvestism is most common, several cases of female transvestism have been reported in the clinical literature.
Answer: T
p. 530
Obj. #5

8. ____ The majority of women who discover that their husbands enjoy cross-dressing support this behavior.
Answer: F
p. 530
Obj. #5

9. ____ Many men who engage in transvestism have sought professional help and have successfully altered their behavior.
Answer: F
p. 531
Obj. #5

10. Available research reveals that a large number of people who practice sadomasochism overstep boundaries and become involved in activities that are physically and emotionally dangerous.
Answer: F
pp. 531-532
Obj. #6

11. It appears that people with masochistic tendencies are more common than their sadistic counterparts.
Answer: T
p. 532
Obj. #6

12. It appears that many people who participate in sadomasochistic activities are motivated by a desire to experience dominance and/or submission rather than to inflict or receive pain.
Answer: T
p. 532
Obj. #6

13. A few men who engage in exhibitionism progress to more serious offenses.
Answer: T
p. 534
Obj. #8b

14. People who expose themselves are usually adult males over 40 who have never been married.
Answer: F
p. 535
Obj. #12

15. Autoerotic asphyxia often results in death.
Answer: T
p. 536
Obj. #7a

16. Over 80% of a survey of Canadian women reported having received obscene of threatening phone calls at some time in their life.
Answer: T
p. 537
Obj. n/a

17. People who engage in voyeurism tend to frequent places like nudist camps and nude beaches.
Answer: F
p. 538
Obj. #12

18. Research has revealed that a significant number of people who work in morgues or funeral homes engage in necrophilia.
Answer: F
p. 541
Obj. #5

19. Orgasmic reconditioning is an example of behavior therapy.
Answer: T
p. 543
Obj. #14

20. ___ The four phases in Patrick Carnes' model of sexual addiction are:
Answer: F   despair; preoccupation; ritualistic behaviors; and expression of
p. 544   the sexual act.
Obj. #15

Short Answer Essay

1. Define paraphilia and give examples. Describe how classical conditioning may be involved in the origin of some of these. (Obj. #1)

2. Distinguish between noncoercive and coercive paraphilias, describing three examples of each. (Obj. #3-9, 11-13)

3. Define fetishism and give examples. Offer some hypotheses as to why these develop. (Obj. #4a-c)

4. Define exhibitionism and discuss each of the following in regard to it: how to distinguish commonplace exhibitionistic tendencies from illegal behavior; characteristics of the person who engages in this behavior and the problems with our knowledge base in this area; hypotheses regarding what influences the development of exhibitionistic behavior. (Obj. #8a-c, 8e)

5. Describe some of the characteristics that individuals who engage in exhibitionism and voyeurism have in common. (Obj. #8b, 12)

6. Distinguish among transvestism, transsexualism, and homosexuals in "drag". (Obj. #4, 5)

7. Describe some of the problems in defining transvestism, who tends to engage in this behavior, and how the behavior may develop. (Obj. #5a, 5b, 5d)

8. Discuss several different theories that attempt to explain why people engage in sexual sadism or masochism. (Obj. #6c, 6e)

9. Discuss some of the problems involved in labeling a behavior "sadomasochistic" and make reference to available statistics that indicate how common it may be. (Obj. #6a-b)

10. Have you ever been the victim of an exhibitionist? What were the circumstances and what was your reaction? If in the future you are the victim of an exhibitionist, what do you intend to do? (Obj. #8e)

11. Have you even been the victim of an obscene phone call? If so what were the circumstances and what was your reaction? If in the future you are the victim of an obscene phone call, what do you intend to do? (Obj. #10)

12. Describe and distinguish the four behavioral therapies of aversive conditioning, systematic desensitization, orgasmic reconditioning, and satiation therapy. (Obj. #14c-f)

13. List and briefly describe at least six strategies for treating coercive paraphilias, commenting on approaches or combinations of approaches that appear to be most successful. (Obj. #14a-h)

14. Describe Patrick Carnes' concept of sexual addiction. List and briefly discuss the four phases of the addiction cycle. (Obj. #15)

15. Why do some sexologists have difficulty with the concept of sexual addiction? Discuss Eli Coleman's approach to conceptualizing excessive sexual activity. (Obj. #15)

19

Sexual Victimization

Learning Objectives

After studying Chapter 18, students will be able to:

1. Define all of the key terms and concepts for this chapter listed in the margin of the text and be able to integrate them with all relevant material outlined below.

2. Discuss the difficulties in obtaining accurate statistics on the number of rapes and rape survivors in the U.S. and cite some of the variations in currently available statistics.

3. Identify and elaborate upon five false beliefs regarding rape.

4. Citing relevant research, describe some of the psychosocial bases of rape.

5. Discuss what research has revealed regarding the impact of sexually violent and degrading media on the attitudes and behaviors of rapists and nonrapists.

6. Describe the characteristics of men who rape.

7. Discuss the arguments for and against a sociobiological explanation of rape.

8. Discuss recent research regarding acquaintance rape and sexual coercion, making specific reference to the following:
   a. how prevalent it is
   b. factors that might contribute to people engaging in unwanted sexual activity
   c. the use of the drugs such as Rohypnol to facilitate sexual conquest or to incapacitate victims who are then raped or molested

9. Cite examples of how and for what purposes wartime rape has been used.

10. Explain the short-term and long-term effects of rape on female survivors, making specific reference to the following:
    a. rape trauma syndrome
    b. suggestions regarding how to respond to a partner who has been raped

11. Discuss how frequently the rape and sexual assault of males occurs, who the perpetrators are, and what some of the problems are with the data in this area.

12. Describe some of the physical, psychological and sexual effects are on men who have been raped.

13. List and briefly describe nine suggestions for reducing the risk of stranger rape.

14. List and briefly describe five suggestions for how to deal with threatening situations involving strangers.

15. List and briefly describe six suggestions for reducing the risk of acquaintance rape.

16. List and briefly describe five ways in which a woman may take action if she has been raped.

17. Distinguish between pedophilia and incest, and discuss some of the differences in defining child molestation.

18. Discuss the problem of pedophiles in cyberspace and what might be done to combat this problem.

19. Discuss the sexual abuse of children, citing specific information and current research as it relates to the following:
    a. in what situations and under what conditions it most commonly occurs
    b. how prevalent it is and the problems with these statistics
    c. how incidence of abuse in girls compares to that of boys

20. Discuss the results of a controversial meta-analysis concerning the effects of sexual abuse on children.

21. Describe the factors that contribute to how severely abuse affects the victim and what these effects might be.

22. Identify treatment programs available for child sexual abuse survivors.

23. Describe the characteristics of the person who sexually abuses children.

24. Discuss the controversy surrounding the issue of recovered memories of child sexual abuse.

25. List and describe ten suggestions for preventing childhood sexual abuse.

26. Explain what kinds of responses might be helpful in the event you discovered that your own child had been molested by an adult.

27. Define sexual harassment and describe two types of sexual harassment as provided by the EEOC guidelines.

28. Discuss the various forms that sexual harassment can take.

29. Citing relevant statistics, discuss how common sexual harassment is among men and women.

30. Discuss some of the problems unique to same-sex sexual harassment.

31. Discuss the effects of on-the-job harassment on victims.

32. Outline and describe six guidelines for dealing with sexual harassment in the workplace.

33. Discuss sexual harassment that may occur in an academic setting, making specific reference to the following:
    a. who the perpetrators are
    b. differences between harassment that occurs in an academic setting vs. the workplace
    c. how common sexual harassment is in this setting
    d. how to deal with sexual harassment in an academic environment

Chapter 19 Sexual Victimization 419

34. Discuss how different cultures may punish women who have been raped.

Multiple Choice

1.
K
Answer: c
p. 548
Obj. #2
WWW

One of the **primary** difficulties in obtaining accurate statistics on the number of rapes and rape survivors in the United States is
   a. the lack of standard accounting procedures on the part of law enforcement officials.
   b. that although the legal definition of rape is consistent in every state, people interpret the law differently.
   c. the reluctance of many people to report being assaulted.
   d. the problems in distinguishing between rape and molestation.

2.
A
Answer: a
p. 548
Obj. #1

In a state where the age of sexual consent is 17, which of the following would be the **best** example of statutory rape?
   a. A 19-year-old boy has intercourse with his 16-year-old girlfriend.
   b. A 20-year-old boy forces a 17-year-old girl to have intercourse with him.
   c. An 18-year-old girl is raped by a stranger, and becomes pregnant as a result.
   d. A 22-year-old man has intercourse with a 17-year-old girl.

3.
K
Answer: b
p. 548
Obj. #1

In the United States as of June 1996, the age of consent ranged from _____ to _____.
   a. 13; 19
   b. 14; 18
   c. 15; 19
   d. 16; 21

4.
K
Answer: a
p. 548
Obj. #2

Estimates of the percentage of experienced rapes reported by women to some official agency rungs from about
   a. 11 to 16%.
   b. 21 to 26%.
   c. 31 to 36%.
   d. 41 to 46%.

5.
K
Answer: b
p. 549
Obj. #2

The large scale NIJ/CDC found that about _____ of women had experienced attempted or completed rape.
   a. 9%
   b. 16%
   c. 23%
   d. 30%

6.
K
Answer: b
p. 549
Obj. #2

The large scale NIJ/CDC found that about _____ of men had experienced attempted or completed rape.
   a. 1%
   b. 3%
   c. 5%
   d. 10%

7.
K
Answer: b
p. 549
Obj. #3
WWW

All of the following are false beliefs about rape described in the text **except**
a. Women can always successfully resist a rape attempt.
b. Rape is a sexually motivated crime.
c. Many women make false accusations that they have been raped.
d. All women really want to be raped.

8.
K
Answer: d
pp. 549, 551
Obj. #3

Which of the following statements is true?
a. A woman can always successfully resist a rape attempt if she is willing to behave aggressively.
b. Since a large percentage of women have rape fantasies, it follows that these women, consciously or unconsciously, want to be raped.
c. In the media, male-to-female rape is typically portrayed as more violent and humiliating than male-to-male rape is.
d. Many female rape victims may believe that the rape was their fault.

9.
K
Answer: d
p. 549
Obj. #3

One study of 114 imprisoned rapists revealed that approximately _____ percent did not see themselves as rapists.
a. 20
b. 40
c. 60
d. 80

10.
K
Answer: a
p. 549
Obj. #3

In one study of 114 imprisoned rapists, all of the following reasons were given to justify their behavior and to make the women appear guilty **except**
a. A woman could stop you if she really wanted to.
b. Women say no when they mean yes.
c. Women are seducers who "lead you on".
d. Most women eventually relax and enjoy it.

11.
K
Answer: b
p. 550
Obj. #4

Which country has the highest incidence of rape among all Western nations?
a. Canada
b. United States
c. Germany
d. France

12.
K
Answer: d
p. 550
Obj. #4

Peggy Reeves Sanday's comparison of rape in 93 societies revealed that the incidence of rape in a given society is influenced by all of the following **except**
a. the attitudes boys acquire as they are growing up.
b. the status of women.
c. the nature of relationships between the sexes.
d. the degree to which individuals adhere to particular moral or religious values.

13.
K
Answer: c
p. 550
Obj. #4
WWW

All of the following patterns have been identified in relatively "rape free" societies **except**
   a. women and men share power and authority.
   b. women and men contribute equally to the community welfare.
   c. the majority of people share similar religious beliefs.
   d. children of both sexes are socialized to avoid violence and aggression and value nurturance.

14.
K
Answer: d
pp. 550-551
Obj. #4

Which of the following statements is false?
   a. Rape may be motivated by a desire for sexual gratification as well as the need to dominate and control.
   b. Men who are sexually aggressive are more likely to have male friends who are also sexually aggressive.
   c. Violent pornography can decrease a man's sensitivity to the harmful effects of rape on women.
   d. Men in rape-prone societies frequently have less economic and political power than women, which fuels the anger that is often the motivation for the rape.

15.
K
Answer: a
p. 551
Obj. #4

Which of the following statements is false?
   a. Convicted rapists and rapists who have never been prosecuted and convicted demonstrate similar motivations and characteristics.
   b. Recent research has indicated that while rape may be an act of power and domination, it is frequently sexually motivated as well.
   c. Rape is more often a result of how men are socialized than of the individual pathology of the rapist.
   d. Until fairly recently, what we knew about rapists was based on studies of convicted rapists, which represents a very small percentage of men who rape.

16.
K
Answer: d
p. 551
Obj. #6

All of the following characteristics have been linked to men who rape **except**
   a. anger towards women.
   b. self-centered personality.
   c. adherence to traditional gender roles.
   d. being socially inept.

17.
K
Answer: a
p. 551
Obj. #4

Which one is NOT true with respect findings about the impact of media on rape propensity?
   a. Exposure to degrading but nonviolent erotica may increase the inclination to engage in coercive sex.
   b. Viewing hard-core porno depicting violent rape was associated with judging oneself capable of sexual coercion.
   c. Research is contradictory as to whether rapists are aroused by audiotapes of rape scenarios.
   d. It is most likely that any association is due to people who have become deviant later choosing arousing images.

18.
K
Answer: c
p. 552
Obj. #14

With one is true with respect to avoiding rape?
a. A woman who leads an extremely restrictive life can avoid rape.
b. An extremely cautious life will enable you to avoid stranger rape if not acquaintance rape.
c. There are ways to reduce the risk of rape.
d. One might as well live as you like since there is no guarantee that you can avoid rape.

19.
K
Answer: c
p. 552
Obj. #14
WWW

All but which one of the following was suggested as ways to reduce the risk of stranger rape?
a. Take a cell phone with you when you are out alone.
b. Lock your car while you are driving.
c. Never go out alone when it is dark.
d. Carry a device with you for making a loud noise.

20.
K
Answer: a
p. 552
Obj. #14

A study of 150 rapes or attempted rapes found that
a. women who do such things as scream, kick and run were more likely to avoid being raped.
b. women who don't wear makeup or perfume are more likely to avoid being raped.
c. women who can readily cry are more likely to avoid being raped.
d. there are no patterns as to who is likely to avoid a rape when an attempt is make.

21.
A
Answer: c
p. 553
Obj. #15
WWW

You are a heterosexual single woman who enjoys dating. Which of the following behaviors would be **most** likely to reduce the risk of date rape?
a. Your date insists on paying for everything, ordering your dinner, and planning all activities, and you tell him that you appreciate having him make those decisions for you.
b. You tell your date that you do not want to become sexually involved, but when he begins to kiss and fondle you let him.
c. A man you have just met in a bar asks you out on a date. You agree, suggesting that you meet him for lunch later in the week.
d. It's your first date with a man. You have no intention of being sexually intimate with him, but at the end of the evening you invite him into your apartment for a drink.

22.
A
Answer: c
p. 553
Obj. #15

All but which one was recommended to women if they do NOT want to be sexually intimate with a date?
a. avoid using alcohol
b. avoid using drugs
c. invite the person to your apartment rather than going to theirs
d. cover some of the expenses

Chapter 19 Sexual Victimization 423

23.
A
Answer: a
p. 553
Obj. #16
WWW

If you have been sexually attacked it would be **most** advisable to
   a. report even an attempt.
   b. call a friend to come over while you take a shower so you can symbolically get rid of the memories.
   c. practice your story with a friend or family member and only call the police if they think it is believable.
   d. try to figure out what you did wrong so you can acknowledge it and avoid doing it in the future.

24.
K
Answer: b
p. 554
Obj. #7

The majority of acquaintance rapes are **most** likely to result from
   a. anger.
   b. sexual gratification.
   c. power.
   d. sadistic.

25.
K
Answer: c
p. 554
Obj. #6

Gene Abel's research of over 200 New York rapists revealed that approximately _____ of the men had histories of other types of sexual offenses.
   a. ten percent
   b. twenty-five percent
   c. fifty percent
   d. seventy percent

26.
K
Answer: d
p. 554
Obj. #6

The men in Abel's sample of New York rapists reported histories of all of the following sexual offenses **except**
   a. child sexual abuse.
   b. exhibitionism.
   c. voyeurism.
   d. masochism.

27.
K
Answer: a
p. 554
Obj. #6

Which of the following patterns appears to be a precursor to rape and other deviant sexual acts?
   a. masturbating to deviant sexual fantasies
   b. conflicts regarding gender identity
   c. engaging in paraphilias such as klismaphilia or coprophilia
   d. conflicts regarding sexual orientation

28.
K
Answer: b
p. 555
Obj. #8a

A survey of over a thousand teenage women found that ____ had experienced some form of unwanted sexual contact during the previous year.
   a. 5%
   b. 20%
   c. 35%
   d. 50%

29.
K
Answer: b
p. 555
Obj. #7

Arguments for and against a sociobiological explanation of rape include all but which one of the following?
a. Adaptations, even rape, have evolved over eons.
b. Rape is programmed into men so that his genes are more likely to survive.
c. All men don't rape.
d. Women have evolved to prefer men with the dominating characteristics of men who rape.

30.
K
Answer: c
p. 555
Obj. #7

What are the odds that a rape will result in a birth?
a. We don't have these data.
b. Unusually low as the women being raped tend to reject sperm.
c. Less than 1 in 100.
d. About 3 to 4%.

31.
K
Answer: b
p. 556
Obj. #8b, 8c

All of the following are reasons women gave for saying no to sex when they really meant yes **except**
a. not wanting to appear promiscuous.
b. being uncertain about birth control.
c. being in undesirable surroundings.
d. wanting to be in control.

32.
K
Answer: b
p. 556
Obj. #8a

A survey of Canadian high school students found that ____ of males had experienced some sort of coercive sexual activity, although the coercion was usually NOT physical force.
a. over 5%
b. over 20%
c. over 35%
d. over 50%

33.
K
Answer: c
p. 557
Obj. #8c

What are the effects of taking the drug Rohypnol?
a. acts as a sexual aphrodisiac by increasing vasocongestion in the genital tissue
b. inhibits sexual desire by decreasing testosterone in the bloodstream
c. produces a sedative effect that lasts for several hours and may also cause varying degrees of amnesia
d. increases sexual desire by boosting the level of androgen in the bloodstream

34.
K
Answer: b
p. 557
Obj. #8c

Which is true with respect to laws dealing with Rohypnol and similar drugs?
a. They are not yet in place.
b. Congress has recently added 20 years to the prison sentence of rapists who use these drugs.
c. Penalties are determined by the individual states.
d. These are generally in effect only when the drug is used with minors.

35.
K
Answer: c
pp. 557-558
Obj. #9

Rape during war
a. is usually considered a part of the necessary consequences of war.
b. is fortunately rare in our present age.
c. has occurred from early history through the present time.
d. may have some evolutionary advantage in that it spreads genes worldwide.

36.
K
Answer: c
pp. 558-559
Obj. #10b
WWW

A partner can be **most** helpful to a rape survivor by
a. making decisions for her in terms of how to deal with the assault.
b. having sex with her soon after the assault to reassure her that he is still attracted to her.
c. listening to her.
d. apologizing to her for not being there to protect her.

37.
K
Answer: b
pp. 558-559
Obj. #10b

Suggestions for helping a friend or partner recover from rape include all but which one of the following?
a. Give comfort with words.
b. Insist that the victim call a rape hotline, or see a counselor.
c. Offer shelter at your home.
d. Let her discuss this as often as she wants.

38.
K
Answer: a
p. 559
Obj. n/a

Which one is NOT true concerning sexual response during a rape?
a. This doesn't occur unless the woman is enjoying it to some extent.
b. Even orgasms sometimes occur.
c. These are upsetting to the victims when they occur.
d. These may be considered normal physiological reactions.

39.
K
Answer: c
p. 560
Obj. #17

Pedophilia is **best** described as
a. obtaining sexual excitement primarily or exclusively from feet, shoes, or boots.
b. brother-sister incest.
c. nonrelative child sexual abuse.
d. sexual contact between two people who are related.

40.
K
Answer: a
p. 560
Obj. #17

When a man has sexual contact with his 10-year-old daughter it is called _____; when he has sexual contact with his daughter's 10-year-old friend it is called _____.
a. incest; pedophilia
b. pedophilia; child molestation
c. child molestation; incest
d. pedophilia; incest

41.
K
Answer: d
p. 561
Obj. #17

Sexual contact between first cousins
a. is considered incest.
b. is considered pedophilia.
c. is socially disapproved of but not illegal.
d. is illegal in some states but not in others.

42.
K
Answer: a
p. 561
Obj. #19a

_____ incest is most common.
a. Brother-sister
b. Father-daughter
c. Mother-son
d. Grandfather-granddaughter

43.
K
Answer: b
p. 561
Obj. #17, 19a
WWW

Which of the following statements regarding incest is true?
a. It is prohibited in some societies but accepted in others.
b. It is always illegal regardless of the age of the participants.
c. It occurs primarily at higher socioeconomic levels.
d. Sexual contact between a child and a close family friend is one example of it.

44.
A
Answer: b
pp. 561-562
Obj. #19a

Which of the following tactics would a father who is attempting to pressure his daughter into an incestuous relationship be **least** likely to use?
a. telling her that she is his "special girl"
b. using physical force to coerce her
c. reassuring her that he is teaching her something important
d. telling her he will take her shopping for something special if she complies

45.
K
Answer: c
p. 562
Obj. #19a

Incest occurs with greater frequency in families affected by all of the following problems **except**
a. spouse abuse.
b. alcoholism.
c. physical illness.
d. unemployment.

46.
K
Answer: d
p. 562
Obj. #23

Which of the following would be **least** characteristic of a pedophile?
a. does not relate well to other people
b. has problems with alcoholism
c. sexually victimized during his own childhood
d. liberal attitudes toward sexuality

47.
K
Answer: d
p. 562
Obj. #23

Some evidence suggests that the man who engages in father-daughter incest tends to be
a. an atheist.
b. a teetotaler.
c. of above-average income.
d. emotionally immature.

48.
K
Answer: a
p. 562
Obj. #23

Which of the following statements concerning pedophiles is true?
a. They are often moralistic or religious.
b. Their victims are typically unknown to them.
c. They have the potential to be very violent.
d. An equal number of men and women are pedophiles.

49.
K
Answer: b
p. 563
Obj. #19b

All of the following are reasons that would account for why child molestation is unlikely to be reported **except**
a. The offender may be a family friend.
b. The legal system is reluctant to investigate allegations of child molestation.
c. The parents may not want to expose the child to stressful legal proceedings.
d. The parents may not believe the child.

50.
K
Answer: c
p. 563
Obj. #34

According to a review of various surveys, the rates of child sexual abuse in various European countries are
a. significantly higher than those reported by most women in the United States.
b. somewhat higher than those reported by most women in the United States.
c. comparable to those reported by most women in the United States.
d. significantly lower than those reported by most women in the United States.

51.
K
Answer: c
p. 563
Obj. #34, 8a

With respect to sexual abuse, which one is NOT true?
a. There are more young boys sexually molested in the U. S. than earlier estimated.
b. Some children are being abused by women.
c. The United States has more child abuse than other countries.
d. The most abuse occurs with male perpetrators and female victims.

52.
K
Answer: c
p. 563
Obj. #8a

A 1997 meta-analysis combined data from 16 studies of child sexual abuse and found that ___ % of women and ___ % of men reported being sexually abused as a child.
a. 33; 3
b. 22; 15
c. 22; 9
d. 9; 3

53.
K
Answer: c
p. 564
Obj. #24

With respect to recovered memories of childhood sexual abuse it is **most** correct to conclude that
a. these are most likely deliberate fakes.
b. these are most likely imparted by overzealous therapists.
c. these are sometimes but not always accurate.
d. these should be considered accurate.

54.
K
Answer: b
p. 564
Obj. #24

Several studies of adults for whom child sexual abuse as children had been reported and substantiated
a. found that the victims did not wish to talk about this.
b. found that a sizable proportion had been amnesic for their abuse for a period of time.
c. found that almost all remembered the abuse, casting doubt on the recovered memory hypothesis.
d. found that males repressed but the females remembered.

428 Test Bank to Accompany *Our Sexuality*

55.
K
Answer: d
pp. 564-565
Obj. #24

Which of the following statements regarding recovered memories of child sexual abuse is false?
a. Numerous studies indicate that false "memories" of events that never occurred can be created in the research lab.
b. The legitimacy of recovered memories has been supported by several research studies.
c. "Repressed memories" may be inadvertently planted by overzealous or poorly trained psychotherapists.
d. As of 1997, therapists are required by law to videotape interviews of victims of sexual abuse.

56.
K
Answer: c
p. 565
Obj. #18

Pedophiles using cyberspace
a. primarily interact with children and avoid other adults.
b. are generally intelligent but lower middle class.
c. exchange information with other pedophiles, including child pornography.
d. are committing an illegal act by even discussing adult-child sexual interaction.

57.
K
Answer: a
pp. 565-566
Obj. #18
WWW

Which one is NOT true concerning the use of cyberspace by pedophiles?
a. The Communications Decency Act now regulates indecent mail sent over the Internet to minors.
b. The main responsibility for protecting children lies with parents.
c. AOL has tried to monitor kids-only chat rooms for inappropriate dialogue.
d. Even with blocking software, children may still communicate with pedophiles in chat rooms.

58.
K
Answer: d
p. 566
Obj. #20

The meta-analytic examination of child-sexual abuse criticized past research for all but which one of the following?
a. Poor definitions of what is meant by child sexual abuse.
b. Research sampling of individuals from those who have been damaged.
c. Combining cases of repeated violation with those from one-time incidents.
d. Not taking into account that children may be lying about this.

59.
K
Answer: b
p. 567
Obj. #20

Your text suggests which of the following about the meta-analytic finding by Rind, et. al. that boys are less harmed by adult-child sexual contact than are girls?
a. This is important new information.
b. This is questionable as girls are more often abused early and with force and their findings did not consider this.
c. We may need to make stronger laws for girls than for boys.
d. This is probably only apparently so because men tend to deny psychological problems more than do women.

60.
K
Answer: d
p. 567
Obj. #21

Some recent studies comparing a variety of factors that might affect adjustment in later life found which of the following to play the larger role?
a. Sexual abuse when a child
b. Serious illness when a child
c. Parental divorce
d. Family neglect or violence

61.
K
Answer: d
p. 567
Obj. #21

All of the following were more frequently reported in sexual abuse survivors **except**
a. sexual difficulties.
b. drug and alcohol abuse.
c. obesity.
d. placing too much trust in others.

62.
K
Answer: c
pp. 567-568
Obj. #20

A recent controversial meta-analysis of 59 studies of college students sexually abused prior to the age of 18 suggested that
a. sexual abuse laws are too severe.
b. the age of consent should be consistent from state to state and lowered to at least 16.
c. sexual abuse appears to have a largely negative effect for a minority.
d. the media need to be regulated for sexual content.

63.
K
Answer: c
p. 568
Obj. #21

Which of the following is NOT true concerning factors affecting a victim's response to child abuse?
a. The longer molestation occurred, the worse the effects.
b. More violent assaults have more negative effects.
c. If the perpetrator was close to the victim the effects are less.
d. More intrusive abuse is more damaging.

64.
K
Answer: d
p. 568
Obj. #21

A recent study of 1500 12-9 year olds reported all but which of the following?
a. Abused males are 11 times more likely to have suicidal thoughts or attempts than their nonabused peers.
b. Emotional problems are more common for the abused, but especially so for boys.
c. Addiction-risk behavior is more frequent for the abused.
d. Criminal behaviors are not related to a history of abuse.

65.
K
Answer: d
p. 568
Obj. n/a

Which one is NOT true concerning Megan's law?
a. This is named for a girl who was raped and murdered by a previously convicted sex offender.
b. This law requires registration and community notification when convicted pedophiles are released from prison.
c. This is an attempt to protect the community rather than to help a perpetrator.
d. This has been declared unconstitutional in some states.

66.
K
Answer: b
p. 569
Obj. #25

All of the following are suggestions given for preventing child sexual abuse **except**
a. Present information to children when they are still very young.
b. Discuss ethics, social responsibility and definitions of appropriate sexual activity.
c. Discuss with the children some tactics adults might use to gain compliance with their sexual demands.
d. Explain the difference between okay and not-okay touches.

67.
K
Answer: c
p. 569
Obj. #25

According to your text, sexual abuse prevention materials
a. are treading on parental rights when presented in the schools.
b. should only use scientific terms.
c. should be given early as up to a quarter of abuse victims are under 7 years of age.
d. should be done with fathers talking to boys and mothers talking to girls.

68.
K
Answer: a
p. 569
Obj. #25

Which of the following was NOT given as a suggestion for preventing child sexual abuse?
a. It might help to get the child a little frightened so she will pay attention and remember.
b. Emphasize that children have the right to control their bodies.
c. Remind them that you will not be angry if they report to you that they have been touched in a way that wasn't okay.
d. Help them understand that they can scream or run away from an uncomfortable situation.

69.
K
Answer: d
p. 570
Obj. #25

Conveying the message to children that _____ is one of the **most** important aspects of abuse prevention discussion.
a. there are men out there who may try to exploit them in some way
b. someone they know may attempt to fondle their genitals
c. they should be wary of any adult they don't know who tries to approach or befriend them
d. private touching can be very pleasurable between adults who love and trust each other

70.
K
Answer: c
p. 571
Obj. #27

The two types of sexual harassment as defined by the guidelines issued by the EEOC are
a. quid pro quo; verbal harassment
b. quid pro quo; physical harassment
c. quid pro quo; hostile or offensive environment
d. hostile or offensive environment; physical harassment

71.
A
Answer: a
p. 571
Obj. #27

Trish's professor has made it clear that he can ensure her success in graduate school if she complies with his sexual advances. This type of sexual harassment is called _____ harassment.
a. quid pro quo
b. hostile or offensive environment
c. coercive
d. verbal

72.
K
Answer: d
p. 571
Obj. #27

According to the EEOC guidelines, which of the following statements is false?
a. Verbal harassment is illegal.
b. Physical harassment is illegal.
c. If a person uses sex to be promoted, his or her co-workers may file suit against the employer.
d. Hostile or offensive environment is in reference to the workplace, but does not apply to academic settings.

73.
A
Answer: a
pp. 571-572
Obj. #28

All of the following are forms of sexual harassment on the job **except**
a. an employer and her secretary flirting with one another.
b. being the constant target of sexual jokes.
c. an employer requiring sexual availability in order to be hired.
d. an employer requiring sexual favors to be given to customers in order for the employee to get a promotion.

74.
A
Answer: c
pp. 571-572
Obj. #28

All of the following are examples of sexual harassment **except**
a. Marin's employer repeatedly asks her out on a date and she refuses.
b. Because of her repeated refusals, Marin's employer suggests that she may be either frigid or a lesbian.
c. Marin's employer tells jokes with a racist theme at staff meetings.
d. Marin's employer stares openly at her breasts, even after she asks him to stop.

75.
K
Answer: c
p. 572
Obj. #29

One survey of 24,000 federal employees as well as a later update of this survey found that _____ percent of the women and _____ percent of the men had been sexually harassed.
a. 10; 3
b. 23; 12
c. 42; 15
d. 76; 32

76.
K
Answer: c
p. 573
Obj. #30

Which of the following statements regarding same-sex sexual harassment is true?
a. Recent legislation has made it much easier for victims of same-sex sexual harassment to obtain satisfactory legal judgments against the perpetrators.
b. Most defendants in same-sex sexual harassment claim that they have a homosexual orientation.
c. The supreme Court has ruled that Title VII does prohibit sexual harassment between an offender and victim of the same sex.
d. Federal law specifically stated that same sex sexual harassment was illegal.

77.
K
Answer: c
p. 573
Obj. #31

Which of the following statements regarding the effects of sexual harassment is false?
a. The victims may feel guilty, nervous and irritable.
b. The victims may suffer a range of physical symptoms.
c. The victims usually enhance their financial status, but their psychological health is negatively affected.
d. The victims feel alienated from other co-workers.

78.
K
Answer: d
pp. 573-574
Obj. #32
WWW

All of the following were listed as guidelines for dealing with sexual harassment **except**
a. File criminal charges against the perpetrator of an attempted although unsuccessful rape.
b. Confront the harasser.
c. Discuss the situation with your supervisor and/or the offender's supervisor.
d. Write a letter specifying the harassment you have been subjected to, distribute copies to everyone in the office, and quit your job.

79.
K
Answer: b
p. 574
Obj. #33

Which is NOT true with respect to sexual harassment in schools?
a. School districts are liable for hostile sexual environments created by school employees.
b. School districts may be sued for damages if a student sexually harasses another student.
c. Sexual harassment occurs even in middle schools.
d. When teachers harass, it is most commonly male teachers who harass female students.

80.
K
Answer: c
p. 574
Obj. #33

Which one has NOT been reported as true for women who report sexual harassment?
a. They are viewed as less feminine by others.
b. They are viewed as more assertive.
c. They are generally viewed positively by their peers.
d. They are generally viewed as less trustworthy by both men and women.

81.
K
Answer: b
p. 574
Obj. #33

Your text suggest that if you experience sexual harassment on campus that you should
a. report it only if it s quid pro quo harassment case.
b. report it to reduce the likelihood that others will also be victimized
c. probably consider civil litigation.
d. be prepared for recrimination if your report is not decided to have a good foundation.

Multiple Choice from Study Guide

1.
K
Answer: e
p. 548
Obj. #2

A woman may be reluctant to report having been raped for which of the following reasons?
    a. She blames herself for what happened.
    b. She fears reprisal from the rapist or his family and friends.
    c. She wishes to avoid recalling a traumatic event.
    d. Her experience of acquaintance rape does not match her idea of rape as a violent attack by a stranger.
    e. all of the above are true

2.
K
Answer: c
pp. 549-550
Obj. #3

The belief that "rapists are 'obviously' mentally ill" is false because
    a. Mental illness is not common.
    b. Sex offenses are not classified as mental disorders.
    c. It describes rapists as crazed strangers and runs contrary to research which shows that most rapes are committed by someone the victim knows.
    d. Mental illnesses are uncontrollable, therefore a rapist cannot be held responsible for acts committed while ill.

3.
K
Answer: c
p. 549
Obj. #3

The notion that "women say 'no' when they mean 'yes'" is false because
    a. women are socialized to be better communicators than men.
    b. women are trained to lead men on.
    c. it helps rapists justify their behavior as normal sex play, not rape.
    d. the role of seducer demands that women act coy.

4.
K
Answer: b
p. 550
Obj. #4

Which characteristic was found in the rape-prone societies studied by anthropologist Peggy Reeves Sanday?
    a. shared power between the sexes
    b. glorification of masculine violence
    c. expectations that both sexes contribute to the welfare of the community
    d. higher rates of psychological disorder among men

5.
K
Answer: a
p. 550
Obj. n/a

The highest incidence of rape among Western nations is found in
    a. the United States.
    b. Mexico.
    c. Macedonia.
    d. Colombia.

6.
K
Answer: b
p. 551
Obj. #6

All of the following are characteristic of men who are more likely to rape **except**
    a. having male friends who are sexually aggressive.
    b. having low self-esteem.
    c. feeling anger towards women.
    d. holding traditional gender roles.

7.
K
Answer: b
p. 554
Obj. n/a

The majority of first rapes occurred before the victim was _____ years old.
a. 12
b. 18
c. 35
d. 50

8.
K
Answer: c
p. 555
Obj. #7

A sociobiological explanation for rape cannot be supported at this time because
a. cross-cultural studies have not been carried out.
b. studies have not been conducted on nonhuman primates.
c. the odds that rape offers an evolutionary advantage are very low.
d. scientists lack the appropriate techniques to study biological adaptations like rape.

9.
A
Answer: b
p. 556
Obj. #4

Ahmet believes that he should be aggressive and make the first sexual advance, whereas his girlfriend Frankie believes she should act passively so she does not appear "too easy". Ahmet and Frankie's behavior **best** illustrates the influence of
a. poor childhood socialization.
b. sexual scripts.
c. sexual personae.
d. poor communication skills.

10.
K
Answer: d
p. 556
Obj. #4

In a study of college women all of the following were reasons given for offering token resistance **except**
a. not wanting to appear promiscuous.
b. undesirable surroundings.
c. uncertainty about a partner's feelings.
d. desire to avoid game-playing.

11.
K
Answer: a
p. 560
Obj. #10

One study of rape survivors showed that nearly 75% had reduced levels of sexual activity for as long as
a. six months.
b. one year.
c. three years.
d. six years.

12.
K
Answer: c
p. 558
Obj. #10

Which of the following **best** describes initial emotional reactions to being raped?
a. hypersexuality and depression
b. drug or alcohol use and sleep disturbances
c. shame, anger, guilt, fear, feelings of powerlessness
d. anger, aggression, and recklessness

13.
K
Answer: b
p. 560
Obj. #17

_____ refers to sexual contact between relatives whereas _____ refers to sexual contact between an adult and child who are not related.
a. Pedophilia; incest
b. Incest; pedophilia
c. Incest; statutory rape
d. Pedophilia; paraphilia

14.
K
Answer: c
p. 561
Obj. #19b

Which type of sexual abuse is the **most** common?
a. father-daughter
b. stranger-child
c. brother-sister
d. uncle-niece

15.
K
Answer: e
p. 562
Obj. #23

Pedophiles who are prosecuted have which of the following characteristics?
a. religious
b. lonely
c. poorly informed about sexuality
d. two of the above
e. all of the above

16.
K
Answer: d
p. 563
Obj. #19b

A summarization of several studies indicated that _____ percent of women and _____ percent of men reported being abused as children.
a. 8; 3
b. 11; 5
c. 17; 6
d. 22; 9

17.
K
Answer: c
p. 564-565
Obj. #24

Which of the following statements **best** reflects the position of the American Psychological and American Psychiatric Associations regarding recovered memories of sexual abuse?
a. Both associations agree that the majority of recovered memories were implanted by unqualified therapists.
b. The American Psychiatric Association disputes the notion that memories can be recovered, whereas the American Psychological Association disagrees.
c. Both associations agree that forgotten memories can be recovered later in life.
d. Both associations agree that memories recovered under hypnosis are more trustworthy than memories recovered using other methods.

18.
K
Answer: a
pp. 567-568
Obj. #21

Which of the following is NOT a frequently encountered effect of childhood sexual abuse?
a. abstaining from drug and alcohol use
b. difficulty forming intimate relationships
c. depression
d. revulsion at being touched

19.
K
Answer: d
p. 569
Obj. #25

In order to prevent childhood sexual abuse it is recommended that prevention programs reach children younger than age _____, as 25% of abuse occurs before that age.
a. thirteen
b. ten
c. eight
d. seven

20.
A
Answer: b
p. 571
Obj. #28

Which of the following is the **best** example of *quid pro quo* sexual harassment?
 a. Janelle finds pictures of nude women taped to her locker at work.
 b. Sarah's supervisor says she can keep her job if she performs fellatio.
 c. Maria's co-worker repeatedly asks her out for dates, even after she refuses.
 d. Teesha's patrol partner regularly makes comments about her breasts, even though she has told him to stop.

21.
K
Answer: a
p. 573
Obj. #31

All of the following are effects of sexual harassment on victims **except**
 a. financial gain
 b. feeling ashamed
 c. feeling irritable
 d. lack of motivation

22.
K
Answer: d
p. 575
Obj. #33c

A survey of high school students revealed that _____ percent experienced sexual harassment.
 a. 12%
 b. 18%
 c. 34%
 d. 50%

23.
K
Answer: c
p. 575
Obj. #33d

The authors suggest that if you experience sexual harassment on campus you should
 a. avoid the harasser by dropping the class.
 b. circulate a petition among students to send to the professor's dean.
 c. report it so that the inappropriate behavior will stop.
 d. find a way to endure the term and then tell other students about the professor's unprofessional behavior, so they won't take his or her classes.

True/False

Students may be asked to answer these questions using the traditional format of marking their answers either "true" or "false". Or, to encourage more active involvement, you may choose to use the following instructions:

If the statement is true, place a "T" on the line preceding it. If the statement is false, place an "F" on the line preceding it and then change the statement to make it true by deleting incorrect information and/or adding accurate information.

1.
Answer: T
p. 548
Obj. #1

___ Statutory rape is having intercourse, even if consensual, with a person under the age of consent for that state.

2.
Answer: T
p. 549
Obj. #3

___ A consequence of the misconception that women want to be raped is likely that rape survivors may believe that the rape was their fault.

Chapter 19 Sexual Victimization 437

3.
Answer: F
p. 551
Obj. #4

____ Rape is typically not sexually motivated, but is rather an act of power and domination.

4.
Answer: T
p. 551
Obj. #4

____ Convicted rapists are less educated and more inclined to commit other criminal or antisocial acts than are rapists who have never been prosecuted or convicted.

5.
Answer: T
p. 551
Obj. #5

____ Research indicates that certain kinds of violent pornography encourage attitudes of violence against women.

6.
Answer: T
p. 553
Obj. #16

____ One suggestion for reducing the risk of acquaintance rape is to avoid using alcohol.

7.
Answer: T
p. 554
Obj. #11

____ It appears that as many as 3% of men have been raped.

8.
Answer: F
p. 555
Obj. #7

____ Your text suggests that sociobiological explanations of rape appear to be fairly strongly supported.

9.
Answer: T
p. 557
Obj. #8c

____ Convicted rapists who used Rohypnol will have 20 years added to their prison sentences.

10.
Answer: F
p. 559
Obj. n/a

____ If a friend or partner has been raped you should probably as soon as possible try to get them to think about something else rather than keep talking about it.

11.
Answer: F
p. 561
Obj. #18a

____ The most common type of incest is father-daughter.

12.
Answer: T
p. 562
Obj. #24

____ The man who engages in incest and the man who is a pedophile share similar characteristics.

13. ___ Over 1 in 5 adult women and almost 1 in 10 adult men report having been sexually abused as children.
Answer: T
p. 563
Obj. #20b

14. ___ Research has demonstrated some support for the legitimacy of recovered memories of child sexual abuse.
Answer: T
p. 564
Obj. #25

15. ___ Screening software when used will largely eliminate the problems of pedophiles in cyberspace.
Answer: F
p. 566
Obj. #19

16. ___ Programs to prevent child sexual abuse must begin early as perhaps 25% of abuse victims are younger than age 7.
Answer: T
p. 569
Obj. #20a

17. ___ "Quid pro quo" is one type of sexual harassment.
Answer: T
p. 571
Obj. #28

18. ___ While sexual harassment is a very real problem for those who experience it, it is not very widespread.
Answer: F
p. 572
Obj. #28, 30

19. ___ Displaying pornographic pictures that create a hostile or offensive workplace environment is considered sexual harassment.
Answer: T
p. 572
Obj. #29

20. ___ Your book recommended that students who experience sexual harassment on campus should report it to reduce the likelihood that other students will experience the same thing.
Answer: T
p. 575
Obj. #34d

Short Answer Essay

1. Outline the false beliefs pertaining to rape and briefly discuss why each is a myth. (Obj. #3)

2. Making reference to relevant research, discuss the social and cultural processes that contribute to a rape-prone culture. (Obj. #4, 6)

3. Summarize Peggy Reeves Sanday's research on rape-free vs. rape-prone societies. (Obj. #4)

4. Making reference to relevant research, discuss the connection between rape and exposure to different types of pornography. (Obj. #4)

5. Discuss how a woman might reduce the risk of acquaintance rape. (Obj. #16)

6. Discuss some of the ways in which an individual may meaningfully participate in his or her partner's recovery from rape. (Obj. #10b)

7. Assume that you are a parent and would like to protect your child from pedophiles on-line. What steps would you take at home? Do you believe that special steps should be taken in libraries or school settings? (Obj. #19)

8. Discuss the results of a controversial meta-analysis concerning the effects of sexual abuse on children. (Obj. #21)

9. Discuss what might be done to help prevent child sexual abuse. (Obj. #26)

10. Discuss the evidence as to whether or not there are differences in the effects upon males and females of child sexual abuse. (Obj. #20c)

11. Discuss both sides of the "recovered memories" debate, citing evidence to support each view. (Obj. #25)

12. Assume that you have been raped. What actions do you believe you would take? Would this differ depending upon whether it was stranger or acquaintance rape? (Obj. #17)

13. Describe the two types of sexual harassment as indicated by the EEOC guidelines, and discuss specific forms that the harassment may take. (Obj. #28, 29)

14. What are some effective ways for a victim to deal with sexual harassment? (Obj. #33)

15. Discuss the differences and similarities between sexual harassment in a workplace vs. an academic setting. (Obj. #34b)

20

Sex For Sale

Learning Objectives

After studying this chapter, the student should be able to:

1. Define pornography and explain some of the problems in establishing a contemporary definition of it.

2. Discuss the legal controversies surrounding pornography as they relate to the following:
    a. evaluating what is obscene from a legal standpoint
    b. freedom of speech
    c. regulating the dissemination of pornography
    d. addressing the dissemination of pornographic material on the Internet

3. Describe the effects of sexually explicit materials, making specific reference to the following:
    a. the outcome of President Johnson's Commission on Obscenity and Pornography
    b. the limitations of research results in this area
    c. three types of sexually explicit materials
    d. the extent to which pornography affects intimate relationships between men and women
    e. the process and outcome of the 1986 U.S. Attorney General's Commission on Pornography (the Meese Commission)
    f. China's laws regarding sexually explicit materials

4. Define prostitution and discuss the ways in which it has manifested itself throughout history.

5. Identify the characteristics of the female prostitute's typical customer.

6. Describe some characteristics of the typical prostitute and explain some of the motivations for being a prostitute.

7. Explain the controversy that exists in this country regarding the legal status of prostitution, and in doing so, distinguish between legalization and decriminalization.

8. Explain how AIDS is a concern for prostitution, and citing relevant statistics, discuss the extent to which AIDS is a problem in the U.S. as opposed to parts of Africa.

9. Discuss teenage prostitution, making reference to the following:
    a. what prompts some teenagers to become prostitutes
    b. common characteristics in the lives and backgrounds of teenage prostitutes
    c. according to one study, who the children are that are used in child pornography
    d. how federal laws have affected child pornography
    e. what many consumers of child pornography have in common
    f. how children who are involved in child prostitution are affected socially, emotionally, and psychologically

10. List and briefly describe three types of female prostitutes and the services they may provide.

11. Define the role that a brothel has played in prostitution.

12. List and briefly describe five types of male prostitutes.

13. Discuss the various people, agencies, businesses and institutions that benefit economically from prostitution.

14. Describe how women and children worldwide have come to be exploited through prostitution.

15. Describe the influence of the Internet on prostitution services.

Multiple Choice

1.
K
Answer: b
p. 579
Obj. #1
WWW

Pornography is defined as
   a. sexually explicit material.
   b. visual or written material used for purposes of sexual arousal.
   c. what doesn't offend community standards.
   d. written, visual or spoken love manuals.

2.
K
Answer: a
p. 579
Obj. n/a

Which one is NOT true concerning the Kama Sutra?
   a. It is Japanese.
   b. It is an example of pornography.
   c. It describes specific sexual techniques.
   d. It includes spiritual views.

3.
K
Answer: b
pp. 579-580
Obj. n/a

Which one is NOT true about the Christian Church during the Middle Ages?
   a. It controlled production of the printed word.
   b. It took over the role of the Roman Empire in producing sexual themes in public art.
   c. It had a restrictive attitude toward sex.
   d. It commissioned the majority of artwork.

4.
K
Answer: b
p. 580
Obj. n/a

Pornography became a multibillion dollar industry when
   a. Fanny Hill was published.
   b. The first issue of Playboy was published.
   c. Deep Throat was marketed.
   d. the VCR became widely available.

5.
K
Answer: c
p. 580
Obj. n/a

Availability of pornography was assisted by all but which one of the following?
   a. Gutenberg and movable metal type
   b. The photograph
   c. The postal service
   d. The Internet

6.
K
Answer: d
p. 580
Obj. n/a

Pornography is a _____ a year industry.
a. 100 million
b. 500 million
c. 1 billion
d. 8 billion

7.
K
Answer: c
p. 580
Obj. n/a

About ____ Web sites sell some kind of sex.
a. 10,000
b. 50,000
c. 100,000
d. 250,000

8.
K
Answer: a
p. 580
Obj. n/a

In January of 1999 _____ people visited the top five free pornography sites.
a. 48,000
b. 98,000
c. almost 500,000
d. about 1 million

9.
K
Answer: b
p. 581
Obj. #3

A study of college student responses to 4 types of video pornography found that
a. males rated as most arousing the highly explicit video.
b. both males and females rated as most arousing the highly romantic and highly explicit video.
c. females rated as most arousing the highly romantic but not explicit video.
d. results depended upon whether or not the participants called themselves feminists.

10.
K
Answer: c
p. 581
Obj. #3

A recent study of pornographic materials found that
a. x-rated videos have the most sexual violence.
b. x-rated magazines had the most violence.
c. newsgroups had the most sexual violence.
d. no difference in sexual violence associated with kind of material.

11.
K
Answer: b
p. 581
Obj. #3c

Which of the following is NOT one of the three types of sexually explicit materials?
a. Violent pornography
b. Masochistic and aggressive pornography
c. Degrading and dehumanizing pornography
d. Mutually consenting and pleasurable erotica

12.
K
Answer: b
p. 581
Obj. #3c

Racial stereotypes presented in interracial pornography are an example of
a. violent and aggressive pornography.
b. degrading and dehumanizing pornography.
c. erotica.
d. masochistic and aggressive pornography.

13.
K
Answer: d
p. 582
Obj. #3d

Which one is **least** true of pornography?
a. It perpetuates the myth that a real man should always be ready for sex.
b. It emphasizes oversized penises and penile performance.
c. It shows women as responsive to just about any stimulation.
d. It teaches that sex is humorous and should be relaxing.

14.
K
Answer: c
p. 582
Obj. #3d

Which one was found concerning the effect of pornography on satisfaction with physical appeal and sexual performance of a partner?
a. This decreases them for women.
b. This decreases them for men.
c. This decreases them for both men and women.
d. This has no major or clear effect.

15.
K
Answer: b
p. 582
Obj. #3f

Two unrealistic expectations that pornography can be consistently accused of perpetrating are that men _____ and women _____.
a. are sexually very knowledgeable; are sexually very naive
b. are always ready for sex; are highly responsive to any stimulation by men
c. have masochistic tendencies; have sadistic tendencies
d. can have multiple orgasms; faint when they have good sex

16.
K
Answer: a
p. 582
Obj. #2d, 3f
WWW

One study found that when men and women were repeatedly exposed to pornography
a. that both sexes became less satisfied with the physical appeal and sexual performance of their partners.
b. that both sexes began experiencing a variety of sexual problems.
c. that men wanted sex more frequently with their partners, and the women wanted sex less frequently with their partners.
d. that it enhanced their sexual activity as well as their communication with their partners.

17.
K
Answer: d
pp. 582-583
Obj. n/a

Examples of the use of pornography as social criticism include all but which one of the following?
a. Hustler
b. Fat pornography
c. Fanny Hill
d. The Tenderloin

18.
K
Answer: d
p. 583
Obj. #2a
WWW

According to the Supreme Court, all of the following are currently criteria for evaluating obscenity **except**
a. The theme of the work as a whole must appeal to prurient interest in sex.
b. The work must be offensive to community standards.
c. The work must be without serious literary, artistic, political, or scientific value.
d. The work must cause corrupt or depraved behavior in at least some of the viewers.

19
K
Answer: b
p. 583
Obj. n/a

The definition of obscenity
a. is essentially the same as for pornography.
b. implies a personal or societal judgment.
c. refers to perverse acts limited in scope.
d. is primarily religiously based.

20.
K
Answer: c
p. 584
Obj. #2a

The problem with the current criteria for obscenity is that they are
a. too limited in scope.
b. too broad in scope.
c. highly subjective.
d. outdated.

21.
K
Answer: a
p. 584
Obj. #2b

The _____ Amendment of the U.S. Constitution refers to freedom of speech.
a. First
b. Second
c. Third
d. Fifth

22.
K
Answer: d
p. 584
Obj. #3h

Which of the following statements regarding sexually explicit materials in China is false?
a. The government believes that exposure to such materials creates sexual offenders.
b. Some people have been put to death for selling these materials.
c. People who publish these materials have been arrested.
d. These materials have been banned since the 1920s.

23.
K
Answer: d
p. 614
Obj. #2d

New legislation has been considered by some communities which would allow individuals to press civil suits against providers of sexually explicit depictions of the subordination of women on the grounds that this pornography
a. has been proven to be physically harmful to women.
b. creates profits at the expense of women.
c. is obscene and offensive.
d. is degrading and dehumanizing to women

24.
K
Answer: b
p. 585
Obj. #3g

The 1986 U.S. Attorney General's Commission on Pornography recommended that
a. prostitution be decriminalized.
b. possession of child pornography become a felony.
c. erotica be made more widely available.
d. "Dial-a-Porn" telephone services should be available but in limited numbers.

25.
K
Answer: a
p. 585
Obj. #3a

What happened after pornography was legalized in Denmark in the late 1960s?
a. The sale of pornography to Danes decreased in the years after legalization.
b. The sale of pornography to Danes increased in the years after legalization.
c. The sale of pornography to Danes remained the same as it was prior to legalization.
d. There was a significant increase in reported sex offenses.

26.
K
Answer: b
p. 585
Obj. #3a, 3d

The 1970 United States Commission on Obscenity and Pornography concluded that sexually explicit materials had what effect on behavior?
a. There were significant, long-lasting changes in behavior.
b. There were no significant, long-lasting changes in behavior.
c. There were changes in behavior, but they were unable to be clearly measured.
d. Behavioral patterns were highly variable and inconsistent.

26.
K
Answer: a
p. 585
Obj. #3g

One reason that researchers criticized the Meese Commission's report on pornography is that
a. it ignored the detrimental effects of violence, whether accompanied by sexually explicit materials or not.
b. it focused on sexually explicit materials that were violent and ignored the effects of materials that were degrading and humiliating.
c. it ignored the results of the Denmark study.
d. it was a sophisticated rehash of the 1970 Commission report and reached similar conclusions without taking into account the results of more recent research.

27.
K
Answer: c
p. 586
Obj. #2c

Which one is true with respect to obscene materials and Federal law?
a. There is no regulation since the Supreme Court ruling of 1969.
b. There is regulation only for written for not spoken materials.
c. They prohibit mailing or broadcasting of obscenity.
d. They apply primarily to importations from abroad.

28.
K
Answer: a
p. 586
Obj. #2c

The private possession of pornography
a. is not a crime.
b. is subject to government regulation.
c. is illegal only with respect to videos.
d. is only for wealthy collectors.

29.
K
Answer: d
p. 586
Obj. n/a

Sex-related businesses
a. are not regulated.
b. are regulated by land-use regulations.
c. are regulated only if they involve a national company.
d. are regulated only for minors.

30.
K
Answer: b
p. 586
Obj. n/a

A Supreme court decision about the Internet
a. is yet to be made.
b. gave it the "highest" protection from government intrusion.
c. allows only fines as punishment.
d. can be superseded by state law.

31.
K
Answer: a
p. 587
Obj. #2c

Which one is NOT true with respect to child pornography laws?
a. They are protected by the First Amendment in certain circumstances.
b. It is illegal to sell images of adult women pretending to be under 18.
c. Internet sting operations are used to locate and arrest child pornographers.
d. Computer generated images of child pornography are illegal.

32.
K
Answer: c
p. 587
Obj. #7

Prostitution is legal in
a. none of the United States.
b. California.
c. Nevada.
d. Vermont.

33.
K
Answer: c
p. 587
Obj. #4
WWW

In which of the following periods in history was prostitution viewed as scandalous but necessary?
a. ancient Greece
b. medieval Europe
c. Victorian England
d. the state of Nevada in the early twentieth century

34.
K
Answer: d
p. 588
Obj. #5

Which of the following **best** characterizes the type of man who would patronize a female prostitute?
a. young, lower-class, unmarried
b. middle-aged, upper-class, married
c. young, middle-class, married
d. middle-aged, middle-class, married

35.
K
Answer: d
p. 588
Obj. #6

Which of the following **most** accurately describes the typical prostitute?
a. a delinquent school dropout
b. a college student supplementing his or her income
c. a well-educated adult seeking adventure and extra income
d. Prostitutes come from extremely varied backgrounds and all walks of life.

36.
K
Answer: c
p. 588
Obj. #7
WWW

All of the following are arguments for maintaining the criminal status of prostitution **except**
a. if prostitution were legal, many women would start doing it.
b. it is the government's responsibility to regulate public morals.
c. if prostitution were legal, it could be taxed by the government.
d. if prostitution were legal, it would be difficult to enforce any restrictions on it.

37.
A
Answer: c
p. 588
Obj. #6
WWW

Which of the following would **most** likely explain why women become prostitutes?
a. high sexual drive
b. emotional difficulties
c. financial incentives
d. strong desire to please men

38.
K
Answer: a
p. 589
Obj. #14
WWW

In regard to worldwide prostitution, which of the following statements is true?
a. In Thailand, the sex trade is more than the agricultural industry.
b. In India, "Bombay disease" refers to prostitution.
c. Younger and younger children are sought for prostitution in developing countries because an increasing number of clients are pedophiles.
d. Industrialized nations such as Japan, Germany and the U.S. have successfully united to combat the sex tourism industry that exists in many developing countries.

39.
K
Answer: b
p. 589
Obj. #14

Sex "tourism" is **most** likely to occur in
a. Africa.
b. Asia.
c. Europe.
d. Central America.

40.
K
Answer: a
p. 589
Obj. #14

When Egyptian women marry foreigners the marriage last more than a few months in
a. about one of 200 marriages.
b. those instances where there is religious compatibility.
c. the majority of cases.
d. those cases where she can produce an heir.

41.
K
Answer: c
p. 589
Obj. #14

The CIA/State Department report estimated that there are _____ women and children who are essentially slaves in the U.S. sex industry.
a. no
b. several thousand
c. 50,000
d. 250,000

42.
K
Answer: b
p. 590
Obj. #8

HIV rates in New York streetwalkers were
a. 5 percent.
b. 35 percent.
c. 85 percent.
d. negligible because New York requires condom usage and offers needle exchange.

Chapter 20 Sex For Sale 449

43.
K
Answer: a
p. 590
Obj. #7

COYOTE is an acronym for
a. the prostitutes' union that has organized for political change.
b. a citizens' group that opposes the decriminalization of prostitution.
c. a civil rights group that advocates no censorship on pornography.
d. an organization that provides support for people who engage in bestiality.

44.
K
Answer: b
p. 590
Obj. #7

When comparing legalization or decriminalization of prostitution
a. there is essentially no difference.
b. legalization would allow regulation and taxation
c. decriminalization would allow regulation and taxation.
d. we need to consider that these would remove protection for teenage prostitutes.

45.
K
Answer: d
p. 590
Obj. #7

A possible consequence of decriminalizing prostitution would include all of the following **except**
a. that women would be allowed to control the use of their own bodies.
b. that criminal penalties for engaging in prostitution would be removed.
c. that its association with organized crime might be weakened.
d. that it could be licensed and regulated.

46.
K
Answer: d
p. 591
Obj. #9b

Approximately _____ percent of teenage prostitutes have been victims of sexual abuse.
a. 25
b. 45
c. 75
d. 95

47.
K
Answer: a
p. 591
Obj. #10

This type of female prostitute is easily subject to arrest and is often from a lower socioeconomic background.
a. streetwalker
b. woman who works in a brothel
c. call girl
d. B-girl

48.
K
Answer: b
p. 591
Obj. #9b
WWW

In one study of adolescent male prostitutes, two dominant themes in their early lives were
a. early experimentation with drugs and unsupervised home life.
b. unsupervised home life and rejection by peers at school.
c. death of a parent and early drug and alcohol usage.
d. parental divorce and rejection by peers at school.

49.
K
Answer: c
p. 591
Obj. #11
WWW

Which one is NOT true with respect to brothels?
a. There were common in the early history of this country.
b. They typically collect about half of a prostitutes' fee.
c. They are presently illegal in all parts of the United States.
d. This refers to a house in which a group of prostitutes work.

50.
K
Answer: c
p. 592
Obj. #10

A man receives a "local" after going to a massage parlor. This means
a. that his masseuse is nude while massaging him.
b. that he received a type of massage indigenous to that particular geographic location.
c. that his masseuse manually stimulated him to orgasm after massaging him.
d. that his masseuse orally stimulated him to orgasm after massaging him.

51.
K
Answer: c
p. 592
Obj. #10

The _____ usually earns more money than other female prostitutes.
a. streetwalker
b. woman who works in a massage parlor
c. call girl
d. woman who works in a brothel

52.
K
Answer: b
p. 592
Obj. #5

In one study, the massage parlor customers were
a. young, blue-collar workers.
b. white-collar businessmen over age 35.
c. young military service recruits.
d. blue-collar workers over age 35.

53.
K
Answer: d
p. 592
Obj. #12
WWW

Men who provide sexual services for women in exchange for money and gifts are called
a. hustlers.
b. call boys.
c. studs.
d. gigolos.

54.
K
Answer: d
p. 592
Obj. #12

Which of the following type of prostitutes does NOT service men?
a. peer-delinquent prostitutes
b. hustlers
c. call boys
d. gigolos

55.
K
Answer: a
p. 592
Obj. #12

The role of the gigolo is **most** similar to that of the
a. call girl.
b. streetwalker.
c. brothel prostitute.
d. pimp.

Chapter 20 Sex For Sale

56.
K
Answer: a
p. 593
Obj. #12

Which of the following tend to work in groups?
a. peer-delinquent prostitutes
b. gigolos
c. call boys
d. hustlers

57.
K
Answer: b
p. 593
Obj. #13

What was the conclusion of the 1959 United Nations Commission study of prostitution?
a. Women enter into prostitution because of their nonconformist attitudes concerning sex and marriage.
b. In order to prevent prostitution, it is important to create other economic opportunities for women.
c. Customers should be arrested and prosecuted along with prostitutes.
d. Any proposal to reduce prostitution should involve a drug rehabilitation program for women.

58.
K
Answer: c
p. 593
Obj. #12

A hustler
a. works primarily out of gambling casinos.
b. caters to rich women.
c. contacts customers in person, e.g., streets or bars.
d. is an Internet businessman.

59.
K
Answer: c
p. 593
Obj. #12

A call boy
a. works from the streets.
b. is usually a teenager.
c. has regular customers.
d. does telephone sex.

60.
K
Answer: d
p. 593
Obj. #13

Which of the following profits financially from prostitution?
a. pimps
b. referral agents
c. hotels and doormen
d. all of the above

Multiple Choice from Study Guide

1.
K
Answer: a
p. 580
Obj. n/a

All of the following expanded pornography and extended access of sexually explicit materials **except**
a. The Miller v. California decision.
b. Photography.
c. the railroad.
d. VCR's.

2.
K
Answer: c
p. 581
Obj. #1

Erotica can be distinguished from pornography because
a. pornography depicts genitalia; erotica does not.
b. erotica is made primarily by females; pornography is made primarily by males.
c. pornography connotes domination of women; erotica portrays sexuality respectfully.
d. erotica is soft-core; pornography is hard-core.

3.
K
Answer: c
p. 582
Obj. #3

Which of the following is true regarding the impact of pornography on sexuality?
a. Pornography emphasizes female pleasure and autonomy.
b. Pornography shows the complex nature of male sexuality.
c. Pornography depicts men as always being ready for sex.
d. Pornography shows women acting coy and shy in response to stimulation from males.

4.
K
Answer: b
p. 581
Obj. # 3c

In the study of college students who were shown four video segments, which video was rated as most arousing?
a. the hard-core video with no romance, by men only
b. the hard-core video with romance, by women and men
c. the soft-core video with no romance, by women and men
d. the soft-core video with romance, by women only

5.
K
Answer: a
p. 582
Obj. #3d

Zillman & Bryant's study demonstrated that when women and men were repeatedly exposed to pornography
a. both women and men became less satisfied with their partner's physical appearance and sexual performance.
b. women became more active and responsive during sexual interaction with their partners.
c. men broadened their repertoire of sexual behaviors to include activities other than sexual intercourse.
d. women and men reported an increased in the frequency of sexual activity.

6.
K
Answer: d
p. 581
Obj. #1

What do violent and degrading pornography have in common?
a. use of hard-core, explicit images
b. aggression and brutality
c. use of nontraditional gender roles
d. imbalance of power

7.
K
Answer: c
p. 583
Obj. #2a

Legal issues surrounding pornography have focused on defining what is
a. degrading.
b. depraving and corrupting to the user.
c. obscene.
d. violent.

8.
K
Answer: b
p. 584
Obj. #2b

Our nation and legal system are still debating whether or not sexually explicit materials should be protected by
a. the Geneva Declaration.
b. freedom of speech.
c. universal human rights principles.
d. United Nations Resolutions.

9.
K
Answer: c
p. 587
Obj. #4

Which of the following statements is false regarding the history of prostitution?
   a. Prostitutes were valued for the intellectual companionship in ancient Greece.
   b. Sexual relations between men and prostitutes occurred in religious temples.
   c. Prostitution was banned in medieval Europe.
   d. Prostitution was considered scandalous but necessary during the Victorian era.

10.
K
Answer: a
p. 588
Obj. #6

Which statement is true concerning the background of female prostitutes?
   a. Prostitutes are a diverse group and no single theory or profile describes them.
   b. Most have a history of sexual abuse.
   c. The majority are poorly educated.
   d. They exhibited higher rates of problem behavior during adolescence.

11.
K
Answer: c
pp. 588-590
Obj. #7

All of the following comprise arguments against the criminal status of prostitution **except**
   a. Prostitution thrives despite criminal penalties.
   b. Prostitution encourages connections with organized crime.
   c. The government has a responsibility to regulate morals.
   d. Penalties against prostitution target prostitutes more than customers.

12.
K
Answer: d
p. 591
Obj. #9

Which statement is true regarding teenage prostitution?
   a. Many are runaways from stable middle class families.
   b. Most have shown remarkable resiliency against the troubles of sex work.
   c. Most work in phone sex or lingerie modeling.
   d. The overwhelming majority have been sexual abuse victims.

13.
K
Answer: c
p. 591
Obj. #10

Which type of prostitute is **lowest** in the hierarchy of prostitution and faces the worst work conditions?
   a. a brothel worker
   b. a massage parlor worker
   c. a streetwalker
   d. a call girl

14.
K
Answer: a
pp. 592-593
Obj. #12

Which term is out of place here among these descriptors of male prostitutes?
   a. pimp
   b. gigolo
   c. kept boy
   d. hustler

454 Test Bank to Accompany *Our Sexuality*

15.
K
Answer: d
p. 593
Obj. #12

_____ often use prostitution as a way to commit robbery and assault.
a. Streetwalkers
b. Madams
c. Call boys
d. Peer-delinquent prostitutes

True/False

Students may be asked to answer these questions using the traditional format of marking their answers either "true" or "false." Or, to encourage more active involvement, you may choose to use the following instructions:

If the statement is true, place a "T" on the line preceding it. If the statement is false, place an "F" on the line preceding it and then change the statement to make it true by deleting incorrect information and/or adding accurate information.

1.
Answer: T
p. 579
Obj. n/a

___ Visual and written pornography still exists as found in ancient Indian society.

2.
Answer: F
p. 580
Obj. n/a

___ Pornography first became a multi-billion dollar industry with the advent of the VCR.

3.
Answer: F
p. 581
Obj. #2a, 3c

___ Research indicates that all three types of sexually explicit materials have a detrimental impact on men's and women's attitudes and/or behaviors.

4.
Answer: T
p. 582
Obj. #3

___ Pornography has effectively been used as social criticism.

5.
Answer: F
pp. 583-584
Obj. #1

___ In recent years, the judicial system has been able to establish a definition of what constitutes obscenity that is objective and clearly understood.

6.
Answer: T
p. 684
Obj. #3h

___ In China, some people have been put to death for selling sexually explicit materials.

7.
Answer: F
pp. 584-585
Obj. #3a, 3g

___ The 1970 commission on pornography, and the 1986 commission made similar recommendations.

Chapter 20 Sex For Sale 455

8. ___ After pornography was legalized in Denmark, the sale of
Answer: F   pornography to Danes decreased over time but the number of
p. 585   sex offenses increased.
Obj. #1, 2

9. ___ The 1986 U.S. Attorney General's Commission on Pornography
Answer: T   concluded that violent pornography caused sexually aggressive
p. 585   behavior toward women.
Obj. #4g

10. ___ Pornography dissemination statutes evolved as a result of the
Answer: F   Meese Commission Report.
pp. 585-586
Obj. #2c, 3g

11. ___ The Supreme Court has ruled that the Internet is entitled to the
Answer: T   highest protection from governmental intrusion.
p. 587
Obj. n/a

12. ___ The primary incentives for becoming a prostitute involve social
Answer: F   and psychological factors.
p. 588
Obj. #6

13. ___ Customers of prostitutes are typically white, middle-aged, married
Answer: T   and middle class.
p. 588
Obj. #5

14. ___ In Thailand, the sex trade is even more successful than the
Answer: T   agricultural industry.
p. 589
Obj. #14

15. ___ In Africa, sex with prostitutes is a primary mode of transmission of
Answer: T   the HIV virus.
p. 590
Obj. #8

16. ___ In Washington D.C. prostitute's customers have their cars seized.
Answer: T
p. 590
Obj. n/a

17. ___ Decriminalization and legalization are essentially the same thing.
Answer: F
p. 590
Obj. #14

18. ___ Brothels presently exist in the United States only in films about our past history.
Answer: F
p. 591
Obj. #4

19. ___ The male equivalent of a call girl is a hustler.
Answer: F
p. 592
Obj. #10, 12

20. ___ A major way to prevent prostitution would be to create other economic opportunities for women.
Answer: T
p. 593
Obj. #6

Short Answer Essay

1. Describe some of the difficulties in establishing a legal definition of obscenity. (Obj. #2a, 4c)

2. Discuss freedom of speech and sex discrimination as they relate to legal controversies concerning pornography. (Obj. #2a–d)

3. Give the definition of pornography and obscenity and then from your own personal beliefs and perceptions give some specific examples of what would constitute each? (Obj. #1, 2a)

4. How did the recommendations and conclusions of the 1986 U.S. Attorney General's Commission on Pornography Report differ from those outlined by the 1970 commission? Briefly describe some of the criticisms of the 1986 Report. (Obj. #3a, 3g)

5. If a potential mate told you that they were interested in watching x-rated movies and examining and possibly using other forms of pornography, would you be interested in continuing the relationship? Why, or why not? (Obj. n/a)

6. What would you do if your teenage child were found examining pornography? Consider magazines, movies, and the Internet. Would it make a difference if it were a son as compared to a daughter? (Obj. n/a)

7. Do you believe that prostitution should either be legalized, or decriminalized? Why or why not for both? (Obj. #7)

8. List and briefly describe three types of female prostitutes. (Obj. # 10)

9. List and briefly describe five types of male prostitutes. (Obj. #12)

10. What sex differences exist with respect to prostitution? (Obj. #6)

11. Discuss some of the various people, businesses, institutions, and organizations that profit from prostitution. (Obj. #13)

12. Describe the existing controversy in this country regarding the legal status of prostitution. (Obj. #7)

13. Discuss how women and children have come to be exploited in prostitution worldwide, what the effects of this are, and what is being done to address this problem. (Obj. #14)

14. Discuss the interaction of AIDS and prostitution, both in this country and others. (Obj. #8)

15. How has the Internet changed the nature of pornography dissemination and the sale of other sexual services? (Obj. #15)